AF680395

Professor Berend presents the first comprehensive inside account of Hungary's economic reforms since the 1950s. Working from Communist Party archives, which have hitherto partially remained closed to scholars, Berend situates the history of these economic reforms within their political context, looking in particular at the role of the Soviet Union. He examines the theoretical background to reform, the obstacles that arose during implementation, and the gradual realization that minor reforms of the old system could no longer work.

The Hungarian Economic Reforms 1953–1988 comes at a time when many centrally planned economies are examining their performance and structure and seeking suitable forms of change. The Hungarian reforms have attracted considerable world attention and are seen as a model for those countries wishing to rid themselves of their Stalinist command economies. Thus the book indirectly sheds light upon Chinese economic reforms and on Gorbachev's Soviet *perestroika*. It will be of interest to specialists and students of East European studies, with special reference to the EMEA, planned economies and economic reform.

THE HUNGARIAN ECONOMIC REFORMS 1953–1988

Soviet and East European Studies: 70

Editorial Board

Ronald Hill (*General editor*), Judy Batt, Michael Kaser
Anthony Kemp-Welch, Margot Light, Alastair McAuley
James Riordan, Stephen White

Soviet and East European Studies, under the auspices of Cambridge University Press and the British Association for Soviet, Slavonic and East European Studies (BASSEES), promotes the publication of works presenting substantial and original research on the economics, politics, sociology and modern history of the Soviet Union and Eastern Europe.

Soviet and East European Studies

70 IVAN T. BEREND
The Hungarian economic reforms 1953–1988

69 CHRIS WARD
Russia's cotton workers and the New Economic Policy
Shop-floor culture and state policy 1921–1929

68 LÁSZLÓ CSABA
Eastern Europe in the world economy

67 MICHAEL E. URBAN
An algebra of Soviet power
Elite circulation in the Belorussian Republic 1966–1986

66 JANE L. CURRY
Poland's journalists: professionalism and politics

65 MARTIN MYANT
The Czechoslovak economy 1948–1988
The battle for economic reform

64 XAVIER RICHET
The Hungarian model: markets and planning in a socialist economy

63 PAUL G. LEWIS
Political authority and party secretaries in Poland 1975–1986

62 BENJAMIN PINKUS
The Jews of the Soviet Union
The history of a national minority

61 FRANCESCO BENVENUTI
The Bolsheviks and the Red Army, 1918–1922

60 HIROAKI KUROMIYA
Stalin's industrial revolution
Politics and workers, 1928–1932

59 LEWIS SIEGELBAUM
Stakhanovism and the politics of productivity in the USSR, 1935–1941

58 JOZEF M. VAN BRABANT
Adjustment, structural change and economic efficiency
Aspects of monetary cooperation in Eastern Europe

57 ILIANA ZLOCH-CHRISTY
Debt problems of Eastern Europe

56 SUSAN BRIDGER
Women in the Soviet countryside
Women's roles in rural development in the Soviet Union

55 ALLEN LYNCH
The Soviet study of international relations

Series list continues on p. 344

THE HUNGARIAN ECONOMIC REFORMS 1953–1988

IVAN T. BEREND
President of the Hungarian Academy of Sciences and Professor of Economic History, Budapest University

CAMBRIDGE UNIVERSITY PRESS
Cambridge
New York Port Chester Melbourne Sydney

CAMBRIDGE UNIVERSITY PRESS
Cambridge, New York, Melbourne, Madrid, Cape Town, Singapore, São Paulo, Delhi

Cambridge University Press
The Edinburgh Building, Cambridge CB2 8RU, UK

Published in the United States of America by Cambridge University Press, New York

www.cambridge.org
Information on this title: www.cambridge.org/9780521108010

Originally published in Hungarian as *A magyar gazdasági reform utja*
by Közgazdasági és Jogi Könyvkiadó 1988
and © Közgazdasági és Jogi Könyvkiadó 1988
This revised edition first published in English by Cambridge University Press
1990 as *The Hungarian economic reforms 1953–1988*
English translation © Cambridge University Press 1990

This publication is in copyright. Subject to statutory exception
and to the provisions of relevant collective licensing agreements,
no reproduction of any part may take place without the written
permission of Cambridge University Press.

This digitally printed version 2009

A catalogue record for this publication is available from the British Library

Library of Congress Cataloguing in Publication data
Berend, T. Iván (Tibor Iván), 1930–
The Hungarian economic reforms, 1953–1988/Ivan T. Berend.
p. cm. – (Soviet and East European studies: 70)
Bibliography: p.
ISBN 0 521 38037 5
1. Hungary – Economic policy – 1968– 2. Hungary – Economic
conditions – 1968– 3. Hungary – Economic policy – 1945– 4. Hungary –
Economic conditions – 1945– I. Title. II. Series.
HC300.28.B457 1990
338.9439′09′045 – dc20 89–7349 CIP

ISBN 978-0-521-38037-9 hardback
ISBN 978-0-521-10801-0 paperback

Contents

Preface

It is a peculiar and by no means easy undertaking to write a history of the present. The task becomes more difficult still when the author is personally acquainted with most of the protagonists in the processes being investigated. Additional problems obviously arise from the fact that I have not only been a contemporary and witness of two out of the three decades discussed in this book, but I have tried to contribute to the process, in my own special field, taking part in a number of debates, and participating in the work of some of the bodies referred to.

Personal involvement has been a strong motivation in choosing the style of presentation: letting the protagonists themselves do the talking as much as possible, letting the original documents speak for themselves as far as I can. The same goes for archive records and contemporary periodical or newspaper articles. The intention has been for the author to be as unobtrusive as possible. After all, he is very much present in the selection, editing and interpreting of the source material, thereby transmitting his own stance to the reader.

I have tried to be an honest and candid chronicler, intending that in this work, too, I should contribute to a better understanding of the Hungarian reform process, and to its further development.

My book discusses the history of the Hungarian economic reforms. Obviously, this is inseparable from the objectives of economic policy and from the real processes of the economy. Nevertheless, on this occasion I will not examine the global economic-historical process of the period, but – resting content with a mere signalling of interrelations – I will concentrate exclusively on the reform process. This exercise covers a period of more than thirty years. I immediately owe my readers an explanation: do the reforms really have such a long history? How, in that case, am I actually interpreting the concept of reform? In this work I identify three phases in the reform process. The first started in the mid-fifties, the second in the mid-sixties and the third in 1979–80. But can one really speak of reform in all of these periods?

It is certainly quite easy to pick holes in this argument. At best one can say of the partial corrections made within a previously adapted Soviet economic model, affecting only one or another sector of the economy, or, say, measures introduced only as an experiment, that they constituted merely a correction, not a real reform of the model, whereas reform implies a comprehensive overhaul of the functioning system. In this sense, it is only in 1966–8 that one can speak of a genuine reform, while the first and third phase can only be regarded as corrective phases. The former strove to 'rationalize' the over-centralized command economy, whilst the latter amounted to a reinstatement and correction of the 1968 model of reform.

Yet one is justified in investigating these thirty years by the historical character of the reforms, which themselves formed a historical process and had a logical continuity over the entire period under discussion. Intellectual preparation and the shaping of economic and political ideas are just as much a part of this as partial corrections, or, say, experiments that in some cases only extended to a few companies and may have resulted in no more than a realization that correction of the old system could not lead to a solution, since it was bound to be frustrated by the reproduction of well-known disruptions. So the ambiguous, corrective experiments are very much a part of the historical process of the reforms without which the theory and practice of comprehensive reform could hardly have matured. Even though I by no means regard the thirty years under discussion as successive phases of genuine reform and consider that only one real reform took place in the period investigated – during the mid- to late sixties – I have none the less to speak about three major phases and about a coherent history of the reform process.

This book was published in Hungarian by Közgazdasági és Jogi Könyvkiadó (Budapest) in 1988. I am grateful to Cambridge University Press for the careful and helpful copy-editing, and for publishing my third book in this decade. I hope very much that this volume will aid an understanding of the exciting experiment of the Hungarian reforms (to replace the Stalinist Soviet economic model) which, to the present, have led to the start of a combined, radical economic and political reform, and thus a change of the whole system.

Introduction

As an ally of Hitler's Germany, Hungary was among the vanquished nations following the Second World War, which led to the total military and political collapse of the Horthy régime. The old ruling class and most senior civil servants, regular officers, landowners and industrialists left the country. An entirely new situation arose from the presence of the Red Army which had driven the Nazi forces out of Hungary and swept away the Hungarian Arrow-Cross government, from the sphere of authority granted to the Allied Control Commission under the ceasefire agreement, and from the vast concomitant political transformation. In political terms, the marks of this new situation were the introduction of basic democratic rights, the first free elections and a coalition government. Developments like the distribution of the great landed estates among the landless peasantry, the reconstruction to clear up the considerable war damage and the success in stabilizing the Hungarian currency without any outside assistance were accompanied by forceful intervention on the part of the state and a gradual, partial process of nationalization.

The early post-war years of democratic transformation were followed in 1947–8 by a dramatic change in the international scene. The wartime system of alliances fell apart and the Cold War set in, causing particularly sharp changes to occur in East-Central Europe. The world had split into two separate, antagonistic camps. The transition in Hungary to a one-party system gathered pace, which was in accordance with the guidelines laid down by a Cominform (the 'information bureau' of communist and workers' parties set up around this time), as was the adoption of political and social structures based on the Soviet model. The exclusive validity of the Stalinist Soviet model as the sole kind of socialism was underscored by such Stalinist policies as the excommunication of Yugoslavia, the denunciation of Tito and the condemnation of the theory of separate roads to socialism.

Accompanying the persecution of the 'enemy' at spectacular show trials, the forced pace of industrialization (to be implemented under a single five-year plan) and the forcible collectivization of agriculture was a radical transformation of the system of institutions. Planning extended down to the minutest detail and market forces and prices were ruled out. All these things took place at great speed in Hungary between 1947 and 1953.

In 1947–8, known as the Year of the Turning-Point, this policy caused the opposition, and even coalition parties, to be disbanded. The Hungarian Social Democratic Party was absorbed into the Communist Party of Hungary to form the ruling Hungarian Working People's Party. Simultaneously, two radical measures of nationalization were taken. In November 1947 the major banks were placed under state ownership. Since the collieries had already been nationalized and the four largest heavy industrial plants were under state management, the state gained control of the key positions in the economy. Then, in March 1948, the shares owned by Hungarians in all industrial companies employing over a hundred workers were nationalized, which gave the state an 83 per cent share of industry. Further nationalization followed in December 1949, covering industrial companies with more than ten employees. Indeed, some industries like printing and pharmacy were fully nationalized irrespective of the number of employees,[1] and it was intended to extend this to all industries and trades. Mátyás Rákosi, who had become first secretary of the merged Hungarian Working People's Party, publicly announced in August 1948 the start of what he described as a gradual, voluntary collectivization of agriculture. But by November of the same year Rákosi was already informing his party's central committee that private peasant holdings (most of them formed only three years earlier under the land reform) would have to be herded into the collective fold within three or four years, although his statement was carefully kept from the public. A campaign of ruthless, compulsory collectivization began.

The early 1950s saw a veritable drama unfold in the countryside as economic pressure was put on the peasantry and the police turned all their powers of harassment against them. Rather than join the new cooperative farms, large numbers of peasants fled the villages altogether, leaving their land untilled. In fact a mere 25 per cent of them signed up. (Meanwhile the size of the state farms increased tenfold, partly through incorporation of abandoned land deemed to have been handed over voluntarily.) Intolerable economic pressure was also placed on private industry and retail trading, in fact on all forms of small-scale ownership and economic activity, through a process even more rapid than the one used in agriculture. Between 1949 and 1953 the number of self-employed tradesmen and their employees shrank from 368,000 to 51,000, in other words to a seventh. The number of small private retailers and their employees fell from about 100,000 to less than 3,000.[2]

Private property in Hungary was eradicated at the turn of the 1940s and 1950s. State ownership, and to some extent cooperative ownership, became all but universal. The dominance of the state was also reflected in the system of planning and institutions that was established. New systems for banking and for industrial organization were set up at the turn of 1947 and 1948. After the major banks had been nationalized in November 1947, the National Bank of Hungary, which already acted as the bank of issue, gained a monopoly of short-term lending. All company transactions were directed through it under what was known as the single-account system. However, new specialized banking institutions were established alongside the central bank after the previous commercial banks had been wound up. The old Credit Bank provided the physical framework for the new Investment Bank, which distributed the sums allocated in the budget for investment projects. The Commercial Bank's staff and premises were taken over by the new Foreign Trade Bank. The extensive branch network of the First Savings and Discount Bank of Pest was combined with some provincial financial institutions in 1949 to form the National Savings Bank, whose principal task was to take deposits from private individuals and lend them money. All the banks were under the direction of the Ministry of Finance.

The reorganization of industry was equally radical. To the new Soviet-style system of planning the joint-stock company framework was as inappropriate as the organizational forms of state ownership which had existed under capitalism between 1945 and 1948.

The new system for nationalized industry involved setting up 750 so-called national enterprises under the direction of the Ministry of Industry, which in May 1948 established a network of twenty-nine industrial directorates. The latter worked partly as organizations of state administration while also performing management functions (drafting of plan details, plan supervision, coordination, pricing and distribution of materials). Companies whose production profiles were similar were grouped horizontally into industrial centres. Production, manpower, energy, materials and so on were managed at company level by the industrial directorates, which were gradually incorporated as departments into the ministry with overall control.

Under the command economy introduced after 1948, there was no more company autonomy. The enterprises, though formally independent, were directed centrally. As a consequence of this, the Ministry of Industry gradually split into a number of sectoral ministries whose make-up and organization frequently changed. In 1949 a National Economic Council was set up to provide overall coordination of the various economic portfolios and directing institutions.

The command economy which was being established suited the requirements of a comprehensive system of central planning. All economic targets were expressed in compulsory plan indices, most of them in quantitative, physical terms such as square metres, hectolitres, pieces and so on that were then 'converted' into indicators of value. This procedure was introduced in the 1948 modification of the Three-Year Plan, known as the Five-Month Plan, and more fully in the First Five-Year Plan that started in January 1950. Under the new system of planning the entire functioning of the economy, including all production and distribution, was directed by central command on the basis of compulsory plan indices that covered everything. Production levels were set in detailed annual plans applying to each company and containing an extraordinary number of indicators. This procedure was considered to be the last word, overall and in detail, in the application of 'economic laws' and the 'interests of the national economy'. The plan's explicit directives told companies how much to invest, how much to pay in wages, how much raw material, energy and labour to use, and what to produce of what range of products, and of what quality. The National Planning Office developed a detailed national energy and materials account on the basis of which it compiled the five-year plan that became law after enactment by Parliament. This plan was then broken down into annual, quarterly and monthly plans, and the national plan was broken down first into sectoral plans for ministries and then into compulsory central plans for individual companies.[3] So the stipulations for production, supply of materials, investment and so forth formed a closed chain of connected plan 'prescriptions'.

Each plan indicator became the personal responsibility of the recipient. Company autonomy became a formality under this system, since even quarterly production targets were prescribed by the ministry. In most cases the central authorities were directly responsible for company management and performed operative, supervisory and controlling functions. The trouble was that under those conditions there was no hope that centralized planning would be able to function. It was all too clearly in the interest of the central planning and controlling organizations and their staffs and officials to be successful, to show good results, to ensure the fulfilment or even overfulfilment of the plan, in other words to aim at a consensus with the companies when drafting compulsory plan indicators. What emerged was 'plan bargaining', under which companies were able to some extent to assert their requirements and ambitions.

What the economic policy-makers were seeking to do was to exert their central will through detailed regulations. They wanted as far as possible, to cut out the 'accidental' attributes of the market. So efforts were concentrated on disconnecting all kinds of automatic market and monetary mechanisms. This was vividly expressed in the price reform of 1951, which substituted fixed prices for the free market.[4] The price of consumer goods under this system had to cover the cost of production and provide a net profit. On the other hand, it was considered superfluous to ensure that the price of investment goods included any profit above the cost of production. So factory and consumer prices started to go their different ways. Energy and raw materials were priced unrealistically low and received huge state subsidies. The clearest instance of a dual pricing structure was in the system of compulsory agricultural deliveries: a tiny fraction of the produce could be sold at free-market prices, but the bulk had to be delivered to the state at unrealistically low prices. In other words, a high proportion of the income produced in agriculture was channelled into the accumulation funds of the state.

Industrial prices in the state sector were regarded simply as a technical accounting instrument. They were not required to reflect real value and they were unrelated to supply and demand. The prices of energy and raw materials were kept low, irrespective of how much they cost to produce. Moreover, the links between foreign trade prices and domestic prices were severed. A manufacturing company would deliver its products to a foreign trade company at the factory price, and the often substantial difference between the two was bridged by a state subsidy. In practice the official exchange rate failed to function, so that domestic prices could often be four, five or more times higher than prices calculated according to the official rate of exchange. In other cases, the state sold expensively imported goods at cheaper prices to domestic firms. The problem was compounded by the introduction in the socialist countries of fixed prices for trade within Comecon at the time of the Korean War, partly to eliminate the awkward price fluctuations the war was causing and partly to produce fixed prices for planning their foreign trade. These fixed Comecon prices were left unchanged until 1957, so that the rigid price structure operating among the Socialist countries became totally unrelated to the price levels and proportions on the world market. Planning was, of course, facilitated by eliminating the unforeseeable influences of market fluctuations.

So the price system provided no incentives to economic activity or to comparison of costs and incomes. Nor was profitability treated as a criterion. This was not in fact expected of prices, since incentives were based on fulfilment of quantitative, material plan indicators. Ultimately, prices only exercised a real price function in a single sector of the domestic market – consumer goods – and even there they did so only in relation to demand, leaving supply unaffected, in accordance with the Stalinist dictum that 'demand necessarily precedes supply'. Companies had no need to market their products, and their performance was no longer influenced by the marketability, production costs, quality or technical standard of the goods they produced.

With prices artificially determined, fixed, unrelated to supply and demand and centrally regulated, all incentives in companies, including the personal incentive for managers provided by bonuses and for company workers through the wage system, were linked to compliance with central commands and plan indicators. But in the command economy, it was impossible at company level to comply with every plan indicator in full, and so companies concentrated their energies on meeting the stipulations most important to them. This should obviously have been those in which they had a determining financial interest. Thus the economic policy made attainment of the fastest possible growth of production the principal incentive. Between 1950 and 1955, the most important and longest lasting of the 200 or so central decrees and regulations on bonuses published in the official gazette was the bonuses decree of November 1, 1952 (456/3/1952.MT.sz), which set as the main qualification for a bonus the fulfilment or overfulfilment of the production plan, which essentially encouraged firms to fulfil at all costs the quantitative targets, the plan index for the 'global production plan of the company'.[5]

Clearly none of this occurred by chance. It must be emphasized again that the plan's main indicator, in line with the economic policy objectives, became the growth rate of industrial production in general and of priority industrial sectors in particular. A quantitative increase in production was seen as the main solution to the contradictions that emerged in its wake. Despite innumerable amendments and changes to the decrees, the government continued to regard quantitative fulfilment and overfulfilment of plan indicators as the top priority and to back that up with financial incentives. This fundamental principle, which was aimed at maximizing results concerning the main objectives, overrode all other economic criteria.

In order to assess the economic mechanism in Hungary after 1948 one must obviously consider that one of the basic issues was to eliminate industrial backwardness and a historically low level of capital accumulation. Before the mid-twentieth century, history has provided few examples of poor countries catching up. The Soviet economic model has withstood the trial of the Second World War and become an attractive one to countries struggling against backwardness. Moreover, the Soviet model was the only socialist experiment conducted at that time: there were no other examples to study. All these factors certainly contributed to the Hungarian government's decision to adapt the Soviet model rather than seek new paths. This statement sounds like a euphemism, because one might well ask whether the move by the Hungarian government was a decision at all, since it was taken under very strong Stalinist pressure under the conditions pertaining in the international communist movement at that time. That fact is well known, but nevertheless it would be a gross simplification in the opposite direction to regard this move as compulsory emulation. One indication of the appeal that the Soviet model had is its adoption during those years by the Yugoslav and Chinese revolutions, even though they were following a decidedly independent course. Above all, this highly centralized system of state interventionism marked an effort to attain the maximum concentration of forces required for rapid industrialization in relatively backward countries. One must also bear in mind that from its very inception this type of planning had been bound up with the aim of building a highly self-sufficient war economy. It was not solely in the Soviet Union of the 1930s that this objective seemed topical; the same held true for East-Central Europe in the early 1950s during the Cold War. The Berlin crisis, the Korean War and Stalin's view that a third world war was inevitable had a determining influence on Soviet policy. So the economic policy of the Hungarian government was likewise determined by the information received from Stalin and Molotov that war would inevitably erupt within three or four years.[6] Closely connected with the First Five-Year Plan launched at the beginning of 1950 and with its forced pace of industrialization and methods was the preparation of a war economy.

So military spending amounted to 50 per cent of the investment in the first year of the five-year plan and to an average of more than a third in the four years that followed. The build-up of a command economy of the war-economy type was also an important part of the preparations. In fact this mechanism did make it possible to concentrate on a chosen few sectors of the economy. The Soviet economic model offered the major advantage of a high rate of capital accumulation. Having had an annual accumulation rate of 5 or 6 per cent of national income before the war, Hungary in the early 1950s managed a rate of about 35 per cent. The command economy had a decidedly macroeconomic bias. By creating hitherto unknown opportunities for increasing accumulation and concentrating investment, the Soviet model that Hungary (and other East-Central European countries) adopted after 1948 made a rapid, forced pace of industrialization possible.

In addition, the command economy had some short-term advantages. Being a centralized system it offered help in running an economy of shortage, made to some extent inevitable by the very fast growth rate and the embargo policy applied by the United States. Centralization also contributed to overcoming the immediate negative impact of the socio-political transformation to be found in the absence of professionals and managers able to guide a new managerial stratum that was inexperienced and in most cases unqualified.

Despite these advantages, the command economy produced negative consequences for the Hungarian economy right from the start. The advantage of a macroeconomic orientation, for instance, was accompanied by the real danger of accomplishing to an extreme extent economic objectives that were badly selected and unrealistic. The ability to handle shortages was accompanied by a mechanism that itself contributed greatly to creating those shortages. The command economy eliminated the influence of prices and the market from company activity, linking financial incentives with the priority central objectives, primarily the highest possible rate of growth. But it soon became obvious that a typical hierarchy was emerging and that other important aspects of the central will (and the plan indicators) were being subordinated to the most important tasks concerning the fulfilment of the plan. Technological development, productivity rises, quality improvements, production-cost reductions and so on were inevitably neglected. One must conclude that an economic system aiming at the most thorough possible eradication of market prices was only able to assert the central will in part and in a contradictory manner. Indeed, in numerous fundamental respects it gave rise to tendencies that conflicted with the original objectives. Soon the negative consequences that conflicted with the genuine plans began to predominate, although these were all joint consequences of the economic policy and of the planning mechanism. Though neglecting the general analysis of economic policy, I would refer here to the all-embracing effort which aimed at the fastest possible development of an autarkic ordnance industry – for which command planning promised to be an excellent tool.

One of the major weaknesses – closely related to economic policy – was the wastefulness of investment and production (as a consequence of eliminating realistic relations of value and price). On the one hand, this ultimately entailed a freezing of vast sums as a constantly and rapidly rising number of projects remained uncompleted. On the other it led to the production of immense quantities of unsaleable products. Since companies drew no particular benefit from lowering their cost of production and were primarily interested in fulfilment of their production plan, the simplest way for them to increase the global value of their production was to use ever more and dearer materials. During the early 1950s such phenomena were common. It could come about, for instance, that whereas in 1949, 100 forints' worth of material were producing 100 forints' worth of new value, the same material turned out to produce only 71 forints' worth of new value in 1954.[7]

A phenomenon known as global plan fulfilment became extremely common. It can partly be categorized again under squandering of material, since companies would often fulfil their production plan by manufacturing vast quantities of unsaleable goods. The frequent overfulfilment of the target for the total value of production turned in reality into a situation quite the opposite of what had been planned, in which there was superfluous production of the articles most easily manufactured or those that required the largest input of material. The targets for heavy castings weighing several tons would be overfulfilled and production of light castings neglected.[8] In the summer of 1951, for instance, the Debrecen Garment Factory fulfilled its global production plan by 127 per cent, but the 'plan fulfilment quotient' covering the assortment produced was only 55 per cent. In the case of the Csepel Auto Works the figures were 107 and 65 per cent. Deviations from the plan led to the accumulation of superfluous stocks of unmarketable goods into which vast amounts of material and labour were locked. Between the last quarters of 1952 and 1954, the production of state-owned industry grew by 12.7 per cent, but the stock of unsaleable finished products rose by 72 per cent![9]

There was no reason why companies should want to modernize their technologies or products. They enjoyed a monopoly position on the domestic market and were protected from the risks of market competition. They had no direct contact with competitive world market either, where the competition would have shown up their technical backwardness very sharply. The price system and the total insulation from real involvement in the market served to seal the economy off from adverse influences such as fluctuations on the world market and from the favourable influences of incentive. Whereas there was no genuine encouragement to update technology, there was a direct encouragement to go for quantitative growth and to fulfil plan indicators that actually hindered technical development. One instance of this was the wasteful exploitation of oils and lignite resources.[10]

By 1950 even the controlling institutions themselves were sending out warning signals: 'In general the erroneous view has emerged in our factories that production alone is important, because that is what they are primarily responsible for.'[11] This attitude, which arose for self-evidence reasons, conflicted with companies' long-term interests and put a sharp brake on research and development. Companies were impelled towards producing traditional goods in the traditional way, since a well-trodden path made it easier to fulfil the plan. Since there was no reason for companies to pursue quality or marketability, a noticeable decline in the quality and range of products set in, despite the numerous indicators and prescriptions to the contrary. These phenomena were frequently denounced in vain by the leaders of the economy: 'What is happening in the field of quality', Ernő Gerő stated as early as June 1951, 'is utterly intolerable and insupportable. It must be said that in 1945, in 1946, in 1947 and in 1948, when we had far fewer means at our disposal and we were far weaker economically, there were not so many justified complaints about the quality of the goods we manufactured for export.' Indicative of the serious decline is the fact that one per cent of the shoes exported had been regarded by the buyers as unsatisfactory in 1950, whereas 25 per cent of the shoes exported to socialist countries in 1951 were rejected.[12] Despite the most varied regulations, the incentive system was unable to produce any change for the better. For instance, the Duna Shoe Factory's proportion of rejects was 20 to 46 per cent of production in 1952. The figure for tyre manufacturing was 21 to 26 per cent, and so on.[13] Meanwhile the variety produced narrowed considerably. Before the war the factory had made eighty different models of men's shoes. By the early 1950s it was making only sixteen. Mass production of consumer goods became general. Shoe factories which used to undertake to produce as few as a couple of thousand pairs of a particular model now regarded anything less than 25,000 pairs as not worth their while. Shortage and lack of competition robbed choice of its importance to producers and trading companies alike. For instance, grain-leather shoes were unpopular, but 'they were all sold within a few days of delivery to the shops, because the customers found no other goods on the shelves'.[14]

So the system of volume-seeking incentives provided no real economic encouragement to fulfil the plan indicators for quality, technological levels, assortment or productivity. Since natural economic and market incentives were lacking, attempts were made to overcome this with a succession of new orders and regulations, the strictest possible control and the maximum degree of operative intervention from day to day to ensure that the central commands were obeyed. In November 1951 the National Planning Office decided to replace the previous system of irregular reporting with daily and ten-daily collection of data on how the main indicators were being fulfilled. All this material was collected from the companies through the ministries.[15] A characteristic example of how bureaucracy inevitably burgeoned was the procedure followed by the secretariat of the Ministry for Domestic Trade, which collected daily sales figures for sugar, lard, flour, bread, meat and so on from the individual trading companies. Meanwhile Budapest City Council called for daily sales reports on twenty-five other items.[16]

Since more and more commands were issued in an attempt to apply the central directives and realize the basic economic objectives, companies became snowed under by an increasingly incomprehensible mass of detailed instructions. For instance, the mining division of the ministry concerned sent out 121 instruction circulars to the mines in the first half of 1951 alone. Adding in the instructions from individual departments and the trust and centres, each received 1,024 circulars and instructions from ministries and other authorities in those six months.[17] In the twenty-eight months between January 1, 1952 and April 30, 1954, the Ministry for Metallurgy and Mechanical Engineering issued thirty-eight new instructions, amendments and supplements, plus two corrections, purely concerning the bonus system.[18]

The voracious central appetite for information and the flood of decrees and regulatory commands caused the administrative apparatus to swell considerably. In 1941 there had been one white-collar to every nine manual workers in Hungarian industry. By 1953 there was one to every four.

Yet in spite of all this, it became less and less possible to ensure that the commands and instructions were followed. The party and economic leaders had high hopes that moral and ideological pressure could be applied to achieve economic results. In May 1951 the Political Committee of the Hungarian Working People's Party passed a resolution declaring the need to create a climate of opinion in the factories 'that will make the position of the squanderers and wasters of material untenable'. But once a wasteful use of materials had become a direct help to companies in fulfilling their plans there was no preventing it by appeals, however frequent, for the subordination of the interests of the group (i.e. company) to the good of the national economy. In most cases where the interests of a company and the perceived interests of the economy clashed, the latter were defeated. However, the mass of instructions, the official controls and the influence of moral and political education were joined by the use of increasingly frequent and strict punitive measures. The various forms of disciplinary procedure, up to and including dismissal, became an important managerial method.[19]

Under a command structure in which company executives had to be compelled centrally to perform basic economic tasks, the ultimate yardstick in the assertion of central objectives (incarnate in dozens of plan indicators) was to enforce the spirit of the planning law by administrative means. As early as the summer of 1950 the economic leadership declared the following to be among the major tasks: 'Stringent measures must be taken to tighten up plan discipline and violators of plan discipline . . . must be brought to book not merely through disciplinary proceedings, but in more serious instances, irrespective of the persons involved, they must be brought before the courts.' The Presidential Council's Decree No. 4 of 1950, which regulated the protection of economic planning under penal law, prescribed a maximum prison sentence of two years for a significant departure from the detailed plan targets for which there was 'no pressing need'. For a serious crime 'involving grave danger to or infringement of the national economic plan or any of its detailed plans' the maximum sentence was five years. Administrative methods came to play a central part in realization of the plan.

But not even the full arsenal of legal and administrative measures could ensure that several plan indicators would be attained. On the contrary, despite the drastic stringency, the economy began to be marked by growing numbers of 'instances of indiscipline'. More serious even than the high material inputs of finished products was the failure to ensure adequate production of labour-intensive components, which caused equipment worth incredible sums to be wasted and export opportunities to be lost. It was impossible to ensure continuous production and eliminate the end-of-month and end-of-quarter rushes, when plan targets were 'met' at the expense of huge quantities of material and labour.

To sum up, it became obvious that an overly centralized system of planning based on compulsory plan indicators had seriously detrimental effects, most of which could already be felt in the early years of the First Five-Year Plan, although in the initial, short term they might conceivably have been considered to be minor deviances compared with the main, central objective and the achievements in forcing the pace of capital accumulation and industrialization. On the other hand, the system employed was no longer adequate in the long run even to further its central purpose, since its contradictions caused it to spring leaks through which a growing proportion of the total social product seeped away during the process of reproduction. The main leaks, which can also be discerned statistically, were the growing stocks of unsaleable goods and the resources 'frozen' in uncompleted investment projects,[20] and there is no doubt that a significant proportion of the national income produced in 1949–53 was lost through them. One can establish that about a fifth of the growth of national income at constant prices during those years was lost in these two ways.[21] Since a rise in the number of uncompleted investments is to some extent an inevitable concomitant of large-scale investment activity, one can only attach an informatory value to this figure, but it is clearly indicative of a process that emerged in the 1950s out of the forced pace of industrialization and the command economy that served it.

Thus the command economy that evolved after 1948 was the product of particular political circumstances. As an economic system it allowed the economy's latent potentials for extensive growth to be exploited, but it by no means provided an economic mechanism adequate for modernization in the latter half of the twentieth century, since it was unsuited to the generation of technical progress and modern production and service sectors. Despite the rapidity of the growth, its lopsidedness and wastefulness contributed to reproducing the country's relative backwardness later, at a higher level of industrialization.

All of this became quite swiftly and dramatically evident, and led to efforts to correct matters. By 1953 it was obvious that the targets for the 1950–4 five-year plan were not going to be met, and obvious too was the political necessity of relieving the social tensions which had been heightened by compulsory collectivization, political terror and a 22 per cent fall in real wages. Moreover, it was vital to halt the decline of agriculture immediately. Stalin's death, the end of the Korean War, the retreat of the direct threat of a new world war and the first signs that international tensions were relaxing cut the ground from under the feet of a policy founded on preparations for war. As Mátyás Rákosi put it in the course of a conversation in 1955: 'we had prepared for war and, unexpectedly, peace broke in on us'[22] and paved the way for the inevitable changes.

Part I

The first phase of the reform process: the intellectual antecedents and the first corrective steps, 1953–1964

1 The first moves to correct the economic mechanism

The need for change was made all the more apparent by the crisis that emerged in the hard winter of 1952–3, with serious disruption of food supplies, the collapse of the energy system, frequent power cuts and widespread shortages that were felt by the whole population. Curiously this coincided with the sudden death of Stalin in the spring of 1953, which generated a demand for change and a 'new course' of economic policy in the Soviet Union. Like the earlier aping of orthodoxy, the adjustment to change was also implied in the processes in East-Central Europe that were designed to produce uniformity. Summoned to Moscow along with Imre Nagy, whom he had earlier set aside, Mátyás Rákosi held talks with the Soviet leaders, who demanded changes in Hungary. The Central Committee of the Hungarian Working People's Party held a dramatic meeting in June 1953 that proved to be a turning-point. In a quite unprecedented way, the clique that held the leadership of the party so firmly in its grasp was obliged to make an emphatic denunciation of the policy it had been pursuing, and indeed to name those (themselves) who had been responsible for the grave errors and crimes committed.

The breaches of legality, the political murders, the unsuccessful First Five-Year Plan, the compulsory collectivization and its tragic consequences, and the dictatorial methods of the party leadership were all roundly denounced. Yet the June Central Committee meeting did not even mention the planning system. At most one finds reference to it indirectly in statements disapproving of the excessive expansion of an overly centralized and overly bureaucratic system of administration. In this respect the resolution 'On the Mistakes Committed in the Party's Political Line and Practical Work and the Tasks Connected with Rectification of Them'[1] confined itself to condemning the circumstance that 'the mistakes committed in the party's general line and in economic policy contributed greatly to the fact that administrative methods have been widely employed against the working masses, [and] the police and the authorities have meted out punishment on a mass scale . . .' In point of fact, the statement mentioned the command economy only in a single specific respect: 'From 1954 onwards', it said, 'a new, simpler system of compulsory [quota] deliveries must be defined.' In this case, too, the practical objective was merely to make a modest adjustment.

On the political level the command economy was still wholly identified with the socialist system. However, some serious political obstacle to change had been removed, and it now became possible to analyse reality and examine and criticize the solutions employed hitherto. Indeed, one must add that a decision to correct economic policy would necessarily involve attempts at least to correct the system of planning and control.

The new government, which announced its programme shortly afterwards, still did not extend its comprehensive criticism to the economic mechanism; however, the first very modest plans for correcting the economic system were formulated in 1954. On January 15, 1954 the (government) Council of Ministers adopted a resolution to eliminate 'damaging official bureaucracy' and to rationalize the apparatus of state. A government commission was set up for the purpose, and guidelines were drawn up, stating, among other things, that 'by passing down a requisite part of the spheres of authority the forces and means required for carrying out the tasks should appear where the tasks are'.[2] The special committees set up alongside the government Commission for Rationalization brought in practical and theoretical specialists and became the first to begin investigations that also extended to a more profound analysis of how the economy was functioning. Particularly important was the investigation carried out under the special committee on planning which was completed in May 1954, since by aiming to simplify planning it was the first to come up with a proposal for alleviating the excessive centralization. In this case, the substance of the corrections concerned a sizeable reduction in the number of compulsory, all-embracing plan indicators. It was this committee that proposed reducing the numbers of ministerial plan indicators from 11,497 to 3,200–3,330 and of governmental plan indicators from 5,899 to 655. (It should be added that this entailed compiling a more concise collection of plan indicators that would none the less cover almost the same sphere.)

Similar cuts were made in the system of compulsory reports on plan fulfilment, which provided the information on which the constant interference by the state was based. As a result came an announcement on September 18, 1954 that 85,000 state staff were to be dismissed, from the administration of state within a month and from state-owned companies by March of the following year.

In October 1954 a more comprehensive and longer-term project to transform economic policy and the planning system was launched under the direction of the government secretariat. The guidelines, which had already been drawn up, declared it would be impossible to accomplish the new goals without a change in methods employed. None the less, the practical work was still pursued in terms of reducing the number of compulsory plan indicators. The number of articles covered by the industrial plans fell from 2,085 in 1954 to 726 in 1955, and the number of agricultural indicators was reduced to a tenth. In July 1956 the National Planning Office carried out further simplification of the central planning process: from 1957 onwards it was decided not to provide a quarterly breakdown of indicators for total production, and it was also decided not to allocate raw materials centrally in cases where adequate stocks were available. Experimental reforms were introduced in the spring of 1956 at the Duna Shoe Factory, and these were followed by similar experiments at another eighty to a hundred plants, starting in the summer. Essentially, these involved reducing the number of compulsory indicators right down to a core, with the idea of according the companies greater freedom of action. In the case of the Duna Shoe Factory, there were just eight such after dozens had been jettisoned.

2 The critique of the command economy: towards a new concept of the economic system

While the modest, practical corrections designed to encourage a modernization and rationalization of the overly centralized, directive system of planning were developing, the first studies were completed and published from 1954 onwards. These demanded a far more radical and comprehensive reform.

In October 1954 the *Közgazdasági Szemle* (Economic Review), a monthly which had a long history, was relaunched and became a forum for arguments and debates in favour of reform. The editors did not immediately publish an already available study by György Péter, but waited until December before doing so. None the less, the first issue contained an article entitled 'Economic Viability and the International Division of Labour' by T. Liska and A. Máriás, in which they attacked the policy of self-sufficiency and import substitution. In arguing that there should be participation in an integral international division of labour they came up against the problem of the price system, which they criticized since it 'does not reflect values'. They emphasized that prices should reflect value even among the socialist countries and that 'the profitability of foreign trade can only be defined on the basis of a comparison of international values'. This concept, which allocates a central place in economic policy to foreign trade, is bound up with essential questions concerning the whole economic system, most of all with the role of market relations and the price system.[1]

The November issue carried an article by K. Szabó and S. Kopátsy on the calculation of agricultural prices. The theoretical stance taken by the authors was this:

> There is a comparatively broad goods production in this country's economy. In economic policy we must therefore assert the law of value extensively . . . According to the experience of previous years, the failure to apply the law of value properly and the substitution for it

> of rigid, administrative instruments impedes the growth of production and the improvement of living standards, and sooner or later will upset the process of reproduction.

In rejecting administrative methods, the authors underlined the importance of the categories of goods and market: 'In determining the price of individual kinds of agricultural product, the profitability of the production of the product concerned must be taken into consideration.'[2]

The sphere of debate was already wide by this time. On November 4, 1954, for instance, the Department of Agricultural Sciences at the Hungarian Academy of Sciences held a public debate on household plots (the smallholdings granted to cooperative farm members and state farm employees), the starting-point of which was an article by F. Erdei with a similar title. Erdei's point of departure was the principle that 'the collective farm and the household plot constitute an integral entity'. Although his stance, which was laden with compromise, involved rejecting the regular produce-producing role of household farms, this was emphasized during the debate by I. Okályi and L. Markó.[3] During the same weeks the journal *Többtermelés* (Surplus Production) carried an article by S. Balázsy bearing a rhetorical title, which went so far as to state in a discussion of organizational methods that the national economic plan 'is not the basis for organizing production'.[4] Even though the approach he employed was primarily microeconomic, he described the kind of corporate behaviour patterns that made it easier for companies to fulfil their central plan indicator for global production (e.g. the manufacture of large, heavy castings, the production of material-intensive goods, the neglect of spare-parts production, etc.) and recommended introducing *net* production value, i.e. an indicator of the *new* value produced by the companies. Moreover, in discussing the reduction of the number of plan indicators, he went so far as to recommend abandoning the 'breakdown' of the indicators for companies, which was the essence of planning based on compulsory indicators, proposing that just two indicators should be used: net production value and the absolute value of accumulation that was to be paid into the budget. Under this concept, companies would only draw up plans for internal use, and only two compulsory plan indicators would apply to them.

So the role of the market and prices was stressed from different standpoints. Whilst the articles just mentioned examined certain details, they stopped short of arriving at general principles. In the December 1954 issue of the *Közgazdasági Szemle* came a comprehensive concept of reform that amounted to a real revelation. The author, György Péter, head of the National Statistical Office, attempted to approach the dysfunctions of the economy not through the resulting specific, partial phenomena, but through their general causes.

> Our leadership's main methodological error lies in excessive centralization and bureaucratism . . . We have tried to solve economic tasks of fundamental importance . . . primarily by the mass issue of central directives . . . Through instructions expressed in several thousand indicators, the national economic and ministerial plans (plan instructions) also interfere in considerable detail in the life of individual ministries or companies.[5]

By contrast the author stressed a fundamentally new requirement of planning: 'What we should aim for is to achieve the required result not with more but with as few central indicators as possible, and what amounts to the same thing: we should ensure greater independence and freedom for the leaders of the ministries, authorities, companies, etc. . . . Companies', Péter stressed, 'are *autonomous* economic entities.'

The author argued that by issuing compulsory directives the government was interfering unnecessarily in company affairs. To make use of the means represented by companies there is no need for central directives. It will suffice to define 'the goals to be attained, the tasks to be accomplished'. This was all the more so, he said, because the implementation of all the detailed instructions cannot be verified, while an incentive coupled with fulfilment of a global production plan only supplies a material interest in quantitative growth. Thus 'production in certain companies has sometimes become an end in itself'.

The solution, Péter said, would be the replacement of the control from above using commands and punishment by 'the greatest possible involvement of those concerned'. Control would then be realized through the market relations 'which exist between the individual companies (and similarly between the companies and the consumers) and derive from goods relations and the operation of the law of value'. For this to happen there must be a change, to use a present-day expression, from a sellers' to a buyers' market: 'We must ensure that the users, the buyers . . . are able to lay down requirements concerning the assortment, quality and price of the products, that they are able to choose and . . . decide whether or not they will buy certain . . . products (at the price it is desired to set).'

However, two basic requirements must be met for this to happen: adequate stocks and variety must be ensured by eliminating shortages, and 'a correct price level and correct price ratios' must be developed. By eliminating 'incorrect, "artificial" price ratios' we must create 'the conditions under which the functions of money are consciously asserted in the running, the control and the planned, proportionate development of the socialist economy'.

Under the new system described, company incentive was to be concentrated not merely on quantitative fulfilment of the plan but on the profit gained on the real market at real prices and expressing the performance as a whole. 'The way to link the financial interest of companies . . . with achievement of the ultimate objective, for which we must strive in the interests of the national economy, is to establish a close correlation between the financial interest of company managers (and indirectly of the other workers) and the financial results of the companies, with as high a profit as possible.

Under the new mechanism of planning and direction that Péter underlined, the free allocation to companies by the state of resources required for investment would also cease, of course, since this results in their 'having no financial stake in utilizing the existing current assets effectively'. So companies 'would also pay a certain fee . . . an "interest" on the fixed assets placed at their disposal and on the investments'.

Obviously all this would radically alter the role of planning, which would then focus on defining

> the direction of development, the main proportions of the economy . . . Basically it is a question of such proportions as the one between the distribution of the national income and accumulation, the accord between the purchasing power at the population's disposal and the supply of goods, the development of the individual social sectors, the development rate of the individual sectors of the economy, the division of investments . . . This work . . . must be considered the main task of planning. However, the results of such comprehensive calculations cannot be of the nature of plan directives.

Though Péter, admittedly, did not wish to do away with compulsory plan indicators altogether, he thought that in order to ensure that the principal proportions were preserved there was a need for 'a few, relatively few, plan directives of a *notificatory* nature that must certainly be carried out'. These he considered essential for 'major investment projects' and 'the quantity of production of a few important export products and the extent of accumulation'. However, stipulations for production would be replaced by a 'system of delivery contracts' concluded between trade and industry.

To encourage acceptance of his concept in practice, Péter thought it important to stress at the end of his study that the principle of gain, profit, supply and demand 'resembles the way they are asserted . . . in capitalist society'. But application of these would not imply some sort of right-wing deviation. Drawing on the arguments put forth by Stalin at the Fourteenth Congress of the Soviet Communist (Bolshevik) Party, he states: 'The main thing is by no means that trade and the monetary system are the method of the "capitalist economy". The main thing is . . . that we should successfully use these methods and means . . . for laying the socialist foundations of our economy.'[6]

Péter provided his comprehensive critical analysis and recommended a new economic system in a mere twenty-five pages. In other words, he could only sketch his concept. No detailed analysis could be undertaken in that particular work.

Another work, completed in 1955–6, and also of decisive importance in the development of Hungarian economic thinking, attained a special significance too.[7] Although it had been publicly debated as a dissertation in September 1956 it was not published until spring 1957. János Kornai, the author, conducted a critical in-depth analysis of the excessive centralization in the case of the Hungarian textile industry and arrived via descriptive argumentation at some generalizable conclusions. In some 200 pages Kornai presented a detailed analysis of the system of compulsory plan indicators and the mechanism of incentives and penalties attached to it, and the practical operation and influence of all this. He had undertaken a novel task. As he wrote in his introduction, the dozens of textbooks 'which describe our methods of economic direction and planning, our system of prices and wages, etc. . . . have one serious fault in common: instead of saying how this economic mechanism functions in reality, they say how it would function if it functioned in the way its authors would have liked'. For his part, Kornai sheds light on how the Hungarian economy was actually functioning. But this demonstration of the functional disorders in the system is far from the book's greatest achievement, for he also proved that the various mistakes were not independent of each other, that they constituted a coherent system: 'We have surveyed the various phenomena of excessive centralization. These', he stresses, 'do not exist side by side by chance; they are not independent of each other, they constitute a *connected, cohesive whole.*' Indeed Kornai convincingly revealed that 'the autonomy of the company is more or less a formality. We can perhaps – with a slight exaggeration – compare it to a company whose sites and workshops are geographically scattered.

The industrial authorities equal the company management, whilst the company equals one of the scattered individual sites and workshops.'[8]

On the other hand, a company robbed of its autonomy and of its ability to carry out central decisions becomes wasteful and will not produce enough. Since the rigid price system fails to respond to supply and demand, it also rules out any automatic coordination of production and consumption, producing shortage and at the same time an accumulation of unsaleable stocks concurrently. Having revealed a multiple correlation, the author was led to conclude that individual elements in the economic system could not be corrected. If you single out the production cost indicator and remove it from its context, connecting it to financial incentive, alongside (or instead of) requiring fulfilment of the global production plan, this 'pushes the company towards a deterioration in quality . . . [and then] the production cost indicators persuade the company to aim, as far as possible, at a narrower assortment and avoid introducing new products'. So the 'quasi-reform [that] many desire today . . . allowing planning and the entire present mechanism of economic control to remain, allowing companies still to be obliged to fulfil the global production plan . . . but be given a far freer hand in their assortment and the compilation of their detailed programme . . . could do as much harm as good'.

It is on the basis of a comprehensive approach to the economic system that Kornai also develops his system of concepts: 'By the expression "economic mechanism" I mean the sum of our methods of directing the economy, the whole organizational form of economic activity, the whole workings of management . . . But it is intended to express at the same time that in referring to the economic mechanism we are not thinking generally of the production relations (in a *class* sense) but of a specific *organizational* form of a defined mode of production. In this sense it is possible for several kinds of economic mechanism to operate on the basis of social ownership of the means of production.'[9]

Although the overly centralized economic mechanism based on compulsory plan indicators is a logical, interdependent system, the facts which are described in detail show up fundamental contradictions in the way it works. 'The inherent contradictions of this kind can be relieved, but in order to resolve them the economic mechanism that engendered this contradiction must itself be changed.'

But if the interdependent economic mechanism is faulty, so that all partial corrections generate as many negative effects as they eliminate, if the existing system of operation cannot be equated with socialist relations as such, and several kinds of economic mechanism are indeed possible, the author comes to the ultimate conclusion that 'fragmentary changes carried out independently of each other cannot yield satisfactory results. What is required is a consistent and comprehensive reform!'

Kornai also outlines the main direction his analytical investigations are taking. 'Is the indicator really the essence of planning, as many . . . believe? The essence of planning: to create the main proportions of the economy on the basis of a consistent central plan . . . The indicator: *one* of the indispensable means for carrying out that task. But in addition, it is possible and necessary to resort to other means as well.' For instance, the bulk of the accumulation fund should be distributed centrally. 'The proportions in which the principal investment sums are distributed amongst the individual sectors of the economy and the sectors of industry, the plan of the most important investment projects – this is an obligatory indicator. This is perhaps the most important area in which directives can be used.'[10] The functioning of the economy must in any case be placed under *economic* 'compulsion' instead of the compulsion of directives, in which case the company is 'compelled by the competition for the customer'. The penalty for failure to fulfil plan indicators is not meted out administratively. The company and the management 'will receive a "monetary penalty" without any administrative intervention whatever', since the penalty 'automatically' accompanies the taking of a wrong step.[11]

These papers by Péter and Kornai clearly agree on a large number of points. Both embody a critique of the overly centralized system of planning based on compulsory indicators, and both propose a comprehensive reform, a new economic mechanism.

To make a critical appraisal of the theoretical foundations of the comprehensive reform would go beyond the scope of this book. These papers, along with several other studies, played a real pioneering role (although the theoretical accomplishments of the Yugoslav reform process and the Polish school of economics at the time had an obvious influence on them) and they defined the course of economic reform for several decades. No reflection whatsoever on the historical part they played is implied by adding that they did not lead in every area to a theoretical understanding of the more profound causes and correlations. Such a cognitive understanding progresses by natural stages as successive new experiences and layers of knowledge accumulate. Merely as a record of fact, and without the smallest intention of preaching with the benefit of hindsight, let me add here that it took even Kornai another quarter of a century to prove, in his book *A hiány* (The Economics of Shortage), that neither the pursuit of quantity and the concomitant, almost insatiable demand from the sphere of production, nor the recurrent shortage and the tendency for stocks to accumulate which the shortage generates are simply the consequences of a particular kind of economic policy or of the economic mechanism that corresponds to it. These 'distortions' are not forced on a company from outside, indeed 'the internal compulsion to expand is even more important because it has an even stronger impact on the functioning of the system. The internal compulsion to expand explains the appetite for investment and the insatiable reproduction of it.' The experiences of executing the reform show that the real difficulties for the economic leadership arise when they stand up against the excessive demand from below. The real pressure for growth, the extensiveness and the expansion, according to this theory, emerge from 'below', since for companies capital does not impose a limit on production.

> The company's survival is guaranteed; where prolonged losses occur, state assistance will sooner or later . . . come to the rescue . . . The growth of a company scarcely depends on profitability. As a result of all this a company's demand for input grows beyond all bounds, all the more because . . . the uncertainties caused by shortage oblige companies to accumulate stocks of inputs.

Kornai links this microeconomic analysis with macroeconomics by adding: 'The lack of genuine risk explains why there is no voluntary restraint on the demand of companies, public institutions or junior and middle investment. We can therefore say the demand for investment is almost insatiable.'[12]

Experience also proved that the company autonomy required is scarcely conceivable while the centralization of investment remains unchanged (or essentially unchanged). So something that both Péter and Kornai in 1954 and 1957 still regarded as *natural*, that investment must be carried out through centralization in the form of plan indicators, conflicts fundamentally with the basic elements of their system of thinking.

At the time when the theoretical basis for the reform was being laid, a fully-fledged concept was still lacking. In most cases the ideas went no further than to envisage curtailing the command economy, not eliminating it completely. Although this is clear from the systems of thinking already described, it is worth quoting explicitly the conclusions reached by the 'reform economists' in the summer and early autumn of 1956. According to Tamás Nagy, for instance, 'the economic mechanism connected with the law of value should function within the framework of central planning'. In this category he clearly included 'centralized disposal over the overwhelming majority of products', 'centralization of major investment projects', 'central direction of foreign trade', and even the 'central instructions to particular companies' on the quantity and assortment of production, when these were necessary.[13]

In September 1956 Péter Erdős expressed his concern in the party daily *Szabad Nép* about the 'limitless unleashing' of the law of value, since by doing this 'we renounce the greatest advantage of socialism' whereby 'we develop our economy directly in accordance with the interests of society as a whole'.[14] While arguing in favour of the reform, Erdős championed the compulsory elements of economic management as well. On the other hand Kornai, writing in the same paper a month later, emphasized that the command economy should be replaced 'to as great a degree as possible' by an economic mechanism founded on the application of economic levers.[15]

As László Szamuely put it in his account of the first wave of debate on reform: 'The conclusion from all this is that in 1954–7 economists were aiming for a rationalization of the centralized planning model known at the time . . . In these ideas there was a relegation of the normative nature of the regulators which would allow companies . . . to create an economically viable and competitive situation.'[16] In short, reform economists were not suggesting a complete change in the existing planning system. At the same time, the analyses were well founded, and the new concept which was developed was comprehensive enough to pave the way for a major reform.

However, there was no chance of realizing it between 1954 and 1956. In a development related to the internal power struggles in the Soviet Union (and the fall of Malenkov), Mátyás Rákosi and his clique regained the upper hand in the spring of 1955. At the March 1955 meeting of the Central Committee of the Hungarian Working People's Party, there was blame and condemnation of Imre Nagy and the 'right-wing deviation' discerned in the resolution of June 1953, and of the 'reformist economists' who were arguing for a new economic mechanism. In the March/April 1955 issue of the *Közgazdasági Szemle* an emphatic piece of editorial self-criticism appeared: 'Our [exponents of] economic science and also our sole theoretical economics journal, the *Közgazdasági Szemle*, bear responsibility for the fact that . . . expression has also been given to incorrect, non-Marxist views.' This editorial categorically rejected 'the overestimation of the theory of the role of value in the transitional period'. This 'overestimation (i.e. the emphasis on the market and its central role in the economy) has spread widely among our economists in the last year and a half . . . [and] certain articles have gone so far in overestimating the role of the law of value as to extend its coverage to the regulation of production in the socialist industry.'[17]

In the same issue of the periodical, Egon Kemenes challenged the views of György Péter, and István Friss those of Imre Nagy. József Nyilas also made efforts, using strong rhetoric, to meet the 'main task' defined in the March resolution: 'to smash ideologically and completely isolate the harmful, right-wing views'.[18]

3 The turn: reform goals of the government and the practice of correction

The turn could only come after the revolutionary people's uprising in October 1956, which destroyed the Stalinist system in Hungary.

In the autumn of 1956 a radically new situation emerged. The grave political crisis, coupled with a crisis of confidence permeating extremely large masses, paved the way not merely for forces advocating a radical renewal of socialism, but also for various trends of outright opposition to socialism. The uprising, which embodied different trends and possibilities, could not settle, however, and no one of the diversing trends was able to consolidate because the second Soviet military intervention of November 4 restored power. The new government, headed by János Kádár, a member of the previous party opposition who had established the new Hungarian Socialist Workers' Party with Imre Nagy in the stormy days of the people's uprising, parallel with the strong repressive measures, started to search for a renewal. The demand for radical change came naturally to the fore. This was done against the efforts at restoring the status quo represented by the politics of the old leadership that had failed. This renewal was all the more necessary as also the economic strategy pursued earlier got into political crisis and lost its credit with the public.

The armed struggles had died down but the atmosphere still resembled a war, with a strict curfew in force at night and strikes paralysing the country, when the Provisional Central Committee of the month-old Hungarian Socialist Workers' Party convened on December 5, 1956 to analyse the course over the previous years which had led to the tragedy, and to decide upon a new programme of action. The events of July to December 1956 had wrought changes which had set the country on an entirely new course, and it seemed as if many things would have to be started from scratch again. The party was rid of its earlier (not least personnel) burdens, and the new leadership, after a debate lasting three days and three nights, declared in the December resolution, its first major policy statement:

> From the end of 1948 . . . the Rákosi–Gerő clique abandoned the theoretical foundation of Marxism–Leninism . . . [and] in directing economic life introduced a sectarian and dogmatic policy . . . [and] bureaucratic methods of planning . . . They forced upon the people an economic policy which disregarded the country's economic conditions [and] hindered the rise of working people's living standards . . . They seriously discredited the agricultural cooperative movement in the eyes of a sizeable proportion of the peasantry. By copying the Soviet example mechanically . . . [and] relegating national interest . . . they seriously offended the national and patriotic feelings of the Hungarian people . . . The Provisional Central Committee maintains that the government, with the involvement of the competent state organizations and best economic experts, must work out as soon as possible an economic policy adequate to the new situation. This economic policy must in every respect rest upon our own economic conditions and characteristics. It must assist far-reachingly in the assertion of individual initiative and professional expertise . . . apply financial incentive in all areas, including the promotion of technical development, the improvement of quality, the reduction of production costs [and] the improvement of the efficiency of labour. The significance of planning is not diminished, but the sphere of its tasks must alter, and its attention be turned primarily to the establishment of the main proportions and line of economic development; where this poses no threat to the building of socialism greater opportunities must be ensured for the development of the private sector. The main concern in our economic policy is for the prime consideration in the redistribution of the national income [and] the preparation of our investment plans to be a steady rise in the living standards of the working people. The Hungarian Socialist Workers' Party regards as one of its principal tasks . . . the constant strengthening of the worker–peasant alliance. Our government's agricultural policy must serve this fundamental purpose . . . With a view to raising the living standards of the working people a powerful uplift of agricultural production must be facilitated on the individual peasant holdings and in the socialist [i.e. state and cooperative] sector of agriculture alike.[1]

These sentences quoted at length from the resolution's analysis of the economic situation and principles for devising a programme reflect a determination to start afresh. The search for *change*, renewal and courses suited to the local characteristics became a political imperative in the historically grave situation at the end of 1956. However, it was equally fundamental and imperative for the new government to ensure *continuity*. It should be borne in mind that the debates and the political groupings that emerged between 1953 and 1956, along with the majority of the political parties that appeared on the scene at the end of October, embraced a range of thinking that extended as far as practical rejection of industrialization and promotion of small-scale peasant farming into an ideal.

In contrast to this concept of a 'garden Hungary', in which agriculture based on small-scale peasant farms would have reigned supreme, the Hungarian Socialist Workers' Party laid strong emphasis on the continuation of socialist economic policy while restoring political power and the former, historically evolved path of socialist transformation (for instance at the party conference in June 1957). The continuation of industrialization and the gradual and deliberate collectivization of agriculture were regarded as principles of prime importance, in terms of politics and economic policy.

The dilemma of change and continuity was no simple one. Should there be continuity of basic principles, but change in the way they are applied? But where does principle end and practical implementation begin? The same dilemma influenced the efforts to transform the mechanism of planning and economic control, with confrontation between diametrically opposed views of radical reform and of partial, gradual corrections to the existing system. The party was indeed in a dilemma, since it recognized both the need for change and the need for continuity. The Kádár leadership itself had been formed under an imperative political compromise, and its constituent groups, to put it simply, did not emphasize the requirements of continuity and change in the same way. In short, there were different ideas about how the dilemma was to be resolved.

Between November 1956 and March 1957, in the thick of the everyday struggles to consolidate power, the need for radical change emerged as the vital political issue, but from the spring of 1957 the unexpectedly rapid process of political and economic consolidation caused the need for stability and continuity to be overvalued. The conservatives gained ground and started to emphasize that radical reform was not required at all – as Andor Berei put it, the need was 'not to do something *different*, but to do it *better*'. According to this interpretation, the continuity of economic policy and the planning system could be strengthened only by minor changes that did not go beyond the curbing of earlier excesses or conflict with the assurance that the old road was to be followed in a more effective way. It was argued that distortions and mistakes had only emerged when the targets of the First Five-Year Plan had been raised excessively at the beginning of

1951 and that the same strategy, coupled with more moderate rates of accumulation and investment, less extreme disproportionalities and, of course, a steady, modest rise in living standards, would provide a first-rate guarantee of continuity. These ideas remind one of the July 1956 resolution of the Central Committee of the Hungarian Working People's Party, and it did indeed become an increasingly widely held view within the party and the state apparatus in the spring and summer of 1957 that a smooth implementation of the July programme would have guided the Hungarian economy on the desired course, and could still do so now.

A great advocate of this view was István Friss, who headed the Economic Department of the Central Committee. Speaking in Parliament on the plan and the budget in July 1957, Friss said that 'after numerous healthy initiatives the party in July 1956 essentially took a position alongside the correct economic policy and economic management . . . [and since October 1956] we have taken significant steps along the path that was previously marked out correctly'.[2] In an address to the general assembly of the Academy of Sciences three years later, Friss placed even stronger emphasis on the same idea of continuity between the 1950s and 1960s, particularly between the principles of July 1956 and the practice since 1957:

> The experience gained in the course of more than ten years and especially in the last three years has demonstrated beyond any doubt the correctness of Leninist democratic centralism as, among other things, the basic principle of our economic organization . . . The economic successes we have achieved since the counter-revolution were in a large measure due to the fact that we have taken, partly in accordance with the party resolution of July 1956, a big step forward in decentralizing the management of the economy.[3]

These views were reinforced by the persisting ideological identification of socialism with the Soviet model, even in detail. Such views remained viable, so that conservative ideology still posed a quite serious obstacle to comprehensive reform. Meanwhile the economic and political consolidation taking place diminished the prestige and political necessity of major change.

There were conservatives who wanted to return to the old policy and drop the reform objectives and slogans altogether. József Révai (a former member of the Political Committee) expressed the views of these groups very clearly in a speech to the June 1957 party conference. Looking back on November 1956, and referring to the exclusion of the old, discredited leaders of the Hungarian Working People's Party,

Révai declared: 'In that situation, so to speak, this was *tactically* absolutely correct. Amid the circumstances of counter-revolutionary pressure it would not have been right to have taken upon ourselves such a burden as legal continuity with the Hungarian Working People's Party or a marked emphasis on political continuity.'[4]

Even to the majority of the party leadership who sharply rejected the view that the party's post-1956 policy was only an inevitable tactical concession, it could also seem as if radical changes might disturb the process of normalization and consolidation. At the same time, the exponents in the state and party apparatus of a modified continuity established a firm hold particularly on the middle and lower positions, where no radical changes in personnel had taken place. Their views, of course, were in line with their self-interest.

Analysis of these complex political processes is beyond the scope of this book, although a few aspects of them will be mentioned later in connection with the examination of economic transformation, where an attempt will be made to demonstrate in greater detail this final conclusion: whereas the emphasis at the turn of 1956–7 had been placed on radical change, it had shifted by the summer of 1957 on to a correctively adjusted continuity with the policy of the Hungarian Working People's Party.

Between November 1956 and the summer of 1957 a determinant economic reorientation took place in Hungary. A few days after the Provisional Central Committee resolution quoted earlier had been issued, the Economic Committee, the government's new, supreme body for economic coordination, met on December 10, 1956. According to the minutes, its chairman, Antal Apró, stated that 'the economic section of the government programme must be worked out . . . In addition, he considers it necessary to set up a broad committee of economic experts, members of workers' councils and industrial and agricultural experts to work out for the government the issues of economic policy and the methods of directing the economy.'[5] This expert committee was soon brought into being and formed eleven sub-committees of between fifteen and thirty members each, to devise policy concepts for domestic and foreign trade wages and labour policy, price and materials management, industrial production and organization, and financial policy. The work of these was coordinated by two main committees, of which one, the Industrial Production Committee, was headed by György Péter, one of the leading figures in the economic debates of the post-1953 period and the principal Hungarian advocate of comprehensive reform. The other, known as the Economics Committee, was the most comprehensive coordinator. It was headed by Professor István Varga,[6] who had been a prominent economist and public figure before, during and after the war, before being shunted aside in the 1950s. The secretary to this committee was István Antos, a leading expert who was later to be Minister of Finance. The choice of members and officers made it obvious that *this* committee of experts was going to present a plan for radical reform. Clearly there were influential groups in the party and government who looked forward to this, although some regarded the 'popular front' character of the key experts committee as significant only as a political tactic and wanted to take the coordination and drafting of the programme out of its hands.[7] However, when the experts committee was convened, this was not the stance that prevailed.

Preparation for radical reform of the planning and management system began straightaway. Indeed, it had actually started before the committees were appointed, and before the party Central Committee had met, with a proposal entitled 'Current Issues in the Organization and Management of the National Economy' drafted by the Ministry of Finance. This formulated extremely clear-cut principles for a radical transformation of the planning system. 'The socialist ownership of the overwhelming majority of the means of production continues to necessitate *planned economic* activity. From this it follows that there is a need for a national programme to ensure the development of the national economy and the correct proportions and correlations for it.' The proposal, completed on December 5, 1956, goes on to say that

> companies are operating on the basis of a plan approved by the workers' councils. The issue to be resolved is how the national programme and the plan of each autonomous company can be coordinated . . . As a general principle the figures in the national economic programme *will not be broken down by companies*. The application of the programme's objectives must be accomplished by means of economic influences. While establishing company autonomy, the assertion of economic influence at the same time requires central direction in certain areas of organization of the economy.[8]

According to this notion, the realization of the central objectives could be ensured by at least a temporary central regulation of investment and through management of the essential materials and of the wage flows. (Concerning the last, the proposal was for a central regulation on the per capita average wage that could be paid in 1957.) It follows from the nature of indirect regulation that 'one of the most decisive problems in the reorganization of the economy is the *price system*. A price system must be established in which . . . a flexibility of adjustment to practical life applies.' The proposal stated that stable, centrally determined prices were required in the case of consumer goods, but the price of the means of production would be the subject of free bargaining, in which the central will would be ensured by official price control over the essential materials. Clearly a new way of encouraging economic activity was also required. According to the proposal, 'The role of profit in the new economic system must be greatly increased . . . All of this justifies the introduction of *profit sharing*.' This was needed immediately and was 'in any case being demanded by the workers' councils too'. (It was considered necessary for companies to establish a profit-sharing and investment-innovation-welfare fund.)

Connected with the proposal drafted by the Ministry of Finance was a more comprehensive project begun in December 1956, with a group of about thirty or forty expert staff from the ministries, the National Bank and the National Planning Office. This proposal was completed in early January 1957 and was discussed in a number of forums during the spring. On several issues, however, there were significant differences of opinion among the members of the panel, and six of them published their own concept in the *Közgazdasági Szemle* in April 1957.[9]

I do not intend to give a detailed account of this proposal for reform, partly because its main principles bear a strong similarity to those of the Ministry of Finance and partly because the main ideas in it were incorporated into the proposal made by the government-appointed committee, which took as its starting-point the idea that the way to bolster planning was to abolish the 'system of compulsory plan indicators based on a breakdown by company'. This inter-ministerial expert committee favoured a system of incentives to encourage the overall activity of companies, basing it on market activity and market prices.

The philosophy behind the proposal was to combine central planning with the market economy. It was generally considered that 'we should drop the management of production mainly by commands. But at the same time we do not consider it desirable to introduce some kind of purely market mechanism (free prices, free production profile, competition in foreign trade, an absence of any central planning organization).' The main production profile of the companies would, for instance, be set by the supervising ministry. 'To expand, alter or perhaps narrow down the profile . . . a permit from the supervisory authority must be requested.' In the same way, important materials would be centrally distributed and the price system would embrace a combination of fixed and free prices.

A restructuring of the institutional framework was called for to expedite the introduction of indirect regulatory methods and the development of company autonomy. 'However, it must not be imagined', the argument ran, 'that this can be carried out if the present company frameworks are maintained . . . The application of the new mechanism requires that we . . . merge companies which have been artificially broken up. Similarly, it is conceivable that we would combine into trusts [i.e. holding corporations] companies which could expediently be run as small "autonomous" companies.'

Here it should be remembered that the reform proposals were being devised under extremely difficult historical circumstances, so that they were influenced not only by the level (and the weaknesses) of theoretical understanding but by tactical concessions to make them more acceptable. Those devising the proposal thought the dysfunctions of the economy could easily be cured by a partial granting of autonomy to companies and even more partial introduction of market prices. Moreover (and in this they were perfectly right in practice), the committee considered that reforms could only gain acceptance gradually.

4 Economic reform and the workers' councils

The ideas for a new economic mechanism that took shape in late 1956 and early 1957 naturally considered the role to be played by the workers' councils.

The earliest of these concepts, contained in the Ministry of Finance proposal at the beginning of December, actually took the workers' councils as its starting-point. As the preamble put it, 'Centralism, the bureaucratic economic system, has been replaced by the workers themselves through the establishment of the workers' councils, workers' self-management. The new situation poses several issues of economic organization upon which a position must urgently be taken, at least at a level of principle.'[1]

The same question was discussed from a theoretical point of view in the *Közgazdasági Szemle* by Sándor Balázsy. He noted that company autonomy and an orientation towards performance constituted precondition for workers' self-management, which 'can only be conceived of on the basis of a direct financial interest that would tie the workers' collective to the successful operation of the company'. But in Hungary the political developments constantly gave rise to this in reverse order. First workers' self-management arose, and only afterwards could 'the condition for it to function, the gradual assertion of company autonomy and the linking of company interest with the direct financial interest of the workers' collective, be accomplished'.[2] Almost in retrospect, therefore, the required system of economic institutions – the independent company – has to be provided for the political conditions which have already emerged.

The political situation, it seemed, had created a curious *fait accompli* in the field of self-management. The November 24, 1956 issue of the official gazette contained the decree of the Presidential Council legalizing the workers' councils which had come into being spontaneously in October. It was stipulated that 'the management of the factories, mines and works is undertaken by the workers' councils elected by the workers of the industrial enterprise'. Under the first point of Article 8, 'The workers' council decides on the company's most important issues, [and] controls the entire activity of the company.' Points 5 and 6 state that the workers' council 'decides the company's plans and the number of workers [and] determines the organizational structure of the company'. Its authority also extended within legal limits to fixing company wages and wage forms, to hiring labour and to deciding how the profits of the company should be used, the proportions of profits for 'production, social welfare and cultural investment and reconstruction, and the repayment of profit to the workers of the plant'. Under the first point of Article 9, the board of the workers' council 'decides the task of the manager of the plant'. Under the third point the employment and dismissal of senior company staff is made conditional on the board's approval.[3]

On the basis of this very wide sphere of authority, the party's daily paper, *Népszabadság*, described the workers' councils as 'the fundamental institution of the new system of economic management'.[4]

The trouble during these months was that the institution engendered by this policy was totally at variance with the existing system of operating and controlling the economy. It is understandable that a debate on the issue raged in the press for months. On December 25, 1956 the chairman of the workers' council at the Zugló Factory for Chemical Products recognized the contradiction inherent in the fact that 'the manager is subordinate both to the supervisory state body and to the workers' council . . . that the law divides the supreme company power, and so provides the opportunity for debate, conflicts and slackness'. To resolve this, he said, 'the plant can only have one master, the workers' council'.[5] But a fortnight later the manager of the Plumbing and Heating Installation Company was arguing that 'the state is the actual owner of the company . . . The mistake in the [Presidential Council's] decree is precisely that it provides an occasion for a misunderstanding in principle by entrusting the workers' councils to carry out tasks which in fact belong to the economic [i.e. company] management. Now direct economic management cannot be the task of the workers' councils, since they are not executive organizations.'[6] Another contributor argued that 'many interpret things as if it were part of the [workers'] council's sphere of authority to decide what to produce from what . . . In my view that is not the case, since the company is unable to gauge the national requirement . . . for every article!'[7] On the other hand, the chairman of the workers' council at the Electrical Appliances and Components Factory, in looking at the changes to be made in economic policy, considered it was precisely the company plans devised by the workers' councils according to guidelines from the higher authorities that would ensure that 'we shall at last be able to talk of real plan discipline'.[8]

The contradiction was expressed thus in a *Népszabadság* editorial (quoting the words of a company director): 'We are being ground between two millstones. From above we are squeezed and commanded by the ministry, from below by the workers' council.' Although the article stated that this contradiction could easily be surmounted, it stressed that the workers' council should provide ideological guidance rather than play an executive role, adding that dual subordination was not a 'newly invented or temporary' phenomenon. It was something that 'should be developed further, not eliminated', the paper said.[9]

The situation really was contradictory, as the government was obviously aware when it set up a committee in mid-December to prepare for a system of workers' self-management. At the meeting of this committee on January 30, 1957, Industry Minister Antal Apró, who was in the chair, emphasized the significance of central planning and said 'firm central direction' was called for until the country had 'overcome the difficulties' of the extreme conditions and the serious raw material and energy shortages. Apró pointed out that 'the company manager is directed both by the ministry and by the local workers' council. But the management of the company is wholly the task of the manager.' He saw this duality as emerging because 'the establishment of the workers' councils means in practice that a dual control – characteristic of socialist public administration – is being applied'.[10]

But a debate and a struggle of a different kind was raging around the workers' councils during these months. János Kádár said in the spring of 1957: 'The workers' councils . . . came into being in such circumstances and under the guidance of such elements that they initially served the interests of the counter-revolution. The situation later improved and the workers' councils continued.'[11] This struggle was motivated to no small extent by the fact that the Budapest Central Workers' Council, which had formed on November 14, 1956, conducted an open campaign against the government, organizing a general strike.

Meanwhile the Budapest Central Workers' Council was also forming ideas about how to reorganize the economic system. It wanted to replace the command economy with a medium-level organization by creating 'chambers' for the companies in each industry which would rush to the assistance of the autonomous companies by supplying materials, coordinating sales and marketing, and allocating production quotas and framework delivery contracts. These chambers would have been grouped into a national chamber of industry, and similar agricultural chambers were envisaged on a regional basis in the countryside, with a national chamber of agriculture as the supreme representative organization. The national chambers, including others for cooperatives, commerce, transportation and so on, would delegate representatives to a self-governing National Economic Council and would set up another self-governing body, an economic planning committee of expert advisers.

According to these ideas, the executive organizations of the government and all the ministries and regional administrative councils would have functioned in parallel with the self-governing organization of the economy. The administrative authority over the economy would have covered supervision, legal matters and industrial inventions, labour safety, theoretical aspects of technical and scientific development, and – on the basis of recommendations by the National Economic Council – the allocation of investment funds and supervision of how they were used. In the event, the government banned the Budapest Central Workers' Council, along with the Budapest district and the provincial county and city workers' councils on December 9, 1956, on the grounds that they had become centres of political opposition. However, the government continued to tolerate the factory workers' councils, even in the spring and summer of 1957, as institutions of factory democracy, so long as some required personnel changes were made. In a keynote speech at the party Central Committee meeting on May 18, 1957 Jenő Fock emphasized: 'Our party is strong, our dictatorship of the proletariat stands on a firm foundation. For that very reason the impatience and hastiness that marks the work of our party organisations in connection with the workers' councils is unjustified. We must make it clear: the workers' councils are fulfilling their purpose provided they answer at least three fundamental conditions' – that they rest on the basis of socialism, that they enhance factory democracy and that they help to resolve economic problems. He said workers' councils which met those requirements must be supported, while the remainder had to be modelled upon them.[12] By contrast, the desire to restore political power at local and factory level caused local party organizations to attack the workers' councils fiercely, not least out of a desire for political retaliation and related personal motives. So in practice the winding up of the workers' councils began. 'In most plants in Borsod County', János Kukucska, second secretary of the county party committee, reported in the summer of 1957, 'the workers' councils have already died out . . . after coming into being and operating as organs of the counter-revolution, not the revolution . . . They organized the strike . . . they were organs for political sabotage and incitement against the government. For this reason the plant workers' councils in Hungary must be institutionally abolished.'[13] But at the national party conference in June 1957 this was by no means the stance finally taken by the majority, and even József Révai quarrelled with it: 'I regard . . . Comrade Kukucska's position . . . as a sectarian position. The workers' councils were, admittedly, the offspring of counter-revolution in this country . . . But the overriding factor is not that but whether there are still sizeable strata of workers who regard the institution of workers' councils as their own . . . We have no right to disregard their views.'[14] Even though for Révai the top priority was again political tactics, these tactics (no rush to abolish the workers' councils while the majority of workers identified with them) were by no means the sole reason for the stance taken by the party leadership and the government. This was clearly expressed by János Kádár in the summer of 1957:

> What should be the correct procedure with regard to the workers' councils? . . . How should we decide? I think it was wrong that certain workers' councils were disbanded in May Day pledges . . . even though people say the workers had insisted on the abolition of the workers' councils. In certain places the workers had actually insisted on this. For instance, in certain mining areas . . . But elsewhere perhaps thirty communist employees took umbrage at them, while seven hundred female textile workers did not . . . This is not the way to resolve the matter. The party must soon work out its position in this respect . . . I think the most important thing is for workers' control . . . to be increased institutionally in the factories. We must ensure that workers' control is carried out by the directly elected representatives of the workers . . . This control cannot of course be allowed to weaken central direction or eliminate the authority of the manager; it must amount to realistic supervision and a say in affairs. This is the decisive thing. Whether it is called a workers' council or something else is a matter of secondary importance. In my view we can safely call it a workers' council.[15]

In the summer of 1957 the preparations for transforming the workers' councils began at the instigation of the Central Committee. The sphere of thinking involved in this exemplified well the unpublished position drawn up at the end of May, which referred back to the plans for developing workplace democracy that had come up at the beginning of 1956. Along with a certain degree of decentralization in the management of the economy there arose 'the requirement that factory workers become directly involved in company management', as the May analysis put it.

> After these precedents the workers' councils came into being in the midst of the counter-revolution. In most cases these turned into counter-revolutionary organizations. At present their role as organizations in the economy has not been clarified. The following ideas are possible about the future of the workers' councils: one can establish centrally which are the companies where workers' councils must and can be set up, at the same time as redefining their tasks; the fortunate strengthening of the trade unions will allow workplace democracy to increase while sidestepping the workers' councils, and so the workers' council can be abolished with the approval of the majority of the employees; the workers' council can be transformed into an advisory body attached to the company manager, of which 50 per cent of the members are appointed and the other 50 per cent elected. On the basis of the Central Committee resolution, the delegated committee will draft a proposal on the workers' councils in the near future.[16]

So a gradual phasing out of the workers' councils began in spring and summer 1957, although the debates still continued over their future as an institution. At top levels of government not only a policy of toleration but the demands for democratization of the workplace were considered sustainable, and the same held true for the institution of the workers' council, *incorporated into the system of central management*. Nevertheless, the question of eliminating or transforming them came to the fore, and the affair in any case showed up in a radically different light than it had during the weeks when the decree on the workers' councils was enacted by the Presidential Council.

The political situation and institutional role of the workers' councils was obviously a factor in the very deliberate division made between the case for workers' self-management and the reform of the economic mechanism in all the concepts of radical reform that followed the earliest ones of December 1956. Not only do they avoid using as their point of departure the need to create the economic conditions for company autonomy on behalf of an institution of workers' self-management that already exists, they go out of their way to point out that the cause of economic reform is independent of the destiny of the workers' councils and workers' self-management. Although all the major reform proposals in the spring and summer of 1957 reckoned with this institution and considered that the operation of the reform and the activity of the workers' councils could be linked, the reform proposal from the inter-ministerial expert committee mentioned earlier underlined: 'The specific tasks of the workers' councils in the management of industrial companies must be defined in detail and – more or less – finally, after the creation of the [economic] mechanism. We do not agree with those who say that creation of the new mechanism has been made necessary by the existence of the workers' councils.'[17]

The expert committee set up by the government and headed by István Varga and István Antos underlined in its proposals:

> It is the opinion of the Economics Committee . . . that the methods of economic management it has proposed can be applied more effectively if the company workforce, in institutional forms, takes an active part in the management and control of the company . . . In view of the fact that according to the measures in force there are workers' councils operating in the industrial companies, it seems expedient for the functions in question to be the responsibility of those councils.

However, the proposal, which was dated May 29, 1957 and entitled 'The Planning of the National Economy and the Factors and Methods of Plan Fulfilment', stressed unequivocally that the proposals 'concerning the new principles of operation for socialist companies would, the Committee is convinced, remain expedient even if the workers' councils were not to cooperate in the management of companies'.[18]

So economic reform in Hungary, as a consequence of the political processes taking place, embarked on a course of its own entirely independent of the destiny of the workers' councils and workers' self-management.[19]

5 The principle of the substantial reform

Returning to the reform proposals, one should emphasize the desire of the political leadership at the turn of 1956 and 1957, as expressed in the Central Committee resolution of December 1956, to introduce comprehensive reform. This desire was closely linked with its rejection of industrialization at a forced pace and of compulsory collectivization, and with its determination to raise living standards. Great political importance was attached to the idea of reform, which received a great deal of publicity.

At the beginning of January 1957 the party daily *Népszabadság* carried an article by István Földes 'On the New Method of Our Planning System'. The previous economic system in Hungary 'in which everything was ordered from above, through a mass of compulsory plan indicators . . . stifled company autonomy . . . [and] made it impossible even to recognize the genuine interests of the national economy'. An extensive debate on a reform of the economic system which would mobilize the internal forces of the economy had already been going on: 'However, there have been impediments to this work, primarily . . . as a result of resistance by economic and party leaders who stubbornly adhered to the old ways . . . With the removal of these impediments the work has now speeded up. A separate section at the Planning Office has been created to work out the guidelines for the new economic mechanism . . . *The principal instrument of state direction will not be the obligatory plan indicator, but planned influence by economic methods.*'[1] A week later the paper was saying that 'the faulty system of economic activity did not give people an interest', and economical, profitable activity by plants which had now 'come of age' could develop on the basis of individual interest.[2] At the beginning of February, light was shed in a series of interviews on the government programme that was being prepared. An interview was published with György Péter on the work of the reform committee which he headed and on the application of the 'economic accountability and financial incentive' which was to replace direct commands. A piece by Jenő Wilcsek reported on plans for transforming the price system.[3] Another week later the *Népszabadság* underlined the importance of the work done by these committees in preparing for the democratization of industrial management, which it described as 'an important condition for the success of our socialist construction work, one that we neither want nor intend to abandon'.[4]

It is worth comparing the newspaper articles for the general public with an unpublished position. In February 1957 the Central Council of Hungarian Trade Unions expressed its impatience in a briefing on the economic situation:

> Not even the outlines of the new economic mechanism have been clarified. Our present economic situation makes temporarily justified a degree of centralism (for instance, in raw material and energy allocation) even greater than the old, yet in the individual regulations and statements . . . we do not express decisively the temporary nature of the currently justified centralized measures, indeed we not infrequently underline to an exaggerated extent the longer-term necessity for centralism . . . *Not infrequently, we identify the requirement for a planned economy with the damaging method of excessive centralization . . . Concepts must be developed both for the structure of the economy and for the new economic mechanism.*[5]

In the early months of 1957, the political authorities were trying to hasten radical change in economic activity. The government, or more precisely the expert committees, certainly got straight down to work, since they had only a month in which to present their proposals. The first comprehensive proposal for reform was completed in early March 1957, and the first part of it was submitted to the government at the end of April. The second part ('The Planning of the National Economy and the Factors and Methods of Plan Fulfilment') followed at the end of May, and the government received the full draft on June 1.

The significance of these proposals is enormous, since they constituted a comprehensive reform proposal, covering every sphere of the functioning and organization of the economy, of planning and of state and company activity in terms of their relations to the new objectives of economic policy and of how to achieve them.

The full proposal presented below[6] was divided into three chapters. The first summed up the prevailing situation of the economy and the second the principles from which the new economic policy sets out. (Despite their close correlations with the substance of this book, they will not be presented here since this investigation is intended to focus on the historical path taken by the reform.) The third chapter sketched a draft of the new economic mechanism. 'Remaining firmly within the basis of a centrally controlled, socialist planned economy', the introduction declared, 'we must also search for the means and methods that can render the management of our economy more flexible, but exclusively in order to make it more effective, a still better instrument for implementing the central plans.' The full proposal continued: 'In certain respects, direct intervention will always be necessary. However, the majority of compulsory plan indicators . . . become superfluous.' Elsewhere it said that 'drafting of annual plans will continue, based on the long-range plans for the economy, for whose implementation the government within its own sphere of authority will be responsible. The breakdown into individual plan tasks at company level, however, will only be done in exceptional cases, since the government will ensure plan fulfilment by indirect means. For this very reason, the instruments and methods that ensure the fulfilment of the plans must be defined within them.'

The proposal sees the government as 'regarding company independence as one of the basic principles of the new economic mechanism'. For this it was, of course, indispensable that producer prices should correctly reflect the corporate and social costs of production.

The price reform was envisaged as ranging from industrial producer prices through charges for services to consumer prices. Both the introduction of a system of fixed, maximum and free-market prices and the gearing of consumer price ratios to value ratios were judged to be essential: 'At the same time as the new price system comes into force . . . the composition of the cost of living should be established according to more correct proportions.' Within this process, major price increases in rents, transport and services would be effected over a period of three to five years and in turn be offset by wage increases (as 'rent supplement') financed out of money gained from the reduction of payroll taxes incorporated into industrial prices. Moreover,

> our specific Hungarian conditions . . . increasingly demand that in developing the new price system we pay due regard to world-market price relations. The correct establishment of import prices requires above all the production of realistic rates of exchange . . . The prices of imported raw materials must reflect actual expenses incurred, [while] exporting companies must be given a maximum interest in the price to be obtained abroad. The production company will receive the price obtained abroad, converted at a realistic rate of exchange.

In this way companies would be oriented by market prices while receiving an incentive. So the proposal was for an immediate implementation of profit-sharing. The laying of the foundations for company independence also necessitated a transformation of the system for investment and financing: 'We shall introduce a system for supplying fixed and current assets to companies that abolishes the previous practice of giving companies free use of fixed and current assets and requires of them a utilization fee for fixed assets, and the payment of a comparatively high rate of interest for current assets.'

The draft also covered the institutional side, envisaging as the supreme managing body of the new system a National Planning Committee in which other economic experts would be involved alongside the ministers with economic portfolios and the chairman of the National Bank. 'The Ministries would be relieved of much of their executive work.' Their task would mainly consist of preparing development and investment concepts, gathering market information and monitoring company activity. Direct ministerial control would be abolished, as would the other controlling institutions, whose place would be taken by supra-company trusts and associations, which would support individual groups of companies and maintain direct contact with the ministries. As an earlier version of the draft put it: 'It is worth examining whether the establishment of a single ministry for industry would not be more appropriate after a certain interim period.'[7]

However, the reform proposal contained a large number of guarantees that government policy objectives and central plans would be carried out. The first of these guarantees was that the system of centralized investment financed from the budget would be retained.[8] Central management of materials was accepted over quite a long interim period and would only be dispensed with once a 'surplus of goods' had arisen. Similarly, the proposal incorporated central price regulations and viewed free-market prices in certain areas as conditional on a satisfactory goods supply.[9] On top of all this, the system of compulsory plan indicators was also regarded as sustainable within certain unspecified limits.

All in all, the reform proposal tried to consider a variety of prevailing conditions and struck compromises with them. Necessarily, therefore, it fell short of the level of economic understanding at that time, which was partial in any case. With hindsight, it is clear that implementation of the proposal would not wholly eliminate the dysfunctions in the economy.

More and more concessions were made even while the reform was being prepared. One confirmation of this is found in a letter of June 17, 1957 from István Varga and István Antos to Antal Apró, who chaired the government's Economic Committee. They informed him that four members of the reform committee had appended their personal opinions to the commission's second report of May 29, giving as the reason:

> The original draft was built on the idea that the system of compulsory plan directives (with the exception of investments) would be abolished and the implementation of the plan would be ensured within the system of economic incentives. In the course of the negotiations at the sessions of the Economics Committee, this idea was modified. The document now submitted starts out from the premise that under certain conditions the methods of compulsory plan indicators must also be applied.[10]

The backtracking is clear even from a comparison of the committee's first draft of March 2, 1957, signed by István Antos and István Varga ('Proposal Concerning the Formation of the Economic Structure and Mechanism') with the full report at the end of May, mentioned already. By contrast with the stringent restrictions we have noted in the full report, where free-market prices are regarded as possible only for goods of secondary importance, the first draft stated: 'Once a surplus of goods has been created, supply and demand will influence the prices *in every case* in which a surplus can be ensured.' Another general, unqualified statement was that 'state subsidies must in principle be abolished all along the line'.

The ideas on the price system were naturally connected with the concept of systematically eliminating command-style planning. 'In company economic activity', as the draft of early March put it, 'planned economic activity will continue to apply. Each and every company will continue to draw up a company plan, even though these will not have the character of a directive.' The companies, the ministries and the National Planning Office were to keep one another informed, but the plans of the central organizations were not to be binding on companies. 'To direct and influence companies various instruments of economic policy assume a greater significance, including credit, pricing and fiscal policy.' Among the proposals of the Industrial Organization Committee was an emphasis on the same idea: 'Under the new economic mechanism, the role of *indirect* economic methods will gradually gain predominance . . . These methods, first and foremost, are the price system, the various methods of deduction from [company] income . . . the credit system and the more intensive application of financial incentives, which manifests itself in the wage system and the system of awarding bonuses.'

Under this concept the state as proprietor 'leases the fixed and current assets and the "goodwill", the value of the name, to the company workforce'. In return, the company pays a usage fee of 5 or 6 per cent for the fixed assets placed at its disposal, a rate of interest set by tender on the sums received for renovation and investment from the centralized share of the depreciation fund, and an interest rate of 18 to 20 per cent on the current assets placed at its disposal. On the other hand, the company can establish a reserve from the retained company profits to ensure flexible economic activity, while with the remainder it will pay a profit share to the workers. Companies which do not perform well could even become insolvent. 'In certain cases', according to the draft, 'liquidation procedures might even be taken against insolvent companies.'

As Varga and Antos put it in their letter quoted earlier, the basic idea was to retain the direct central sphere of power and intervention only in the single area of investment policy. Indeed the committee's draft in early March states unequivocally that 'sums to be allocated for investment purposes will continue to be subject to detailed planning of a command character'. However, the draft also linked centralized investments with the principle of company autonomy, for 'although the cost of the new investments should be allocated from budgetary resources, on the basis of strict planning, these would not be free of charge but based on an interest rate like the one we have generally prescribed under the heading of the usage fee for the independent funds'. The new company would be formed before the launching of the investment project and its managers would be appointed, having from the outset a stake in ensuring that the investment was as cost-effective as possible and a responsibility for the management of it. Although profits could also be a source for company investment under this system, these would be far smaller in scale than the investment from the budget.

Finally, it should be stressed in connection with the reform programme that the expert committee linked with the reform the prime task of restoring the equilibrium of the economy. Initially, amidst an acute shortage of goods, it regarded it as important to have a relatively high degree of central intervention. These areas of intervention were gradually to be eliminated once the equilibrium, or 'surplus of goods' as it was often described, was ensured. The experts thought recovery could be achieved in 1957–8. Bearing this in mind, they stated that the new 'economic mechanism can only be accomplished gradually'. At the same time they unequivocally expressed (in Supplement No. 1, already quoted, of the original reform draft) what they did and did not understand by gradualism: 'Gradualism cannot mean that the practical introduction of the proposals should or could be postponed for years. The old methods of controlling the economy cannot be pursued any longer; they would not resolve our grave current difficulties.'

6 A counterproposal for partial corrective measures

Before continuing to follow the career of the draft reform prepared by the government-appointed committee of experts, let us consider another aspect of the story. From the outset there had been a strong current of opinion in conservative circles that the system of planning based on compulsory indicators was fundamentally correct. All that needed doing, they considered, was to trim its 'excesses' and 'distortions'. They sharply rejected the idea of radical, comprehensive reforms, arguing that the Hungarian Working People's Party resolution of July 1956 had pointed the way for the economic mechanism. Consolidation would have been effectively accomplished by the Second Five-Year Plan (prepared for the years 1956–60) through a process which the 'counter-revolution' of 1956 had interrupted. Once political power was gained back, they continued, the task was to return to the course set in July 1956. A clear formulation of this view was made in June 1957 by István Friss, head of the Central Committee's Economic Department, when he addressed Parliament on the plan and the budget:

> After many healthy initiatives, the party in July 1956 adopted a stance in favour of the essentially correct economic policy and economic management [of an] extension of democracy, large-scale decentralization, greater local autonomy, individual incentive and a more correct approach to financial incentive in economic life. [Since October 1956] we have taken significant strides along the path which had earlier been designated correctly.[1]

While the elaboration of a new economic system had begun and been making some progress in the first half of 1957, in accordance with the December resolution of the party, the advocates of the other concept had been working to clarify and validate their own solutions. Their position was stated very clearly in a memorandum of May 24, 1957 entitled 'The Party's Economic Policy':

> We firmly adhere to the Marxist–Leninist concept of central direction and plans that cover the whole of the national economy . . . At the same time we must obviously learn by the mistakes and rectify them . . . Planning extending over the whole economy, along with central control, must be combined with local autonomy and encouragement of local initiative. This is the direction in which the party resolutions of July 1956 point, and this is the path indicated by them, along which we were moving before the counter-revolution and along which we have been progressing since the defeat of the counter-revolution.[2]

A few days later, in a revised version of the memorandum, the clause 'Leninist democratic centralism must be asserted in economic life' was added.[3]

But the history of economic ideas demonstrates that such a thing as an eternal Marxist–Leninist concept of planning has never existed. In the final years of Lenin's life, after the revolution had been won, planning was linked first with the system of war communism and direct, central allocation, and then with the New Economic Policy (NEP), based on market relations. There can be no argument about the way democratic centralism, the Leninist principle of party organization, can be applied in the management of the economy (although this concept of what to do about the economy was never expounded other than in slogan terms). Translating it into the language of planning, 'democratic centralism' can only imply the institutionalization of 'plan bargaining' well known from the practice of compulsory planning. Under it companies may argue and express their points of view, and the authorities have an interest in bowing to them up to a certain point, but in the end the companies are obliged to abide by the central decision. Ultimately, emphasis on 'democratic centralism' in the economy merely implied some kind of corrective, partial decentralization of the command economy.

Extremely interesting from this point of view is the investigation carried out during these months under Friss's supervision with the aim of rationalizing the old system of planning. While the government-appointed committee of experts were busy drafting their proposal for reform (the main ideas of which were known by the spring), a quite different corrective process was developing as well. The project involved analysing the cases of thirty industrial companies in early 1957. As Friss wrote in his summary,

> It was indeed characteristic of this period that the pre-October 23, 1956 system of economic planning had ceased, while no new method of economic management had yet been developed. Under such

circumstances the companies themselves developed the most important deciding factors in economic activity, applying the methods they considered best. This means at the same time that in industry, and in other sectors of the economy as well, an experiment on a national scale has gone on.[4]

The lessons were interesting. As the manager of the Csepel Auto Works reported,

In December last year and in the months of January and February 1957, we could not talk about . . . a planned economy . . . All our company received was a single figure as a target, which fixed the attainable production value at 60 per cent of the figure for the previous quarter. The company acted quite independently in fleshing that figure out with goods, by seeking links with cooperating companies and with buyers. Based on their requirements we compiled production, labour and production-cost plans.[5]

The situation at the April 4 Engineering Factory was similar: 'The two main indicators laid down for the company were the profit on completed production and fulfilment of the export plan . . . So it became the company's task to determine all the connecting plan tasks arising out of the two compulsory tasks.'[6]

From all this Friss drew the conclusion that 'one of the most undoubtedly positive experiences of the most recent period has been that the commonplace and the stereotyped in planning have ceased . . . [and] plans are better aligned to the characteristics of the sector and the company concerned'.[7] For the National Combing Mill, for instance, there were central prescriptions for investment, the quantity of finished products, the quantity of raw material and yarn to be used, the average wage level and the profitability. In the case of the Kőbánya Pharmaceutical Factory, compulsory indicators were set for the output of three priority lines, for the forint value of export deliveries, for the volume of exports of two particular products, for the utilization of the two main raw materials, for the wages fund and for the sales. In practice, the custom of prescribing a 'global production value' was disappearing, although it was still used, mainly in the food industry.

On this basis, Friss proposed the following:

From the experiences with the current system of planning it also follows that it is expedient to prescribe the production volume for the products most important to the economy, the export plan, the maximum quantity to be used of the materials most important to the economy, one factor regulating wages, along with the company's results and its total expenses. These indicators . . . are justified by

> several circumstances . . . otherwise it would be left to chance to decide which companies . . . are able to obtain materials for producing which products and how, not to mention the inevitable speculation and corruption.

However, Friss proposed increasing company autonomy and reducing the number of compulsory plan indicators: 'It is desirable to institutionalize this situation which has developed spontaneously and to obstruct the attempts which will undoubtedly be made by ministries to restore the earlier constraints of planning without exception.' There is an important lesson to be drawn for the rationalization of planning, according to Friss. If the ministries no longer provide precise prescriptions for particular products 'these are developed by the production and wholesaling companies concerned', which allows demand to be met in a better way.[8]

A similarly large number of spontaneous changes took place in the wage system.[9] During these months the previous, direct wage regulations were replaced by prescriptions and control of average wages. 'The control of average wages is not very popular', one report stated. 'Companies fiercely attack it. The main objection is that it prevents the growth of wages', and also that 'it increases unemployment within the factory gates, because superfluous workers are hired at low wages in order to push down the average. It obstructs the growth of productivity . . . It prevents the introduction . . . of an incentive wage system.' None the less, the proposal stated categorically: 'It was necessary to prescribe average earnings, and it remains correct to keep average wages . . . in central hands, lest . . . wages should follow widely differing patterns of increase. This would, on the one hand, cause a large-scale migration of labour, and on the other bring excessive wage increases in some places.'[10]

To sum up, the Friss proposals amounted to a correction of the command economy and were designed to conserve the old centralized planning, while allowing slightly greater scope for company independence. At that particular moment in history it was not merely designed to improve the economic system. It was concerned far more with providing an alternative to comprehensive reform, a substitute for it that would seemingly satisfy the demand for change.

7 Immediate corrections to the operation of the economy

While the divergent concepts of comprehensive reform and of correcting the command economy were taking shape, there also arose a need for immediate, practical action which it would have been dangerous to postpone in the current political and economic situation. More and more rational, corrective measures were proposed to the authorities and discussed one after the other by the Economic Committee and other organizations of government, with a view to implementing them straightaway.

Of the more important of these, one of the first to be taken concerned the price system. The government's Economic Committee had already discussed a suggestion to establish a Prices Office in December 1956. As the proposal under consideration phrased it:

> The democratization of our economic activity and the development of the new economic mechanism make it indispensably necessary for a position to be taken on the role and regulation of prices . . . Under the new economic system to be developed state regulation of prices need not embrace the whole of goods production and turnover; a significant part in the setting of prices must be given to the companies . . . [and] indirect or lesser forms of price regulation must be used over a wider area.[1]

A month and a half later, Béla Csikós-Nagy, as president of the new National Price Office, was putting these basic principles to the Economic Committee in a document 'On the Current Tasks of Price Regulation in Industry': 'The Economic Committee has established that the application of the subsidy system is not reflecting the requirements of the socialist price mechanism, and this system can therefore be maintained only temporarily. After the normalization of the production level of costs in industry, the system of industrial producer prices must be completed by December 31, 1957, so that [these prices] can come into force on January 1, 1958.' The proposal links the emergence of prices proportionate to value with the demand for company autonomy and the existing fact of workers' self-management. Csikós-Nagy warned that the 'atrophy of financial incentive would [otherwise] occur precisely at a time when we would like to incorporate the system of workers' self-management into the economic mechanism'.[2]

In March the government made temporary arrangements for regulating industrial prices in order to defend consumer prices, but the decision was accompanied by a statement of principle that the subsidy system 'fails to comply with the requirement of a socialist price mechanism' and could only be retained until an overall settlement of producer price was made.[3] In fact, the work of setting producer prices in order began, the objective being a system of prices proportionate to value and inputs which would work in favour of economic clear-sightedness, orientation and incentive.

The most important and consistent reform measure was taken in agriculture, the starting-point clearly being political, since it became vitally important from the point of view of power to win over the peasantry, for which a mere cessation of the enforced collectivization and official harassments of the 1950s would not have sufficed. In addition, the abolition of the hated system of compulsory delivery became inescapable, all the more because the government of Imre Nagy had already announced its abolition in October 1956. Any return to the old way was now out of the question even from the political point of view. A similar position had arisen with the other agricultural bulwark of the command economy, the system of compulsory sowing plans.

The government's announcement that compulsory deliveries and other such obligations would be abolished came in November 1956. Unlike other sectors of the economy, agriculture was shorn of the basic institutional foundations of the command economy. Previously, compulsory deliveries had been linked to artificially low prices unconnected with value, assisting in a kind of exploitation of agriculture in favour of accumulation and industrialization. But in agriculture's case the command economy was not merely corrected, it was brought crashing to the ground. Compulsory delivery was replaced by market relations between the state and the peasantry, leaving the government the weapon of price incentives. In the spring of 1958 the Minister for Agriculture declared: 'After the abolition of the compulsory delivery system, the administrative relationship between state and peasantry was primarily replaced by commodity relations of a commercial character.'[4] The logic of market relations and the absence of administrative compulsory prescriptions elicited and assisted in the development of an increasingly realistic price system that abolished, among other things, such artificial administrative discrimination as the paying of higher prices for cooperative and state farms than to private farmers: Government Regulation No. 3263/1957 provided for a uniform system of farm prices.

Of course the government had a struggle on its hands with the new agricultural policy. For instance in the summer of 1957 the district council of Edelény in Borsod County sent round 'offer-collection' sheets. 'In some places', a confidential report notes, 'a dangerous phenomenon, especially on the part of the councils, can be observed, manifested in the application, out of a desire to meet plans for free purchases, of the old methods, which do more harm than good . . . Excesses can easily occur, or rather enforced "offers" produce meagre quantities . . . We must emphasize particularly that . . . producers are now really beginning to believe that compulsory delivery has ceased.'[5]

Nor can abolition of compulsory sowing plans be regarded as the natural consequence of issuing the regulation. In a variety of covert forms, sometimes simply through 'emphatic' advice, the local authorities strove to apply their plans, and the old habits persisted for years.

Various corrective measures arose out of indispensable, day-to-day practical requirements in other fields as well. For instance, a proposal for correcting the previous system was made in March 1957 by the Minister for Light Industry. It was designed to create more flexible incentives and apply the profit motive, but the ambivalence of the attitude behind it is quite clear: 'It must be borne in mind that companies will neglect the production of certain less profitable or loss-making products . . . We wish to prevent this by having the authorities . . . issue *directives* ordering the products concerned to be made and reducing the size of the profit in cases where the manufacture of them is neglected.'[6] In a word, this was compulsory planning and direct state intervention again, although not in such detail as before, surviving as a last resort. Incidentally, this behaviour was not merely characteristic of ministerial bodies, for companies themselves found their bearings in the new environment only with difficulty. When central planning relaxed around the turn of 1956 and 1957, confining itself to a few compulsory plan directives and ensuring companies greater autonomy, primarily in product assortment, sales and purchases, the majority of managers themselves sought to arrive at firmer centralized planning. Of course, this was partly because the compulsory nature of planning was still unchanged in spite of the lower number of indicators employed and partly because partial independence created a somewhat ambiguous situation. Moreover, most of the managerial staff had become accustomed to central planning under which they had only to carry out central orders, and so found it easier for them. Finally, companies wanted safeguards in relation to their suppliers. As a consequence 'the ministerial and *corporate* organizations for business activity pressed for the restoration of economic discipline, in order to gain the grounding for the fulfilment of their plans'.[7]

With uncanny speed there was confirmation of the emphatic warnings some economists had made about corrective changes in 1956: 'The solution cannot be sought in a mere quantitative reduction in the number of indicators, the columns of figures or the roster of administrative staff.' Indeed, some wittily pointed out that such a partial simplification, if the foundations of the mechanism and the command economy were left unchanged, 'would only strengthen the improvisation that operates in an unhealthy direction, and so engender a self-defeating trend: an attempt to restore the plan indicators and bonus criteria which had been abolished'.[8]

Despite the contradictory situation, the government successively initiated a variety of corrective measures. For instance, partial changes were prepared for the mechanism of foreign trade. In January 1957 the Economic Committee discussed a joint proposal by the Ministers of Finance and Foreign Trade for revising the price-equalizing system which had been hitherto applied in foreign trade.[9]

They saw 'a need for resolute measures that encourage more economic foreign trade activity . . . their introduction also being justified by the expansion in the number of companies with direct foreign trading rights'. It was proposed that the difference between the unrealistic official rate of exchange and the real rate be offset by domestic surcharges from April 1957 onwards. 'The present exchange rate . . . acts as a brake on exports and an incentive for imports. [Moreover] the practice of automatically offsetting from the state budget the real price differentials that arise must cease.'[10]

All in all, the government strove to overcome the disruptions caused by the malfunctions of the economy and to assert the new economic policy objectives not by comprehensive reform but by provisional, partial measures.

Part and parcel of this correction process was an aim to allow greater scope for the private sector, which had been almost entirely eliminated. This was underlined, for instance, by the existence of private farms, which it was thought would continue for a long time, and by the role accorded to the household farms tilled by members of cooperatives. As for the policy towards private industrial and servicing activity, it is worth quoting a report from mid-December 1956: 'The National Planning Office, in starting to prepare the plan for the year 1957, took the following main considerations into account: . . . (d) Substantially more scope than before must be allowed for private initiative, in both production and commerce, and to this end private investments advantageous from the point of view of the national economy must also be encouraged.'[11]

A daily paper reported on January 5, 1957: 'The self-employed working in the building industry, carpenters, bricklayers, painters and decorators, electricians, etc., will receive . . . permits as quickly as possible, within one or two days.'[12] On January 26 the government passed a resolution on the development of small-scale private industry that included a 20 per cent reduction in the rates of tax applying to them. It allowed the self-employed to undertake work for the public sector and ensured supplies of materials through a public tender system, at the price the state sector was paying. It also altered the regulations that constrained export activity.[13] A month later, the tax break for self-employed craftsmen was granted to self-employed shopkeepers and freelance members of the intelligentsia.[14]

Encouragement of private enterprise was also the intention behind a decision by the government's Economic Committee on February 1, 1957 to allow certain state-owned shops to be leased. State-owned retail and catering outlets that were operating 'with great difficulty under company management' could be rented out to private individuals. This was to be 'introduced experimentally for 200 units, after which *c.* 1,000 units, a round 6 per cent of the retail network, will be rented out'. At the same time greater scope was to be given to wholly private retailing. Under the proposal, the figure of 9,500 private retailers already operating could be 'raised to a maximum of 20,000' by issuing new permits.[15] On February 19 a government decision to this effect was published as well,[16] but nothing much came of it. Róbert Hoch stressed in the *Közgazdasági Szemle* the strength of 'the unjustified resistance to the expansion of private activity, the obstructiveness and hairsplitting, the panicky fear of private trading (and private craft industry). Yet the gratuitousness . . . of this must clearly be seen . . . Were I to presuppose for a moment the *absurdity* that private retailing's share of turnover was going to increase tenfold by comparison with 1955, it would still, even then, be less than two-thirds of what it was in 1950.'[17]

The situation with nationalized housing also came up for reconsideration.[18] The nationalization policy of the early 1950s had gone to such extremes that an astonishing 30 per cent of the state-owned houses contained only one dwelling and another sizeable percentage between two and four dwellings. The plan was to resell to individuals the 200,000 dwellings in some 70,000 houses with not more than six rooms in them.[19]

So, without the theory or practice of according almost total predominance to state ownership being altered or the need for private activity to play a bigger part and have a right to exist in a society proceeding towards socialism, a modest adjustment to the structure of ownership began. The breadth of the area in which the various corrective measures were taken is illustrated by the examples given. Many thought that adjustments of this kind were going to make the economy run smoothly and resolve most of the defects in the overly centralized command economy. A few years were to pass before it was realized at government level what a failure this policy of corrective measures had been.

8 Intervention against the comprehensive reform plans as 'economic revisionism'

Correction and rationalization of the existing economic system was called for by all who regarded any substantial deviation from the Soviet model as fundamentally incompatible with socialism. In their eyes the corrections being introduced were in no way initial steps towards a more comprehensive, radical reform, they were a substitute for it. Moreover, they firmly rejected any break with the comprehensive system of planning by command. Confronting them were the reform economists seeking a comprehensive strategy for change, whose view was shared by the economists of the expert committee: after a brief period of transition comprehensive change had to come. Introducing a bit of their proposal here and a bit there was not going to work. The proposal for reform devised with extra speed in December and January by the interdepartmental panel of experts took express issue with any notion of procrastination, gradualism or corrective tinkering. Their position document, quoted earlier, was quite adamant: 'In our view it is likewise impermissible to treat *full implementation* of the mechanism as a distant prospect . . . we must also consider how economic policy and the economic mechanism exert a reciprocal influence on each other.' Without a comprehensive reform of the economic mechanism, the change of direction in economic policy – discarding forced quantitative growth, the 'iron and steel' programme, aiming at a new development policy relying on the conditions and traditions of the country, involving the development of agriculture and the raising of living standards – which the government also professed would be endangered. There was no way of 'supporting the correct economic-policy objectives with the mechanism employed up to now. Indeed with this mechanism, under which even clear economic discernment cannot be achieved, it is hardly possible to develop a proper economic policy at all.' At the same time it was clearly stated that previous measures to simplify the system of planning indicators and increase company autonomy had 'not proved effective. These measures, even at best, have produced only a minor *quantitative* change, and they have not resulted in any qualitative change.'[1]

This view became extremely prevalent among economists, some of whom argued heatedly against partial tinkering. While the exponents of comprehensive reform sharply rejected such partial corrective measures as to cut the number of compulsory plan indicators, the advocates of them launched a devastating counter-attack that coincided with the reconstruction of the monolithic political power structure.

It was clearly not a mere clash of conflicting ideas. Those who saw comprehensive reforms as 'reformism' or a betrayal of socialism equated socialism with the Soviet economic model. The Soviet economic system that had emerged at the end of the 1920s and the beginning of the 1930s, and that still existed in those years, was an inalienable component of their image of socialism and the only model they could conceive of for a socialist economy.[2] The fundamental traits of this planning system were seen as something inviolable; only minor corrections to it could be reconciled with socialism. This political and ideological stance appears very typically in a lengthy study entitled 'Ideological Struggle against Revisionist Economic Views', dated May 24, 1957 and intended for publication. The author was Andor Berei, an economic adviser to the previous party leadership who had served as president of the Planning Office, and in October 1956 emigrated to the Soviet Union. An indication of the significance of the views it contained is given by the fact that it was discussed at the request of Jenő Fock by the Provisional Executive (i.e. Political) Committee of the Hungarian Socialist Workers' Party. It is certainly worth tracing its line of argument and main conclusions.

'Revisionist views', Berei writes, 'appeared with frequency in our economic writings before October 1956 . . . These views still exercise an influence – not to be underestimated – on our economic scene. This article . . . applies a critical analysis to the manifestation of economic revisionism currently most fashionable, which appears under the banner of the "new economic mechanism".' Although real mistakes are the starting-point for these economists, 'they exaggerate them and generalize from them'.

After his introduction Berei raises his main question:

> Is planning of the national economy . . . possible without compulsory plan indicators extending to every sector of the economy and every part of the country? Plans for the economy at the present stage in the

> development of the socialist economy can only be state plans that are centrally devised . . . Uniform, central plans can only be implemented safely and unequivocally by state methods, primarily by *making plan indicators regulating production, allocation, etc. compulsory*. If the plans did not assume the form of *plan directives*, they would be shorn of their chances of fulfilment. How can one describe as a plan at all an economic concept which is neither a law nor a command?

Having asserted that traditional planning is the only option, Berei goes on to elaborate:

> Economists who advocate the new mechanism argue that abolition of the 'system of commands' does not rule out the implementation of national economic plans, since the state is able to divert company activity into a planned channel by the indirect means of financial and other measures . . . Yet financial, credit and other, similar, measures in themselves cannot guarantee that the thousands and tens of thousands of companies will produce and deliver at the time and in the quantity the uniform plan for the national economy requires.

In Berei's eyes elimination of the so-called plan breakdown, of compulsory plan directives, will lead to nothing other than a return to capitalism:

> There emerges clearly before us the unbridgeable contradiction that exists in the new economic system between acknowledgement in principle and practical denial of planning. By abolishing the leading economic role of the socialist state it will actually end planned economic activity as well. Willy-nilly, the new mechanism will amount to anarchy of production, a dominion of 'blind laws' . . . and will day by day increasingly 'reproduce' the capitalist elements in the economy . . . The revisionist critics of the planned economy . . . dethrone the specific development laws of socialism and place on the vacant throne not a new but a long-familiar idol, the image of the law of value.

In considering the received interpretation of 'Leninist principles' and the 'principles of socialism' to have an exclusive monopoly as a natural right, he is categorical and unequivocal:

> Although the views and theories emerging under the title of the new economic mechanism contain some correct ideas in their details, they amount basically to a cardinal revision of the Leninist principles of building a socialist economy and important tenets of socialism's political economy . . . *We reject the new economic mechanism as a manifestation of revisionism* and as a misleading concept.

It is clearly no insignificant coincidence in an article written in the spring of 1957, while the government-appointed committee of experts chaired by István Varga and István Antos were working feverishly to prepare the reform proposal, that Berei should have included in his article a personal, if 'courteous', slight on Varga:

> [The new mechanism,] as István Varga, who with praiseworthy candour professes himself to be a non-Marxist economist, writes, can function 'only when the national economy is in equilibrium' . . . The advocates of the new mechanism obviously hope that if equilibrium prevails at the moment of introduction not even the new system of economic activity will upset it . . . The final verdict on the new economic mechanism is delivered by the admission that this system cannot bring about 'the establishment of national economic equilibrium' – either initially or continuously.[3]

It was worth spending some time on the line of thinking in this article, which was never published, because it illustrates the views of those opposed to comprehensive reform with great clarity. For the same reason, it is worth quoting Berei's conclusion in the article:

> The way to rectify the mistakes is not to demolish the foundations of the planned economy, which alone meets the requirements of the socialist economy, but to overcome, radically and thoroughly, the anti-democratic, bureaucratic and voluntarist distortions manifest in the application of the Leninist principles of the socialist economy . . . To the economists who demand a different mechanism our reply is, not a different one but [the same] done better! It is not a different mechanism that we need but a better and more perfectly functioning one of our existing system of a planned economy.

From this logic it follows self-evidently that 'the revisionist views pertaining to the new economic mechanism do not merely fail to enhance the extremely necessary efforts and researches aimed at' real improvement, they 'constitute one of the greatest obstacles to them . . . The new mechanism is not an economic wonder drug but among the most harmful manifestations of revisionism. Against it we must wage an ideological struggle of convincing force.'[4]

Similar positions were expressed from the spring of 1957 onwards. In a debate on March 19 among the economists working at the National Planning Office, several staff members took issue with those of their colleagues who were advocating radical reform and spoke up for the system of planning by directives.[5] A few days later, a new paper called the *Gazdasági Figyelő* (Economic Observer) carried an article by Géza Ripp entitled 'Planned Economy or Anarchy'. This quite lengthy piece, bitterly opposed to reform, made the following accusation against the reformers:

> On the pretext of criticizing the errors that actually exist they have launched an attack on the Leninist principles of directing the socialist economy . . . and proposed something new instead . . . Rejection of centralized planning [and advocacy of] decentralization . . . signify that we turn from the path of planning to the path of spontaneity. The independence of companies from central control, [and] competition between companies . . . inherently contain a real danger that the direction of economic processes will slip out of society's control. Spontaneity . . . can lead only to the emergence and enhancement of anarchic tendencies, which will inevitably obstruct the development of socialism and strengthen economic forms based on the private ownership that still exists.[6]

Early in April, the *Gazdasági Figyelő* carried an editorial comment, 'Restoration of the Capitalist System', which denounced the reform as a stand-in for counter-revolution: 'Frontal attack having proved a dismal failure in Hungary, the recipe for counter-revolution has changed . . . They are seeking to advance patiently, inconspicuously, step by step. We therefore emphasize unceasingly that we must be watchful in [taking] decisions on economic issues . . .'[7]

Many argued that the cause of the earlier economic problems should be sought merely in the economic policy, not in the command economy itself. László Háy, who was editor-in-chief of the *Gazdasági Figyelő* and rector of the Karl Marx University of Economic Sciences in Budapest, was among those to do so, picking out the 'excessive scale' and 'excessive tension' of the plan, and declaring that 'the basic problem lay in economic policy'.[8]

In a joint article in the April issue of the *Közgazdasági Szemle*, Ilona Bieber, József Fábián and Emil Gulyás likewise rejected the idea that the mistakes of the early 1950s originated in the system of planning and control: 'In our view the errors derived not from the economic foundation, the production relations, but from the economic policy. The economic policy was oversized . . . The rectification of the mistakes made in economic policy did not require the kind of qualitative change that would demand an alteration in the socialist production relations.'[9]

Arguing against this, a number of economists came out firmly against divorcing issues of economic policy from those of the mechanism and disputed the categorical rejection of comprehensive reform: '[When] an economist raises new ideas with a view to improving our socialist planned economy, there are some who immediately blow the whistle and, generalizing their condemnations of socialism's overt and covert foes, oblige these well-intentioned people to retract as well, damping their creative inclination.'[10]

None the less, the tide of condemnation and sharp criticism continued to rise, particularly from the summer of that year onwards. Endre Molnár had sharp criticisms to make of several contributions to the *Közgazdasági Szemle* in an article entitled 'Revisionist Views on the Economic Role of the Socialist State' in the theoretical journal of the party, *Társadalmi Szemle* (Social Review):

> In the course of the efforts to work out the new economic mechanism the attacks have been centred on the Stalinist assertion that 'our plans are not plan forecasts, not plan guesses, but plan directives'. The common feature of the proposals demanding a new economic mechanism is precisely the way they are directed against the strongly centralized state control of the economy, a state control embodied primarily in the national economic plan that embraces the whole economy and has a compulsory validity . . . There are many discrepancies and differences among the advocates of the new economic mechanism. However, many concur in their willingness to accept the compulsory plan, the command [system] in the state control of the socialist economy, only as a necessary evil, and they labour nostalgically to construct an economic structure in which the system of price and value mechanisms and economic incentives would automatically provide regulation.

By contrast, the writer himself makes a categorical assertion: 'If the economic activity of companies is unregulated by state plan targets of validity . . . if production is therefore regulated essentially by the law of value and the mechanisms of the market (which is characteristic in a capitalist economy), the damaging phenomena characteristic of the capitalist economy will necessarily arise.'

Whereas Molnár's reasoning is also connected with the international struggle between capitalism and socialism ('From the antagonism between the imperialist and socialist camps follows the necessity for a powerful proletarian state and a consistent, centralized state leadership in the field of the economy as well'),[11] the line of thought pursued by István Friss brings him to a similar conclusion by way of an emphasis on the technical trends of development apparent in capitalism and socialism alike.

> In discussing the main identical influences of technical advance on countries with differing social systems . . . we wish to mention one last fact. This is the growing weight of state intervention . . . The question of the direction in which the socio-economic consequences of technical advance ultimately point extends to the other question of whether or not technical advance increases the necessity for central control of economic activity . . . The answer supplied by the facts [the

> author claims, making a rather arbitrary selection from them] . . . is quite plain. The growing weight in the non-socialist countries of state intervention in economic activity, the growing number of attempts by non-socialist countries to develop a sizeable proportion or the whole of their economies on the basis of a plan for several years, points to the fact that *centralized control of economic activity is increasingly becoming a constraint, a necessity.*[12]

Heated public debates took place in the summer. In June a dispute broke out in the *Gazdasági Figyelő* between István Varga and László Háy. Varga objected to several articles in the paper which had attributed to 'some' an intention of furthering revisionism and the restoration of capitalism. These articles, Varga said, were grappling with erroneous views not in fact subscribed to by Hungarian economists at all: 'There may be "certain people" in Hungary who genuinely espouse . . . the opinions stigmatized in the articles concerned. But it is curious none the less that I, for example . . . should only have come across "others" so far.'[13]

Háy, who edited the paper, listed specific examples in his reply as evidence that 'revisionist views . . . have in fact arisen'. He included among the examples the views of all who have not sought the cause of the problems in mistaken economic policies and had rated the pertaining system of planning and control as bad. 'This means', he said, 'that once the new mechanism . . . develops, the administrative methods [such as] . . . specific plan indicators, must vanish.'[14]

The debate spilled over into the daily papers. In August 1957 Tamás Bácskai reiterated in the *Népszabadság* how it had been a serious mistake in 1953–6 'not to have sought requisite methods of planning and control for our new economic policy in time, instead creating a dangerously ambiguous situation by trying to patch the old methods belonging to a different course'. On the subject of György Péter's concept of reform, Bácskai declared that its substance was not 'for the plan to be a function of the spontaneous mechanism of the law of value, but for the law of value to be placed in the service of the plan . . . [while] the so-called economic mechanism, the methods of planning and control, undergo a radical perfecting process. However, this radical change . . . does not amount to revisionism.'[15]

But three weeks later, a diametrically opposed position was taken in the same paper by István Friss's deputy, Edit Varga, in a full-page article entitled 'Improvement or Revision of our Planned Economy'.[16]

By October 1957 the readers of the *Népszabadság* could have been in no doubt about which view had prevailed. István Friss, in his lecture 'On a Number of Practical and Theoretical Issues Pertaining to the

Direction of the National Economy' to the Political Academy of the party, expressed the objectives of partial, moderate corrective reform unequivocally, while dealing in detail with the 'revisionist tendencies' arising in Hungarian economics, among them the position taken by György Péter, whose views, he concluded, 'really come very close to revisionism . . . Even though he himself is not a revisionist, this line of thinking contains the danger, for him or others, of engendering revisionism.' As for János Kornai's concept of the mechanism, it amounted to 'Kornai's rejection of our entire socialist-type economic system' according to Friss, since it embraced the entire machinery of the economic system, which it considered had to be changed. 'For lack of any other alternative, he would presumably like to replace it with capitalism', Friss charged. However, wishing to come to a more differentiated assessment, Friss stated that the majority of the economic studies did endorse the planned economy and come up with useful proposals for improving it, and so he preferred to interpret their controversial character as a 'revisionist tendency' rather than revisionism, and he recommended caution 'in using the epithet revisionist', particularly because 'some people have been accused of this entirely without foundation'.[17]

The closing chord of the public debate was a resounding rejection of the reform concept expounded by the expert committee and of the one put forward on the basis of it by István Varga in the *Közgazdasági Szemle*. Edit Varga was particularly categorical in stating in her introduction:

> István Varga's article, which contains a number of statements of detail which are correct, is none the less incorrect in its substance and overall effect . . . István Varga claims he . . . wishes to further a strengthening of the planned economy; the train of thought and the logic of his article, however, have just the opposite influence on the reader . . . So his train of thought with its slogan of improving planning actually ends in the blind alley of the impossibility of planning.

Against the anxiety and doubts the author expounded what she considered a full guarantee that the economic laws would be correctly identified: 'There is no reason for supposing that we shall not . . . become more familiar with the laws of the socialist economy or that we shall not be able to approximate to them in our plans to a far greater extent than hitherto.' On the other hand, the planned economy fitted into the system of proletarian dictatorship, for whose economic policy 'the plan is the main instrument . . . If the plans are realistic and in accord with the laws of economic development, accomplishment of them depends primarily on the activity of the agents of the socialist state. Can the economic programme of proletarian dictatorship be executed without directives? Clearly it is quite impossible.' And since István Varga, in his controversial study, had turned even to Stalin for arguments to underpin his position, quoting Stalin's remark that 'we must not forget that apart from the elements which can be influenced by our planned economy, our national economy also has elements that cannot for the time being be subjected to the planned economy', Edit Varga proved with philological accuracy that it was her critique Stalin was confirming, for István Varga had only quoted half of Stalin's sentence, which goes on to say there are antagonistic classes 'which cannot simply be overcome by having the state planning office elaborate plans', and so 'issues which cannot be regulated by the plan must be resolved by means of class struggle'.[18]

The criticisms of reform were given a final, official endorsement in a study entitled 'A Few Remarks on the Ideas and Proposals of the Economic Experts' Committee', which was also discussed by the party's Working Group on Economic Theory. Its author, István Szurdi, likewise considered several detailed proposals by the committee to be usable and useful, but he asserted: 'It must be stated here unequivocally that the instructing of companies in state ownership is a concomitant and fundamental characteristic of the socialist planned economy, and the chief method of state regulation.'[19]

Thus the leading figures in the determining of economic policy[20] had said their final word and delivered their political and ideological verdict on the basic issues of the reform, so closing the debate. Indeed, the public debate was closed for a time, but only for a time. In the mean time, while the debates had been going on, the economy had been consolidating with surprising speed after the serious disruption around the turn of 1956 and 1957, which was accompanied by the threat of inflation and unemployment.[21]

In the autumn and early winter months, production had still been paralysed by strikes, but from January 1957, when average daily output was running at 72 per cent of the figure for the same period of the previous year, the situation returned to normal. In February, daily output was 17 per cent higher than it had been in January, in March almost 28 per cent higher, and in May 35 per cent higher, which meant it only fell short of the figure for May 1956 by 4 per cent. In an article headed 'The First Quarter and a Few Lessons', the *Népszabadság* reported that industry under ministerial control had attained 80 per cent of the previous year's production level.[22] The change for the better was particularly spectacular in mining, the most critical sector. In December, average daily coal production had been 14,700 tonnes, but in April it was 67,312 tonnes,[23] and in May 1957 it was back to the level of 1955. The pre-1956 level was approached in power generation and steel-making, and it was surpassed in cotton and shoe manufacturing. Domestic stocks, which had dwindled in value from 14,500 to 8,700 million forints between October and December 1956, began to grow again, reaching 12,500 million forints.[24] International financial commitments, the significant trade gap and the budget deficit could be financed from the commodity and foreign-exchange loan made available by the socialist countries.[25]

Accompanying this process and partly attributable to it was a remarkably swift political stabilization. In April 1957 and again on May Day there were enormous rallies backing the government. Just as the shock of the serious collapse had strengthened the inclination to comprehensive reforms, so the swift economic and political consolidation did the opposite. Comprehensive reform was rejected and the policy of retaining the command economy's fundamental characteristics, while correcting it only in detail and gradually, became the dominant, official line.

It was in this essentially altered environment that the decision was taken between partial corrections, which had already begun in many fields, and radical economic reform, which was seen as a potential disturbance to the smooth process of consolidation. The outcome was clearly influenced by numerous practical and political considerations. A big factor was certainly the aim of sustaining the favourable, calm and less shocked atmosphere, in order to ensure an effective process of consolidation. So were the ideological and political considerations. Under the prevalent historical conditions, the fundamental features of the Soviet economic model which had emerged in the early 1930s under rather special conditions were still considered tantamount to Marxism–Leninism and the laws of socialism. Various views and objectives jostled in the political leadership, particularly in the summer of 1957, when the old dogmatic wing made a strong attempt at a comeback during the June national conference of the Hungarian Socialist Workers' Party by trying to alter the policy of the new party leaders. The main concern under the circumstances was to ward off this attack and defend the new political line. This called for open counter-attack,[26] and also for some tactical compromises behind the scenes.

Aggravating these factors was the new political leadership's lack of economic experience. From their level it seemed as if the malfunctions of the economy could be remedied by eliminating certain causes from which the mistakes were considered to derive. They thought primarily in terms of resolving single problems and for quite some time failed to see how these were related to each other. So the recognition by certain groups of economists that the whole economic system needed changing was unmatched by a political recognition of this at the level of government policy. One reason why this transference failed to occur may have been the political and moral crisis affecting the intelligentsia, a sizeable proportion of whom supported a policy of socialist reform. They shied away from politics and involvement in government, considering that economic issues had lost importance to political ones. So the reform camp was weakened from within as well.

This process at home was initiated by changes in the international communist movement. In 1957 came a conservative backlash from the Twentieth Congress of the Communist Party of the Soviet Union and the Chinese party programme of letting 'a hundred flowers bloom'. In China, a sharply 'leftist', conservative turn took place almost immediately, while the Hungarian and Polish crises, which had alarmed Central and Eastern Europe with their open attacks on socialism, caused the majority of the communist and workers' parties meeting in Moscow in the autumn of 1957 to declare revisionism to be the main danger. Although the communiqué adopted at the conference stated that 'dogmatism and sectarianism . . . can constitute the main danger at certain stages in the development of one party or another', it stressed that 'while denouncing dogmatism, the communist parties maintain that under the present conditions revisionism is the main danger'. Once again, the conflict with Yugoslavia sharpened and principles of the Yugoslav party leadership such as the system of self-management and the restructuring of the economic model were sharply criticized as an embodiment of revisionism. In Hungary the proclaimed and active 'struggle on two fronts' against both dogmatism and revisionism continued, but as Ferenc Münnich put it in the journal *Társadalmi Szemle* when describing the Hungarian party's experiences, it 'has considered and still considers revisionism to be the main danger'.[27]

So it seemed as if this combination of factors had blocked the road to economic reform for some time. Not only was comprehensive, radical reform taken off the agenda for 1957 (understandably enough in a year that at best could only have been one of preparation), it was not envisaged for the coming years either. This had been signified earlier in several official statements and in the resolution of the national party conference of June 1957. Though the 'struggle on two fronts' had been endorsed in the resolution, the economic conclusion from the heated debates was this:

> The party conference states in connection with the system of economic leadership that it attaches decisive significance to the state's role of central direction . . . [and] rejects the erroneous views which deny the necessity for state central direction and control. If these views were applied . . . they would lead to anarchy, a strengthening of capitalist elements [and] serious injury to the socialist economy and the people. The party also takes into consideration that the centralization of the economic system in recent years was greater than necessary . . . Some of the measures leading to excessive centralization have already been abolished and work is under way on devising the most suitable [kind of] economic leadership.[28]

Shortly afterwards came the news that the reform studies initiated by the government had been discontinued. István Friss, in his address to the party's Political Academy quoted earlier, informed the public of this in a rather one-sided way:

> It is part of the party's and government's economic policy . . . to involve the experts in practical and scientific activity for consultations prior to government decisions. The most significant in this respect has been the work of the eleven committees of experts [on which] . . . over 200 experts have worked and raised a great many useful and good ideas. *It followed from the nature of the proposals made that the majority of them could not yet be implemented directly*, but the government . . . has used several ideas in working out its economic measures.[29]

The confidential report on the activity of the Economic Committee in 1957 was far more explicit:

> The [state of] incompletion in the working out of the measures for developing further the system of economic direction and management is well known. As early as January 1957 the government instructed the Economic Committees to begin a reappraisal of the system of economic management at the same time as [devising] proposals for averting the threat of inflation, and to work out the proposals necessary for developing the economic system further. Although work on a broad scale to elaborate the proposals had begun – with the involvement of some 200 economic experts – *the completed proposals have not yet been debated* [and] a plan of the specific measures to be taken has not been prepared. And apart from a few minor measures, no change has ensued.[30]

The appraisal that follows paints an even more precise picture of the fate of the draft reform that the expert committees forward: 'The committees completed their work almost a year ago and prepared a summary of their proposals. *Since then, the state of our national economy has changed significantly*, we see a great many things more clearly . . . The government has used some of the proposals in its economic measures.'[31] It goes on to list the proposals from the expert committees which have been applied. Of these partial, corrective measures it mentions the emphasis given to reconstruction as opposed to new investment projects, the acceptance of the views on modernizing the railways and the introduction of a profit-sharing system. Certain proposals, like the transformation of wage differentials, were seen as applicable at a later date. But it then pointed out:

> The summary proposal by the Economics Committee contains alongside the correct proposals listed some erroneous ideas which do not accord with the requirements of Marxism–Leninism [and] depart from the declared objectives of our party and our government . . . Members of the Committee firmly and sharply dissociated themselves from the dogmatic theory and the sectarian practice of the past, but they by no means did so fully from revisionist, right-wing theory and practice . . . [They declare] that the majority of compulsory plan indicators become superfluous . . . [and] a breakdown of plan tasks by companies will be made only exceptionally . . . In 1957 we, too, took significant strides towards increasing company autonomy. Most of these measures have proved successful although in certain areas like materials allocation and investments, we have gone to extremes . . . It will be correct for us to place certain economic factors entrusted to the autonomy of companies back in the sphere of central planning.

Ultimately the concept of partial, gradual corrections prevailed in the search for a solution around the turn of 1956 and 1957, although certain elements of the comprehensive radical proposals for reform were taken into consideration as well. A host of partial corrections were introduced from the end of 1956 onwards in response to immediate practical needs, and the command economy was retained. A National Planning Office report dating from the spring of 1959 noted the taking 'in the years preceding the counter-revolution of numerous steps to simplify planning which were supplemented by further measures in the course of endorsement of the plan for 1957. The basic aim of the 1957 measures was to increase the effectiveness of planned economic activity by increasing the autonomy of the ministries and companies. These measures were accompanied by a further reduction in the compulsory plan indicators.'[32]

The planning system that began to emerge in 1957 certainly differed in a number of ways from the one that preceded it. First and foremost, the number of plan indicators laid down by the government was reduced. None the less, it is worth specifying the sphere in which commands continued to prevail: the value of global production; the quarterly output breakdown of the most important articles (only 17 per cent of the items covered by the plan stipulation of 1954); compulsory deliveries to domestic trade (prescribed in terms of value and broken down quarter by quarter, although the lists of items were only 25 to 50 per cent as long as they had been in 1954); the quantity and value of compulsory export deliveries, again in a quarterly breakdown (and again in a list of articles only 25 to 50 per cent as long); the supply plan for the major raw materials (a third of those on the earlier list); the whole wage fund: the costs per hundred forints of production value; the investment funds (in a financial and technical breakdown with a separate, itemized endorsement system for individual investment projects); the construction proportion of company renovation projects; the average wage of workers (assessed annually and in terms of the quarter in which the level has been highest); and the allocation for employees' bonuses.

The National Planning Office report goes on to point out that 'in developing the indicators endorsed by the Council of Ministers . . . the aim has been to exercise control only through the few plan indicators most decisive to management and requisite to the professional characteristics'. This assertion is a gross exaggeration of the restraint exercised, since the indicators mentioned wholly determined the functioning of companies and made it depend on the decisions of central authorities. The only substantial exception was the partial abolition of the production directives. However, the 'major items' to which they were now confined were not so great a reduction as a straight comparison with the number in 1954 would suggest. In fact, the reduction to between 17 and 50 per cent arose partly through the merging of previously separate items on the list. Indeed, lower-level supervisory bodies even expanded the sphere of priority and central stipulations. Moreover, 'the ministries and authorities usually published, alongside the approved indicators, as a calculation or guideline figure, the other plan indicators as well'.[33] Not surprisingly, under a system of central, compulsory planning, the guideline figures played the practical part of a quasi-plan. The various ministries sometimes used different planning methods, and the number of plan indicators they issued varied as well. 'The most radical reduction in the number of plan indicators was made by the Ministry of Light Industry.'[34]

So the greatest achievement cited in granting companies greater autonomy was, ultimately, the cuts in the number of plan indicators and priority goods, particularly numerical prescriptions, and the abandoning of the practice of making quarterly breakdowns by production value.

In summing up the various views on this corrective process, the National Planning Office document quoted earlier also published some company opinions that reflect real conditions:

> Nor do companies agree unanimously about whether the reduction in the number of indicators and the change in planning and direction has significantly increased their autonomy. Certain companies seriously question this by saying that although the number of indicators has certainly fallen, those that remain – which control precisely the most important activity of the company – ultimately tie the company's hands just as much as the many previous indicators did. Admittedly, the lower-level controlling bodies and the companies are receiving fewer compulsory indicators, but in practice they are still receiving governmental or other indicators in the form of guideline numbers or partial indicators, so that in the opinion of these companies the situation as compared with the past has not changed at all . . . The companies regard as a lack of autonomy the fact that there are few, indeed almost no means at their disposal for speeding up from their own resources the development tasks they regard as most important.

The degree of centralization in the management of labour was also relaxed, by abolishing the compulsory payroll prescriptions. (However, this also was still controlled through prescription concerning the wage allocation and the average wage.)

A similar attempt to remedy the previous overly rigid and bureaucratically centralized system of planning and control can be seen in the discontinuation of the direct central regulation of the range of products in many fields, particularly light industry. 'The actual production', according to the National Planning Office, 'is taking place on the basis of demand, through constant negotiations between industry and commerce.'[35]

The all-embracing, account-like stipulations for material allocation were also restricted to a narrower sphere.[36] Companies were involved to a greater extent in the preparation of central plans.[37] Of course, this can at best be seen as a degree of institutionalization of the 'plan bargaining' which existed already.

The direct exporting rights introduced experimentally into foreign trade were supposed to provide a market incentive for industrial producers to merge production and foreign trade activities. The incentive to engage in foreign trade was itself changed: the imperative to fulfil plan indicators was replaced by a relationship to the size of the price subsidy received.[38]

Partial change occurred in the investment system,[39] but without bringing a substantial change in the mechanism of investment activity, since 'the means available for investment purposes are still almost exclusively placed at the disposal of companies free of charge', so that they continued to aim for 'acceptance of the largest investment demand possible'.

Some rationalization took place in the system of incentives and material interest. The previously one-sided incentive to fulfil or overfulfil plan indicators (which was bound up with the implementation of the global production plan) ceased to apply. But again one presumes that this corrective measure had more theoretical significance than practical impact. It certainly dealt a blow to the ideology of the compulsory planning system by officially acknowledging that the plan indicator was not the sole yardstick for company activity or incentives. Companies now had control of part of their bonus allocations, which itself diminished considerably (from 50 per cent of the total wage bill to 25 per cent). Although still included in the indicator-based planning process, the profit-sharing system, which gave prominence to company performance, was an attempt to replace quantitative by qualitative criteria. However, in the current economic environment (including the price system and the limited scope open to company management), the Planning Office study justifiably pointed out that 'the profit-sharing system is not what its name implies; in its present form it could well be called a collective bonus or an annually calculated managerial fund'.

All of these changes certainly made the planning system more flexible and attempted to eliminate several of the major contradictions it had contained. But the only sector in which the planning system underwent major changes in 1956–7 was agriculture, where it was allowed to serve the purposes of economic policy more effectively. In industry and other sectors of the economy, continuity reigned despite the changes. Although the partial and gradual transformation of the planning system at the turn of 1956 and 1957 did mean that the Hungarian economy had embarked upon a path of change, far more important than the actual results of this was its effect on attitudes and the experiences it provided. It proved that the economic mechanism was no longer a taboo subject and that it could be corrected.

The next few years saw a continuation of the moderate, corrective policy line and attempts to overcome conflicts that arose by making further partial changes. Partial though they were, the corrections came to be a natural concomitant of the economic processes, which helped to erode the rigid ideological notion of the socialist economic system. By doing that, it also helped to undermine the previous identification of comprehensive reform with reformism or revisionism.

9 Minor corrections to the mechanism between 1958 and 1964

The government did not regard the corrective measures taken in 1956–7 as the end of the change to be made in the system of planning and control. The process continued because changes which had already been prepared needed implementing, but equally because of the change in outlook, under which not all elements of the planning and control system were still regarded as taboo or unalterable. However, even though the idea of a radical reform had been rejected, the years after 1957 were a time in which a wide variety of experiments, far from unified in their nature or direction and in many respects mutually contradictory, were carried out. Meanwhile attempts to remedy faults in the workings of the economy in a variety of fields were made in a way that tied in with the corrective approach taken in 1957. The most important of these was the correction of the price system.

It had become obvious in 1953–6 that the price system had serious faults. On the one hand the system of fixed pricing prevented producer prices from reacting to changes in input and production costs. The prices of some things, fuel and raw materials in particular, were fixed so far below the costs of producing them as to make economic appraisal impossible and actually to encourage maximum use of them. As a result, work had started early in 1956 on setting producer prices (and haulage rates) in order. It was more than a matter of continuing the correction of the price system where it had been left off. Prices had played a particularly important part in the ideas for radical economic reform, and in addition, extensive debates had begun about planning and prices in several other socialist countries over those months. The very principles of pricing policy in a command economy were being criticized and questioned.

The main feature of the price system introduced in Hungary in 1951 and prevalent in the socialist countries at this time was that the centrally fixed producer prices for articles produced by state-owned companies and utilized by the state sector were set in principle at production-cost level. They included no profit, which would be indispensable to any degree of self-financing, and they were free of tax. Moreover, the cost level used was less than the total of the real costs. In fact, subsidized prices were deliberately set in the case of major basic materials for industry. 'In previous years, low basic material prices were considered correct', Béla Csikós-Nagy wrote in 1957, 'on the grounds that the price in turnover within the state sector was merely a technical accounting instrument, and in this way the "distension" of the prices for semi-finished and finished products could be prevented.'[1] By disrupting the unified price level between means of production and consumer goods, the costs of the products produced and used in the state sector only had to be covered in the price of consumer goods – in other words, when the product moved out of the state sector to an outside consumer, a cooperative, an individual or a foreign market. So the price of consumer goods included a high turnover tax. Since the producer and consumer price spheres were separate, they moved divergently and had no direct influence on each other.

It should be mentioned in the first place that the differing ideas about direction and planning were reflected in the price debates, which produced a wide range of proposals for changing the system. At one extreme was the position that if the right market balance and abundance of stocks could be provided there was no need for officially set prices at all. Producer and consumer prices had to move together, and the price movement had to be guided fundamentally by the market. Others considered that the system of official prices had to be retained, but a radical change made in the system for setting them. As a basic principle, the real costs of the reproduction process had to be reflected in the production-cost figure. Many experts proposed keeping the system of fixed prices by linking producer and consumer prices.

It is obviously beyond the scope of this book to give a detailed account of this voluminous price debate. Quite soon, compromise views began to emerge:

> The price system should not be viewed *exclusively* as a system of fixed prices or *exclusively* as a system of freely determined prices; instead the two must be combined . . . In fact every price system today is a combination of the two. The problem [as one contribution to the debate underlined] is not the necessity for the combination but first the proportions of the two kinds of price system, and even more, deciding what subsequent difficulties and contradictions will be

> caused by the combining of the two conflicting systems. It would be naïve to think . . . that the blending of the two different price systems will resolve their various separate contradictions, end the negative effects and allow only the positive effects to be asserted.[2]

Proposals were put forward for tackling the problem of the lack of market interest (in quality, modernity, etc.) for production companies by 'taking the consumer price as the starting-point for determining the producer price, and . . . from this price subtracting the wholesale and retail margins, and the . . . turnover tax, and accepting the remainder as the producer price'.[3]

For the calculation of industrial producer prices alone several proposals were aired. The prevailing system of a net producer price based on production cost was placed against a proposal that net income industry by industry should be realized in proportion to wages (a value type of price system). Another group did not merely choose labour input as their starting-point. They proposed realizing the net income in the producer prices in proportion to the fixed and current assets used by the sector (a producer-price type of price system). Finally, there were those who proposed that producer prices should adjust to the price ratios of the world market, an idea that first developed during the 1956 debate on the Polish economy and was espoused in the Hungarian debates by Tibor Liska (but only published subsequently – a fact to which we shall refer later). In this case domestic prices would be set not by the socially necessary costs of the particular country and industry but by the price relations on international markets. In its more moderate version, the system would only have applied to the major raw materials, and in its more extreme version to the whole of manufacturing industry.[4]

The choice between the various proposals for the price system was, of course, primarily and fundamentally determined by the degree of radicalism allowable in the reform of the planning and direction mechanism. Market-type price reforms were ruled out by the retention of the directive type of planning even at company level. In other words, the preservation of the basic features of the mechanism decided the nature of the 'price reform' as well.

On July 1, 1957 the government-appointed Economic Committee adopted a resolution on a general reorganization of industrial producer prices. The new producer prices which were planned to be introduced from July 1, 1958 had, according to the resolution, 'to make serious progress towards the development of a unified system of industrial prices geared to value'. To this end, 'the cost factors previously omitted without cause must be reincluded in the production cost'. The resolution also declared: 'We cannot . . . subsidize the products of the basic industries, and so the state price subsidy on coal and on metallurgical products must be ended.' The resolution took the line that the price proportion should reflect the social inputs of labour.

It naturally followed from the corrective concept which had now become established that the modernization of the system of producer prices did not extend to the main features of the price system, or the main issues of the almost general use of fixed prices and the strict separation between producer and consumer prices. 'In general the present system of fixed prices must be retained', the resolution stated.

In the same way, the resolution went on: 'The operations of reorganizing producer prices must be carried out in such a way that . . . with exceptions, consumer prices should not be affected. In cases where the new producer prices are not covered by the consumer prices', it adds, 'the maintenance of the consumer prices must be ensured by the prescribing of a state subsidy.'[5]

The new producer prices were finally introduced on January 1, 1959, and there is no doubt that the price system characteristic of the 1950s had been altered. The most significant change was the abolition of subsidies (and the consequent higher price) for basic materials produced at home. In 1958 the proportion of subsidy to return from sales had been 85 per cent in coal mining, 22 per cent in metallurgy, 27 per cent in the wool industry and 15 per cent in meat-processing. The heavy subsidies on basic materials had distorted production-cost relations in the entire economy. Taking the level of production costs as a base, the new prices were significantly higher. The prices of coal, industrial power and foundry coke jumped by more than 300 per cent. The prices of bauxite, manganese ore and lead rose by 250 per cent, while those of iron ore, heating oil, wool and timber exactly doubled, and those of wheat, rye and sugar-beet rose by some 150 per cent. The prices of imported basic materials and capital equipment were also changed, cutting out the previous practice of supplying companies with imported materials at the domestic price, which was far lower than the actual cost of purchasing them. After the price reorganization the domestic prices of imported goods were calculated on the basis of the historical average world-market prices over a number of years. The whole idea was to replace a system that was encouraging the wasteful use of materials and energy and oriented towards a one-sidedly quantitative type of growth by price proportions that would encourage more modern and less material-intensive production.

The change in the system of producer prices also aimed to encourage technical modernization by raising significantly the depreciation rate on equipment. To make the implementation of it more consistent, the book value of buildings and machinery was reassessed. Although it was not a genuine market assessment, the figure was increased by an overall 70 per cent in state-owned industry.[6]

The result of this partial price reform was to raise producer prices in industry by an average of 53 per cent. The structure of the cost of production changed, with the proportion of materials increasing from 68.8 per cent to 72.4 per cent and of depreciation from 5 per cent to 6.9 per cent, while wage costs fell from 23.9 per cent to 18.2 per cent. Company profits, which had been planned at between 3 and 8 per cent, finally settled at 9.3 per cent of total production value in the first half of 1959.[7]

While the reorganization of producer prices did rationalize the system by taking real costs into account, the objectives set for it, as we have seen, were only modest and partial. No effort to link producer and consumer prices was even attempted and no limitations were placed on the virtually general validity of fixed prices. This in itself perpetuated the neglect of realities and actual expenditures. The new prices were based on the value proportions and production structure and on input conditions prevailing in 1958, but no provision was made for automatic price adjustments for subsequent *changes* in these. So the scene was set for a repetition of the whole problem, a rapid deterioration in the balance between producer prices and production costs and a return of all the other distortions accompanying a system resting on subsidies.

Since the partial results of the price reorganization were ephemeral, the president of the National Prices Office was prompted to suggest in a proposal to the Economic Committee that fixed prices should be adjusted with greater frequency: 'The question arises', Béla Csikós-Nagy wrote, 'of making certain modifications . . . in the practice of state price regulation followed so far, under which we generally raise producer prices every five or six years . . . We must consider . . . whether it would not be expedient to review the prices regularly, at least every two years, and modify them as necessary.'[8]

So a year after the first, extremely modest price regulation came another alteration whereby the fixed prices were at least changed more frequently, and a more flexible price system under which there was adjustment to the value relations pertaining was accomplished at government level.

10 Organizational corrections – the transformation of company structures

The subsequent corrective measures extended into other fields. On March 6, 1959 the party Central Committee announced that it would put forward at the next party congress 'a proposal for improving the work of government and the direction of the economy'. A few weeks later, Prime Minister Gyula Kállai said at the party's Political Academy: 'We must thoroughly investigate our methods of directing the national economy . . . The required changes in direction must be implemented without delay.'

The announcement of further corrective measures had been helped along in this case from two sources. First and foremost, there were developments in other socialist countries. A large-scale *organizational* transformation of economic direction had been carried out in the Soviet economy in 1958: the sectoral ministries had been replaced by national economic councils organized on a regional basis (although these regional centres themselves exercised a sectoral type of direction). In Czechoslovakia at about the same time the middle-level industrial directorates had been largely abolished, although the sectoral ministries had been retained. This measure was linked with a radical reduction in the number of companies through mergers. In Poland, the industrial directorates were replaced by company associations. 'One concomitant of the Hungarian measures to reorganize the economy, as it has been in the other socialist countries, might be to reduce the number of levels of direction', was the conclusion reached in an article in the *Közgazdasági Szemle.*[1]

As the organizational changes got under way in the neighbouring socialist countries, the leaders of the Hungarian economy began to take a second look at some of the discarded elements of proposals for reform made in 1956–7, and this was the second source for the further spate of partial corrections. In March 1957 the planning economists and the National Planning Office held a debate, during which it was, for example, almost universally accepted as a principle that 'the precondition for transition to the new economic mechanism . . . is a requisite organizational change . . . [and] the formation of organizational units which are, on the basis of their standing, size, homogeneity of profile, provision of qualified staff, etc., capable of functioning within the frameworks of the new mechanism in the production of the specific product'.[2] In this context it is again worth quoting the idea from the comprehensive reform proposals of the inter-ministerial expert committee mentioned earlier, of recommending an organizational transformation as well as a way of strengthening company autonomy: 'However, it must not be imagined that this can be carried out if the present company frameworks are maintained . . . The application of the new mechanism requires that we . . . merge companies which have been artificially broken up. Similarly, it is conceivable that we would combine into trusts companies which could expediently be run as small "autonomous" companies.'[3]

It was obviously an important factor in these proposals that companies, which were envisaged as the pillars of the comprehensive reform, could hardly have been granted genuine autonomy while the organizational framework for companies in the 1950s remained: the natural company entities had been broken up, and in numerous cases what had previously been units of a company had been turned into 'independent' companies. For instance, Manfred Weiss of Csepel had been split up into the Steel Works, the Tube Factory, the Metalworks, the Motor Cycle Factory – in fact into eighteen separate companies. These were then controlled from January 1, 1955 by the sectoral directorate. The intention of reconstituting the companies which had been prised apart, or of combining several smaller companies making the same kind of products, had already emerged in the mid-1950s. A contributing factor was obviously the general belief in the benefits of the concentration process and the establishment of entities as large as possible. One of the first examples of industrial reorganization was the Hungarian Silk Industry Company, which was formed by amalgamating ten independent factories on January 1, 1955. The concentration of a whole industry – a yarn-preparing centre, a spinning mill, two weaving mills and a finishing factory – seemed to offer an advantage, in that 'management . . . within an industry organized into one company is highly centralized. On the other hand, the company's economic autonomy is far greater than that of companies functioning under industrial directorates.'[4] A similar measure was prepared in 1956, but only carried out at the end of 1958. From that time onwards, however, the process gathered pace: on October 18, 1958 the Economic Committee adopted a resolution on establishing the Hungarian National Brewery Company, which grouped the four earlier large breweries into one at the beginning of 1959. 'Under the new structure', the resolution ran, 'the separation of the management from production organization must cease.'[5] At the turn of 1958–9, ninety-three companies were merged into thirteen new companies, while the paint factories and gasworks followed the lead taken by the brewing industry.

But these later mergers were already fitting increasingly into a comprehensive process of corporate restructuring. On January 16, 1959 the programme was presented to the party's Political Committee by Antal Apró from the preparatory committee on the reorganization of industry.[6] The main guidelines stated that 'local initiative must be encouraged by increasing the autonomy of factories . . . The new management bodies must be set up . . . so that there are as few intermediate steps among them as possible.' But until the end of 1961, only the first and quite modest wave of the reorganization took place.

The partial corrective measures taken at this time were concentrated almost exclusively on structural reorganizations, but this coincided curiously with the answers sought to the growing tensions that appeared in the Hungarian economy in 1959–60. As the rate of growth and development picked up, the negative effects of the system of planning and control began to re-emerge. (The moderate growth rate in the previous years had naturally had a more muted effect.) Once again attention and statements focused on the economic mechanism. 'Faster building of socialism', Jenő Fock emphasized in a contribution to the 1960 general assembly of the Hungarian Academy of Sciences,

> demands, among other things, that the methods of planning and directing the economy should develop constantly, that the control of the economy, the so-called mechanism, should be in accord with the development of the forces of production, that it should not impede their development but make it speedier . . . However, there has not been adequate progress recently in perfecting our economic methods . . . There is no debate on the issue, there is no search for a path, the various views do not clash.

In his address, Fock mentioned that the majority of economists were obviously avoiding these issues because 'at one time they were closely connected with them . . . [and this being so] strayed unwittingly on to revisionist ground . . . There are also economists who dare not venture on this rocky ground having been "put wise" by the example of the others.' At the same time, Fock drew attention to a negative tendency hiding behind the banner of stronger centralization, whereby certain organizations were aiming to retrieve spheres of authority they had previously relinquished. Referring to the 'struggle on two fronts' (against revisionism on the one hand and sectarianism on the other) Fock underlined that 'by treating our own narrow-mindedness and our sectarian and dogmatic thinking and deeds as a "venial" sin . . . we feed revisionism. I have said all this', he continued, 'because I would like to encourage economists to analyse the new phenomena in the building of socialism in a bolder, creative way.'[7]

Speaking after Fock, Árpád Kiss, president of the Planning Office, emphasized the qualitative sides of economic development, underlining that the growth rate itself is not an expression of development. János Hont, Deputy Minister of Agriculture, emphasized the effectiveness of the new mechanism introduced in agriculture:

> For more than three years we have been influencing and directing agricultural production in a planned way while eliminating administrative methods and using economic methods (price, taxation, credit and purchasing policy . . .), and the experiences have indisputably proved the correctness of this policy. Our present system is substantially more effective and ensures a greater degree of planning than the pre-1957, predominantly administrative system did . . . Efforts to apply 'greater planning' by administrative means through unit plans for cooperative farms must be rejected as an incorrect method whose consequences are harmful.[8]

The intentions of those in charge of the economy were to revive the debate and seek new, practical solutions. Slowly arguments in favour of reform began to surface in the economic press. András Hegedüs, for one, was theoretical in his approach and argument:

> The specific system of planned economic activity is a model developed from the economic angle on the social reality of the socialist nation . . . One characteristic trait of the dogmatism that appears in the science of economics is that it often restricts the sphere of economic systems applicable under socialist property relations to *a single form* . . . even though various different economic forms amount to the optimal solution at stages of development . . . There can hardly be any doubt about the need to alter the specific economic forms from time to time . . . The modification of the specific economic forms . . . does not affect the substance of production and economic relations.[9]

Considerable headway in the theoretical expression of the economic reform's potentials in principle had been made by Tibor Liska, who had stood alone since the debate had broken off in 1957. He was not content merely with a reformulation of the 1954–7 principles for reform (although it must be added that not even this was done during the conspicuous silence observed by economists on the matter of reform in the early 1960s). Liska admittedly took as his starting-point what he had already said in October 1954, in the first issue of the *Közgazdasági Szemle*. In the autumn of 1963 he began a study entitled 'Critique and Conception. Thesis on the Reform of the Economic System' by saying:

> Our economic leaders have become more thoughtful and more professional in recent years, but the economic system has not changed in substance . . . Our economic leaders can and must contemplate developing a new, more up-to-date mechanism, because not only the individual elements but the whole of the present system is out of date . . . In planning a new, up-to-date mechanism the economic leadership must start out from a reform of the price system.

Liska rejected the notion of a price system on the basis of domestic production costs in all its variants; in other words, he dismissed the principles concerning the price system that had featured in the earlier debates and proposals for reform, arguing that to base the calculation of prices on the cost of domestic production 'impedes technological development', 'encourages autarky' and 'by sanctifying the limitations of the domestic market slows the pace of economic growth'.

Such a price system, Liska argued, was unsuitable for gauging the profitability of production, and so was an impediment to 'international specialization' and in turn to 'catching up with world standards'. From his comprehensive critique of the price system, Liska went on to state that the substance of reform of the mechanism should be the introduction of world-market prices:

> The work socially required . . . today is clearly equal to the labour input required by the general world economic conditions and to that which can be realized on the world market . . . So what is the solution? A domestic price system based on world-market prices and an economic mechanism based upon it! . . . Under a domestic price system based on world-market prices the price centre of every single product which constitutes or potentially constitutes . . . an object of foreign trade would be the world-market price, at an exchange rate uniformly converted into forints, currency by currency. Thus the prices would merely be discovered, not 'calculated'.[10]

Liska dealt not only with the price system but with the relationship between the state and companies, thus going far beyond the requirements of the reforms proposed in 1957. He tackled the essence of the operative economic system and by focusing on the automatic mediation of world-market influences sought to create the decisive instrument for leading the Hungarian economy on to a new course. However, the proposal at this stage did not elicit any practical response. Although published, it remained an isolated manifestation, mentioned here to exemplify the sporadic and isolated demands for reform that began to appear again at that time.

Publication of Liska's study in the *Közgazdasági Szemle* in a column entitled 'Debate' was far from implying that a wave of debate was in sight. The implication was rather that the article was open to debate, and although a real debate did not emerge, the journal appended two essentially dismissive replies to the article in the same issue.[11] Discarding 'the primitive ideas of the market-price mechanism of classical capitalism', Béla Csikós-Nagy sharply disputed the assertion that 'the socialist countries . . . cannot bring realistic prices into being, and that for them to be able to have a market economy in goods they must adopt prices from the capitalist world'.[12] It should be added that what Csikós-Nagy rejected was not the idea of taking world-market prices into consideration. Indeed he considered this to be a natural consequence of the existence of the price phenomenon. What he argued against was the automatic introduction of world-market prices, based upon convertibility. The principal issue, 'which must be debated', is the *way* in which the world-market price was to be taken into consideration.

Only very slowly did the prolonged silence on the issue of economic reform begin to be broken in the early 1960s, and at a political level it still did not cause any modification of the corrective approach which had developed in 1957. The time for that was not thought to have come yet. The party Central Committee adopted a resolution of February 2, 1962 on 'Further Development in the Direction of the Economy' in which solutions were still sought through organizational changes. 'To promote the desirable concentration of the productive forces of industry and construction, companies representing a small productive force must be merged' so that they became more economic. On the other hand, their autonomy had to be increased, and the intermediate levels of industrial control, the industrial directorates had to be abolished in a reorganization that was to be completed by the end of 1963.[13] On September 5 of the same year the government's Economic Committee discussed a plan for industrial reorganization, with Jenő Fock in the chair and János Kádár and Sándor Gáspár taking part. 'Modification or alteration of the system of planning is not timely', it was stated, but the next sentence contrasted with the categorical negative of earlier years: 'This issue must be examined at a later date.' The objective of improving the functioning of the economy, which was described as the immediate task, 'can basically be attained by concentrating the productive forces'. By embarking on a large-scale merger of industrial companies they sought most of all to promote this concentration. (Similar methods were also being applied in other Comecon countries.) This purpose reflected the idea that bigger companies would automatically be more economic. At the same time 'a decided aim of the reorganization is to abolish the industrial directorates, [and so] reduce the number of intermediate levels of direction'. Under this system the now more independent and uniform large companies could be linked directly with the ministry. This, it was thought, would bring a strengthening of central direction (by eliminating the bureaucratic and unwieldy process of transmission from layer to layer) *and* make companies more autonomous. So 'the number of central plan indicators must certainly be reduced at the time of the reorganization'.[14]

In the autumn of 1962 the Economic Committee, acting almost like an assembly line, discussed a series of proposals from the various industrial portfolios for merging companies. Ten independent foundries were formed into a nationwide Foundry Company. Eleven sugar refineries and a research institute were combined into the Sugar Industry Company, while eight state-owned wine-cellar concerns, plus the Cork Processing Company, were first combined (on January 1, 1963) into the Wine Industry Trust and a year later into a nationwide company called the Hungarian State Wine Cellars. During the reorganizations of 1962–3, six confectionery companies were merged as the National Confectionery Industry Company, and a National Rubber Industry Company covering the whole industry was set up.

'The reorganizations', it was reported, 'were largely completed by January 1, 1964.'[15] The result was a radical transformation of Hungary's industrial structure under which whole industries, in several cases, were grouped under a single company. As István Szurdi, a secretary of the party Central Committee, put it: 'Not in every case is it possible for merger to result in a whole industry, or even a major area of it, embracing a homogeneous line of products, being represented by a single company. In such cases, trusts have been formed to gather together and direct the companies.'[16] The number of state-owned industrial firms fell from 1,427 in 1950 to 839 in 1965, while the average number of employees in each rose from 336 to 1,183. This unprecedented centralization had resulted to a considerable degree from organizational change. But in most cases the legally and administratively established larger companies, which could represent a whole industry, only signified in terms of their internal make-up a largely formal association of several smaller plants, although the major changes of personnel that accompanied the reorganizations improved the professional standards of company management.

However, from the point of view of the subject we are examining, the processes within the companies are not primarily what deserve attention. Even the title of the resolution on reorganization adopted in February 1962 spoke of further development in the system of direction, and, as has already been mentioned, aimed at greater company autonomy and the phasing out of the intermediate levels of control, in other words at a further rationalization of the system of command economy.

In fact, the structural reorganization, under which the industrial directorates lying between the ministry and the company were abolished, caused substantial changes. Only five directorates and one chief directorate remained, although some of the directorates survived in a different guise, controlling the companies as trusts (of which seventeen were created). Ultimately, the intermediate level of control, functioning in a number of forms, covered 7 per cent of companies, but these accounted for 50 per cent of the workforce in state-owned industry. So not surprisingly, the party Political Committee was informed in the spring of 1964: 'In several areas the organizational changes are still only formal, and there are therefore some who dispute even the economic justification for the mergers.'[17] Nor had any real change in the basic features of the economic system taken place in the other half of industry, where the intermediate level of control had really been eliminated. Substantial change remained blocked by the unaltered system of obligatory indicators and the incentives based on fulfilment of them, in short by the old frameworks of the economic system.

But the real problem did not in any case consist in the lack of real change or in the formality of the changes made. In practice, the merger of companies foisted hierarchical monopolies on the economy. The bureaucracy of the control hierarchy was reproduced in the bureaucratic set-up within the new monopoly companies. Since the creation of them narrowed the market significantly, it led to a substantial reinforcement of directive planning, not to a correction of it. Despite the aim of corrections, the company reorganization ultimately became a powerful and resilient obstacle to reform, whose extremely adverse effects were to be felt for a quarter of a century.

11 The new model for agricultural cooperatives

Meanwhile, far more significant and positive changes were taking place in agriculture. When the authorities placed the emphasis on the *political* conditions at the end of 1958 by putting the mass collectivization of agriculture on the agenda again, they were following a general trend in East-Central Europe. However, the intention was not to force Hungarian agriculture into some doctrinaire mould but to ensure that the mass reorganization would include some system that would give the peasantry an interest in the results of production. This was to be achieved by introducing forms of cooperative that were tailored to their needs.

The political leadership rejected the idea of retaining the private peasant holdings. Once the political system was re-established once more, a long-term plan was developed in the spring of 1957 for gradual collectivization by strengthening the existing cooperatives and making them more attractive to the private peasant farmers. In other words, the Hungarian Socialist Workers' Party did not choose a course any different from the one that had been or was being followed by the other Comecon countries. This entailed to some extent, inevitably, a reawakening of the old instincts and attempts to force the pace of collectivization, particularly among the local apparatus.

None the less, when the process of organizing cooperatives recommenced, important new elements were built into it. Step by step, as the socialist transformation of agriculture progressed over the years that followed, a new cooperative model was brought into being. Of course the situation had changed substantially since 1957. A truly gradualist approach had been planned in the party's 'Agricultural Theses': the higher level of development on the cooperatives was going to persuade peasant farmers to join them of their own free will, since their living standards would be higher if they did. But the requisites for large-scale farming could not be provided now, amidst a campaign of mass collectivization. Since this collectivization took place with quite unexpected speed in 1959 and 1960, special attention had to be paid immediately to providing the right financial conditions retrospectively and ensuring the *consolidation* of the cooperative farms which had been set up.

The situation was summed up like this by one representative of agricultural policy: Although the vast majority of the peasantry had now joined the cooperatives in some counties and districts, 'can we say that in these places the socialist large-farm system of agriculture has already developed? . . . This juncture is *not the end, but only the beginning* in resolving the complicated and quite difficult task that constructing the system of socialist large-farm agriculture . . . represents.'[1]

Though traditional, the method of collectivization that the party leadership adopted was also different, for instance in rejecting the use of ruthless administrative methods to make private peasant farming impossible. Bearing in mind the 'dual task' of combining collectivization with the development of agriculture, attention during the traditional process of mass collectivization was turned to new procedures which took into account the individual aspirations and proprietorial instincts of the peasantry and sought to combine private and large-scale cooperative farming within the traditional cooperative framework.

The development of large-scale cooperative farms was seen as a long-term process in which the actual formation of the cooperatives was merely a decisive initial stage. It followed self-evidently from this that the development and application of various *transitional forms* would receive support. Of course, something quite different had been meant by transitional forms in 1957–8 from what was meant by them in the early 1960s. In 1957 there had been support for what were known as lower forms of cooperatives that extended in some cases from collective organization of buying and selling as far as collective arrangements for some actual farming activities, and they were supposed to prepare the ground for true cooperative farming. During the debates of late 1958 it was suggested that collectivization should proceed through the organization of what were called specialized cooperatives offering back-up services, while private holdings were retained. In other words, only certain activities, by and large marketing and some parts of the farming process, would be collectivized. This was only put into practice in certain regions, particularly Bács-Kiskun County and some of the wine districts. However, some break was made with the rigid Soviet model by applying transitional forms and types of association of 'a lower type' *within* the new cooperatives. One of the most typical of these inventions was *share cultivation* within the cooperatives, known also as 'family work organization'. Under this system, used mostly for root crops, the land of the cooperative was divided into shares worked as family holdings by the cooperative members. (Lack of machinery was one factor that encouraged the adoption of it.) Despite its simplicity, share cultivation at once created a firm incentive for the peasants working on the cooperative, ensuring that labour-intensive tasks were completed in good time.

Imre Szabó, chairman of the Béla Bacsó Agricultural Cooperative in Aba, summed up his experiences in this respect in the *Népszabadság* in February 1960:

> For a time there were a great many problems on our cooperative farm as well. . . We began to ponder what we could do and applied a new method of dividing the land for crop cultivation . . . We divide or 'parcel out' the root-crop area into stips, from sowing to harvest time, among the members of the crop cultivation brigade . . . Apart from receiving the value of the work units earned from the divided area, the cooperative member who has tilled and harvested the crop also receives 25 to 50 per cent of the surplus produce in kind. There are 86 members working in the crop production brigade, and last year we counted as many as 250 people a day out hoeing in the cooperative's fields on the area divided up. The children and wives came, and even relatives from town helped . . . The strength of the brigade had trebled.[2]

Three months later this system was introduced on eighteen of the twenty-four cooperatives in the district of Paks. The general meeting at the Constitution Agricultural Cooperative in Dunaföldvár decided that those who harvested more than 15 quintals (1,500 kilograms) per *hold* (0.57 hectares) of distributed land would receive 50 per cent of the surplus. In the case of potatoes, the norm was to be 70 quintals, and 40 per cent of the surplus could be retained. There were places where peasants were also guaranteed a share of the surplus over the norm after haymaking.[3]

The part played by private peasant activity in livestock farming was even more important. Even though large expenses were incurred, the conditions for large-scale stock-breeding could not be provided on the cooperatives. Common stalls and sties could not be built for much of the peasantry's livestock. 'Let us examine how cooperative stock-breeding is established and what remains on the household farms' of the members, the daily paper *Népszabadság* wrote in the spring of 1959, in a report on the cooperative village of Kapospula.

> Máté Kovács, the brigade leader, leafs through the cooperative's plan and his own journal . . . 'We went from house to house and took an inventory', he says. 'There are 365 head of cattle in the village, of which 180 will soon be incorporated into the cooperative, while 185 remain on the household farms. There are 276 swine . . . These will all remain with the members for the time being. We shall be bringing four breeding boars into the cooperative, and when there is fodder [for them] . . . we shall bring in twenty breeding sows.'

Neither the number of livestock nor the sales of livestock produce had fallen since the reorganization. In fact, the latter had risen from 68,900 to 74,800 kilograms. 'Others, elsewhere, can learn and draw lessons from the example of Kapospula while establishing collective farms', the *Népszabadság*'s writer concludes.[4] 'By its very nature the process of establishing a common stock of animals takes quite a long time', Lajos Fehér warned during the reorganization. 'Any haste, impatience or importunity in this regard does harm to the national economy [since] it reduces the size of the herd . . . It is foreseeable that our scope for investment will not allow the livestock to be gathered under one roof in many places, however much we would like to do so; *temporarily they will have to be left on the household farms*.'[5] In fact, the household swine stock was three-and-a-half times the size of the common stock, and more than 60 per cent of the cattle remained on the household plots.

Making a virtue out of necessity, the special part played by household stock-breeding was eventually incorporated into the classic pattern of cooperative farming.

During and even after the period of mass collectivization, the old ideology continued to work, of course. In many places, where the traditional criteria of the Soviet model were identified with socialism and applied in a doctrinaire way, it was argued that a cooperative into which the stock were not incorporated immediately was not a real cooperative at all.

As early as 1959 a report to the party's Political Committee noted that 'household stock-breeding is looked down upon in many places, which manifests itself in a failure to provide pasturage or other fodder for the household livestock'.[6] The government acted immediately (Government Decree No. 37/1959) to provide a legal barrier against such conduct, yet Lajos Fehér was demanding a year later in the columns of the *Társadalmi Szemle*: 'Let legality again prevail in this. For experience shows that errors are being committed in this field in many places, and that veiled actions are being taken to eliminate household livestock in practice by withholding pasture or setting unrealistically high rents for pasturage.'[7]

The government used legislation, commands and persuasion to try to assert its policy of tolerance to household farming. Strong emphasis in combating this doctrinaire 'concern' for socialism was placed on the *transitional* part it was to play, so that one is puzzled as to whether the makers of agricultural policy themselves saw it as an inescapable transitional stage lasting for a few years, something forced upon them by the limitations on investment and the temporary weaknesses of collective farming, or whether they merely regarded this as an effective debating tactic against the local, executive apparatus that favoured the orthodox, narrow concept of a cooperative prevalent in the early 1950s. It was probably a bit of both. It was less a question of devising theoretically a new model to replace the old, which was downright harmful, than of adapting and altering the old model to everyday requirements. In so doing they were scarcely in a position to distinguish the 'final' from the 'transitional', the features which could be replaced by the 'ideal' at a later date.

'The *artely* type of cooperative, along with the household farm, will survive through the whole period of socialism', one reads in the *Közgazdasági Szemle*.

> But as the collective farm develops rapidly, the household plot gradually loses its significance, at first to a relative extent and later to an absolute degree . . . Initially [household farming] is also significant from the point of view of supplying the country . . . In the later period, when socialism has developed, its role in producing commodities steadily diminishes until it finally disappears, and its role in the members' personal consumption gradually falls as well. On several *kolkhozes* in the Soviet Union, for instance, household cattle raising has ceased.[8]

But the crux of the matter was not long-term concepts for the future or clarity of principle but flexibility in practice. The aim was not to match cooperative farming to doctrines but to adjust it to the interests of the population and the economy. The logic behind this thinking and its political application shows up clearly in this passage from the article quoted earlier, which Fehér wrote in the summer of 1960:

> The transitional measures issued are satisfactory . . . Some of those working in the party and state apparatus, and particularly some of the

> cooperative farm leaders, *do not understand* this policy or *do not agree with it* . . . Household farming is an *integral complementary part* of cooperative farming . . . It will be needed so long as the economic activity of the cooperatives, namely the production of goods by them, *has not reached a high enough level* for collective production to take over the supply . . . of the peasant family needs of cooperative members, and their proportion of production . . . Then, and only then and on that basis will household farming become superfluous and meaningless. Until then, there is a need for it, and this issue must be taken very seriously . . . In many places the transitional measures are being branded in a sectarian manner as 'capitalist tendencies' or regarded as some sort of 'sin and act against socialism' . . . These damaging, narrow-minded ideas *must now be forcefully eliminated*, and everybody must understand . . . that the country needs meat![9]

Toleration of household farming, if only temporarily, due to the pressure of investment limits and as a necessary evil, also emerges from a confidential brief addressed to the party's Political Committee by the National Planning Office while the Second Five-Year Plan was being prepared: 'The targets, *even up to the end of the five-year plan – for investment reasons* – reckon to a large extent on the goods-producing role of the household farms.'[10]

Yet the agricultural policy-makers had to wage an almost daily struggle against narrow 'concern for socialism' among local officials. Let us look at just two of the innumerable documents that show the difficulties, and to indicate how protracted the struggle was, let us choose them from the mid-1960s:

> We must take it as a serious warning that between March 1961 and April 1963 . . . the household cattle stock fell by 66,000. The picture is similar for the stock of sows . . . [which] had dropped by 90,000 head . . . Contributions to the decline in household production, and particularly in household stock-breeding, have been made by both subjective and objective factors. One can consider as a subjective factor the various erroneous views. Very many cooperative leaders have helped to cause the decline with their views and their concomitant actions.[11]

Some three months later, Károly Németh was repeating the same point:

> In practice, there has not been consistent application everywhere of the principle that the strengthening of the collective farm must be assisted simultaneously by the household farms. Some people mistakenly contrast the collective with the household, saying that household farming impedes the development of the collective farm . . . A

> stop must be put to the efforts directed at winding up household farming without consideration for the real living requirements . . . The household farms are providing a large proportion of the food supplies for the rural population . . . and these farms have provided 22 per cent of the produce bought up [centrally] . . . So it is easy to understand what difficulties the country would face if we gave way to the attempts to eliminate the household farms and failed to assert the principle that the household farms must be regarded as an integral part of the collective farm.[12]

The message slowly got through that there had to be an accommodation to reality in the case of household farming. Considering it initially as a transitional form and a concession until large-scale farming had developed and the big investment projects could be made, the agricultural policy-makers fought a consistent battle for auxiliary private activity, arriving at a practice in which the collective and household farming were treated as an integral, mutually complementary unit, that was ultimately seen to have the value of a *model* and allowed to become institutionalized.

Another factor of great importance in the development of cooperative farming and of the conceptual model for practising it was *mechanization*. Unlike the earlier model, this provided the basis for *autonomous large-scale farming*.

The changes in Hungary were greatly assisted by a reappraisal taking place at the same time in the Soviet Union, where the system of machine stations was abolished. On March 27, 1958 Khrushchev put a resolution before the Supreme Soviet on further development of the *kolkhoz* system and reorganization of the machine stations. His premise was that the political function of the machine stations in organizing the cooperatives and their production had become superfluous.[13]

Nevertheless, the process in Hungary was not a speedy one. Experiments had begun back in 1957 with turning the machine stations into companies responsible for their own accounts, Orosháza being the first, and in September of the same year the government decided to allow cooperatives to make limited purchases of machinery themselves. This was introduced nationally on April 1, 1957 by Government Resolution No. 1026/1957.III.2. A transformation had begun, although the existence of machine stations as such was still not being questioned. During preparatory discussions in the Economic Committee in February 1957 it was agreed, in line with a proposal from the Minister of Agriculture, that 'the network of machine stations should be retained'.[14] The consequent government resolution, already quoted, confirmed that transforming the machine stations from budget-financed institutions into financially separate companies made no change at all in their main function, which remained 'economic and political assistance to the socialist reorganization of agriculture'.[15]

Despite this, and despite the fact that the cooperatives bought a mere 270 tractors that year, the state monopoly of owning agricultural machinery had come to an end. More significantly still, the function of the machine stations began to change from one of political control to one of providing a service. Abolition of councils of the machine stations along with their role as a base for agriculturalists helped to erode the power the stations had exercised over the cooperatives. As Imre Dimény put it at the end of the 1950s: 'It is clear now that it was incorrect to assign direct control of cooperative farming to the machine stations. This amounted to unjustified meddling in the internal affairs of the cooperatives, so restricting their independence and cooperative democracy.'[16]

In April 1957 the daily *Népszabadság* gave space to a debate on mechanizing the cooperatives, launched by László Horváth in an article entitled 'Should the Cooperatives Buy Machines?' He noted that several had bought tractors last autumn, and as interest in doing so grew, experts began to argue about 'whether it is right for the cooperatives to buy machines . . . We would like above all to say a word against instances of rigid one-sidedness, against measures and notions that tend to disregard the growth of yields and the development of the cooperatives in favour of forms and stereotypes.'[17] Another writer who took part in the debate stressed that machine stations were necessarily equipped with big machines: 'The situation in the case of machines for sowing and cultivation differs from that of the light tractors required to pull them. Without *these* machines being available on the spot, a high quality of intensive crop cultivation and large yields are inconceivable.'[18]

The rejoinder was swift. Gyula Marosujvári, who headed the Chief Directorate of Machine Stations and Mechanization at the Ministry of Agriculture, pointed out that

> the machine stations had become one of the targets last year of the ideological preparation for the counter-revolution . . . The management of a good many cooperatives which began working with their own machines this spring have now realized it was quite superficial to think it would be a lot cheaper to work with their own machines . . . [One] cooperative loses 11,500 forints a year on the running of a single Zetor tractor . . . So what should the cooperatives do? . . . To make

> better use of the machines at the machine stations we must give the cooperatives the chance to avail themselves of them.[19]

Hence the counter-rejoinder: 'Our cooperative peasantry, at this very time, are showing their affection for machinery', József Hodek, chairman of the Kisbér-Battyánpuszta cooperative, said in his contribution to the debate, 'when we hear that the cooperatives without any cash are prepared to sell their breeches to buy machines. Whereupon they say that this is not right.'[20]

The government view was put plainly to the party Central Committee by Jenő Fock on May 17: 'We must also make the strengthening of the existing cooperatives possible by permitting them to purchase universal tractors and engines.'[21]

The purpose of the machine stations and the path the cooperatives were to follow in mechanizing were defined more specifically in the party line on agricultural policy laid down in July 1957:

> A major role awaits the machine stations. Above all they must ensure . . . the mechanization of basic agricultural tasks (ploughing, harvesting, threshing) . . . Cooperatives may buy all the agricultural machines required for farming (power-driven and manually operated machines) with the exception of combine harvesters, threshing machines and, in general, tractors for ploughing. With the assistance of these machines they can complement the work carried out by the machine stations.[22]

But only a few weeks later it emerged from a resolution by the party's Political Committee that mechanization by the cooperatives was only to be regarded as exceptional after all: 'The mechanization of agriculture', it declared, 'must still be carried out primarily through the machine stations. Accordingly, the fleet of machines in the machine stations must be constantly developed.'[23]

Matters swung the other way again in the autumn of 1959, when the burdens of mass collectivization began to weigh very heavily on the budget, and it became essential to make as full use as possible of the cooperatives' own resources for investment by allowing them 'to buy machinery out of their own resources to a greater extent than hitherto', according to the Central Committee in October 1959. Yet the paramount role of the machine stations was still being stressed even for the next five-year period: 'Until the socialist reorganization has been completed, the mechanization of agriculture should take place fundamentally through the machine station network', it was stipulated at the Seventh Congress of the Hungarian Socialist Workers' Party in December 1959.[24]

Even so, mechanization by the cooperatives was fairly slow, as many of them were short of funds themselves. One development was a decision at the beginning of 1961 to allow machine stations in six counties to sell off their obsolete machines and to turn the machine stations at Turkeve and Székesfehérvár into repair shops. At the end of that year cooperatives still owned only a quarter of the more than 44,000 tractors in the country. At a time when collectivization was complete, a mere twenty-eight cooperatives had managed to mechanize their production fully, while another seventy owned most of the machinery they required. At that point the decision was taken at the top of the party: 'The experiences with cooperatives operating machinery prove that it would be best from the point of view of the economy for the cooperatives to establish the conditions for secure functioning, to employ full mechanization and to carry out all work with their own machines.'[25] By 1962, the bulk (at least two-thirds) of the new agricultural machines available were intended for sale to cooperatives, and the direct objective was to sell off the fleet of 20,000 tractors in the machine stations, while gradually transforming the stations into repair shops.

Finally, the following was decided in February 1964: 'As a result of the mechanization of the cooperatives, some three-quarters of the tractor stock . . . will pass into cooperative ownership this year. It has now become a timely issue to reorganize the machine stations.'[26] During the months of 1961 when collectivization was being completed there were still 235 machine stations in the country. Of these 143 survived until early 1964, but only 63 into the following year and a mere 20 by 1967. By the end of the 1960s the machine-station system had ceased to exist. (Simultaneously, just two machine stations were converted into repair shops in 1963, but 57 in 1964 and 131 in 1967.)

Again, it had taken almost a decade for policy and practice to change, in this case for the earlier model of cooperative to develop into one that was fully equipped with up-to-date machinery and allowed to operate as an independent concern.

Over the same period, from 1957 onwards, the way the cooperatives paid their members was beginning to be revised. Heated debates arose over the system of payment according to 'work units' and over proposals for introducing various new forms of payment instead.[27] Again the change-over was gradual. A resolution in the summer of 1957 still spoke of suppressing 'methods of distributing dividends that depart from the basic socialist principle of income distribution' and said methods acceptable in principle, 'based on a further development of the work unit, must be investigated in terms of their practical application and consequences, and the findings utilized'.[28]

The inertia of adherence to the old model was strong again. Even at the beginning of 1961, Sándor K. Nagy was fighting on two fronts when he wrote in the *Társadalmi Szemle*: 'Some regard the work unit as a necessary evil and [now] reject it outright . . . Others think that under cooperative conditions of ownership the socialist principle of distribution can only be applied through the work-unit system. So it is claimed that where they depart from the work unit they abandon the principle of socialist distribution as well.'[29] A number of experimental wage systems began to be tried. The simplest transitional form was to combine work-unit payment with advances of cash: 'This year the cooperatives have paid great heed to increasing material incentive. One of the best methods', the daily *Népszabadság* quoted an Agriculture Ministry representative as saying, 'is regular cash advances. We have achieved great progress in this respect. Almost 80 per cent of cooperatives have regularly distributed advances in cash on work units performed.'[30]

But far more was involved than this. 'We have been seeking new forms of income distribution since the spring of 1957', the chairman of the Hunyadi Cooperative at Tetétlen told the same paper. 'The present system of work units does not provide members with an adequate incentive in relation to the final results of production. One who tills the land badly will receive the same according to work units performed as one who has done the task conscientiously. So I consider it expedient and just for each member to receive income according to the value of what he has produced.'[31]

The best cooperatives made a bold break with the classic work-unit system. The Red Star Cooperative in Barcs switched to cash payment based on work norms. At the Progress Cooperative in Tótkomlós yield-related distribution of income was introduced. By 1960, 200 out of the 230 cooperatives in Pest County had switched to new forms of distributing income. At a *Népszabadság* forum, István Tömpe, First Deputy Minister of Agriculture, expressed his support for these efforts, reminding his audience of the Central Committee's resolution of October 1959 and criticizing the formerly rigid practice of his own ministry: 'The newly tried forms of income distribution must be spread more widely . . . Unfortunately the initiators of these have not received much support so far, but the ministry's leading officials now agree with these initiatives and are assisting these endeavours. The methods of the Progress Cooperative in Tótkomlós or the Red Star in

Barcs are . . . worth following.'[32] In many places the payment system was adjusted to the requirements of members, while elsewhere they used systems devised by the Academy of Sciences' Institute for Agricultural Management. The work there was directed by Ferenc Erdei, who had much to do with the weaning of the cooperatives from the earlier, doctrinaire systems and ideas about production relations and the distribution system, and the beginnings of treating them as business entities, in which the organization of the work, the wages and the other management factors could be adjusted to provide members with an incentive and comply with their requirements. Not least, it was through Erdei that the best traditions of the Hungarian cooperative movement between the two world wars were incorporated into the search for a new direction. The overall result was a steady and substantial increase in the incentives to produce. In 1961 the *Társadalmi Szemle* accorded considerable space to the new wage system in the cooperatives:

> Some people are worried . . . To them we can say only one thing: that adherence to a stereotype divorced from real life and disregard for changed circumstances is very dangerous. If we can produce more by this method, the application of it is effective and necessary to the development of socialism and the cooperatives . . . We have calculated that in Heves County last year the work of every cooperative member would have been required for the area growing vegetables, grapes, vinestocks and root crops. There would have been no members left to produce the cereals and the fodder crops, for the stockbreeding or to drive the teams if the work had merely been organized . . . by the customary brigade system based on work units . . . After careful preparations, however, we decided that from January 1, 1961 we would switch over from using work units to direct cash payment.[33]

In the case of labour-intensive root vegetables and other crops that require hoeing, many cooperatives turned over to income distribution based on yields, and some more advanced forms of this were calculated on an income-sharing system based on added value. One of the simplest transitional forms was to supplement the work-unit system with bonuses consisting of 20 to 50 per cent of the surplus produced above the target, paid in kind or in cash. In the early 1960s the new system spread rapidly:

> Already there are many efficiently managed . . . strong cooperatives, which have been guaranteeing the value of the work unit for years, and in fact some have switched to direct cash remuneration of work performed. The party and the government supports . . . further

> development of the traditional work-unit system . . . The narrow-mindedness apparent in a number of places, causing a feeling that socialism is threatened by these changes and so a rejection and prohibition of them, should be overcome . . . Experience shows . . . [that] direct cash assessment of work, relating cash payment directly to performance . . . best suits all the requirements of socialist payment for work.[34]

Yet in spite of the wide introduction of various bonus systems, Imre Dimény was able to point out even three years later that 'we are still only at the very beginning with the utilization of material incentives . . . So there is still a great deal to be done in extending direct incentives to those working in every sector.'[35] In other words, the evolution of the new wage system extended over the full ten-year period that we are discussing.

The last of the principal features of the new model for cooperative farming to be mentioned is the concept of the cooperative farm as a comprehensive entity, and this deserves special attention. As has been seen, the idea of the machines being in cooperative hands had been rejected earlier. Albeit gradually, the view emerged that the cooperative should not merely be a ploughing, sowing and stock-breeding concern but an entity with a complex of functions in which certain *industrial activities* had a place as well. It was seen that if cooperatives had their own machines they needed shops to maintain and repair them. Moreover, they should be equipped to process their own products industrially. Even the party's agricultural policy document of July 1957 already declared: 'Cooperatives must be given the chance to process their own produce . . . So it must be possible for them to set up small processing plants (milk-processing, milling, distilling, etc.) or to take such plants over from the state and other bodies.'[36]

Since the process of mass collectivization and transformation of the cooperatives intervened, it was not until the mid-1960s that the industrial activities of the cooperatives really began to develop. But the food-processing, canning and other plants that were none the less set up had a greater significance than the contribution they directly made, since they helped to evolve a comprehensive notion of the cooperative farm. Even the success of the mass collectivization of 1959–61 would be incomprehensible if one did not take into account that the new economic role of the household farms, the new opportunity for the cooperatives themselves to mechanize, and the spread of new payment methods that provided a material incentive, made cooperatives far more attractive and left plenty of scope for auxiliary private activity. Another big contribution was made by the involvement of an agricultural intelligentsia in the management of the new cooperatives. All these factors, even in the early stages, helped to make the cooperatives acceptable to the peasantry.

These motifs in the process of transforming the cooperative pattern exemplify how the changes developed steadily until the mid-1960s and were by no means over then. By the end of those ten years, however, the model was very much in the making, and the ground had been prepared for a spectacular boom in Hungarian farming. That, however, required the right external economic conditions as well, and of course a high rate of investment in the sector. But the basis of transformation was the introduction of market and value relations, for which only the foundation had been laid by abolishing the compulsory delivery system at the end of 1956 and introducing purchasing prices to replace the artificially low delivery prices which had accompanied the system. In fact, the purchasing prices introduced in 1957 on the basis of earlier market prices were more than 80 per cent higher than the compulsory delivery prices had been. The impact of this was soon offset by a general purchasing price reduction of 10 per cent in June of the same year, and then by an increase in industrial prices and taxes. After that, the wholesale agricultural price index rose only slowly – by slightly over 4 per cent between 1958 and 1961.

Obviously, value and price relations have been restored partially. For instance, in the spring of 1961 the Public Finances Committee of the party was compelled to face up to the lack of incentive in cattle-farming. The costs of keeping a cow only brought a return after seven or eight years. It took 2.80 to 3.20 forints to produce a litre of milk even on efficient farms, while the purchasing price was only 2.40 forints.[37] After the various price measures introduced at the turn of 1956 and 1957, and again at the end of the 1950s, agricultural prices rose by another 7.5 per cent between 1961 and 1965, but the discrepancy between agricultural and industrial prices remained significant even in the mid-1960s. 'The purchasing price of agricultural products is low', Imre Dimény stressed in his spring 1965 report to the Public Finances Committee, 'lower by 32 per cent at the value price and 26 per cent at the producer price . . . At the same time, calculating at the value price, industrial prices are 16 per cent higher and at the producer price 11 per cent higher than the level of socially required expenditures.'[38] The purchasing price in agriculture, the party Political Committee concluded in the summer of 1965, 'is unjustifiably low'. By contrast, according to the calculations of the Prices Office, the price in 1965 of the industrial materials and implements used in agriculture exceeded the 1958 level by over 16 per cent. 'Under the circumstances', the resolution concluded, 'the cooperatives are incapable of laying the foundations of a material and technical basis for up-to-date farming, which requires substantial investment . . . Under the Third Five-Year Plan [1966–70] it is justified to create an agricultural price level that allows the majority of cooperatives to cover their outlay from their earnings, including a part of the requirements for expanded reproduction.'[39]

In the same year, the problem of the mounting debts, of the cooperatives, exacerbated by the gulf between agricultural and industrial prices, had to be settled if agriculture was to be economically viable again. In accordance with the Political Committee resolution, the state cancelled a total of 12,700 million forints' worth of debts owed by 3,090 cooperatives, out of a total of 20,500 million forints owed by 3,181 cooperatives. The deadline for repayment of a further 5.400 million forints was extended. 'After the credit settlement', the resolution said in conclusion, 'the debts of the cooperatives amount to 19.7 per cent of the net value of fixed assets, as opposed to 73.6 per cent before the settlement.'[40]

So the evolution of real opportunities for self-management was slow but steady. In 1964 only 6.5 per cent of the cooperative farms' investment for production came out of their own resources. In 1966 the proportion was already 37 per cent. There were more substantial increases in farm prices in the mid-1960s, as the preparations for the economic reform began: some 10 per cent in 1965–6 and another 8 per cent before the new price system was introduced in 1968. As a result, 50 per cent of the cooperative farms' investment in 1967 was covered from their own resources.[41] But the gulf between agricultural and industrial prices was not bridged during those years or even later, and the conditions for agricultural profitability only improved gradually, even though the ground was undoubtedly prepared on the cooperatives between 1956 and 1964 for the more radical reform that was to affect the whole economy.

12 First criticisms of the ineffectiveness of the corrective policy

Clearly, the comparative success with the mechanism applied in agriculture made it more apparent that the partial, sporadic corrections to the way the state sector operated were not having the desired effect.

'No substantial progress has been made in increasing company autonomy', the party Political Committee was told in a report in May 1964.[1] A confidential party assessment made in December 1964 was equally blunt: 'Work of a more forward-looking, principled character has scarcely come to the fore at all in the work of the ministries . . . [and] the executive work at the ministries has increased, not decreased.' In other words, the direct running had passed from the intermediate organizations of control not to the companies but to the ministries, and this had reinforced neither central control nor company autonomy. The December report reaches this conclusion: *'For there to be a more significant change in the authority, responsibility and rights in essential, substantial issues, reforms in our whole system of economic activity are required.'*[2]

Although the partial, corrective measures had been unsuccessful, they are none the less links in the chain of the Hungarian economic reform as a process. One might say that the conclusion of the corporate reorganization of industry coincided with the last of the partial, corrective changes made to the mechanism, for in January 1964 a system of charging companies a 5 per cent fee on the gross value of their fixed assets was introduced (having featured in the 1957 proposals for reform), with the purpose of encouraging companies to use them more economically.[3]

The tinkering then came to an end. As the party statements just quoted make quite plain, eight years' accumulated experience showed that partial corrections were not going to have the desired effect: there had to be 'reforms in our whole system of economic activity'. The corrective measures had hardly affected the overall functioning of the economy at all. What the president of the National Planning Office had said of the 1957–60 period remained all too true: 'Certain simplifications have been accomplished, but the 1954–6 system has not substantially changed.'[4] Amid the economic tensions and functional disturbances of the first half of the 1960s this continuity was now considered downright damaging: 'Opening moves have been made in the system of central direction of the economy in recent years', it was stated in a study prepared by the Central Committee apparatus in the spring of 1965. 'These measures have proved effective in some particular fields but they are incapable of creating satisfactorily the desired accord between our planning objectives and our system of control.'[5]

The recognitions that emerged from the system of making changes and minute corrections to the mechanism on a day-to-day basis brought comprehensive reform on to the agenda once more.

Part II

The 1966 decision on comprehensive reform: the second phase

13 Disequilibrium, tensions and shortcomings in the workings of the economy

The transformation of the country's economic structure and a decade of rapid industrialization had made it apparent that the Hungarian industry was approaching the pre-war level of the advanced European countries. The manpower resources which had previously seemed unlimited were beginning to run out by the mid-1960s, so that the industrialization process could no longer be based on increasing the input of labour into the economy by creating new jobs. This is quite apparent from the figures for annual growth of industrial employment: 5 to 6 per cent over the previous fifteen years, slowing to one per cent in the mid-1960s. By the early 1970s the national workforce had begun to decline.

This all amounted to a substantial change from previous decades, particularly when one adds in the structural factors. No increase in the labour force employed in the services had taken place, and it was vitally necessary to begin developing them, which would involve a transfer of labour from industry.

Future industrialization could no longer derive from increasing manpower, so that labour mobility and productivity gained immediate importance, and so did technical development. The economy had to function in a new and more efficient way and incentives had to be introduced.

This did not escape the attention of either economists or the government. The practical justifications for economic policy, the main arguments for introducing the reform, and in most cases the subsequent evaluations of these, explained the acceleration in the pace of reform, the strategic change in economic policy and the significant transformation of the model for the economy in terms of the industrialization which had occurred, the change in the economic structure and the exhaustion of the manpower surplus. The correlation is quite correct, but to emphasize the necessity of comprehensive reform only in these terms would be to tell only part of the story. A more important factor, indeed the prime mover behind the change, was the inadequacy and serious weaknesses of the prevailing system of economic policy and planning, despite the adjustments made to it after 1956. The decade after 1956 had brought a failure to attain economic objectives which had been set around the turn of 1956 and 1957, hence the sharp economic tensions of the early 1960s and the consequent effort to find new methods and solutions.

The functional problems of a command economy were quite well known from earlier experience. Economists had explored how its workings led to periodic overheating that resulted in regular stop–go cycles. Also understood was the connection between the command economy and the economy of shortage, with shortage appearing simultaneously with the accumulation of unsaleable stocks.[1] It was the reappearance of these problems in the early 1960s that convinced the government it had taken certain erroneous measures and failed to take certain necessary ones.

Particular mention must be made in connection with the period of the Second Five-Year Plan (1960–4) of the recurring disequilibrium in the economy, of which the most conspicuous sign was Hungary's mounting indebtedness to non-Comecon countries. Debts of 1,600 million forints in 1959 rose to 2,200 million in 1960, 3,000 million in 1961, 3,700 million in 1962 and 4,100 million in 1963. More revealing still is the fact that Hungary's debt-servicing commitments to these countries in 1962 had exceeded the value of its exports to them. According to a confidential report, 'The [balance of payments] deficit has had to be offset by further borrowing and the rescheduling of existing credits.'[2]

But even this does not represent the full threat posed by the loss of economic equilibrium. A report prepared for the members of the party's Political Committee in 1962 makes the immediacy of the problem plain:

> It should be noted in connection with the growth of capitalist debt and appraisal of our foreign exchange situation that some 80 per cent of the growth in debt has involved short-term credits . . . The proportion of the short-term credits that expire within three months is overwhelming. This is the main reason why the sum of our repayment obligations in every month of the first half of 1962 was more than twice as large as the foreign exchange earnings from goods exported were able to cover.[3]

The economic disequilibrium continued throughout the five-year period. Nor did the mid-1960s promise any speedy recovery: 'In the coming period of constantly growing weight of . . . repayment obligations beyond the trade turnover', the Political Committee concluded in April 1965, 'will make it even more difficult than before to restore equilibrium to the balance of payments.' The forecast for the second half of the 1960s was that 'the deficit in the balance of trade will impose decisive limitations on economic development not only in 1965 but in the years that follow'.[4]

Of course, the growing trade and payments deficits and the difficulties with repayments were not of financial or commercial origin. This needs emphasizing, because world-market prices and the structure of Hungarian foreign trade (based primarily on the export of finished industrial products and the import of raw materials) were basically in Hungary's favour, which had not been so during most of the twentieth century. In the longer period since the First World War, Hungary's terms of trade had deteriorated by 40 to 50 per cent. For the first time, the terms of trade were improving slightly: 'In 1964 the changes in market prices continued to improve the balance of trade, although to a lesser extent than in previous years', it was reported in 1965. 'We gained an extra 214,600 million forints' worth of foreign exchange compared with the prices planned for.'[5]

Needless to say the imbalances were only outward signs of deeper economic troubles, but they affected the most sensitive point of the economy. During the years of autarky in the 1950s, the objective had been to eliminate the links with the Western countries as far as possible, even though this had not completely succeeded. The principle of Comecon self-sufficiency had weakened in the late 1950s, and the ideology of 'two world markets' had waned. Hungary, like the other countries of Central and Eastern Europe, had begun to think in world-market terms. Trade with Western countries had become something natural, not something to be thought of as temporary or undesirable. However, these East–West economic links were transitional in character in the decade after 1956. As an article in the daily *Népszabadság* put it in the summer of 1957, they 'differ radically' from trade among the socialist countries and 'contain irreconcilable contradictions'.[6] At most they were seen, metaphorically speaking, as a safety net for the 'Comecon world market', and thus as a necessary evil. This outlook gained practical expression, for instance at the 1958 Comecon session in Bucharest, where it was stated: 'The socialist countries must make efforts to maintain and develop exports to [Western] countries with the primary purpose of being *able to purchase the goods of which there is a shortage in the socialist countries.*'[7]

Imports from the West were gap-fillers, easing acute shortages, sometimes of wheat, occasionally of meat and often of various raw and basic materials and part-assemblies that could not be obtained within Comecon. Under an economic policy that favoured rapid growth and under the conditions of an economy of shortage, these additional imports were extremely necessary. One might add that the very high level of investment required for import-substituting industrialization could not be covered within the Comecon framework either, partly because all member states were suffering from similar shortages, and partly because planning was rigid and a flexible market was lacking.

But the roots of the problem were deeper still. One of the pillars of Hungary's economic strategy after 1956 might be described as purchasing 'raw materials for machines'. Complementing this was the principle that Hungary should make fewer material-intensive products. Ultimately, neither goal could be attained, least of all to the extent dictated by the rapidly rising energy and material requirements of swift economic growth. It became increasingly clear at the National Planning Office, as Miklós Ajtai pointed out in the guidelines drawn up for elaboration of the new five-year plan in the spring of 1964: 'We cannot assert on a large scale the principle that we should extensively import materials or material-intensive products in exchange for exports of goods requiring highly qualified labour and a small input of materials.'[8]

About the same time Péter Vályi was explaining: 'We have convinced ourselves that a consistent assertion of the principles following from the country's shortage of raw materials is not possible for several reasons, even though in themselves they would be to our advantage . . . The notion of buying "raw materials for machines" is only partially applicable.' For Hungary's trading partners, particularly the small Comecon members, were in fact after materials for materials. In his analysis written for governmental use in the mid-1960s, Vályi put forward an appraisal quite different from the earlier one that had sprung from the enthusiastic and naïve zeal of the late 1950s. Whereas the partner countries 'can sell a good part of their unprocessed products on the capital world market as well, just as we can, the same materials are far less competitive in processed form'. Without modern technology and the assurance of quality and profitability, Vályi concluded, 'the division of labour we consider correct cannot be fully successful even among the Comecon countries . . . On the basis of experience with plan coordination our machinery exports are able to serve the purpose to an ever lesser degree. In machinery turnover . . .

the objective of a 1:1 proportion largely applies', which made it essential to reappraise the principles advocated for the last ten years.[9]

If an 'order of hardness' were emerging, in other words, if a good bargaining position could only be obtained with products qualifying as valuable on hard-currency markets, and if the price of imported materials had to be earned either in other materials or in high-value, technically up-to-date products competitive in terms of quality and the cost of producing them, Hungary in the long run could obviously not rely exclusively on exporting machinery of a middling quality and degree of sophistication. The logic of the situation required a turn towards products competitive abroad rather than import substitutes, as the National Planning Office underlined in the spring of 1966: 'So foreign trade becomes the crucial issue in the industrial policy of our five-year plan . . . industrial exports on an increasingly large scale are required . . . Alongside a target of 32 to 36 per cent growth in industrial production over the five years, [the plan] set an objective of a 50 per cent increase in industrial exports.' However, the rider was added: 'Industrial exports must be grounded in a firmer production structure.'[10]

A radical change in the structure of production, based on the international division of labour, had been decided upon at the turn of 1956 and 1957, but it had not taken place to any substantial degree. This failure, and the policy of import substitution, were largely behind the imbalances of the economy. The results of pursuing import substitution were not least apparent in the failure to build up competitive, up-to-date, export-oriented industries to a sufficient extent, and they were felt all the more strongly as the scope for further rapid development of foreign trade within Comecon diminished: in fact turnover stagnated for two years. In the mean time continued wasteful investment and chronic infrastructural underdevelopment fuelled the demand for imports. The role of non-Comecon trade had to be reassessed. It could clearly be thought of no longer as a gap-filling process of goods purchases if the hard currency for it was not being generated and it had to rely on credit, most of it short-term.

The prevailing assessment was still less tenable because it became increasingly obvious that trade with Comecon and trade on the world market could not be conducted independently of each other. For the priority industries required not merely an overall growth of imports but imports of materials, part-assemblies and capital equipment that could only be bought for hard currency. This requirement is convincingly illustrated by a calculation the National Planning Office made at the beginning of 1966 concerning the incidentally successful bus programme. The envisaged export for roubles to the socialist countries of 6,000 buses worth 1,300 million forints of foreign exchange in the year 1970 would mean importing from the West, for dollars, machinery worth 327 million forints.[11] In other words, the hard-currency requirement came to almost exactly a quarter of the targeted rouble receipts. To balance trade, it was not enough to export profitably for roubles. The dollars had to be earned as well, otherwise the more Comecon exports grew, the more dollar imports would grow, and in the absence of suitable goods to sell in the West, the more the unrepayable dollar debts would mount up.

Since there was hardly a Hungarian industry that did not require a hard-currency input into its products, some of the exports of these products should have been sold on the world market to cover it. This was often impossible because of the uncompetitiveness, low quality and so on that resulted from a policy of import substitution. The Western exports came nowhere near to covering the hard-currency imports (components, materials, etc.) incorporated into Hungarian export products: the convertible-currency balance of trade and balance of payments were firmly in the red. The objective of economic relations with the developed Western countries had to change. Instead of plugging shortages they had to promote modernization of the economy, allow technology to be obtained, improve long-term investment policy, and thereby enhance Hungary's export potential on the world market. But this would require not only a straight exchange of goods but economic relations of a more comprehensive kind. 'An active credit policy can and must be pursued, for certain forms of foreign credit are advantageous to the Hungarian economy', József Bognár was already arguing in 1957. 'It is an old-established and prevalent business custom for supplier companies . . . to extend short-term credit (of three, six or nine months) to a foreign customer. There is absolutely no reason why we should not avail ourselves of such credit . . . It is desirable to raise investment credit . . . in connection with the development of certain Hungarian factories.'[12] Before a credit policy could gain a final place in economic practice, political circumstances and attitudes had to change a great deal. This was pinpointed by Péter Vályi in his confidential reappraisal of economic relations already quoted: 'The changes in the international situation and the need to ensure up-to-date products present us with the task . . . of preparing ourselves to establish cooperation in production with the advanced capitalist countries for the sake of the country's development.'

One might regard as symbolic of the change of attitude the decision by the party's Public Finances Committee in the autumn of 1963 to give priority to 'the chance of developing the domestic nitrogen fertilizer industry on a large scale with capitalist credit' rather than to the grain purchases from the West which had been envisaged.[13] Early in 1964 the Political Committee came out in favour of raising long-term Western loans for investment in priority industries over the following three years, for instance to buy equipment for gas and oil prospecting and accelerate development in iron and steel and at certain large chemical plants.[14]

As foreign trade became a central issue in the Hungarian economy, reassessment of the export and production structures came to the fore in other respects as well. One side of the coin was the constant pressure for imports imposed by shortage, and the other was the low standard of the exports intended for the world market. It was recognized how unsuitable the command economy had become and what an obstacle it represented to achieving all these new objectives and changes.

It is worth noting that the first signs after 1956 of economic tensions had emerged in 1960. The phenomena were noted, but the causes were not investigated in any depth, and the attempts to eliminate them elicited the old reflex reactions. In the autumn of 1960 the Political Committee took the following view:

> The heads of the industrial portfolios are primarily responsible for our failure to implement the resolutions of the party and the government on investment projects, on the raising of productivity and on the alteration of the industrial structure of industry, including the product structure . . . A proportion of economic leaders are insufficiently imbued with . . . a sense of political responsibility . . . and generally speaking do not apply the guideline adopted by congress that ministerial, local, sectoral and company interests must be subordinated to the interests of the national economy.[15]

Two months later, the same body confirmed its position: 'The socialist awareness of economic and production managers in important positions has not strengthened, and this is now . . . slowing down our progress. The real root of this, along with numerous other, equally important factors, is that local interests are being promoted above national economic interests.'[16]

This attitude had also been reflected in an article in the daily *Népszabadság*, entitled 'Our Industry and the World Standard', published in the winter of 1959, which demanded to know what was holding things up, when 'our social system has created all the objective conditions for technical advance'. In such an approach, volition had clearly overriden objectivity, and the solution was seen in terms of changing man's nature and behaviour. 'Our factory managers must shoulder the risk, and under no circumstances sacrifice the good name of the factory to possible greater bonuses and profit shares.'[17]

Clearly the attitudes in politics and political journalism were lagging a good way behind what the economists had realized and expressed earlier. Even three years later, in December 1963, the Central Committee was still declaring in a resolution:

> The importance of exports to the development of the economy requires that . . . export committees be set up alongside the regional party committees which play a big part in export production. The committees' task will be to keep account of export tasks and supervise the implementation of them . . . In order to improve the relations between the major industrial companies and foreign trade companies . . . the foreign trade companies should inform the managers and party organizations of each industrial company regularly (monthly or quarterly) on the principal market requirements [and] the problems arising with export products.[18]

The efforts to treat economic symptoms with propaganda, moral exhortation and non-economic institutions (such as regional party export committees) was a natural consequence of the command economy and the lack of a market and profit incentive, reflecting incomprehension of economic processes and a doctrinaire isolation from reality. However, it was not typical of the Hungarian political leadership, who had learned a great deal from the early 1950s and from the tragedy of 1956. Meanwhile new experience had been gained from the partial corrections of the early 1960s. The moralizing and stroke-of-the-pen approaches to economic problems were in fact waning by the mid-1960s.

In 1957 it had still been believed in the corridors of government that the dysfunctions of the economic system could be remedied by reducing further the number of compulsory plan indicators and taking other, similar corrective measures. This attitude proved remarkably resilient but ten years later the weight of evidence against it was causing a reconsideration. A study entitled 'Evaluation of our Economic Development, Experiences in the Realization of our Economic Policy', commissioned from the National Planning Office by the party Central Committee in March 1965, stated: 'Compared with the mainly "quantitative" achievements the progress with the "qualitative" characteristics of our production is meagre . . . The problems with the quality and [level of] technical development of our products are also heightening . . . It is fundamental to our continued development that we bring these "qualitative" characteristics to the fore in production.'[19]

Despite the significant industrial and economic growth, serious errors familiar from the 1950s were recurring in the economy. In practice rapid growth remained the top priority, and inevitably the so-called 'national economic interest' was relegated. The push for quantitative growth created a pointless 'company interest' in fulfilling or overfulfilling the plan for its own sake. Vast quantities of superfluous and unsaleable products were being produced, and although these helped to inflate the figures for production growth and surpassing of the global production targets, they consumed huge quantities of mainly imported materials and energy, and of manpower.

The build-up of unsaleable stocks began again in 1958. Even in the spring of that year, at a time when shortages of goods were rife in most areas, the Central People's Control Commission stated: 'Mistakes are also common in the technical design of textile goods, haberdashery, garments and shoes, which the public are therefore unwilling to buy.'[20] Although the wholesale garment trade had put down 3.2 per cent of its total stock as 'frozen' at the end of the first quarter, the Commission pointed out: 'It is . . . in the financial interest of companies not to register their frozen stocks as such.' So in reality, according to an estimate by the Ministry for Domestic Trade, the proportion of unsaleable stocks was more like 5 to 10 per cent, and the Central People's Control Commission found even higher levels of frozen stocks during its investigations.[21]

Still more significant were the stocks of unusable materials, semi-finished and finished goods, components and so on accumulated by the manufacturing companies. One might regard it almost as symptomatic that even in the first quarter of 1957, a year in which there was a critical shortage of materials and goods, the problem had become acute: 'The Ministry of the Metallurgical and Engineering Industries, according to preliminary estimates, will surpass its production plan by some 300 million forints in the first quarter', the Political Committee was told, 'but the National Planning Office calculates that for only 70 to 80 million forints' worth of the extra output is there an actual need or demand at home and abroad . . . *The manufacture of superfluous products must be prevented by every means.*'[22] The extent of the failure to do this is well demonstrated by a survey three years later: 'In some companies', according to a National Planning Office report at the beginning of 1960, 'the proportion of superfluous stocks to total stocks has reached as much as 20 to 60 per cent.'[23] When placing their orders for materials, companies might well not know what their plan targets for the following year would be. Changes in the plans could also make materials or components superfluous, and so could overfulfilment. For instance, it was stated in the summer of 1958 that 'a significant proportion of the [goods produced through] overfulfilment of the plan by the foundries . . . is not required by the engineering industry'.[24]

The Political Committee heard from a report in the summer of 1961 that year-on industrial production was 13 per cent higher, but 'a higher proportion of the growth of industrial production than last year has not been serving the purposes of domestic trade, foreign trade, investment and renovation, and instead has manifested itself in a rise in the stocks of materials and semi-finished and finished products. This phenomenon is not a new one.'[25] In fact, Statistical Office reports show that stocks increased by 5,000 million forints in 1958, by 7,200 million in 1959 and by 9,200 million in 1960.

A comprehensive picture of this serious malfunction in the economy emerges from an enquiry by the Public Finances Committee of the party Central Committee in January 1962: 'A significant proportion of the national income consumed domestically consists of the 45 to 47 per cent growth . . . in current assets. The stocks of the national economy grew to a greater extent in 1961 than in previous years, and serious attention should be paid to the relatively fast growth in the proportion of national income attributable to the growth of stocks. (In 1959, 2.3 per cent, in 1960 5.4 and in 1961 *c.* 8.5 per cent of national income went on increasing stocks.)'[26] The process proved unstoppable. According to the president of the Planning Office in March 1965, 'Significant quantities have been placed "in stock" of industrial products (and raw materials, semi-finished products, manufactured goods and imported articles) for which there is no demand on either domestic or foreign markets. In the years 1961–3 . . . in other words in the space of three years, these stocks have risen by 33 per cent.'[27]

The bare figures can hardly convey the burden on the country of the superfluous stocks accumulated because of the way the economy was operating. This dead weight ranged from ill-cut, and thus unsaleable, children's clothing to substandard machines and materials and goods other companies did not want. In addition, a huge quantity of investment was frozen into too large a number of projects which were therefore running very late. It is more revealing to point out, for instance, that the proportion of national income squandered on accumulation that brought no return was more than double the country's defence spending.

This all tied up with the whole system of command economy. It was recognized as early as the summer of 1958, in the Planning Office report on industrial stocks quoted earlier, that the 'undesirable growth of stocks in most cases is merely a projection, a consequence of deficiencies in other areas of economic activity'.[28]

This wanton accumulation obviously tied in with the technical backwardness of industry and the inferior technical standards of its products, which curbed sales at home as well as abroad. It followed logically from import-substituting industrial development that the main criterion should be to ensure domestic production, and where economic policy objectives came into conflict with it, that technical standards should give way. Modernization of technology would have required a strategy of selective development that eliminated the imperative of autarky and concentrated on a few up-to-date, competitive, export-oriented sectors. However, the chances of applying this appeared only partially and in a very few areas. Meanwhile vast investment sums were spent on ambitious programmes to extract energy resources and raw materials and on the continued effort to substitute for imports. In addition, the limitation imposed on Hungary's participation in the international division of labour were a serious obstacle to updating technical standards.

Yet another obstacle was the maintenance of the existing system of planning, which remained insensitive to technical development despite the corrective measures introduced in 1957. The priority accorded to quantitative growth was a direct impediment to technical development that encouraged the conservation of outdated technology. But there was a big difference from the early 1950s in that the government was constantly trying to counter these problems. According to a proposal in the autumn of 1958:

> The continuous, day-to-day work of technical development – which is basically carried out at company level . . . should be advanced not with masses of indicators but with the requisite financial and moral incentives. In many cases the financial incentives to companies often influence them towards the conservation of technology . . . [and] we must devise and introduce methods of providing a financial incentive that influence them towards the development of technology and the interests of the national economy, instead of the conservation of technology and local interests.[29]

It is worth referring again at this point to the measures introduced in

1957 partly with this objective in mind. Several of the measures to correct the mechanism were taken in order to overcome previous functional problems. Since the company's interest in fulfilling and overfulfilling its compulsory production targets actually obstructed technical development, which was disadvantageous to the company, a technical development fund, of which news was given as early as the autumn of 1957, was set up to balance this. 'Incorporation of the technical development fund into the producer prices is certainly advantageous, since the sum which can be spent on the development of technology automatically increases with the development of production', or so the story went.[30]

Other corrective measures were designed to improve technical performance by easing the bureaucratic restrictions. The distinction between investment and depreciation funds was abolished, to give companies a free hand to combine them as they would and 'dispose freely on the proportion of the write-off for renewal'. But as a confidential report concluded, it soon became obvious that 'sums set aside for renewal purposes in the joint investment-renewal plan . . . were being used for starting new investment projects and continuing major investment projects already in hand'.[31] Again, correction of single elements in the economic mechanism failed to serve the purpose, since the whole system of functioning and incentive continued to propel companies in the opposite direction.

The new depreciation procedure, the creation of technical development funds and other, partial measures brought no real change, and the command economy continued to cause the conservation of obsolete technology. Companies were not even prepared to scrap machines whose cost had long been written off. A company would 'prefer to pay the sums for depreciation rather than scrap [machinery] at the expense of company profits. The machine which can be acquired from the renewal fund will not generate in one year the kind of sum involved in the loss arising from scrapping a machine', it was pointed out in an evaluation by the Planning Office early in 1960. In other words, the scrapping of obsolete, run-down machines would appear in the company accounts to be a 'deterioration in performance'; since the company might be called to account for this, it blocked 'the path of rational writing-off'.[32]

As the columnist István Földes put it in the daily *Népszabadság* in the summer of 1957:

> The statement that awareness is not enough to build on also holds

> true for technical development, especially when the price system and bonus arrangements not merely fail to encourage technical development but actually slow it down, as often happened in the past and still happens even today . . . So one cannot on the one hand work towards raising of the technical standard if on the other hand one fails to create the requisite methods for providing a financial incentive.[33]

In fact, the conditions for doing so had still not been provided by the mid-1960s.

So despite the significant growth of industrial production in the period under discussion, the level of productivity did not appreciably improve. In fact, in terms of production per unit of fixed assets, the figures showed a downward trend by comparison with 1958. Taking 1960 as 100, the index of production divided by stock of machinery and installations in 1966 was down to 84. The relative lag in productivity increased along with the growth of production. Whereas Hungary stood seventh among thirty-five countries in the mid-1960s in terms of number employed in industry per thousand of population, it stood only twenty-second in terms of per capita net industrial production.

It was partly the technical standard, partly the overall market indifference of companies, and ultimately the whole system of incentives based on plan indicators that resulted in the poor quality of products and the amassing of huge unsaleable stocks. In the spring of 1961, for instance, István Friss told the Political Committee:

> The number of complaints about quality made against industrial products and particularly products for export has grown . . . The 500 AR-321-type radio sets offered by Orion in April were not accepted because of quality shortcomings . . . 15.6 per cent of the export deliveries of the Duna Shoe Factory, as much as 54.5 per cent from the Fashion Shoe Factory, 16.3 per cent of cotton fabrics and 60.3 per cent of silk fabrics were declared unfit for export. Thirty-two per cent of the cotton fabrics for export prepared by the old-established Goldberger factory were rejected.[34]

Eighteen months later it was reported that half the refrigerators sold needed repairing within six months, and each television set had to be mended an average of three times during its warranty period.[35]

In a command economy the profit-sharing system was incapable of producing an incentive for companies to update their technology and improve quality. For the profit-sharing itself was distorted by state intervention (not to mention the inadequacy of the price system). In fact special corrections were constantly being allowed to companies. According to an estimate compiled by the Public Finance Department of the party Central Committee, these factors combined influence over 40 per cent of profit shares in 1963. 'It is worth noting', according to a report by the department to the Political Committee, 'that as a result of the various corrections, profit shares are gradually being divorced from their original basis, the growth of profitability. This brings with it the danger that the incentive nature of profit-sharing will diminish.'[36] With the basis of the economic mechanism unchanged, the profit-sharing system was distorted into a kind of bonus or a fund for distribution at the manager's discretion.

Despite the measures of decentralization taken and the efforts to rationalize and simplify the overly bureaucratic system of control made between 1956 and 1967, Hungarian industry remained governed by a host of directives, for which the centres, trusts and other supervisory authorities still demanded reports with an insatiable thirst for information. 'The number of data and reports passing between companies and outside authorities and between company headquarters and factories has grown', it was concluded at the end of 1964. The same report pointed out that 'in 1958, companies in the construction industry sent the ministry various reports on 64 occasions, containing 77,000 pieces of data; by 1963 the figures had risen to 133 and 560,000 respectively. Under the Ministry for Heavy Industry's data-provision system 558 reports had to be compiled in 1964, as opposed to 487 in 1963.'[37] So while companies in the construction industry were compiling almost three reports a week containing over 10,000 pieces of data, those in heavy industry were sending in more than ten reports a week.

Apart from generating a quantitative growth in production, these traditional methods were proving less and less effective, and were leading, as they had in the early 1950s, to a considerable absence of planning. The consequent problems and wastage on the domestic market were severe enough, but the gravest effects were on exports, particularly those to countries outside Comecon. There was a chronic lack of products that could be sold competitively on Western markets.

In fact this was inevitable, partly because the structure of production was unfavourable and partly because quality and technical standards were too low. But one main reason was the lack of market incentive for companies. In 1959, for instance, 24 per cent of exports were not produced 'in accordance with the prior requirements of foreign trade or the contracts previously concluded'. In 1960, 21 per cent of the products supplied for foreign trade consisted of 'stocks of unplanned goods'.[38] Under the circumstances, methodical, firmly based export activity on the world market was scarcely possible.

The malfunctions of the economy came into direct conflict in the mid-1960s with the now central issue of exports, and raised again the still unresolved problems with the structure, high energy requirements and low technical and quality standards of industry, which had come to the fore a decade earlier. What the decade had shown was that greater changes had to be made if greater changes were to be expected. Clearly, import substitution had to be replaced by a consistent export orientation in the key sectors of the economy, and this entailed reappraising the entire economic system and the basic features of incentive and material interest. The ten years of partial and moderate corrective measures had provided, if nothing else, rather more favourable conditions for making real progress. People saw that it was no good simply applying ready-made formulae: real requirements had to be analysed and real solutions sought. The political leadership now realized, as economists had done earlier, that treatment of a symptom here and a symptom there was not enough. Comprehensive reform was required.

The role played by all these factors was expressly stated by Rezső Nyers in a lecture to the Political Academy of the party Central Committee in December 1966:

> Ultimately . . . these tensions have a principal root in common . . . the problem manifest in the balance of trade . . . At present the exchange of goods does not ensure us the requisite optimum . . . We are compelled into constrained exporting and a brake on imports. This is all because the composition of our production, in the final analysis, is not such as can ensure we are competitive on foreign markets and able to exploit the advantages of the market.
>
> The assessment of the tensions has played a big part in bringing us to recognize the necessity of a reform of the economic mechanism. We have recognized that it is impossible to combat these tensions effectively by trying to resolve them one by one.[39]

The reform camp was far from homogeneous. There were some who expected it to prevent or circumvent more serious conflicts and wanted to restrict the reform to the unavoidable economic rationalization measures, and others who saw it as a point of departure for a comprehensive reform of the Soviet model. But the existence of this reform camp, diverse though its aims and ideas were, provided a basis for proceeding further.

The sense of openness and realism that emerged in practical policy led to a break with the kind of economic methods inspired by doctrine, preconception and wishful thinking. (As János Kádár put it in a lecture, theory is not something to be tested out on people, it is something with which to promote their interests.) The attention paid to the social consequences of the practical conflicts and processes taking place in the economy – in a word, the values deriving from policy – found expression in a search for new responses. So the course followed between 1956 and 1965 of applying partial, corrective measures was not all in vain, since it broadened into a historical process of genuine reform.

14 Plans and preparation for reform in other socialist countries

Closely related to the recognition by the administration in Hungary of the need for comprehensive reform were the reforming efforts and debates in the Soviet Union and Czechoslovakia, not to mention the economic reform begun in Yugoslavia in 1965. One might go so far as to say that economic reform was in the air in East-Central Europe in 1964–5. It could hardly be a coincidence that periodicals and even central political daily papers in the neighbouring countries were publishing a growing number of articles on the subject at this time. On August 17, 1964 *Pravda*, the daily paper of the Communist Party of the Soviet Union, carried an article by V. A. Trapeznikov entitled 'What Specifically Worries Soviet Economists?' Ideas were formed of updating the economic system through prices, profits and financial incentives. The initiatives of what has come to be known in the history of socialist economic theory as the Liberman Debate represented a forceful criticism of the command economy. As Y. Liberman wrote:

> The position is that industrial companies are still tied by the large number of blanket indicators set from above . . . and so the paradoxical situation occasionally arises in which a company does itself harm when aiming at something useful from the point of view of the national economy. As a consequence, the introduction of new technology and the whole cause of improving production suffers delay . . . Thus many Soviet economists propose that companies be assessed and impelled mainly on the basis of their actual profitability . . . Companies ought to know what they need to produce . . . Plan tasks must . . . gradually . . . turn into 'orders' . . . It is not the state that needs to place the orders . . . which the companies must 'chase'. It is impermissible to eliminate the competitive character of production organization.[1]

In January 1967 the *Közgazdasági Szemle* carried an article by G. Popov providing a summary of the reform debates in the Soviet Union in general and of the series of pamphlets on reform published by Ekonomika in Moscow. The first pamphlet in the series was 'The Necessity and Essence of Economic Reform' by S. P. Pervushin. In 'Some Issues of Economic Reform and Economic Theory' L. A. Leontev wrote of the 'utilization' and necessity of the law of value and commodity production in a way and with a terminology familiar from the Hungarian debates quoted earlier. This all tied in with a categorical assertion by V. V. Novozhilov: 'If the law of value functions under socialism, it cannot be restricted . . . The plan can no more restrict the law of value than it can the law of gravity.' Professor Z. V. Atlas spoke of how industrialization, an inevitable phase in Soviet development, 'demanded a specific economic mechanism', and described this centralized, directive planning model as the tool by which 'rural Russia can break . . . into the world of machines'. He regarded reform as necessary at the level of development attained so that profitability and economic efficiency could be asserted through the introduction of market relations. Subsequent pamphlets in the series dealt with the role of profit, the new system of material incentives and the price reform.[2]

The writings of Soviet economists in 1965–6 bear a considerable similarity to those expressed in the Polish, Hungarian and Czechoslovak debates on reform. However, a great deal more was involved in the case of Czechoslovakia. In 1964 a decision on the reform had been taken at government level, and in 1966 the man leading the preparations, Professor Ota Šik, put forward in an interview also published in Hungary a concept for a Czechoslovak reform which was based at that time on principles remarkably similar to the ideas current in Hungary. 'The new central plan', he emphasized, 'is fundamentally macroeconomic in character.' Elsewhere he stated:

> The factories are not given a quantitative indicator of production, so that the company also decides, for instance, by assessing the sales prospects, the extent to which it is worth utilizing capacity.
>
> Under the new economic system in Czechoslovakia the company will pay two kinds of tax (levy) out of its net income after the deduction of the cost of materials and depreciation, the first being a certain percentage of the net income, which is to be set uniformly for all companies, and the other being calculated according to the assets tied up and deducted as a sum from the net income. The latter is intended to encourage effective utilization of fixed assets. What remains after these deductions will, one might say, be used by the company as it would be by a capitalist company . . . i.e. the company will set aside a reserve fund and a certain sum for technical development, and is free to spend the rest on wages. Wages are composed of

> two parts: a basic wage and a bonus . . . Company managers will have a free hand in the distribution of the bonuses.
>
> The price system will also alter significantly. 'Genuine market prices' are required, the formation of these is still a big problem today, and not merely under the socialist system. For the time being we shall resolve this with three kinds of prices. The most important foodstuffs, energy and the important raw materials will have fixed prices, which will be set and monitored centrally. The second kind of price applied will be the so-called restricted price, which will leave producers a measure of freedom of movement, and finally there will also be free prices, although the inflation that may arise in connection with these must be forestalled.[3]

In the spring of 1966 O. Bogomolov stated in *Voprosi Ekonomiki*: 'The economic reforms applied and planned in the Soviet Union and the other socialist countries are marked by a diversity of forms. The introduction of reforms has been necessitated in the individual countries by similar causes, but the problems are receiving . . . different remedies.'[4]

In the summer of 1967 an article appeared in the *Economist* grouping the socialist countries according to the intensity of their reform aspirations. Yugoslavia, Czechoslovakia and Hungary were placed in the first group, Poland, the Soviet Union and the GDR in the second, and Romania and Bulgaria (since they were not embarking on experimentation with reform at all) in the third. According to the *Economist*, in practice all the reforming Eastern European countries were pursuing identical purposes to some degree, some with more daring and some with more moderation: to reduce the number of indicators, to grant greater freedom to companies, to shift greater emphasis on to net instead of gross performance or costs, and to link all this up with some kind of price reform.[5]

It seemed that the Hungarian party and the government could safely embark, along with other socialist countries, on introducing reforms. So the *Népszabadság*, in the spring of 1965, could put the following question to Rezső Nyers, a secretary of the party Central Committee, in an interview entitled 'On the Transformation of the System of Economic Management': 'Comrade Nyers, you mentioned that . . . you are paying attention to the experiences of the other socialist countries that could be useful here. In what direction do these . . . experiences point?' His answer was this:

> In their broad outlines and courses our ideas and the foreign experiences coincide, although in terms of practical measures there are naturally divergent points of view as well. As far as the course of

> change is concerned, one can sum it up by saying that we, like most of the friendly countries, are aiming at a more expedient combination of central planning and commodity–money relations.[6]

János Kádár was also able to speak with optimism on the eve of the introduction of the Hungarian economic reform: 'A similar reform of economic direction to ours is now on the agenda in several [other] socialist countries . . . I think this is an international necessity placed on the agenda by development.'[7] Reform has been given a green light in Hungary.

15 The political background to the reform

All these factors were important in influencing the Hungarian government to return to the idea of comprehensive reform, which had received a rough ride in 1956–7, but they obviously do not explain the decision in full. In fact, one can point to junctures in both Hungary and the neighbouring countries where the patent necessity of change did not lead to reform at all. Similarly, there were occasions when open debates on reform and even some practical measures in some socialist countries failed to have any effect whatsoever on others, and were not even publicized there.

The main factors behind the return to a policy of reform were the domestic political processes which had taken place in a favourable climate. Western observers of the Hungarian reform have reached an almost banal consensus of opinion that the price for the Kádár régime being allowed to embark quietly on reforming the economy was that it should not attempt to meddle with external relations and political structures. The pragmatic stereotype of 'goulash communism' and the legitimacy earned through the improvement in living standards obscured the fact that no comprehensive economic reform could even have been contemplated had there not been a substantial transformation and renewal on the political scene.

Although these political processes can obviously be traced back earlier, they began to unfold *properly* in the early 1960s. By this time the hard line of dictatorship involved in the restoration and consolidation of power had been relegated. The political intention of the leadership in general, and the political wisdom of János Kádár in particular, was directed to applying in the long term the tragic lessons of 1956. In the strict sense of institutional transformation, one can hardly speak of a Hungarian 'political reform' at all, but although the transformation processes left the institutional frameworks intact, they caused far-reaching changes.

It is time, therefore, to identify the main features and trends of political change that paved the way for economic reform.

Although we are concerned here with domestic processes, mention must first be made of two international events. First, on June 3–4, 1961 a historic summit meeting took place in Vienna. The encounter and talks between Nikita Khrushchev and John F. Kennedy marked the end of the disastrous years of Cold War and the beginning of détente. Two years later (after the perilous, if educational, interlude of the Cuban missile crisis) the Soviet Union and the United States signed their 'hotline' agreement in Geneva, an act of both symbolic and practical significance. Obviously not independent of this was the return at the Twenty-second Congress of the Communist Party of the Soviet Union, which began on October 17, 1961, to the course marked out at the Twentieth Congress of breaking with the Stalinist past and embarking on new paths of dynamic change. The Soviet party leadership spoke emphatically of the need to 'eliminate the consequences of the cult of personality'.[1] Despite the return to realism, this policy was, nevertheless, influenced by some powerful illusions as well. Communism was to be attained within twenty years, and a programme of overtaking the world's advanced Western countries in every respect was put forward.

Once the international conditions were more favourable and the bitter domestic conflicts were over, it was possible for genuine, substantive political change to commence in Hungary. Since the summer of 1957 the threat from 'right-wing revisionism' had been underlined.[2] Now the sharp edge of political struggle was again turned against the conservatives, the advocates of 'dogmatic, left-wing adventurism'. In 1962 the party returned to the case of Mátyás Rákosi and the pre-1956 leadership. The expulsion of Rákosi, Gerő and their associates from the party[3] was a step with a more than symbolic significance, and so was the Central Committee resolution on completing the rehabilitation of the victims of the show trials in the early 1950s.[4] Around the same time, on March 22, 1963, the Presidential Council decreed a general amnesty for political prisoners jailed after 1956, which was a decisive step towards national reconciliation. Moreover, the secret police were purged and placed under strict and solid political control.

These years brought a political opening-up that transformed political practice even though the institutions remained essentially unchanged. The first steps were taken towards segregating party and state, so as to diminish the direct party control previously exercised at every level. Another important change was to open up the borders, which had been almost hermetically sealed. Before 1956 travel had been impossible not only to the West but even to neighbouring socialist countries. To the latter travel had become possible to a very restricted extent in the spring and summer of 1956. In 1961–2 an institution called the 'tourist passport' was born and it was possible to travel abroad, once a year, even to the West. After a break of more than twenty years, younger generations of Hungarians were able to discover Europe.

In October 1963 an agreement was concluded with Czechoslovakia (the Hungarian delegation being headed by János Kádár) on abolishing the passport and visa requirements between the two countries, and this was enshrined in an inter-governmental agreement on January 2, 1964. Later the same year, similar agreements were concluded with other neighbouring countries, and on September 20 another measure to open up the borders was announced: foreigners wishing to enter Hungary could receive visas from Hungarian consulates within twenty-four hours.

As the borders were being opened up, and the institutionalized suspicion, the search for an enemy and the witch-hunting 'class warfare' of the previous period were dispelled, a real symbol of the openness of a new era came in the form of a statement made by Kádár in a famous policy speech in 1962. 'Whoever is not against us is with us!' In that light the Political Committee of the party adopted a resolution in April 1963 calling for the abolition of classification according to family background as a criterion for university entrance. By this means a sizeable proportion of society ceased to be second-class citizens. There was no more exclusion of the children of 'class aliens', and the discrimination by reference to worker-peasant policy against people with 'other' backgrounds, the intelligentsia, came to an end.[5]

Consistent adherence to the policy of 'whoever is not against us is with us' entailed a reconciliation between the state and the churches, and tolerance instead of impatient stigmatization and repression of church-goers. The same policy was applied in the villages, where the earlier, extremist policy of curbing, and indeed eliminating, the wealthy peasantry even by police harassment and economic sanctions was abandoned. So another stratum of society was free to develop its talents in the new cooperatives, and even to join in the management of them. Certainly measures like these were effective in promoting national reconciliation.

No less significant was a fundamental change of cultural policy which concurrently laid the basis for political alliance with the intelligentsia. The years of a narrow-minded dictation of tastes, of imposing artistic and cultural uniformity and exercising an ideological monopoly, were followed by a toleration of diversity, recognition of artistic freedom and guarantees of freedom of scientific research (if not of equal opportunity to publish). The limits of toleration were constantly extended, for instance to the group of writers who had been known as the populists before the war. They had produced rural 'sociographical' 'studies and to a large extent seen the peasantry rather than the working class as Hungary's future salvation. Their works were now reappraised and they were readmitted into the artistic and political fold. Also rehabilitated were the advocates of trends in the arts which had been condemned in the early 1950s. They were now judged on their merits, and the act of doing so had a significance extended far beyond the cultural sphere. In fact, it became a major pillar of the new political practice.

The political system became much less repressive. The overwhelming majority of the old 'caste' privileges, such as special shops, were also abolished. Leading politicians, too were obliged to pay rent for their housing. There was no cult of an 'infallible leader' any more, and the supremacy of the legal system over political expediency was strengthened. All these changes laid the foundations of a new political style and became a stepping-stone for efforts at restoring the kind of human rights which had previously been disparaged and set aside. Even though most of the alterations were paternalistic government concessions that involved no change in the monolithic system, the developing 'enlightened absolutism' of the 1960s helped to create the main preconditions for economic reform.

Under these circumstances, the Hungarian authorities did not resort to the traditional administrative intervention or to organization and reorganization, nor did they opt for a course of inefficient, partial corrective measures when confronted again with economic trouble. Kádár's policy right from the outset had been to avert a repetition of the sharpening of domestic economic and social conflicts and to seek satisfactory solutions before the conflicts could shake the fabric of society. The political trauma of 1956 was still fresh in people's memories, and having learned the lessons of the previous ten years, the Hungarian authorities were prepared to face facts.

16 The reform decision

Let us now return to the economic problems that were emerging.

In the first half of 1964, during the difficult year of the Second Five-Year Plan, pregnant with economic tensions, unsettled by disturbances to the economic equilibrium and aggravated by mounting foreign debt, some truly novel recognitions were made. In February 1964 Rezső Nyers established that 'some of our economic policy objectives have attained particular prominence . . . technical development, foreign trade effectiveness, productivity, economic viability'. But Nyers, as the Central Committee secretary responsible for economic affairs (he had taken over only just over a year before), did not believe that the old methods of more and more central regulations and resolutions were going to work. He believed in the need to transform the planning and economic mechanism: 'The methods of directing the economy and the financial incentives', he emphasized in an article in the *Társadalmi Szemle* at the beginning of 1964, 'must accord at all times with the dominant economic and political goals . . . It would by no means be correct to identify the essence of the socialist planned economy with a particular planning method. The Marxist–Leninist economic concept of socialism provides scope for a wide variety of methods, indeed for the periodic change of methods and mechanism, which is, moreover, part of it.' He therefore believed the time had come 'to review the methods and incentives of economic management . . . In our present investigation the basic principle could be to bring company activity and national economic interests closer together.'[1]

An article in the same issue of the *Társadalmi Szemle*, the party's theoretical journal, clearly referred back to the debates of six or seven years earlier and the branding of comprehensive reform as 'economic revisionism' when it stated in connection with the tasks of developing economics as a discipline:

> If economists criticize the system of economic management with appropriate scholarly gravity and political responsibility, they are not, in doing so, questioning the basic principles and institutions of the socialist economic order . . . To make further, well-grounded headway in eliminating our present economic problems, we must have some kind of conception of the direction in which . . . steps must be taken in order to perfect the regulation of the national economy. While remaining in touch with reality we must also tackle . . . the present 'mechanism' as a whole. It is the right and the duty of economists to work for the development of it.[2]

But it was not only economic attitudes that were changing around the middle of the 1960s. Once the economic realities had been faced, active steps were taken to reappraise and transform economic policy and the economic mechanism. On June 22, 1964 the party's Public Finances Committee discussed the guidelines for the Third Five-Year Plan (1965–70) compiled by the National Planning Office and concluded that a new version of it had to be drawn up. This revised plan should 'take as its basis a halt in the growth of the capitalist foreign exchange debt'. In other words, the plan should not embody a policy grounded in the growth targets traditionally preferred: 'The decisive criterion of the plan variant should be the requirement of the foreign exchange situation.' Naturally, this approach went beyond any quantitative objectives of import substitution and necessarily shifted the emphasis on to the export requirements. The committee told the planners to find out

> in which groups of products capitalist exports can be increased and to what extent . . . what overall effect (on the product structure) this will have, in which groups of imported goods an absolute reduction of domestic consumption is possible and to what extent . . . in which fields cooperation with capitalists can be counted on and what overall effect this is likely to have . . . [and] what measures are necessary in planning methods and management outlook and incentives

so linking up the objectives in reorientating economic policy with the requirements of the economic mechanism.[3] The intention of replacing a policy of import substitution with an outward-looking one was phrased very succinctly at the meeting of the same committee in January 1966. The forthcoming Ninth Congress of the Hungarian Socialist Workers' Party was to 'analyse the open nature of our economy and the efforts to achieve domestic autarky, working out an economic optimum between these, and to draw requisite conclusions'.[4] A number of traditional ideological taboos were still operating concurrently during these years, and a campaign had to be waged against political spectres. None the less, the government sought new ways of tackling the trade imbalance without resorting to administrative restrictions. The command economy was no longer being equated with socialism.

Starting in 1963, the idea of reforming the mechanism of planning and the direction of the economy came gradually to the fore again. Rezső Nyers established an informal, twelve-member economic advisory body in 1963, so providing an institutional link of a new kind between economists, theoretical and practical, on the one hand and party and governmental direction of the economy on the other. Even in that same year the idea that a comprehensive economic reform was necessary began to emerge in the discussions within this 'brains trust'.[5] To put this into practice, the Public Finances Department of the party Central Committee completed, at the instigation of the Central Committee secretary concerned, a proposal 'on the direction and programme for the work of developing the economic system further'. Its introduction stated: 'The system of economic direction currently operating emerged essentially in the period 1957 to 1960 . . . Accomplishment of the present economic policy requirements . . . is made difficult, or not assisted adequately, in numerous fields by the mechanism employed in the direction and present organization of the economy.'[6] The decision of the committee, which Rezső Nyers chaired, came a week later, on July 21,1964:

> The Committee has resolved that in order to ensure a better foundation and more effective implementation of the objectives of our economic policy it will commence a comprehensive reassessment of economic management extending over our system of production, pricing, incentives, financial affairs, financing and economic activity and over the organization of the economy . . . The objective must be that implementation of the proposals to be devised should produce an increase in the autonomy and responsibility of companies . . . Based upon analytical work carried out from various angles, a critical assessment of the present economic mechanism and system must be prepared, and on the basis of this a comprehensive concept whose application will result in modernization of the economic mechanism and system.[7]

A group of experts was formed to undertake the examination, which was expected to last for two years, and 'a number of distinguished economists' were asked 'to summarize their experiences in writing and express their opinions'. A three-member committee, on which Nyers was assisted by István Friss and Imre Párdi, was set up to direct the task.

Since Friss has already been an important figure in this book, it is necessary to point out that a part in the eventual acceptance and victory of the reform line was played by Friss's ability to re-examine his earlier position and give his support to comprehensive reform, clearly in the light of what he had experienced in the previous years. He gave his reasons in theoretical terms as well to the general assembly of the Hungarian Academy of Sciences in the spring of 1967: 'Initially', he said in a clear reference to his earlier position in 1957,

> it appeared that reform of the mechanism would not affect the theoretical issues of the socialist economy. But it emerged that a re-examination of practice necessitates a re-examination of the theoretical basis for practice as well. Marx wrote of socialism, contrasting it with capitalism, as follows: 'Only where production is genuinely under the planned control and supervision of society does society establish accord between the labour expended on the production of certain articles and the social need to be satisfied by these.' According to this, planned social control, in short the national economic plan, will distribute the total labour precisely in accordance with the social needs.
>
> However, if we confront our plans with reality, it emerges that they have by no means created such an ideal situation . . . So in the sense in which Marx used the phrase, production in this country is not under the planned control and supervision of society . . . There is no need any more to attribute to our society characteristics which exist only in our imagination . . . According to all our experience so far *one cannot rationally control from a single centre* the activity of every economic unit . . . The only correct place to take the economic decisions is where *the local and professional knowledge* required for doing so in the particular case is greatest . . . It is for us, *the descendants*, to establish the laws of the socialist economy from an analysis of our own experience.[8]

The preparation of the reform began in 1964, and on December 10, in relation to the results and problems of the first four years of the Second Five-Year Plan, the Central Committee stated:

> [it] regards as necessary a comprehensive, critical analysis of the present economic mechanism (including the system of planning, finance, and price and material incentives) and a modification of it appropriate to the situation. The purpose to be achieved by the further development is a more effective utilization of the economy's total production capacity, an increase in autonomy and responsibility, and the reduction of bureaucratic practice. The reappraisal of the entire mechanism must be carried out under the direction of the Central Committee's Public Finances Committee, supported by the activity of experts, by the beginning of 1966.[9]

The analysis was begun under the direction of Rezső Nyers through eleven working committees: for planning (headed by István Hetényi), the company mechanism (Ottó Gadó), the agricultural mechanism (János Keserű), the connection between the economic mechanism and technical development (János Sebestyén), the new system of investment (József Bálint), the price system (Béla Csikós-Nagy), the new wage system (István Buda), the mechanism of foreign trade (Gyula Karádi), domestic trade (Imre Fenyő), the new function of local councils (Mátyás Timár), and participation of employees in management (András Hegedűs).

The working committees had completed their critical analysis of the existing system of operation by March 1965, and on this basis a secretariat which had been established in the mean time prepared the initial outline for the reform in April, followed in June by the proposals for perfecting the operation of it. In October 1965 the preliminary draft of the principles of the reform was ready.[10] Simultaneously a 'summarizing material' on the reform concept was prepared in the Ministry of Finance under the direction of Mátyás Timár, and the personal reform proposals of a number of experts – György Péter, József Bognár, Jenő Wilcsek and others – were gathered by the Economic Committee.

At the beginning of 1965 the steering committee for the preparatory work had stated that the work has

> a reform character, i.e. it is not aimed at a simple improvement of the existing economic mechanism, nor at a revolutionary alteration of it. The various reform concepts must be confronted with each other and care must be taken not to allow a single conception to become predominant in the initial stage of the work on an administrative or reputation basis.[11]

At this stage significant differences of opinion appeared on the actual reform committees, among the experts and even within the small secretariat, since the Central Committee's position was interpreted in various ways:

> In the course of the work, naturally, numerous problems of principle and differences of opinion have arisen . . . It is also apparent that views deriving from an adherence to the old principles and practice and to the retention of existing spheres of responsibility and authority feature in the development of certain of the positions taken.[12]

There was an argument, for example, between the Foreign Trade and the Metallurgy and Engineering Industry Ministries over the foreign trade mechanism and independent import–export rights for companies. It was reported that the expert staffs of the two ministries 'subscribe to disparate interpretations of the principles for developing the relationship between foreign trade and industry'. Meanwhile the Foreign Trade and the Finance Ministries were at loggerheads over export subsidies.[13] In the spring of 1965 the reform committee's secretariat reported:

> During the elaboration of the initial concept, a fundamental difference of opinion arose within the Secretariat over which objective should be pursued in the reform of the economic management system. The difference culminated in the assessment of the part to be played by plan directives, compulsory plan indicators. Of the third chapter [on national economic planning] two versions were prepared, but the difference strongly affected other chapters . . . although no second versions of them were prepared.

The most essential difference between the two versions of the initial concept was that the first considered direct state commands to be exceptions in the management of companies, while the second saw plan indicators as essential and integral to the management system, in which they had an indispensable part to play.[14] As one advocate of the latter put it: 'The direct commands, the compulsory indicators finding expression in the plans in the second concept are not an exceptional but a regular phenomenon.' There was to be no abolition of the command economy, merely 'an appreciable narrowing of direction resting on direct plan commands'. He summed up by saying it was clearly a question of 'two concepts of the reform which have a great many elements in common [and] significant points of contact. None the less, the difference is insurmountable . . . and fundamental from the point of view of development prospects. A difference that appears abstract and overly theoretical today will signify a radically differing practice in terms of five or ten years.'[15]

Although the idea of retaining the plan directives even partially was rejected by the steering committee, the wide-ranging conflicts of views and interests were often resolved by compromise. The work went on with a tremendous intensity. In 1966, purely on preparing the price reform, 'some 10,000 people are now working nationwide in the directing organizations and in the production units', it was reported.[16] The legal preparations for the reform were particularly extensive:

> The work amounts to a new kind of assignment. On many issues critical re-examination of legal stipulations so far considered inviolable has had to be faced. The apparently most suitable legal solutions have had to be found for new economic solutions known only in outline . . . For this reason we cannot regard the work as completed, and it will require further years of work and the concerted efforts of

> science and practice, of economic, legal and other social sciences, fully to clear up in principle the majority of the questions which have arisen.[17]

Once the proposals had eventually been formulated, incorporating to a great extent the work done by the reform committee of early 1957, on which no small proportion of the economists taking part had sat personally, it was possible for them to be debated and decided upon. This the party Central Committee did on November 18–20, 1965, adopting a document entitled 'The Initial Guiding Principles for the Reform of the Economic Management System' that radically revised the party and governmental position taken up eight years earlier. 'From the critical analysis we have unambiguously and uniformly ascertained', the resolution ran, 'that essential changes are required. The main shortcomings established are strongly related to one another [and] cannot for the most part be eliminated other than by interrelated and comprehensive measures.' When referring to the previous policy of partial, corrective measures, the resolution was content to repeat the customary, correct-in-their-time formula, but the Central Committee supported the notion that 'in the situation today . . . more than these is required'. As the resolution declared:

> It is a fundamental problem that . . . the extensive degree of centralization and the low degree of independence of companies, the strict and direct state regulation of economic processes largely through compulsory plan indicators, the limitation on the active role of commodity–money relations and market impulses . . . have remained in our economic management system . . . Our entire economic mechanism fails to assist sufficiently in exploiting the advantages obtainable by broadening the international division of labour . . . Our present system of economic management . . . has come into conflict with economic policy and is impeding the application of it.

The resolution breaks new ground in the history of socialist planning internationally with the following assertion:

> *The present system of 'breaking down' the national economic plan for ministries and companies is particularly ripe for change* . . . Often the 'plan breakdown' is the source not of a planned situation but of quite the opposite, an unplanned situation . . . The typical error in our entire price system is that the prices of products differ to a large extent and in an economically unjustified way from the socially necessary inputs; moreover . . . the prices are overly rigid and incapable of bringing supply and demand into accord. The idea has become predominant that

> commodity relations and the law of value also exist and exert an influence in the socialist economy . . . We must allow commodity relations and all the economic categories connected with them – the market, prices, production cost, profit, credit, etc. – to play an essentially greater and more active part in the socialist economy than they have done so far . . . [for] *it is historically imperative that there should be an integral connection between socialist planning and the active role of commodity–price relations*.

The resolution of the autumn of 1965 continues with wording reminiscent of the resolution of December 1956:

> The fundamental task of economic planning is to plan the main targets . . . and main proportions of economic development. We should substantially expand the autonomy of the state companies . . . This is possible if . . . the realization of the plan is directed not by breaking down the various indicators, i.e. not by administrative prescription of the individual plan indicators, but chiefly by economic means.[18]

The principal ideas of the resolution demonstrate that the party had returned to the concept of comprehensive economic reform worked out in 1957, which was seen as the vehicle for a strategic change in economic policy. 'The reform of the economic mechanism', the resolution stressed, 'can also be regarded as a highly significant measure of economic policy.' The reform of economic management was designed 'to exercise a particularly positive effect on the accomplishment of our prominent economic objectives'. It was supposed to promote technological development, so that Hungary could become increasingly involved in the international division of labour. To mention a few of the key expressions, the reform of the mechanism was expected to end the practice of an 'excessively "protectionist" (i.e. essentially autarkic) economic policy', and the effects of encouraging imports and 'insufficiently promoting an improvement of the export structure'. It had to assert the principle that 'the economy of shortage is terminable' and to produce 'the balanced economic growth required' for development to become intensive (based on technical advance and increasing productivity), and agriculture and the infrastructure to catch up with industry, to which they had been subordinated. All these arguments were accepted by the Central Committee, which stated in its resolution: 'We must not . . . delay in [applying] the necessary reforms; instead our declared purpose, having identified the causes behind the mistakes, is to start applying considered and forceful measures to resolve the problems.'[19]

The same resolution set January 1968 as the deadline for introducing a radical reform of producer prices, which gave an enormous fillip to the reform preparations. Huge numbers of expert staff were drawn into them, and by the spring of 1966 it was possible for the Central Committee to cover every detail of the new mechanism of planning and direction in a resolution passed at the session on May 25–27 which saw the reform in both an economic and a political light:

> Based on analysis of our economic scene and in support of our future development, the HSWP Central Committee is initiating implementation of a reform of our economic mechanism . . . The reform will above all be one of the economic mechanism, but it will also be a reform of the system of economic management; at the same time it will connect closely with the economic policy of our party and be directed towards the further development of it . . . The reform will serve as a means of bringing the economic mechanism into conformity with the new tasks that are coming to the fore . . . The reform has economic and political grounds . . . It is a political objective . . . to eliminate . . . excessive restrictions [and] repress bureaucratic tendencies . . . Finally, it is a political objective to create through the reform more favourable conditions for the further development of socialist democracy.[20]

This decision by the Central Committee in favour of the reform also contained guidelines, arranged in twelve chapters, that determined in precise detail the new method of planning, the price and income regulating systems, the new system of investment, and the credit and trading systems.

The substance behind the new economic mechanism, one might say the philosophy behind the new operating system for the reformed economy, was expressed as follows in the resolution:

> The system of plan indicators – the breakdown of the annual national economic plan through the ministries to the companies . . . must be abolished. Companies themselves should draft their plans, which are their own working programmes, and these need not even be endorsed. But we must at the same time cause the active role of commodity relations and of the market to unfold . . . *So the fundamental feature of our economic mechanism is to link together the central, planned control of the national economy, the commodity relations and the active role of the market on the basis of socialist ownership of the means of production.*[21]

The reform was not intended to introduce a genuine market economy with a system of market prices. The aim was to combine central planning with the automatic processes of the market by linking them through what were described as regulators (taxation and regulation of wages, prices, etc.). These regulators were to take the place of plan directives and *simulate* the market, as a means of providing companies with a stake in their own performance.

17 Debates on the reform and compromises before its introduction

Before describing the workings of the reformed mechanism, let me mention briefly the social and political debates that accompanied the preparations for it. For the work of preparing it certainly did not take place in a neutral environment, and it was by no means decided upon solely in terms of economic rationalism and recognitions.

During the years of economic consolidation that began in the later 1950s, the gradual improvement in living conditions and the increase in personal consumption sparked off a debate about the emergence of the 'lust for possessions' and a 'consumer orientation'. These were perceived by some as tendencies that endangered and conflicted with socialist ethics, and even as a threat to the traditional values of the people and the nation.

The characteristic example of this, the debate over 'refrigerator socialism', arose in the autumn of 1961 along with the first, modest increases in the standard of living, when household appliances and private cars were just beginning to appear. The literary journal *Uj Irás* (New Writing) initiated a discussion on the Soviet party's draft programme and its objective of achieving communism in the space of two decades. It should be said straightaway that similar programmes reflecting similar thinking were drawn up in Hungary as well. The National Planning Office put forward a confidential proposal, in other words not a propaganda statement at all, which envisaged a growth of production up to 1980 that would 'not merely exempt our people wholly from problems of livelihood but allow the attainment of consumption targets . . . sufficient to satisfy the harmonious physical and intellectual needs of man'. Indeed, this report to the Public Finances Committee of the party Central Committee put it more plainly and categorically still: 'According to our present knowledge, the proposed levels of consumption will arrive at a standard of *saturation* on a society-wide scale.' Moreover, 'the targets for the major consumer durables will signify *full supply* in terms of the number of families.'[1] In February of the previous year, the *Társadalmi Szemle* had declared in an assessment of a Moscow conference of the socialist countries on agricultural development that 'all the necessary conditions exist in the socialist countries for them . . . to achieve in a short time the highest living standard in the world'.[2]

With eyes glued to the Utopias which had been unleashed on planning and politics and quite blind to the meagre conditions of real life, the poet who wrote the article in *Uj Irás* spoke of 'a plan for the *final* manœuvres . . . for the *ultimate* conquest of the material world'. Taking the triumph envisaged in twenty years' time quite for granted, he spoke of 'the almost total disappearance . . . of the gap between need and satisfaction'. Out of this faith arose a question: 'What can we do to prevent the rising masses, supplied with consumer goods and no longer compelled to make great efforts for their livelihood . . . those alighting on the restful and cheerful banks of communism, from stretching themselves out with a sigh on the warm sandy beach of material welfare?'[3]

Some 130 articles and comments arrived at the offices of *Uj Irás*. Summing up the debate in the summer of 1962, the editors wrote that many had interpreted the introductory contribution as saying that 'it was the enhanced standard of living and the concomitant more comfortable life-style (refrigerators, motor cycles, cars, weekend cottages, travel, etc.) which would give rise to and reproduce the petty bourgeois attitude, and so what was to be done?' Indeed, some of the contributors spoke no longer of the broader future in general but of the existing Hungarian conditions. 'Does the car or the little weekend cottage, and the spread of private possessions in general, not propel us towards an imitation of the bourgeois way of life? And does it not intensify the spread of individualism? In my experience, it does!' This was stated categorically by another poet, who went so far as to speak of 'the prevalent greed for selfish "acquisition" '.[4] One teacher had done a social survey of his class in an average school, and outlined 'the bad, indeed awesome' results of 'a dangerous level of supply or over-supply'.[5]

The debate threw up some rational counter-arguments as well, but it was revealing for the sheer number of instances of Utopian, doctrinaire thinking and lack of touch with reality that were displayed. Condemnations of the acquisitive instinct, even of the 'horror of aimless possession of cars and weekend cottages' and of people playing the lottery when the country was but 'a few steps from communism' were frequent.[6] Though the purpose of this book is not to give a blow-by-blow account of the debate on 'refrigerator socialism', it is worth recalling the kind of reaction that even a modest rise in living conditions and consumption could elicit. The political and moral 'peril' of the refrigerator as a symbol of a pragmatic orientation towards consumption was being preached almost before refrigerators were to be found in Hungarian homes.

In 1965–7, as the idea of reform came to the fore again and the preparations for it were under way, the arguments about the possibly negative social and political consequences of applying the reform principles flared up again.

Péter Veres, one of the leading writers to concern themselves with issues of 'people and nation', felt a duty to ask whether 'some new species of sponging will not be bred by the new mechanism, some new parasitism against which we shall have to struggle anew for the substance of socialism and genuine collectivism'. Published, albeit as a polemic, in the party daily *Népszabadság*, Veres's piece used the traditions of collective action among the peasants and workers to denounce the 'realism of sustenance' and its credo of 'Will I profit by it?' Veres had no doubt about it: 'In the midst of the building of socialism, this kind of "individualization" is taking place among a fairly large proportion of citizens.'[7] His repeated criticisms of this reflected the traditionally 'anti-mercantile' attitude of the pre-war populist movement, to whose revolutionary left wing Veres had initially belonged: 'Some zealously diligent people today earn more after work, through private work on Saturdays and Sundays, than they do the whole week in the factory . . . Diligence is all very well . . . but if the aim of it is no longer a good flat, a fine home and a secure livelihood, but some kind of affectation, one may well ask the question: What is this? Is it good?'[8] But Veres also questioned the rightfulness of group (i.e. company) interests, warning against the growth of it: 'The natural selfishness . . . of individuals is translated into that of groups, and the "chauvinism" of companies and factories . . . can take its place . . . Still more so under the new economic mechanism than before it.'[9] Warning against 'individualization' and the dangers of a society motivated by individual and group interests, Veres stressed repeatedly that a socialist society 'must develop into a caring society, so that it can then develop into a society of democratic collectivism'. But a 'caring' society does not merely care for material things: 'Material supply is necessary too, but it is never sufficient in itself . . . We must likewise work for a change in thinking.'[10]

So the debate on 'petty bourgeois attitudes' and the lust for possessions arose again in the mid-1960s. One journalist, though prepared to accept that even a 'life of luxury' was permissible to those who did 'substantially more work of greater value', complained bitterly in the *Népszabadság*:

> It seems in recent years as if greater confidence had been gained by those who see in the life of us all only their own little joys, which are sometimes despicable and sometimes just morally reprehensible: those who are prepared to work only for their own purposes . . . We failed to notice that these hoarders do not always cause the greatest harm by taking a rake off our desires, riding on the back of our natural aspirations, or taxing us on something that is our own property in the first place . . . It is almost impossible to keep track of the plague that these people spread about them by *their life-style and cynicism alien to the outlook of our society*: the plague of petty bourgeois selfishness, the 'self-made man' effect, and the way they despise and ridicule honest toil . . . We must make those to whom this applies understand, and make them understand it in every possible way, that poplars are tall but they don't after all reach the sky.

Though he repeats that the better workers and better qualified deserve a better living standard, the journalist rails against the '*bourgeois–petty bourgeois egoism* fed by Western injections and aimed at breaking up all around it . . . This we must fight against, we must take note of every manifestation of the hoarding instinct, we must expose the pits in which the infectious outlook of a rat lies hidden.'[11]

Certain familiar motifs in the debate on 'refrigerator socialism' emerged again three weeks later in another article by the same writer:

> What have we done with our pride when we marvel indiscriminately at everything great and trifling so long as it is from the West? What is this rapture? Why do we crawl on our bellies before cars and trinkets, nylon lace and refrigerators, so that the mud splatters all our faces? . . . The Zulus must have wondered like this once upon a time when the first white men brought them strange precious stones and glass beads. The Eskimos must have got drunk like this on their first bottle of liquor . . . But our boulevard louts gaze after a Western car that sweeps by as if it were the first motor vehicle they had seen in their lives. They gaze at a lacy rag held before them as if it were the only thing ever discovered to hide their nakedness.[12]

The columns of the *Népszabadság* continued to carry numerous articles reflecting this debate in subsequent years. The arguments were scornfully listed in an article on the other side of the debate by Jenő Faragó: 'They say, for instance, that selfishness has run veritable riot nowadays, that people are dazed with a desire to possess.' He recalls the frequent query:

> What will happen when we switch over to the new economic mechanism? The fact itself, they argue, that value relations will gain a growing part in the economy, that individual earnings will depend on individual performance, that competition between companies based on financial interest will come to the fore – these factors together will all provide still greater scope for petty bourgeois egoism and a strengthening of the urge to hoard.

To illustrate the mood of the country it is worth quoting from his counter-arguments: 'Are all who own a car, a summer cottage and a mechanized household hoarders and dishonest men? Have we not been fighting so that as many as possible may have all that is needed for a comfortable, peaceful life?'[13]

'Of all the themes expressed in writing and words concerning the new economic mechanism there is one that inexorably recurs', the *Népszabadság* wrote in December 1967, on the eve of the introduction of the reform: 'The question of whether, by extending material incentive, we have not unleashed the instinct of individualism, or whether we are thereby defending and indeed strengthening the collectivist thinking in people's minds.'[14]

The weekly *Élet és Irodalom* (Life and Literature) carried an article by the writer Gyula Csák in which he furiously condemned a 'nephew' of his, chosen as an example, whose sole preoccupations were the latest type of television and how it could be obtained, and how he could possibly afford to buy a car. 'My nephew is not an eccentric; he merely thinks like millions nowadays . . . Do you not understand', the writer wailed, 'that Man is far more than this? And will you degrade yourself to this level?'[15] The very next issue of *Élet és Irodalom* carried another indignant piece, by the writer György Timár: 'I, in defence of the Tables of Testimony of socialist morality, rather take aim at the golden calf. This golden calf roars along at 120 kilometres an hour, scrubs floors, washes, refrigerates and dries.'[16] The *Népszabadság* published a retort to the moralizing writers, who in principle accepted the need for reform: 'Timár's antipathy, felt for the parvenu, for petty bourgeois ostentation and worship of material objects is transferred to the objects themselves. It is almost in them that he sees the tempters of socialist morality.'[17]

In the years when the reform was being prepared there were fears even stronger than the ideological ones. These by no means groundless anxieties were practical ones of inflation, unemployment and not least loss of privilege, advantage and prestige – in other words, that the reform would conflict with certain interests in society.

An article dating from 1967 summed up the main features of the debates and anxieties:

> Understandably, the general public is concerned above all with the impact of the reform on working and living conditions. People often ask whether our new price system will not lead to a constant and excessive increase in prices, whether the system of income distribution and material incentive does not violate our socialist principles, and whether an incentive to increase profitability will not lead to unemployment.[18]

The central party authorities received an account in the autumn of 1967 of the anxieties and objections raised by some 1,600 party officials at courses at the party's Political Academy in 1966–7:

> Those taking part in the courses raised a great many questions . . . One group of questions (those raised in the first period) concerned the necessity, justification and general interpretation of the reform. (Is there a need for change? Does this change accord with the nature of socialism? Will we be able to solve our economic problems more successfully than before? Is the planned economy reconcilable with a more active utilization of the market? . . .) At the courses so far we have only been able to reduce and moderate some of the anxieties raised, but not to eliminate them. (Despite all the precautions will there not be a more significant rate of inflation that also affects the standard of living? . . . Will there not, temporarily, be a quite serious clash between company and social interests? Will consumers not be increasingly at the mercy of producers? Will company workers not be too much at the mercy of the compulsion and whims of company managers? . . . The fourth group of questions embraces the probable social, political and ideological impact of the new economic mechanism. Even at present the course lecturers and discussion leaders are unable to give adequate answers to all of the unclarified problems that students raise in this respect.[19]

During the nationwide debate on the Central Committee's reform resolution, strong counter-arguments were voiced, particularly in the administrative apparatus: 'A number of important questions of principle came up in connection with the debates', the Thirteenth District of the Party Committee of Budapest reported. Among these were 'the substance of the new economic system: we intend to employ the various economic categories, market, price, etc., more intensively . . . [which] raises the question of their opposite poles – crisis, unemployment, inflation – occurring to a greater extent'. 'On the whole, the comments made at party forums', the Political Committee was informed in the spring of 1966,

> were in a question form . . . whereas in the case of ministerial and administrative bodies there were doubts and objections as to whether the total and unequivocal abolition of compulsory plan indicators was a viable course in every area of economic activity . . . The role of central planning ought to be strengthened in the face of statements emphasizing market relations. Reference was made to the fact that the application of the more recent achievements of science (mathematical optimalization) is creating a better opportunity for objective and correct central planning.

Among certain circles in the party apparatus, the report continues, 'objections were raised to the assertion that "the party apparatus does not consider . . . the implementation of plans to be its direct task since it lacks the means for doing so". According to these people the necessary means are provided and "the practice so far must be followed unchanged" ', in the words of the Csongrád County Party Committee.

The leading committees in the trade unions raised fundamental objections from the point of view of employment. In the debate in the Central Council of Hungarian Trade Unions, it was emphasized, in opposition to the fundamental aim of the reform, that 'institutions for ensuring workers' security of employment must be established. Companies should also have an interest in the stability of manpower.'[20]

Describing the atmosphere at the time the reform was introduced, the Nineteenth District of the Party Committee of Budapest reported in the spring of 1967 that the companies themselves were in favour of compulsory planning:

> At present everybody is examining the new economic mechanism from the angle of their own interest, or the interest of their own company. The most characteristic example is for a company to be concerned only about a monopoly situation if it emerges against itself . . . They do not see a sufficient guarantee that the system of incentives in the new economic mechanism can ensure good cooperation between companies.[21]

One very typical statement of the vested interest of the official apparatus was expressed in ideological terms like this:

> Special mention must be made of the atmosphere at Nikex [foreign trading company] which is strongly defeatist . . . On the one hand an

> explicit opposition can be sensed to the idea of the new mechanism, while on the other people raise certain problems and try to divert them on to a wrong course using party interest and party-political criteria as a pretext . . . The extension [to production companies] of foreign trading rights conflicts with the struggle against the policy of loosening up, since the industrial sphere is far more heterogeneous and so less reliable than the sphere of foreign trade.[22]

Speaking in an interview of the experiences in preparing for the reform, Károly Németh also mentioned the 'uncertainty' which 'is characteristic of the party organizations' concerning their role in company management after the reform.[23] The trade unions were worried about their position too. Central Committee secretary Rezső Nyers stated in an article in the spring of 1968 on the 'likely social and political impact' of the new mechanism that 'the trade unions are above all bodies representing the interests of workers in various occupations. I cannot say that they are bodies representing the interests of the "workers".' Indeed, Nyers added that the trade unions could not represent the political interests of the working class with sufficient weight, since their ability to do so was restricted by their representation of occupational interests. The reply was swiftly forthcoming in the central journal of the party. Gábor Somoskői reminded Nyers of the Political Committee resolution of May 10, 1966 – 'The trade unions are the class organizations of the working class in power . . .' – and, 'The protection of rightful class interests . . . has remained to this day the prime objective . . . Under the circumstances of [working-class] power, the statutes of the Hungarian trade unions also define more general political goals.'[24]

Strong concern was apparent in 'the views surfacing among the masses' and still more in the reservations expressed in the governmental and political apparatus, among certain groups of party members and in the trade unions. Speaking of the role that party organizations played in preparing for the reform, József Bálint said it was often asked 'whether or not the new mechanism would "act counter" to the political work of the party organizations and our socialist goals and socialist ideals'.[25] The party's daily paper *Népszabadság* served a dual function in 1965–7, providing the persuasive debate indispensable to preparing for the reform but also acting as a forum for the reservations and concerns. The value of following this debate in the press lies in the arguments advanced, which were largely unchanged, rather than for the political weight that they gained.

In the autumn of 1967 *Népszabadság* sought to question anxieties over unemployment:

> In previous debates on the possible effects of the new economic mechanism the problem of reorganizing the . . . ministries and trusts cropped up recently with growing frequency, but inevitably the problems of reorganizing the factories, particularly the large works, were mentioned. Above all, the debates focused on the employment of workers made redundant during the reorganization. There were some who considered this task insoluble in the first place, who judged the situation to be one in which the reorganizations would inevitably cause hundreds of human tragedies and mass-produce bitterness and resentment. Most judged all this to be the least damaging of the many evils; they forecast the worst problems in manufacturing. Even well-prepared and highly qualified professionals with managerial experience drew the conclusion that the changes at the higher levels of direction would, by their very nature, filter down to the factories, where people in their thousands would become redundant.[26]

During the debate in the press on the new role for party organizations in the factories, the secretary of the Borsod County Party Committee thought it worth reiterating 'that never, anywhere can the party organizations take over the direct management of business enterprises. This is no new principle, although it has not infrequently been flouted by direct interference and operational intervention by the party organizations. In the future it will be even less permissible than it is today. We must warn against this, because even now one encounters concern that "if the party organization does not keep a direct hold on the management of the economy it will lead to anarchy in production and distribution".'[27] The first secretary of the Békés County Party Committee took issue with the petty-minded and obtuse critics:

> Some members of a number of our branches argue that the party's leading role can really apply only if there are communists in every post . . . [and] some still gauge the party's leading role by the assertion of individual, personal interest. *If the satisfaction of individual interest is excluded* the immediate response is, 'Look! The party has no prestige. Where has the leading role gone?' . . . If somebody's child is not admitted to college or university it is sometimes said that the party's leading role has not been asserted . . . There have been cases when a comrade, *for want of the right qualifications*, has not been given a job he would have liked to have, and the question is instantly heard: 'What has the party come to now?'

But while arguing against attitudes like these, the county first secretary himself reflects the deeply rooted ideological and political reservations and concern for vested interest aroused by the reform: 'To exaggerate [the importance of] professional qualifications . . . is to apply our principles incorrectly, and rightfully draws criticism from our party members.'[28]

The editor of the *Népszabadság*'s economic page was certainly justified when he said:

> The motives of those expressing anxiety are of many kinds. Some – perhaps the most numerous group – do not understand certain things . . . Others – for come what may, life decides thinking – do not consider their own personal future or the future of their company to be secure under the new circumstances, and wittingly or not this motivates their opinions on the whole mechanism. What will happen to our company, which unfortunately performs rather poorly, or to our admittedly overgrown or slightly cumbersome institution? Or what will happen to me, since I am not, to put it mildly, among the best? These are the first questions in the minds of these people when the subject of economic reform comes up.

But he appends to this candid assessment of the situation a mention of a decision taken during the reform preparations which can be regarded, in fact, as a compromise indispensable to introducing it at all: 'The party's position is clear: *the reform of the mechanism does not amount to any kind of changing of the guard. For that there is no need at all!* . . . In general, staff changes will only be necessary where the time for such a change has long been ripe in any case.'[29]

These quotations exemplify the anxieties, some genuine but most springing from concern for vested interests and ideological taboos, from the unchanged Stalinist interpretation of socialism and from equating the Soviet model with socialism, that arose in the party organizations, in the government apparatus and among company executives, and not least among the general public. The governmental and political authorities had to respond to them all in a manner that would not violate ideological taboos nor change the image of socialism.

The political response was lucid and realistic: 'There is also anxiety as to whether moral decay will not result from material wealth, i.e. from everyone striving hard for a higher standard of living', Rezső Nyers said, reacting to the debates on the social impact of the reform, and his answer was a rational one: 'How far are we still from having to worry about the effect of an abundance of material goods on manual workers? A long, long way, that's for sure!'[30] Rational arguments were put forward for the necessity of reform and the untenability of equating a 'levelling down' with socialism. It was reiterated that an efficient economy and a rising standard of living would strengthen socialism, not weaken it. Rather than running through a long list of official declarations, let us take one authoritative statement of the Central Committee position in the spring of 1965, to be found in the guidelines on 'current ideological tasks': 'Our party rejects the ascetic, pseudo-revolutionary views of those who maintain that the well-being emerging in the socialist countries is a capitalist excrescence that causes "petty bourgeoisification" and moral distortion. To embrace these views would be to render the struggle for socialism meaningless.'[31] One should add here that the political leaders did not confine themselves to declaring principles in the debates on reform, they launched a veritable ideological offensive. It was regarded as integral to the reform preparations that there should be a massive propaganda campaign to win over the man in the street, the intelligentsia, and particularly those working in the apparatus of the party, the state and the trade unions. A motion of this propaganda effort was passed by the party's Agitation and Propaganda Committee in May 1966:

> Our chief propaganda task is to acquaint our whole society with the reform of the economic mechanism and make it accepted, to reinforce an economic attitude at every level, to make the substance of the economic processes embodying the essence of the economic reform known, along with the part to be played by the reform in fulfilling the assignments of our economic development . . . One chief task is to explain to and convince people how the reform assists and serves the purposes of the current assignments in the building of socialism . . . to prove . . . that in all fields the reform will strengthen the socialist economy and socialist relations and further increase the democratization of our society . . . Accomplishment of the propaganda tasks . . . requires that swift use should be made of the advances in economic theory and that the teaching of the political economy of socialism should be updated in its substance and methodology. The Agitation and Propaganda Department should take steps to ensure that the results of the theoretical researches done by the Institute for Social Sciences and by the Academy of Sciences are swiftly included in economic propaganda.[32]

In the autumn of 1966 a confidential report on the preparatory operations related how two- to four-week courses were being arranged for 'several thousand functionaries (county, factory and cooperative party secretaries, council leaders and leaders of mass organizations, etc.). In 1967 in different courses and seminars, around 300,000 people will study the fundamental issues of the reform.'[33] Looking back after the reform had been introduced, it was noted with satisfaction that the issues involved were tackled by 'almost 270,000 students on three [types of] mass propaganda courses'. It was reported that 'views arising out of a confusion of ideas prior to the economic reform lost considerable ground . . . It was generally considered that the new economic mechanism is an indispensable tool for attaining the political objectives, that it assists in modernizing the economy and making better use of our resources . . . It was generally understood . . . that the party's leading role is not the same as direct and regular intervention in economic activity . . . The recognition was imparted that the fundamental task of the party organizations is concern with the people, information, persuasion and mobilization.'[34]

Mass explanatory and educational work of a similar kind and on a similar scale was carried out by the trade unions: 'In 1967 the instruction of some 2,110 leading trade union officials and 250,000 other trade union officials and activists has taken place in the trade union movement. During this educational work . . . what needs to be known about the economic reform takes a central place.'[35]

But the party leadership and the government had sound political reasons for thinking it essential to combat anti-reform feelings and neutralize vested anti-reform interests by building into the new management system compromises that would take the edge off the undesirable social and political conflicts. Liberally mixed in with the political and tactical considerations, even at government level, were ideological considerations, influenced by taboos about the concept of socialism which had changed in many respects but were unchanged in many others; and most of the party leaders considered this to be a natural phenomenon. So the official party and government declarations during the debates prior to the reform reflected a struggle on two fronts. While criticizing the ideas of the anti-reformers, they also opened up a front against the potentially negative effects of the reform. For instance, the Central Committee resolution quoted earlier followed up its condemnation of 'ascetic, pseudo-revolutionary views' by saying: 'Systematically improving prosperity may on occasions reinforce reprehensible characteristics: hoarding, greed, selfishness . . . The mentality of regarding acquisition as the principal meaning in life is incorrect and harmful. With moral and ideological incentives . . . we appeal to enthusiasm and consciousness, and concurrently wage a battle against gross materialism.'[36]

On the eve of the price reform, the *Népszabadság* stressed with an almost didactic clarity that 'temporary' and 'permanent' brakes were being built into the system:

> Much has been said recently in connection with the introduction of the economic reform about the incorporation of certain brakes into the

> 'machinery' of the mechanism, lest it should, instead of resolving the existing contradictions, create new ones. If required, the socialist state can use these brakes, or rather safety regulations, to intervene administratively in any case where the general interest of society is being damaged somewhere. These economic regulations are *temporary* in character, and the lifting of them can occur at the same rate as the positive driving forces of the reform develop not only in individual companies but on a social scale . . . However, mention must be made of another kind of system of brakes, which can certainly not be temporary, and whose significance will indeed increase in parallel with the development of the reform. This is the system of *political and moral* brakes: *socialist awareness, socialist norms of morality, and a human behaviour in accordance with the ideology of our society*. All these have already provided a tremendous impetus in creating and building our new society. But now – just as the economic reform is placed on the agenda – their role *multiplies*. This follows logically from the situation, and from the living and working conditions the reform creates.[37]

This statement is noteworthy since it not only mentions safety measures regarded as temporary, but reflects an idea that the reform – which was limited even in the economic arena – was not to affect the realms of society, politics or the institutional system. On the contrary, it was the very inviolability of these that was seen as providing permanent safety devices to counteract and overcome the expected perils of the reform. This concept did not challenge the traditional ideology and values, but considered them to be natural starting-points.

Right from the time the reform was introduced, safety measures against the socially and politically undesirable side-effects of it were sought, with the intention of institutionalizing them. These guarantees and brakes, particularly in the early years after the introduction of the reform, in fact destroyed the consistency of the system and restricted the degree to which the principles formulated earlier could be applied. Béla Csikós-Nagy, who had played an active part in preparing the reform, asked in December 1967: 'How faithfully can the reform measures to be introduced in 1968 reflect the guiding principles taken as a basis?' Not wholly, he argues: 'All the important elements in the guidelines will be applied, but at the same time the limitations on the "pure" assertion of economic efficiency and autonomous (decentralized) economic decision-making will be slightly stricter than we had envisaged at an earlier stage in the preparations.' He then adds: 'It was clear from the outset: in the purer form, the guidelines for the economic reform can only obtain validity after a longer or shorter period of transition.' In this connection Csikós-Nagy referred to the predetermined framework of the 1966–70 five-year plan, to the investment projects already under way, to the establishment of reserves, which could not be ensured before the reform, and to the requirement of caution 'dictated by responsibility towards society'.[38] But let me quote two politicians best placed to know about the matter. Rezső Nyers, delivering a report before the Central Committee on November 24, 1967, dealt at length with certain arguments that 'so great a difference' existed between the original guidelines and the final version of the reform system 'as to have violated the economic substance of the guidelines'. The critics said that as a consequence 'price regulation will excessively divert prices away from value relations', that 'companies will have too few resources of their own to invest' and that 'real competition will be impeded by the relatively large number of trusts and associations'. What the critics were ultimately complaining about, Nyers said, was the fact that 'we shall approach declared economic objectives more slowly and gradually'. In response, he said that all of these restrictions 'cannot render the new mechanism ineffective and do not conflict with the fundamental principles, but instead assist in a smooth application of the reform amid politically favourable circumstances'.[39] In that Nyers was obviously right: without compromises it was certainly not going to be possible to introduce the reform at all. But one can question whether the institutional system should have been left unchanged and the socio-political environment intact, to limit the price reform and to retain a strong central control over investment. Thus, to realize the reform in an extremely restrained and partial way was indeed a violation of the fundamental principles that greatly impeded a real application of the reform.

Under the particular circumstances the Hungarian government was faced with an insoluble dilemma: without making significant compromises, the reform could not be introduced, but those very compromises made it impossible for the reform really to unfold. Hopes of resolving it centred on the passage of time and the making of further political progress.

The most open and unequivocal contribution at that meeting of the Central Committee came from János Kádár:

> I think that sufficient guarantees have been attached to the reform as far as our commitments and capabilities are concerned, to the limit that will still allow it to be a real reform . . . It is impossible to introduce and establish a price system that reflects real values immediately, for the implementation of such a system can only be the

> culmination of a process. In certain fields it is a programme lasting decades . . . The gradualness is necessary and correct . . . we have very consciously used brakes which may subsequently be reduced or perhaps even eliminated.

Kádár openly expressed how important a part of the reform preparations it had been to 'inform and win over all the leading officials working in the state economy . . . the party organizations and the trade unions, and in many other fields'. The introduction of the reform depends *'on the two or three hundred thousand leading officials'*, since 'the workers who actually operate the machines, the peasants who till the land or the masses of white-collar workers in ordinary jobs . . . cannot exert an operative influence on the actual realization . . . of the reform'.[40]

The compromises made and the winning over of the apparatus were very closely connected; the 'checks and balances' allowed the introduction of the reform, while also narrowing down its scope of manoeuvring. In the light of all this the architects of the reform looked upon the economic mechanism that was introduced in 1968 merely as a first step in the reform. A second step was to follow in the 1970s, not least in connection with the 1971–5 five-year plan. 'From the outset', Béla Csikós-Nagy writes, 'the second stage in the further development of the system of economic management was in our minds', from the 1970s onwards.[41]

Thereby the reform principles became subject to a dual limitation. Right from the time when the guiding principles were being worked out, the intention was to apply temporary brakes to the 'pure' concept of reform. For instance, companies were in theory to have had a free hand in managing their profits and depreciation funds, but this was to be curtailed from the start by a higher than justified tax on profits and by centralization of 40 per cent of the depreciation contingency. Similarly, under the general stipulations companies would in principle have been allowed to pursue an independent wage policy. In practice a ceiling on the increase in average wages was imposed (4 per cent in 1968). Moreover, an unchanged quota system for certain goods put a strict curb on the market, despite the introduction of a free market for raw materials.

It was openly stated that political considerations were behind the fact that '45 to 55 per cent of the turnover in consumer goods will take place at officially set prices', so restricting significantly the sphere of market prices. But economic reasons were given for setting agricultural prices 'at a lower level than justified by the costs of production'. The state was to have returned the difference to the state and cooperative farms in the form of non-price supports. Again this was a restriction on the principles of the reform, and one that caused farm income to flow from the more efficient and profitable cooperatives to the weaker.[42]

But when reform was being introduced, a second layer of compromises was built into the system. 'The state deduction of company income is a little greater, the official price regulation a little stricter . . . the foreign-exchange restrictions stronger, etc., than we had envisaged . . . These and other factors may arouse feelings that the final stage in the preparation of the reform . . . was marked by a "loss of courage" and "excessive caution" about something over which there had been agreement in principle.'[43]

The brakes built in were designed to promote even the goals of government economic policy in a cautious, gradual way with tough restrictions. There was no desire at the time the reform was introduced to bring about the kind of rational selection that would encourage economically viable, competitive production and allow loss-making production to be run down on the basis of market forces. 'One must cast doubt', according to the official government position at the time, 'on the views of those who consider it a basic requirement that there should be standard regulation based on identical conditions . . . who consider it a basic requirement for rational behaviour that a standard yardstick should be set for every sector (or company).' So in order 'consciously to restrict the application' of rational selection, the ' "pure" assertion of economic efficiency', a balanced stability was ensured for all sectors and companies under which individual sectors and companies were granted exemptions and privileges (concerning payroll tax, levies on assets, profits tax, etc.) and state subsidies (price supports to offset losses). As Béla Csikós-Nagy put it, 'This intricate system of exemptions is of a transitional nature in the particular form in which it comes into force in 1968. But these methods of preference will remain for a long time, adjusting to the circumstances that change with development.'[44]

While normative regulation was rejected, a whole series of built-in brakes remained in effect because the institutional system was left essentially unchanged. For instance, before real market competition could emerge, it would have been necessary to abolish the company monopolies and dismantle the companies spanning whole sectors of industry which had come about through the extreme centralization carried out earlier. But this did not happen. The system of sectoral industrial ministries was also left unchanged, and as institutions for direct intervention in company management, they conflicted by their very nature with the principle of company autonomy.

In the cases of both these important institutions the indispensable change was put off. As was stated on a party committee in the autumn of 1964, 'During the preparatory work for perfecting the system of economic management one must treat as an essentially unchangeable factor the reorganization of the industrial companies which has taken place. Comprehensive proposals for reorganizing the structural forms of the highest direction of the economy must be worked out only later.'[45]

Two years later the Political Committee dealt with the matter in a separate resolution:

> The requisite stability in the structure of state administration dealing with economic activity must be ensured in the coming years to allow good and untroubled implementation of the reforms to the economic mechanism. The only changes it is necessary and correct to make in the coming months are those which assist in applying our economic policy and accomplishing the reform consistently . . . The structure of state administration should remain basically unchanged until 1969 . . . The present company structure should be retained essentially unchanged; changes on a large scale should be averted.[46]

Both central price controls, which were a guard against inflation, and central wage regulation, which effectively prevented unemployment (we shall come back to this later), were severe curbs on the reform, placing consistent and wide-ranging restrictions on the way the devised and adopted principles of the reform could be asserted. A high degree of gradualism was imposed.

In this connection it is worth mentioning particularly the question of institutional democratization which was supposed to link up with the reform. One of the expert committees preparing the reform, the group headed by András Hegedüs working on a system of worker participation in management, sought during 1965–6 for a suitable necessarily compromise solution. Understandably, the political decision was decisively influenced in advance by the previous experience with the workers' councils in 1956–7. This is how the working group saw the matter in the spring of 1965:

> The prime task in the years after the counter-revolutionary events of 1956 was consolidation of power. Development of forms that might have promoted worker participation in management more effectively was impeded by the fact that the so-called workers' councils had come into being as institutions of the counter-revolution, which to a certain

> degree discredited the idea of social self-management, or at least made it appear not to be a timely task from the angle of socialist power.
>
> At this time, when conditions have ripened for a significant reform of the economic system, the problem understandably arises again as to how the workers can be involved in the management system, and what kind of institutions appear to the purpose in this respect . . . The economic reform is probably proceeding towards . . . a growth in company autonomy, and at the same time a growth in the responsibility of management. In this situation the need to involve the workers in management gains a particular significance, as does an ineffective institutional guarantee of workers' rights in this respect. The various company units, on a basis of socialist ownership relations, will at least receive rights of an entrepreneurial character . . . However, one must raise the question of who the people receiving these greater rights will be? The workforce, whose collective work is the basis for the functioning of the company institution, or the manager appointed by higher authority and the management he brings together? . . . This dichotomy, in our view, hallmarks socialist management as an objective necessity: consequently some decisions must remain in the hands of the higher organizations and the manager who is responsible for his own collective, while the other decisions can necessarily be ceded to a body elected by the collective.[47]

In January 1966 a proposal was prepared for involving workers in management. Based on Central Committee guidelines, this took as its institutional point of departure company supervisory committees, councils (boards) of professional management and meetings of company workers. 'During the reform of economic management', the proposal stated, 'the company supervisory committees could become the most important institution of social control.' It was felt that 'by establishing company supervisory committees, an effective social control over professional management, making it socially dependent, can be achieved without, however, replacing professional management, who are a social necessity in the present situation, by direct social self-management'. According to the draft, the supervisory committees would have been attached to Parliament, with their chairmen appointed by the appropriate industrial, agricultural or foreign trade committees of Parliament. This link to a parliamentary committee was regarded as advantageous from several points of view. For one thing it would have increased the role of Parliament, and for another it would have done the same for the company supervisory committees, while increasing their separation from the management apparatus. 'All other solutions raised, in our view, make the supervisory committees dependent on the local management, i.e. render them superfluous bodies since in that way all that would be created would be new forms of an already widespread controlling activity of a bureaucratic and managerial nature.'[48]

In the end, a political decision taken in November 1966 drew a sharp distinction between the state and cooperative sectors, rejecting self-management for the former but accepting it for the latter:

> It would not be correct to link the extension of company autonomy with the system of worker self-management, because one could not expect either a growth in economic efficiency or a development of socialist democracy from doing so. It remains correct to start from the position that in the case of state companies, not only is the owner the state but the manager is the state's representative. However, it is correct to recognize to a great extent and to apply the principle of self-management in the cooperatives, in whose operation the state cannot intervene from a position of ownership. It is concurrently correct to work in the case of state companies for a more comprehensive representation of the interests of society as a whole . . . and for a more direct and substantial involvement of the employees.[49]

A great many different kinds of compromise were built into the edifice of reform while it was being prepared. It should in addition be mentioned that the reform measures were strictly limited to the economic sphere, while the framework of (political) institutions was left intact. It is extremely difficult, perhaps almost impossible, to define precisely what were the measures necessary and inevitable if there was to be a comparatively smooth transition, and what were the measures that impaired the effectiveness of the reform through excessive cautiousness, making the new system of management overly self-contradictory and thereby less viable.

But I should like to repeat that under the historical circumstances of the time, no strictly consistent reform free of brakes and an element of gradualism could have succeeded. A complete transformation that overturned the established, indeed fossilized, systems of values, ideological principles and vested interests would have elicited a domestic resistance and a foreign suspicion so strong as to have endangered the implementation of the reform altogether. This can be seen particularly clearly when one considers the overall turn of events in East-Central Europe at the time the Hungarian reform was being decided on and introduced. In the previous period one can rightly point to a reforming orientation in certain other socialist countries as one of the deciding factors behind the Hungarian decision; but after 1968, when the Hungarian reform was implemented, efforts at reform in other socialist countries, most significantly in the Soviet Union, came off the agenda, partly because of a conservative turn in domestic policy and partly because of the intervention in Czechoslovakia. In Czechoslovakia, a reform following similar principles to those of Hungary's had been prepared and introduced at the beginning of 1967; it was not only halted, but denounced as 'revisionist' and even as an attempt to 'restore capitalism' following the political events in that year. The very word reform came under suspicion and was equated again with reformism and revisionism. In Yugoslavia, a radical reform introduced in 1965 had in fact been followed by inflation and mass unemployment.

So the Hungarian reform and its intention of combining planning with the market was isolated. This worsening of the political conditions for the reform meant that it would have been a hopeless undertaking without a heavy dose of compromise, caution and gradualism, as well as avoidance of the political and ideological sphere. One can certainly describe as justified circumspection the idea of introducing the reform in two stages, a fairly moderate introductory stage followed by a more consistent version. Under the second stage, envisaged for the 1970s, the brakes would have been gradually taken off and the limitations on the central principles of the reform would have been reduced.

It is hard to dispute that gradualism, compromise and limitations played a big part in ensuring that the reform broke through. On the other hand, they undeniably resulted in a system with grave internal contradictions, under which old and new elements that not infrequently conflicted with each other existed side by side. The brakes and the unchanged institutional system, which had been intended to prevent the reform having negative side-effects, blocked the path towards economic rationality and market selection as well. What was lacking was the initial momentum to provide a clean break with the command economy. Moreover, the distinction between a temporary brake and rejection of a solution on ideological grounds was hard to make. Thus the way was paved for debates on the policy to be followed and for interpretation and reinterpretation of the reform itself. The unchanged framework of the system of political institutions did not allow the creation of an adequate social medium for the reform and, later, made it possible for anti-reform interests and conservative forces to reorganize.

But, warts and all, the Hungarian economic reform that came into force in January 1968 was the first comprehensive, substantial and radical reform ever undertaken in a Comecon country. It produced a type of socialist economy that differed from both the existing economic models – the 'classical' Soviet command economy, and the emerging self-managerial Yugoslav model at the other pole – and lay somewhere between them.

One should add here it had been obvious from the outset to those planning the reform that the transformation would also cause a transformation of thinking. 'The Idea of Reform – A Reform of Our Thinking' was the title László Rózsa chose for an article in the *Népszabadság* in the spring of 1966, since 'a reform of economic management cannot be carried out well without a reform of our thinking'. The author correctly noted that even the preparation for the reform had been accompanied by a significant transformation of thinking, because up till then many had considered that the economic difficulties and errors arising could be ridden out – we had only 'to convince ourselves to "restore order" '. The article went on to say how many had believed that the party and the government should resolve to intervene forcefully:

> It ought to declare that it will not tolerate irresponsible work, disorganization, negligence and postponement of decisions, and that it will tighten up control. And if everybody works just a little better, the results will also be different . . . But the real stimuli to speedier progress are to be sought much deeper . . . There are those who do not regard the reform as a renewal and development of Marxist thinking and are disturbed by the fact that our concepts are undergoing changes. In many people's minds Marxism has adhered to the methods and practical forms which they have become accustomed to over the years and imagine to be final and unchanging. In their eyes a great many things today seem to be a step down from a higher rung: a concession or simply a move away from socialist principles. Yet in this case too, *it is a matter of dismantling a system of illusions, which . . . we must pursue very persistently* . . . We are even held back today because a proportion of the socio-political issues, unlike the specifically expressed economic issues, can only be defined in outline, since they are born of the specific conditions and we shall have to adjust them to the economic changes.[50]

In this article the *Népszabadság*, the central daily paper of the party, had done no small thing in coupling support for comprehensive economic reform with expression of a need for a change in outlook. Nor had it excluded the possibility of a rethinking of theory and ideology, including the idea that at a later stage of the reform, as an 'adjustment to the economic changes', it would be possible and indeed necessary to return to the 'socio-political issues'.

18 The main features of the new reform system

After several years' work of analysis and preparation, the economic reform came into force on January 1, 1968.

But the introduction had been preceded, almost from the moment the decision to apply the reform had been taken, by measures of detail designed to ensure a graded transition to the new system: 'Over the next two years [1966 and 1967] we must expand company autonomy in planning and economic activity in such a way that the individual elements of the mechanism already accord with the requirements of the reform, or at least signify an approach in that direction.'[1] Significant steps had been taken immediately in farming. Rezső Nyers had this to report in the spring of 1967:

> In 1966 we raised the agricultural price level by some 9 per cent. In accordance with the Central Committee resolution, the producer prices must rise by a further 10 per cent in the years 1968–70 . . . In connection with the meat-supply situation which had arisen it is justified for the announcement of the increase in the producer price of fatted pigs to be made in the middle of the year and for us to introduce the higher producer prices before the end of the year.
>
> The rise in producer prices introduced in 1966 was followed at the end of last year by the general settlement of agricultural cooperative loans. Nationally, 12,700 million [forints] out of a debt burden of 20,500 million was cancelled.[2]

The transition also began in the state sector, with an 'easing' of the system of compulsory plan indicators. A report compiled for the Political Committee in the autumn of 1966 was able to state:

> In order to assist the transition to the new mechanism, certain elements of the old in several fields come up for further development on January 1, 1967. Direction methods will be simplified, company autonomy increased and direct links between companies be given greater importance in issues in which broad changes of a general nature will take place at the time the reform is introduced.

> The system of plan approval will be simplified further. Under this, the number of compulsory plan indicators requiring approval will be fewer in several fields. In the product management field, the sphere of central management will narrow down [and] the number of centrally allocated products will reduce . . . In several fields central management of materials will cease . . . The system of plan indicators connected with foreign exchange affairs will also be simplified. In order to simplify the investment system, the number of compulsory indicators will fall. The plan for technical design work and the central allocation of design capacities will be discontinued.[3]

Certainly these modest steps had a 're-educating' influence, providing a link between old and new for the economic authorities and the companies. But despite the considerable degree of gradualism built in, the real turning-point came after January 1968, when planning based on compulsory indicators was replaced by a combination of planning and a market functioning under regulators. But this market could only be a (restricted) market of products, while the markets of labour and capital did not come about at all.

Planning continued to play an important part even under the new economic mechanism, but from then onwards the central plan that formulated the goals of economic policy was only compulsory for the government; it was no longer broken down company by company. Only in part were the objectives of the plan pursued through central government decisions and commands or by direct governmental investments incorporated into the budget. Most of the targets had to be met through indirect methods of economic regulation instead.

The five-year plan and the annual plans continued to play an important part in the functioning of the economy, but in a radically different way. The plan no longer contained company tasks (prescriptions for production and sales), and no longer made stipulations about the means companies were to resort to (investment, labour, materials, products and foreign exchange funds). In policy terms the planning of production ceased. At one time quantitative planning had extended to several thousand products, and it had covered almost a thousand even in 1967, the last year of compulsory planning. As a transitional measure to smooth the change-over, the plan for 1968 still contained calculations for 280 products based on the old system of a national material balance, and some kind of turnover-regulating measures for 40 to 50 others. (This applied to products decisive to the economy or a sector of it.)[4]

Apart from such temporary remnants of direct control, planning was intended to retain in the long term an influence over economic processes by quantitative determinations of economic processes. Quantity-based prescriptions of the exports required of and imports allowed to the companies were attached to the central plan. (These defined foreign trade relations without regulating the foreign trading activities of companies.) So were certain export and domestic supply obligations. But even during the early years of the transition, the role of central intervention to ensure continuous production and sales was subordinate compared with the sphere in which companies could decide for themselves.

Direct central decision-making and stipulations persisted to a far greater extent in matters of development and investment. Infrastructural investments were decided on entirely centrally and financed out of the budget. But the government also retained the right to control large economic investments singly and directly. Indeed by centralizing 40 per cent of companies' depreciation funds, the government turned the whole depreciation sphere into one of central distribution. The maintenance of a centralized investment system was reinforced by the fact that in practice bank credit was almost exclusively granted to companies whose investments were linked with state projects.

In spite of all the direct intervention still institutionalized in the plan, it was no longer intended to embrace every aspect of the production and distribution process, or even all the significant ones. Instead the *system of regulators* was designed to ensure, along with the plan targets, that the policy objectives of the government embodied in the central plan were met. 'By extensively employing economic regulators, the national economic plan also regulates the market itself', it was explained at the time. 'Companies produce for the regulated market and must strive to meet the market requirements as fully as possible. The same economic incentives prompt companies to do this as help to regulate the market itself.'[5] But this 'regulated market' was more a piece of wishful thinking contained in the reform model than an economic reality. So the regulators began to be used by the state to regulate the companies more than the market. Whereas under the command economy the central plan had *prescribed* the resources to be used and the production and delivery obligations of companies, regulators were now introduced to give the companies an incentive to pursue the plan's economic objectives.

The government devised an arsenal of regulators to persuade companies to meet these. There was a tax on the wage bill and the company social insurance contribution, a levy on fixed assets, interest on current assets, company production tax, a system of state price supports (export and other subsidies), exchange-rate multipliers, export rebates, company profit tax, wage regulation, tax (both flat-rate and graduated) on company investment and employee profit-share funds, tax thresholds, and so on.

'The regulators worked out in 1966–7 ensure as the essence of the new economic mechanism the closest possible adherence to central plans by financial means', it was explained in the leading economic journal.[6] But again, the 'ideal-typical' functioning of the model was distorted by financial favouritism, by lack of norms of procedure, and by direct intervention, which persisted informally.

So under the new system, regulators that could provide either a boost or a damper and be used in conjunction with each other and the main economic policy objectives enshrined in the plan became among the most important factors in planning. Of course if companies were to run smoothly, the regulators would have to remain stable for quite long periods. But when the reform was introduced there equally naturally arose a need to keep adjusting the regulators, which had been worked out on paper without any previous experience of how they would work. 'The role of the regulators', according to one of the chief directors of these operations, 'is to guide company decisions in a certain direction and to encourage or limit company activity. So the aim of the regulators is to assist in the realization of the main tasks laid down in the national economic plan.'[7]

Of all the regulators, the *price system* was certainly the most important from the point of view of introducing the influences of the market.

Under the command economy, the producer price system had no connection with real costs or value relations and had merely performed a checking and accounting function. Nor had it had any connection with consumer prices (which were also intended to influence demand). It was now the price system, primarily, that was supposed to project market influences. Through prices, companies were to receive the requisite economic feedback and the incentive to sell, since this was how they would make a profit.

So the essence of the price reform was to create prices which better expressed the social costs of production, the value relations and the changes in prices on the world market. Of course these would all have been expressed far more consistently if world-market prices had been introduced, but it was also obvious (and extensive debates during the reform preparations had drawn emphatic attention to this) that a consistent application of world-market prices would have subjected the frail Hungarian economy to world-market forces from which it had been sheltered under the old price system. The world-market yardstick would have measured modernity and efficiency very clearly and unequivocally, pinpointing what was uncompetitive and out of date, and ensuring the advantage of greater profits to what was good and competitive. Under such influences the objectives of economic policy in the 1960s would have been properly realized, but the difficulties of the change-over had to be reckoned with. The government was seeking guarantees that an immediate assertion of world-market influences would not cause irreparable economic damage. (It would have been as if the windows of a hothouse had been opened wide in the middle of winter so that the plants might acclimatize to natural circumstances.)

Moreover, account had to be taken of the possible inflationary effects of market prices. Béla Csikós-Nagy, who had supervised the working out of the price system, put it like this:

> The approach to the market price system makes the price a suitable signalling system in such a way as to make the economy, at the same time, *more sensitive to inflation*. We had therefore to be careful about freeing prices. We also realize that price-setting is no remedy for the *causes* of inflation . . . Of course, price-setting places obstacles in the path of price rises. But *in this case the negative influences take another direction*, with concealed price increases being one of the more, if not the most, serious consequences. *The chief casualty is economic efficiency*.[8]

When those in charge of the Hungarian economy undertook the risks of a reform that was radical in certain respects, they also wanted to avert the undesirable and socially and politically threatening side-effects. So in instituting the reform, they sought to change the old economic processes while regarding the change in the light of a process. Consequently, brakes were also built into the price system (and in the knowledge, as the last quotation shows, that the price of controlling inflation was at least a partial sacrifice of economic efficiency). This was embedded even in the initial principle of the 1968 price reform, which started out from the domestic and not the world-market costs of production. (The adoption of world-market prices would have sent most Hungarian companies into liquidation.)

The new system of producer prices provided further guarantees that it could be controlled by the state. It was a *mixed price system*, in which centrally set (or ceiling) prices and free market prices existed side by side. Of the producer prices, those of energy, timber, a few chemical feedstocks and the majority of semi-finished products (for example, 85 per cent of iron and metallurgical products, 75 per cent of textile fibres), amounting to 70 per cent of raw materials and semi-finished goods produced domestically, had fixed or ceiling prices. Slightly less than 30 per cent of these goods were sold on a free market. The situation was radically different with manufactures, of which only 3 per cent had a fixed price (certain chemical products and foodstuffs), and another 19 per cent a ceiling price (certain chemical, engineering, textile and food products), as against 78 per cent of finished products which were sold at free prices. In building construction, price regulation was largely discontinued. By contrast, almost 60 per cent of farm products had set prices, those of a further 10 per cent were allowed to fluctuate within a narrow band, and some 18 per cent were permitted to fluctuate more freely. All in all, only 12 per cent of food products (including only 6 per cent of meat and meat products) were sold at free-market prices.

When the reform was introduced into the industrial producer-price system, goods with a set or ceiling price accounted for over 70 per cent of the whole, which also reflected a conscious gradualism. But a few years later, the proportion of fixed and ceiling prices had dropped to 36 per cent, with a corresponding rise to 64 per cent of those whose prices were free.

In order to reflect genuine value relations, several previously unreflected factors were built into domestic prices. For instance, the price of an imported good was calculated on the basis of the actual cost of import in convertible currency, calculated using an average of the different exchange rates and adding a 20 per cent tariff, or as much as 50 per cent in the case of a consumer good. So the fluctuation in foreign-trade prices began to affect domestic prices as well. (Export prices, with the exception of those for farm products, were based on the same principle, in proportion to the net convertible currency earned, although the state did not apply this consistently. Export subsidies were paid in the case of unprofitable exports, and high company profits earned out of artificial exchange rates were cut off, so levelling out company profits.)

A variety of measures were introduced to reflect real cost factors in producer prices. These included a differentiated but substantial rise to 4.8 per cent of the previously unrealistic depreciation write-off of 3.4 per cent, the calculation of a levy on fixed assets, a 25 per cent levy on the wage bill to fund the proportion of social benefits not covered by company social insurance contributions, a ground rent amounting to 5 per cent of the site value, a doubling of the water rates, etc.

These all helped to form a more realistic price system. However, the built-in brakes were powerful. A memorandum on the reform compiled for the Statistical Office in 1968 pointed out:

> We are still in a position where we must frequently say: although some activity by a particular company is losing money, it is useful from the economy's point of view . . . or conversely: something may be useful, i.e. profitable to the companies, that is undesirable, damaging and loss-making to the economy. The system of various subsidies, supports, concessions, deductions, taxes, etc., have also made our price system impossible to survey. Costs still do not manifest themselves where they are incurred . . . On the basis of prices one still cannot decide what it would be more useful to substitute for what in the process of production, or which investments or which foreign-trade transactions are the more useful and profitable.[9]

But in consumer prices, there were even fewer changes than in producer prices. They remained extensively regulated. Fifty per cent of the goods and services purchased had fixed or ceiling prices. 'In shaping a flexible consumer-price mechanism, we started from the premise that the state will continue to guarantee the consumer price of basic consumer goods and services.'[10] In the case of goods regarded as basic, fixed (20 per cent of all goods) and ceiling (30 per cent) prices were employed. But let us add again what Béla Csikós-Nagy had to say:

> Concerning the other 50 per cent of the turnover . . . there were stipulations restricting the free movement of the price of basic consumer goods produced in mass quantities. However, it is characteristic of the products grouped here that the range of them changes quickly . . . For instance, more than half the clothing turnover belongs among them, and so does a significant proportion of household implements. Where . . . the product is not important from the point of view of the living standard, we trust the market to set the prices. This covers fashion garments, haberdashery, leather fancy goods, a proportion of imported consumer goods, etc. To the free-price category also belong products in whose production there are opportunities for competition and it is likely that a balance [of supply and demand] will emerge.
>
> The classification of products by price forms . . . does not signify a *rigid definition* of groups of products . . . Clothing for mass consumption, for example, will be placed in the officially restricted price category, whilst exclusive versions of the same articles will be placed in the free-price category.
>
> In general we do not employ price-setting in the internal relations

> within manufacturing industry, but with products whose price changes have an intensive knock-on effect . . . the price-changing intention must be reported [in advance]. The price authority may exercise a veto over the price increase . . . These [measures] also increase the stability of the producer price of consumer goods . . . The total volume of products for which [price-increase] reporting is compulsory varies between 5 and 8 per cent of industrial production.[11]

Let me add here that price control of this kind did not only serve to keep prices stable. It was also a handy government weapon for influencing companies.

The intention, needless to say, was to keep a strict check and control on price increases. State subsidies remained on a broad range of goods – numerous mass consumer articles, staple foodstuffs, children's clothes, books, records, and so on – and thus prevented the price increases of imported goods from reaching the consumer. The government decided it would not institute a broad reform of consumer prices in the early years, even though a linked movement of producer and consumer prices would have strengthened the market influences and incentives. A gradual change in consumer prices was opted for in order to cushion the increase and prevent social tension arising.

The guidelines for a consumer price reform had been discussed in the Economic Policy Committee of the party Central Committee back in February 1967, when it was stated: 'The consumer price reform of 1968 does not attain the long-term objective of a convergence of prices and values . . . A full consumer price reform . . . must be regarded as a task to be resolved under two or three five-year plans.'[12] In the autumn of that year a report compiled for the Political Committee confirmed that the consumer price reform envisaged 'does not provide for a fundamental change in the existing consumer prices . . . [and] would demand a significant increase in rents and in the prices of other public utilities, services and foodstuffs . . . The economic conditions for this kind of change in price relations are not yet ensured.'[13] Also lacking were the economic conditions for increasing production in response to the shift in demand that a consumer-price reform would cause. 'Under the circumstances', it was pointed out in the proposal, 'the sum which the budget has to allocate to maintain stable consumer prices and service fees will be significant.' The subsidies on food, for instance, rose from 1,750 million forints to 4,314 million, transport subsidies from 2,600 million to 4,192 million, and those on industrial, cultural and communal services from 260 million to 1,133 million. (On the other hand, the subsidies for garments, engineering consumer goods and heavy industrial products fell.)[14]

Compared with the domestic inputs, the 1968 consumer price of coal, for instance, covered only 55 per cent of its cost. The figure for power was 82 per cent, for meat, dairy and bakery products 80 per cent, and for haulage and telecommunications 74 per cent, while rents remained at less than a third of the break-even level. By contrast, the prices of light industrial and chemical products were almost a third above cost, those of building materials a quarter above and those of engineering consumer goods almost a fifth above.

So the price reform of 1968 did not essentially affect the main consumer price relations, which differed markedly from the real values. The far greater degree of radicalism in the reform of producer prices made it necessary to bridge the resulting difference with a fairly complex system of taxes and subsidies. The whole matter was regarded as strictly temporary. As the president of the Price Office declared: 'We continue to regard it as a fundamental task to bring consumer prices and inputs *closer together*. This is a *long-term* goal, which . . . we wish to accomplish gradually, over a period of *ten to fifteen years*.'[15]

Despite the lack of major changes in the sphere of consumer prices, it was possible to relate producer and consumer prices, which had previously moved independently of each other. To link the two spheres, the 1968 price reform changed the system of turnover tax, switching it from the manufacturer to the wholesaler, so that the parallel movement and interaction of the two kinds of price could be ensured. Instead of the 2,500 rates of tax valid previously, producer and consumer prices were now linked by 1,000 rates of tax. This still excessively complicated system was explained by the intention of avoiding a sudden and broad increase in consumer prices. But it was planned gradually to simplify and standardize the turnover taxes. Over the next few years, the number of rates fell to 300–400, and an even greater reduction was carried out later.

The price reform was only partial and gradual, but it did create the minimum conditions for ensuring (or at least simulating) a market situation, with a profit motive and incentive. Comparing producer prices with the notional price that would cover production costs plus an adequate profit margin, the level for industrial products rose from 76 per cent before the reform to 106 per cent after. For agricultural products the rise was from 63 per cent to 83 per cent, and for goods transport from 75 per cent to 100 per cent.[16] This meant that producer prices as a whole rose to a level that covered inputs, although the price levels in the individual sectors of the economy did not yet match: 106 per cent for industrial producer prices and only 83 per cent for those in agriculture, compared with the notional costs mentioned above. If one deducted the taxes on consumer goods, the price level in the two sectors became largely uniform. 'From the point of view of the return from sales in the productive sectors, the question of bringing the price proportions closer together seems to be settled.'[17]

The price reform also affected the linkage between producer and consumer prices, ensuring that they moved in parallel, so bringing companies into direct contact with the market and the consumer. This, almost at once, put an end to the mass production of unsaleable goods and to the indifference of companies towards sales.

The price system became a medium for market influences and incentives despite the built-in compromises, which were not significant by comparison with the requirements of the logic of the system. It was through prices that companies acquired income on the market. Since the revenue of state companies was the principal cover for state expenditure, the state appropriated over half of the companies' income in the form of levies on assets and income, and diverted it into the budget. But companies were able to save a significant proportion of the rest of their profits, since they were taxed at a flat rate. In other words, they had a strong motive for increasing their income.

The share of the profits that remained with companies was used to finance investment, and in the form of profit-sharing to motivate managers and employees. But the proportions of profits to be used for each purpose were regulated by the state. A number of funds had to be established out of company profits. The reserves were of comparatively little significance (although by contrast with their original purpose, they eventually became a way of funnelling off net income). The welfare and cultural fund, introduced a little later, was the basis of company social welfare policy, but was not great either. The two funds that took the lion's share of retained company profits were the *investment and the profit-sharing* funds. The former paved the way for independent investment, while the latter provided a motive for profitability.

At the time the reform was introduced the proportion of profits to be placed in each fund was strictly prescribed. Clearly the regulation was designed to apply central ideas about increasing the managerial stake in success and substantially upgrading managerial work. There were detailed regulations laying down the proportion of profits to be distributed through the profit-sharing fund to various categories of manager and employees. Originally the workforce were classified under three categories, and the shares were related to wages, in a hierarchy extending upwards from the workers to the managing director (worker, middle-level management, top management) at rates of 15, 50 and 80 per cent respectively. (The 15 per cent rate was counted as a wage cost while the managerial shares were taken from profits.) This rigid system immediately elicited a powerful and largely rhetorical flood of criticism based on slogans about preference for the workers in a workers' state. As was pointed out in the confidential proposal for correcting the system in the summer of 1969, 'The correctness of the proportions between the profit-share categories is disputed by the majority of workers, who still refuse even today to accept the official explanations.' By May it was already being stressed, 'Classification is dividing the workers into isolated "social groups", turning workers against managers and engendering an anti-management sentiment. The workers' pride has been injured because they feel they are being socially discriminated against.'

The government responded quickly by retreating and declared that 'the present . . . central regulation of profit-share categories must be abolished. But in order to ensure the differentiation of income, a lower and an upper ceiling must be prescribed for profit-sharing categories.'[18]

Also introduced along with the reform were direct regulations determining the proportion of the profit that could be channelled into the profit-share fund and the investment fund. (In 1968 some 8,000 million forints of manufacturing profits went into the investment fund and 5,000 million into profit-sharing.) After a short time, these detailed, direct regulations were replaced by indirect regulators. For instance, it was no longer laid down centrally what proportion of company profits had to be placed in the investment and profit-share funds and the decision was left to the company itself, but the central will was asserted through taxation: if the ratio of profit share and wages rose at the expense of the investment fund, a high rate of tax became payable. In the end, this left companies with no motive to distribute too much of their profits to their employees at the expense of investment.

After a few years, companies had increased their investment funds to an average of 27 forints per 100 forints of profit, leaving 10–11 forints for profit-sharing, which was less than the scale of incentive envisaged originally. Generally speaking, the regulations allowed companies to pay a profit share equivalent to five to six weeks' wages, depending on how profitable the company was.

Using the investment fund, companies were able to take investment decisions on their own, whereas previously all investment had been financed out of the budget at no charge to the company. In 1968 a new system of investment was introduced, in which major, centrally financed investment remained predominant. New, large investment projects in industry, along with public investment, continued to be financed centrally, out of budget revenues (including about half of company profits, which were funnelled off in various ways, along with 40 per cent of the depreciation contingency). Ultimately some 35 per cent of national income was concentrated into the budget. In 1968 the position of uncompleted state investment projects was quite significant, accounting for 23 per cent of all investment spending. But it was expected that this would fall to 17 per cent in 1969 and to a mere 8 per cent by 1970. In spite of the central investment projects started in the meantime, this would reduce the share of central investment to 46 per cent by 1969 and 43 per cent by 1970, as opposed to 61 per cent in 1968.[19]

Company investment accounted for only 39 per cent of all investment spending in 1968. The figure was expected to reach 54 per cent in 1969 and 57 per cent in 1970. So gradualism applied in investment too: 'Because of the determining influence of investment projects previously begun and other commitments binding on the investment fund . . . the freedom of decision . . . is significantly limited . . . For the most part, the impact of a more extensive sphere of decision-making by companies can only be expected in 1971–2.'[20]

A sizeable proportion of company investments was represented by *bank credit*. Loans could be raised when the company's development objectives exceeded the bounds of its investment fund, so long as the company's plans were in accordance with the national economic plan and profitability seemed assured. The credit applications were reviewed by the National Bank, and if given the green light, the loan would be repaid later by the company out of its investment fund.

In the event, budget-financed investment still accounted for 47 per cent of all investment spending five years after the reform had been introduced, while 43 per cent came directly from companies, and bank credit accounted for only 10 per cent. But in fact company freedom to invest was less than these figures would indicate. A high proportion of the investment financed by companies and out of bank loans had basically been decided centrally in accordance with the national plan. Either the company investment was linked to bank credit (which in practice was largely allocated to the bank under the central plan), or it was carried out in response to 'proposals', not officially compulsory, from the ministry in charge. Not infrequently the companies concerned joined in central investment projects. According to some estimates independent company investment accounted for less than a sixth of investment as a whole.

In short, an 'informal' centralization had remained, and was far more powerful than what would have followed from the profit management of companies.

Market activity and the profit motive were also restricted by other regulations and forms of state intervention. One kind was *wage and income regulation*. If the principles of the reform had been realized consistently, companies would have been impelled towards a rational manpower and wages policy, and the reform did in fact take quite a significant step in that direction by abolishing the old central prescriptions about labour and wages, and lifting the administrative curbs on labour mobility that had practically fixed labour to the workplace. (Before 1968, leaving a company 'without permission' would be followed by severe sanctions, including the loss of years worked, resulting in a much lower level of wages and pension, and the loss of certain social welfare benefits and other rights.) The migration of labour power was no longer subject to control after the reform, and it became a matter of course for people to leave one job and take another.

However, the reform did not give companies a free hand in wages policy. Average wages were centrally determined, and if companies wanted to pay more to outstanding employees, they had to pay low wages to a similar proportion of generally unskilled workers to balance this out. By regulating the average wage level, the government was seeking, and indeed found, a guarantee that superfluous workers would not be sacked. It also blocked the path to paying the same overall wages for the same work if done by fewer employees. Obviously, if the principles of the reform had been applied consistently and companies had been given greater independence in their wages policy, the overemployment would have ceased and a proportion of the labour force would have been fired. This would have caused a degree of structural unemployment (although restructuring of employment would have occurred as well), but it would have given a great boost to efficiency. However, the idea of even temporary unemployment had been sharply rejected in the debates before the reform. Full employment was to remain a basic ideological principle. In other words, the government wanted to solve the problem by keeping full employment but gradually absorbing the superfluous industrial labour in other fields, particularly the services. The obvious economic disadvantages were outweighed by the social considerations.

The matter was put very clearly by Central Committee secretary Rezső Nyers in a lecture to the Party Academy before the introduction of the reform:

> What we envisage, in fact, is a slow, gradual, but systematic redirection of the labour force, and so we shall arrange matters through these measures, and not by allowing the regrouping of the labour force to happen all of a sudden . . .
>
> In devising the partial elements of the mechanism – whichever I take, the system of financial incentives, the profit motivation or the appraisal of superfluous staff . . . we have sought to and will in fact apply this gradual approach. By this economic policy we can and will make the process free of jolts.[21]

So the fears of unemployment never materialized. But this was one of the compromises that slowed down real progress towards greater efficiency, although it should be repeated that the idea behind this measure was gradually to eliminate the safety measures and so pave the way for a fuller realization of the original purposes. This is indicated by the fact that in 1972 five years after the reform was introduced, a proportion of companies were allowed, initially as an experiment, to introduce what was known as wage-bill management. This gave them greater freedom and flexibility than the system of regulating the average wage, since they could distribute the same wage bill among fewer workers and salaried staff. (However, despite its obvious advantages, it did not offer an alternative as a general method of wage control, since its basis was the year prior to its application and it only allowed wages to be regulated in single companies.)

There were other factors that also played a part in the regulation of wages and incomes. Most important of these were the upper and lower limits set by wage scales for particular occupations, and the central wage measures that were taken. However, all this regulatory activity applied only to the wage element of income, which was far less than the whole in the case of those earning both wages and other income. For that reason the establishment of the wages–output ratio became a particularly important factor in regulation, because it thereby established the sphere and proportions of the *benefits* received irrespective of performance. In the years that followed the reform, two parallel processes were at work on incomes. On the one hand, greater differentials were made in payments for performance, while on the other there was a market rise, for social policy reasons, in the proportion of income made up of benefits, which reached an average of 27 per cent. These free benefits, some of them provided by companies from their social welfare funds and some by the state from the budget, ranged from child allowance to health and education benefits. In part they sought to ensure that the basic social needs were satisfied irrespective of performance and the living conditions of larger and more deprived families improved. So they had the effect of counteracting and evening out income differentials.

Another important feature of the economic reform was the impetus it gave to agriculture, in particular to the development of a specifically Hungarian model for the *cooperative farm*. There had already been a significant measure of reform in the farming sector, but this was now developed in almost every respect. The price scissors between agriculture and industry were closed by a further, more substantial rise in farm prices. After the measures taken at the beginning of 1966, in the autumn of 1967 (in the case of pork) and at the beginning of 1968, the producer prices, as already mentioned, were raised by an average of 17 per cent, which was a significant step towards reflection of the real values.

The policy on farm prices and the narrowing of the price gap between agriculture and industry became a key factor in financial motivation. As Lajos Fehér, the Deputy Prime Minister, pointed out, the level of farm prices, using 1964 as a base, was 26 per cent lower than that of industrial producer prices, according to the National Price Office, but 11 per cent higher than the value of the inputs. (Only two-thirds of the 27 per cent rise in the prices of industrial products used in agriculture between 1958 and 1964 had been compensated for by the government in the form of various supports.)

The alteration in the price relations was not the only big change in agriculture at this time. The reform was accompanied by a radical step towards eliminating the paternalism of the state towards the cooperatives and making them truly independent and self-managing.

Beginning in the mid-1960s, the directing function of the rural district councils had been steadily reduced. It became general for local leaders to succeed ones who had been appointed centrally, through a democratic process of election. Let me quote an admittedly very partisan article published in the *Népszabadság* early in 1966 on what had been happening in the Cegléd rural district of central Hungary:

> Since 1961, twenty-nine people have held the post of chairman in the ten cooperative farms in the district. There has been a similar turnover among the chief agronomists, chief accountants and party secretaries. Clearly this cannot be ascribed entirely to cooperative-farm democracy, and there is no disputing the right of party organizations to remove . . . incompetent party secretaries . . .
>
> We are well aware that it is not easy to choose the right person for the right job . . . But there is another circumstance that contributes to the frequent turnover: successive trials with cooperative-farm leaders who have already proved themselves incompetent. Not infrequently a cooperative chairman, chief agronomist or party secretary is relieved of his post only to be recommended to another cooperative farm and be entrusted with a similar post. There he works for a year or two, and then sets forth once more, starts again and always has his slate wiped clean. What is the explanation for this? Usually these migrants who keep receiving executive appointments are honourable, upright men, but as cooperative-farm leaders they cannot do their job . . . One often hears it said, 'We don't want to offend these comrades.' . . . By sparing the pride of certain men one can make aggrieved people out of the entire membership of the cooperative farm . . . Equally grave problems are caused by another phenomenon. Half the leaders of the cooperative farms in the district are not local men; they have arrived in their present posts in accordance with Government Order No. 3004 . . . Most have not been living on the cooperative farm, merely travelling there to work and going home at night by train or car. In fact they have managed matters for years while they and their families have been living far away, in a quite different village . . . The failure of the appointees to come and settle . . . is a fact that must be reckoned with in the future as well. So *it is not a solution of any kind for people to be brought in again, from other parts [or] from Budapest to fill the post of cooperative-farm chairman, chief agronomist or party secretary. We must raise cooperative leaders among local people* – and this is the most important lesson of . . . the survey.[22]

Also important from the point of view of curbing the paternalism of the rural districts and the state towards the cooperative farms was a change in the economic relations between state and farm. The 'administrative' character of state central purchasing and other institutions gave way to a commercial basis of partnership only after the reform decision had been taken. The Central Committee resolution on the reform stressed the need to base this relationship 'on mutual economic advantages and abolish all disruptive administrative stipulations to be found in this respect today'. The guidelines that the Central Committee adopted declared: 'In future, the purchasing organizations will only be allowed to function as equal partners of the state farms and cooperatives. They will not be able to act as transmitters of official prescriptions or control means whose exclusive granting or withholding can influence the farms coercively.'[23]

The end of paternalist state intervention and the consolidation of market relations turned the cooperatives into genuine businesses, while reinforcing a cooperative self-management that ranged from free decision-making about production and liberation from the monopoly of the state purchasing organization to the liberty to sell under market conditions. Moreover, a nationwide organization to protect the interests of the cooperative farms developed out of self-managing associations, usually two or three to a county, and the establishment of the National Council of Agricultural Cooperatives. In fact these were the years when the new, post-1956 cooperative model actually matured.

In this new operating climate of corporate independence a great impetus was given to the *industrial, non-agricultural side activities* of the cooperatives. In the spring of 1966 the *Népszabadság* explained what was envisaged:

> Let no one be misled . . . by the figures that say some 14,000 auxiliary units and sideline operations can be found on the 3,300 cooperative farms. For the bulk of this figure of 14,000 is made up of auxiliary operations, machinery repair shops and blacksmiths', locksmiths', wheelwrights' or even tractor repair units that essentially link up very closely with the basic agricultural activity.
>
> It is indicative of the modesty of the achievements and the tasks still ahead of us, for instance, that only 1,393 cooperatives undertake contract haulage and 309 cooperatives earn income from timber processing, while only 352 have beehives. A mere 47 cooperatives pursue cottage industry. Only 725 cooperatives possess shops, retail booths or simple market stalls. Processing activities are particularly backward on the cooperative farms. The present position is well indicated by the fact that only about 10 per cent of farm income derives from auxiliary, sideline and miscellaneous activity, and the ancillary activity of a non-agricultural character accounts for a mere 2 per cent.
>
> Few in this country now dispute that the time has come to expand the economic activity of the cooperative farms. *New opportunities are offered to the cooperative farms by independent sales, preparation and processing of farm produce, and servicing and other ancillary activities as well.* This has been recognized after many setbacks as well as many encouraging experiences.[24]

Another article in the same paper had reported on the case of the Vörös Hajnal (Red Dawn) cooperative farm in the village of Nagykovácsi, just outside Budapest. Here a pickling plant, a stone-grinding plant and a lime kiln had been set up earlier. The chairman, Lajos Kovács, remarked during an interview:

> Here in Nagykovácsi, as on many other cooperative farms, an atmosphere of uncertainty arose about the sideline activities. The membership's uncertainty was prompted by the uncertainty of the supervisory organizations . . .
>
> We had an efficient building team as well, but we broke it up because all the supervising and badgering was really getting on our nerves by then. In a single year there were 50–60 inspections at the cooperative with around 250 inspection staff taking part. It's worth noting that the cooperative farm's membership is 170 people.
>
> Soon there was such a poor opinion of us in the making that we felt affronted. By then they were calling me plain *'Limey Kovács'* and the cooperative 'Foggy Dawn' . . .
>
> (The pretext for this) has gone now because, sad to say, we wound up the building team as well. But the antipathy towards the auxiliary and sideline activities hasn't diminished a bit. Some see it as a necessary evil and in many cases they hold it back by interpreting the legal regulations in a rigid way . . .
>
> For my part I'm against even using the term sideline activity. After all, in practice all this kind of work counts as an important activity with us and elsewhere as well. Still, you have to take the cooperatives' local conditions into account.
>
> . . . What's known as produce rescue is useful and important as well, when the produce that hasn't sold fresh – tomatoes, peppers, cucumbers – is processed by the cooperative. That means the goods don't go rotten and increase the cooperative's income instead.
>
> In my view more independence needs to be given to the cooperatives over sideline activity. This would greatly increase the willingness of the membership and management to take initiatives and bring a substantial gain to the economy as well. They should be bolder about trusting the membership to decide what kind of sideline activity they want to pursue. We aren't going to work against our own interest either, and we only work at things that are useful to everybody.[25]

Innumerable arguments were put forward by the press and the politicians in support of sideline and industrial activities. Let us quote Central Committee secretary Lajos Fehér, as the most competent to speak on the matter. In a lecture entitled 'The Main Trends in the Development of Agriculture' delivered at the party's Political Academy in the spring of 1966 he put it particularly clearly:

> At present, the auxiliary activities of agricultural units in general and the cooperative farms in particular are prohibited by numerous earlier regulations or placed in practice within very tight limits. This restriction, the artificial repression of auxiliary activity, *is causing serious damage to the economy*. It is doing so primarily because it results in the

> destruction of a lot of useful raw materials in agriculture, for want of a processing opportunity. On the other hand, this restriction, *meaningless* in national economic terms and favourable only to the state processing companies in their monopoly position, in practice condemns the *labour force on agricultural units to idleness for part of the year, especially in the winter months.*
>
> With the intensification of agriculture and the improvement in its financial and technical supply position, the need for a certain *local activity of an industrial nature* on the farm is appearing in more and more areas. We are convinced that rather than persecuting and limiting these activities of an industrial nature or making efforts at all costs to separate them off from agriculture, *we should support the farm in developing this activity* . . .
>
> The need for more regular, if possible all-year-round employment for the cooperative-farm membership and thereby some improvement in the earnings relations . . . makes it increasingly urgent today for us to re-examine and alter the obsolete, restrictive legal regulations and practice which are having an adverse effect on the cooperatives . . .
>
> In future the agricultural units must be free to pursue every kind of auxiliary processing activity:
>
> - that allows favourable use to be made of natural or other local endowments and can be organized by the farms profitably;
> - for which there are orders, or for which local, national or export demand arises, so that the satisfaction of these is beneficial for the economy . . .[26]

Food-processing activity by cooperative farms more than doubled between 1968 and 1971. Building activity increased more than two-and-a-half times over and other industrial activity more than doubled.

Finally, reform measures in 1967 reduced the legal restraints on commodity production by cooperative members on their private plots, which had been curbed for ideologically motivated reasons of income policy. In fact the decision on the reform brought a thoroughgoing change in political and practical attitudes to the household farms. In the early 1960s the significant part they had been allowed to play was in a sense a grudging concession considered as temporary and contrary to socialist principles. So the curbs placed on them had been tough, and associated in official minds with a process of building up the collective farming effort. Once the decision on the reform had been taken, this doctrinaire position was reversed. In January 1966 the *Népszabadság* spelled out the political message in an article on the part household farming was playing in Somogy County:

> *Significant progress* has been made in this county as well, compared with the conditions three or four years ago . . . At that time certain

> rural district and cooperative leaders considered it necessary to repress and indeed suppress household farming. They spun theories about how 'the household farm is the chief obstacle to collective performance', how 'the development of household farms is solely in the individual's interest and not in the national economy's' and how 'the cooperative membership can only be accustomed to collective work in the absence of household farms'. These provided grounds for arbitrarily limiting them and in some places even setting about the partial or total *elimination* of household farming.
>
> By now it is clear: significant damage has been caused by these erroneous views, whose effects can still be felt in many places . . .
>
> One can hardly find a cooperative leader who can walk round his village with his eyes open and not see that a serious mistake would be made if we left unused the stalls and sties that stand in the peasant farmyards. For putting them to use subtracts nothing from the large-scale investment projects and requires no additional state support. Space for 26,000 head of cattle and 40,000 pigs has been built on the county's collective farms since the socialist transformation of agriculture. However, all this comes to very little, and . . . *a major part of livestock can still be found on the household farms.* Of the total stock, 52.5 per cent of the cattle, 59 per cent of the pigs [and] 92.5 per cent of the poultry are raised on the household farms . . .
>
> It is well that over a year ago a system of management and organization came into being for the household farms – the so-called *household farming committees.* Their task is to work to coordinate the interests of collective and household farming [and] exert influence to instil the notion that *collective and household production are a uniform whole.*[27]

The new law on cooperatives which came into force the following year devoted a separate clause to stating, as the *Népszabadság* put it, that

> collective and household farming are a closely cooperating, integral entity . . . From this it follows above all that there is a need to broaden and strengthen the cooperation of the collective and household farms by coordinating interests within the cooperative farm. In this framework the household farm is a part of the collective *from the angle of production*, buying and selling.

The writer of the article pointed out that alongside provision for the family concerned, 'commodity production can also be carried out on the household farm'.[28]

Whereas in the case of agriculture the comprehensive reform complemented earlier important processes of reform confined to the sector, in foreign trade only limited experiments had been introduced since 1957 and one can refer to the new initiatives as a turning-point.

The state foreign trade companies which had enjoyed an almost complete monopoly were joined by production companies which were granted foreign trading rights on their own account, and after 1968 handled 23 per cent of the exports and 11 per cent of the imports. But it emerges from the data, too, that that interpretation of the state monopoly of foreign trade which secured the power for the highly centralized foreign trade companies in a monopolistic position was essentially preserved.

Another target of reform was the *private sector*. The reform envisaged not only a growing importance for household farming but some expansion in private activity designed to improve services to the general public and, in some cases, avoid the losses the state sector was making on providing them. In the retail and catering industries, for instance, the idea of expanding small-scale private ownership and of leasing out small state-owned units arose, as it had in 1956–7.

The policy towards private retail trading was reviewed in the summer of 1967 during the reform preparations:

> There will also be a need for private trading activity – to a certain, slightly greater extent than at present – after the introduction of the reform . . . We would like to provide an opportunity . . . for smaller units with fewer than five people [working in them] and whose operation is necessary . . . but unprofitable to the state . . . to be leased to persons with a trade certificate, or for one-person units with a small turnover to be sold.[29]

In 1968 a proposal before the Economic Policy Committee of the party began by saying:

> Our investigations reveal that some units, around 1,000–1,500 shops (or 2 to 2.5 per cent of units) . . . would still be unprofitable to the company if run on a free-till [accounting] principle.[30] At the same time, these units are required from the point of view of public supply. To resolve the problem, we recommend new forms of operation that represent a transition to private from state and cooperative trading without the dangers of privatization.

Four such forms were proposed, under which state companies could have units that were separately or strictly accounting, free-till accounting, or operated under a contract or lease by someone who was classified as a private trader. Catering units run under the free-till system would be exempt from central turnover and staffing prescriptions, and managers would be appointed on an open competitive basis. Finally, both the managers and staff of these units were to have a personal stake in their profitability, and the employment of family members was to be allowed. 'Units important to maintain from the supply point of view may be leased out if the number of employees, excluding family members helping out, is not more than three in the retail trade and five in catering.' The tenant was to rent the fixed assets and premises, and using these sell goods that would constitute his own property. He would pay a rent on the fixed assets, and this rent would ensure a set margin of profit for the company issuing the lease.[31]

Clearly there was an intention of allowing slightly greater leeway for private business. But to interpret this it is important to recall the salient facts: Between 1960 and 1966 the share of self-employed craftsmen in the provision of maintenance services had fallen back from 71 to 46 per cent, and the number of those self-employed in this sector had dropped from 88,000 to 71,000. The 9,000 self-employed retailers in 1966 did only 2 to 3 per cent of the trade: 62 per cent of them were over retiring age and a further 8 per cent were disabled.[32]

The significance of the self-employed had fallen even from the already low level in the late 1950s, and the modest expansion of private activity that was planned was certainly not intended to alter this dramatically. In general, the government's Economic Committee pointed out at the end of 1967: 'it is desirable to *maintain the present proportion* of private activity and the private sector. This requires . . . a reproduction of private activity on the present scale . . . Private activity [must] not afford greater scope to speculators who want to get rich quick on little work.'

A proposal entitled 'The Place and Task of Private Small-Scale Industry in the New Economic Mechanism' put before this committee expressed the ideological position very clearly: 'With the advance of socialist production and the strengthening of socialist awareness, *the social and economic importance of private small-scale industry will slowly and steadily diminish.*' In areas where 'it is indispensable, its functioning must be made possible for a very long time to come', but even under the new mechanism 'private retailing can still only perform a marginal, gap-filling function in public supply'.[33]

In fact adjustment of property relations and private activity received a very modest place in the new economic mechanism that emerged in the late 1960s. Even so, it helped the economy to function better and improved the services to the general public, while providing useful experience in how collective ownership and private business might be combined.

The economic system that arose out of the reform in Hungary was a far more flexible one. The abolition of plan indicators did not, it soon emerged, lead to a kind of 'market anarchy' and the government proved capable of controlling economic processes and applying its economic policy objectives through the system of regulators. The targets of the Third Five-Year Plan (1966–70) were fulfilled to a greater extent than ever before: it was calculated that the target–fulfilment gap was half what it had been under the Second Five-Year Plan (1961–5), far less than half of the gap under the Second Three-Year Plan (1958–60) and hardly a quarter of the shortfall experienced under the First Five-Year Plan (1950–4).[34] The achieved rates (and targets) were as follows: 6.3 per cent (6 per cent) annual growth of industrial production; 2.8 per cent (2.7 per cent) for agricultural production; 2.1 per cent (1.4 per cent) for housing construction; 8.6 per cent (4.9 per cent) for investment, and consequently 10.1 per cent (0.47 per cent) for construction. Under the Fourth Five-Year Plan (1971–5) the targets were adhered to even more closely. Meanwhile the market influences ended a substantial proportion of the malfunctions which had occurred so persistently in the past. No longer were plan targets fulfilled and overfulfilled by turning out unsaleable goods and using up more costly materials. Since companies now had a stake in sales, supplies improved significantly and so did the product range. Big strides were made in overcoming shortage, which was wholly eliminated in foodstuffs and sharply reduced in consumer goods.

To sum up, one can say that a new type of socialist economy, a model of a planned economy with a regulated market, began to emerge in Hungary in the late 1960s and early 1970s. At its heart was – as formulated by those actually participating in its creation – an ensemble of and a relationship between the economic organization and the institutional system of control under which the economic units (production and services companies and their consumers) generally made their decisions under the influence of direct market impulses such as price, supply and demand, credit terms, etc., although the market was monitored, influenced and regulated by the state, as the owner of the fundamental means of production, through economic regulations, and in some cases through direct intervention.[35]

The multiple checks, balances and compromises built into the reform, the indirect interference with the activities of companies, the regulations going into details and operating with innumerable exceptions as well as the market simulated with regulators instead of a real market, could not, after all, produce the mixed system expected from the reform and thought to be ideal. In spite of the abolition of mandatory instructions, indirect state interference through the regulators persisted which allowed the functioning of the market, which had only partially been rehabilitated from the outset, with individual, enterprise-level regulations replacing plan-instructions, interfering with the financial situation of companies. The constraints of the reform were extremely strict and harsh; for the implementation of the planned economic model they had to be lifted.

Thus, although the model which had been planned in theory was certainly not applied in full, the elimination of the command economy and the impact of the new economic mechanism secured substantial progress. Obviously, the economic performance in the five years after the introduction of the reform does not provide a direct indication of how effective it was, because the performance of the economy was also determined to a substantial extent by the prevailing economic policy and the influences of the world economy. They were years that saw the peak of the biggest world boom in modern times, from which Hungary also profited. Having said all that, the favourable economic performance provided evidence that the reform was successful.

The annual rate of growth rose from 5.3 per cent in the previous ten years to 6.2 per cent. Far more importantly, a big factor in that growth, for the first time since the war, was improved productivity. In agriculture this had begun to happen earlier. Now almost all the industrial growth came from an annual average productivity improvement of 6 per cent. Only in the services was there any major increase in labour input (an annual 2 to 2.5 per cent).

The accelerating rate of economic growth fuelled increasingly by an improvement in productivity also helped to eliminate the earlier structural disproportions. From the late 1960s onwards, the restoration of a more harmonious development trend was among the most conspicuous economic policy features. This was reflected in a deceleration of industrial growth (to about 6 per cent a year) and an acceleration of agricultural growth (to 4–5 per cent or more) and particularly of the services (over 8 per cent).

Accompanying a structural transformation in line with the modern trends of this century and the gaining of ground by sectors which had been somewhat neglected and backward was a process of technical modernization. The structural changes in industry also made progress, as can be seen from the steep increase in the imports of up-to-date machinery and the substantial modernization of the machine stock – hardly more than a third of the fixed assets were ten or more years old.

It is estimated that less than a fifth of products were up to world-market standards, however. It remained a weakness of industry, particularly engineering, that too wide a range of products were made and the level of selectiveness was quite inadequate. In fact over half the products were of a standard substantially lower than the world market required.

The most spectacular advance came in agriculture, through a vast programme of technical renewal that lifted the sector from the age of craft industry into the industrial era. In the late 1960s the mechanization of all the main work processes was completed, and the use of artificial fertilizers trebled. Industrial-scale agriculture, involving a revolution in technology and management and a process of concentration, spread over grain and other field crops and fruit and vegetable production. The result, on the pioneering farms if not nationally, was a threefold increase in yields. The major branches of stock-breeding, particularly pigs and poultry, gained an industrial character as well.

The infrastructure and the service industries had long been neglected and fallen far behind. From the mid-1960s onwards the stock of assets in these two sectors grew by an annual average of 5 per cent, as a result of a conscious effort involving price policy and regulation. The most dynamic sector of all, averaging a growth rate of 9 per cent, was construction.

Parallel with this broad development came a rise in living standards. Per capita real income had been rising by an average of 4 per cent a year in the 1960s, a period of steady improvement. After the introduction of the reform, the improvement rate shot up to 6 per cent, covering the manual, white-collar and agricultural workforce alike. For manual workers and white-collar staff the annual increase in real income averaged only 3.7 per cent between 1961 and 1967. This increased to 5.8 per cent after the reform. Continuing the tendency begun in the early 1960s, the income of peasants caught up, although the same could not be said of their living conditions, the 'quality' of life.

As incomes grew more rapidly, so did income differentials, which could not have been allowed to happen until general living standards were rising. Earlier measures to equalize incomes had been a way to improve the wretched condition of the poor strata in society. Now differentials were encouraged so as to provide more incentive to better and more highly qualified work – to speed up progress, in other words.

This increase in income differentials brought about by the reform meant that skilled workers were paid about 25 per cent more than the semi-skilled and about 33 per cent more than the unskilled. The earnings of an engineer or technician in industry would be 160 to 170 per cent of a manual worker's, while top management could earn three to three-and-a-half times as much as a plain manual worker or a clerk. Between top and bottom the income differentials increased to a multiple of eight-and-a-half to nine, and they were larger still if opportunities for extra earnings were counted in, since overtime and bonus opportunities varied widely from group to group in society. The chances of earning extra money were quite good in certain trades (motor mechanics, television engineers and others paid on a job-by-job basis) and in some white-collar occupations (through extra part-time jobs and consultancy activities). Managers too did well in a number of cases, receiving substantial performance-related bonuses. In a few occupations, earnings were increased through tips or even corruption. But such opportunities were entirely lacking for large sections of the manual worker, administrative and professional strata.

As the excessive levelling down of earnings ceased, greater opportunities for spending appeared. Shortages eased and a wider range of consumer durables became available. (The proportion of imported consumer goods in consumption, for instance, rose from a pre-reform figure of 8 to 10 per cent to 20 per cent.) An incentive to do better was provided.

However, the new income differentials had numerous side-effects poorly tolerated by society. It became possible to earn more without contributing more labour, better quality or higher qualifications, by exploiting a monopoly position that allowed higher profits to be made by raising prices. Certain of the small-scale private businesses (which accounted for a mere 3 per cent of those in employment) managed to do exceptionally well by exploiting shortages or anticipating fashions with a flexibility the state companies were quite unable to match. The situation was similar in what came to be known as the second economy, where moonlighters could profit hugely from gaps in the supply of goods and services through their, partly illegal, activities. All of this became the more irritating, as it came into conflict with the basic theorems of the old, obsolete ideology, which was declared to be valid and maintained as attributes. Quite a few elements of reality conflicted with the declared 'values of socialism'.

But despite several problems, incompleteness and conflicts, the success and effectiveness of the reform was vindicated by the performance and balanced growth of the economy, the development of the infrastructure and the trade surplus that emerged.

19 The plan and preparations for continuing the reform after 1968

Although the achievements of the reform were quite apparent, those in charge of the country's economy saw them only as initial successes. The gradual way in which the reform was introduced and the brakes built into the new system made it essential that further steps should be taken under a 'second stage' which would be applied in the early 1970s. Preparations for this began almost as soon as the first stage had been introduced in January 1968. On September 30 of the same year, the Central Committee's Economic Policy Committee, as the party's highest authority on economic matters, was already discussing a proposal entitled 'The Subject Matter for Further Development of the System of Economic Management and the Organization for the Task': 'The performance of two kinds of tasks are indicated by analysis of the workings of the economic management system in order to develop more fully and continue perfecting its influence.' One of the tasks was 'a theoretical analysis . . . designed to develop and augment the reform . . . and outline the possible variant long-term approaches [for this]'. To oversee this side of the preparations a committee was set up consisting of István Friss, Péter Vályi, József Bognár, Lajos Faluvégi and Tamás Nagy. At the same time preparations began of further steps towards 'the creation of a uniform foreign exchange rate . . . (convertibility – uniform exchange rate – domestic price system)', and analysis of 'the extent to which banking and other institutions meet the requirements [and] the principles and direction for developing these . . .' In addition, study began of 'the methods of developing social control over the economy, the role of the [company] supervisory committee . . . the advantages and drawbacks of filling leading [executive] positions on the basis of open applications, etc.'.[1]

At the same time as these broader preparations were started, so was work on a gradual expansion of the 1968 system as it stood. In November 1968 a 'Report on Economic Development in 1968 and the

Economic Reform, and a Proposal on the Chief Economic Tasks for the Coming Year' was compiled by the party's Political Committee for the Central Committee to consider. It was already suggesting something as specific as a consistent price system: 'A further simplification of the turnover-tax system is justified by [the effect it would have of] bringing prices even closer to the input proportions. It is proposed that the 1,500 rates of turnover tax or price support should be reduced to 700.' In the same document appeared a proposal for 'expanding the sphere of free-price forms from 23 per cent to 30 to 33 per cent of the consumer goods supply'.[2]

By the following spring the party's Economic Policy Committee was subscribing to a far bigger step towards price reform when it accepted a submission from the president of the National Materials and Prices Office: 'The long-term tasks in price policy spring precisely from the fact that the criteria for the 1968 price reform could only be applied in part', due to the lack of competition, the exceptions built into the regulatory system, the big discrepancy between consumer and producer prices, and the limiting influence of the remaining set prices. 'These circumstances', as the submission put it, '. . . cannot be fundamentally changed within a short period', but further reforming steps must be taken to ensure that 'world-market price relations have a more consistent impact than they do now . . . on price development'. For the early 1980s the aim must be to have 'consumer prices that actually encourage supply and demand to develop in a rational direction'.

At the same meeting the Economic Policy Committee reached a highly important decision of principle: 'In preparing the policy concept on prices we must assume that convertibility of the forint and a currency reform will be placed on the agenda in later years.' Later the resolution goes on to state: 'In further [moves towards] perfection of the price system, effort must be made to ensure that the domestic price relations reflect world-market price relations better, and so exert an influence on transformation of the structure of production.'[3]

In 1969 the plans for taking the reform further began to spread to areas which the inescapable pressure towards compromise had caused to be omitted from the 1968 reform, in particular institutional transformation, which had been deliberately left out. In the summer of 1969 the Economic Policy Committee discussed a proposal 'On Further Development of Large-Scale Company Organization', in which it was pointed out:

> It is impermissible to retain a monopoly situation in the production

> and distribution of consumer articles . . . where the monopoly situation is detrimental from the public-supply and price-structure points of view . . . There is no need to bring new middle-level controlling bodies into being as the large companies and trusts are wound up . . . We must examine the areas in which economically viable small and medium-sized plants with modern equipment need setting up and the means for doing so.[4]

When the committee returned to this resolution and how it was being implemented eighteen months later, it was possible to report that a comparatively minor investigation of 70 to 80 companies had been carried out in 1970,[5] and a quite detailed plan for reforming the structure of companies was drawn up later that year. The report on this submitted to the party's Economic Policy Committee declared quite specifically:

> The corporate structure which has emerged in the past does not provide the most favourable structural framework for the development of the reform in several respects . . . However, it did not appear expedient to re-examine the company structures at the same time as the reform was being introduced . . . [This] re-examination and correction is now required in order to increase the effectiveness of the reform.
>
> In accordance with the working programme of the Economic Policy Committee, we have initiated a re-examination of the individual organizations in industry, construction, transport and trading . . . During the centralization process carried out intermittently in 1962–4 . . . a great many companies were amalgamated into a large national company, and in many industries one large company or a newly established trust came to operate in a monopoly fashion . . . A monopoly situation arose in several fields in which it prevented . . . healthy competition . . . The role of the large monopoly organizations is frequently detrimental in [its effect on] consumer and producer price movements . . . The root of the problem lies in the unjustified monopoly situations, in the unaccomplished concentration of production for which centralization was to be a substitute, and in the shortage of the healthy small and medium-sized plants indispensable to the satisfaction of consumption . . . The emergence of competition must be assisted by breaking up companies and organizing individual factories into separate companies . . .[6]
>
> The number of separate companies must be increased by organizing into separate companies certain factories – often employing several thousand people – that are viable in themselves . . . There is a lack, in industry, of economically viable small and medium-sized companies with modern equipment, capable on the one hand of producing consumer goods uneconomic for the large companies and [on the other] of effectively assisting the economic operation of the

> large companies through their high degree of specialization and great productivity . . . We must examine what chances there are for establishing such companies [and] what measures are necessary to ensure they operate efficiently . . . In accordance with the guiding principles the types of measures towards the development of the organizations are the following: dividing up of larger economic entities (large companies, trusts) . . . the hiving off of units from large, monopolistic corporate organizations . . . the direct linkage of domestic and foreign trade activity to production organizations, expansion of the sphere of companies with independent foreign-trading rights, and . . . the establishment of new organizational forms.[7]

A supplement to the proposal also contained detailed proposals by the individual ministries for ending the corporate monopolies and splitting up certain large companies.[8]

Though some may be surprised by the length at which this 1970 draft for breaking up large companies has been quoted, it is not unjustified in view of the importance of the measure of reform being planned. It also exemplifies the observance of the principle of gradualism and the strength behind the strategy of applying the reform principles consistently, progressing step by step.

The preparatory work done between 1968 and 1970 on the 'second stage' of the reform had already begun to impinge on the problem of the flow of capital and labour. Following a resolution by the party's Economic Policy Committee, the Economic Policy Department of the Central Committee set up a working committee to devise a method of promoting the flow of social capital. This working committee reported back to say it had

> carried out wide-ranging analyses and compiled recommendations . . . for allowing temporary or permanent regrouping of decentralized investment resources and introducing partial commercial credit, expanding the forms for regrouping fixed assets between companies, legally regulating the issue and purchase of bonds, and establishing an institution to organize and transact the flow of capital in a planned fashion.
>
> The Economic Policy Committee . . . has discussed the committee's recommendations and taken note of them with approval . . . In the view of the Economic Policy Committee help must also be given in reconciling producer, consumer and accumulation demands and the resources for satisfying these through a flow, guided in a planned way and influenced centrally, of social capital.

It considered it necessary for a freer flow of resources to come into being in a decentralized form and with a supplementary character.

'The temporary or permanent redeployment of decentralized investment resources between companies has not so far been permitted under the legal regulations in force.' However, the position statement did say 'the temporary and permanent transfer of development funds' between companies should be allowed:

> This will permit investment funds freed for longer or shorter periods of time to redeploy to areas where their use is more efficient. The development fund can be made over permanently for investment or to finance lasting current-asset requirements, or credit may be extended for such purposes or for the placement of commercial stocks . . . State companies and cooperatives will be allowed to hand over, lease and even cede free of charge to each other their fixed and other assets (machines, installations, etc.) . . . The Working Committee has recommended that the issue and purchase of bonds be allowed because this form of redistributing capital is compatible with our system of economic management, and employment of it will be accompanied by economic advantages. Based on the resolution by the Economic Policy Committee, preparations for legislative arrangement of this matter have begun. It is envisaged that this capital flow would play only an auxiliary, marginal role by comparison with capital flow through traditional channels. But this institution would none the less tie in with the workings of the economy as a major new element. The issuers of bonds might be the central organizations of the state, specific groups of [local] councils, large companies, cooperative centres and financial institutions, while the subscribers could be business organizations (companies, cooperatives), councils and private individuals. Through financial institutions empowered for the purpose, bonds would be liquid, either in the form of a sale or by raising a loan with the bonds as security. The issue of bonds will require a permit, and in order for sufficient experience to be gained (after the enabling legislation) we shall initially allow bonds to be issued in a limited sphere, mainly for the purpose of satisfying local communal needs . . .
>
> As proposed by the Working Committee, the Economic Policy Committee has passed a resolution on the establishment of the Central Development Institute . . . It is envisaged preliminarily that the Institute should concern itself with larger-scale development of operating companies ('raising of capital'), the running down and liquidation of companies ('withdrawal of capital'), the establishment of small and medium-sized concerns . . . The preparations for setting up the Institute are in hand in conjunction with the examination of the issues connected with the development of a rational system of banking.
>
> The Economic Policy Committee . . . in addition considers it necessary for greater attention in economic research to be devoted to

> the problems of principle, the theoretical problems of channelling social capital.[9]

While working on capital flows, those in charge of the economy also started in 1970 to tackle the matter of labour mobility and the wage reform, and wage and income relations that would encourage it. Here an important step had been taken under the 1968 reform, by lifting the old restrictions on changing jobs. The plans and procedures were discussed in the autumn of 1970 at an internal meeting of deputy ministers at the Ministry of Labour, which had been put in charge of preparing for this and developing a longer-term concept of income policy:

> In the middle of this year the Economic Policy Committee charged the Minister of Labour with devising and presenting to the Economic Policy Committee by the end of next year a longer-term programme for the development of income relations . . . The party's Economic Policy Committee recently adopted a resolution declaring that our proposals concerning this matter must be placed before the requisite party organizations by March 1971 and the government bodies must also decide on these matters during the course of next year . . . The following questions must be answered: how the difference between minimum and maximum earnings should change in percentage and absolute forint terms: what alteration of the relations is justified in the present situation: what is meant by high earnings . . . There are both direct and indirect possibilities and needs to influence exceptionally high personal incomes.[10]

All this preparatory work in 1971–2 combined with preparations for a comprehensive political decision to take the reform further. In April 1971 the party Economic Policy Committee set up six working groups to examine the experiences with the reformed system. The subjects investigated were planning, the structural development and regulation of the economy, financial incentive and income regulation, system of producer and consumer prices, and the social aspects of the price policy. In the summer of 1972 the conclusions of these working committees were brought together by a committee chaired by Rezső Nyers, and this served as the basis for the Economic Policy Committee's 'Report on the Examination of the Economic Management Tasks under the Fifth Five-Year Plan: The Experiences So Far with the New System of Management', which was discussed and endorsed by the Political Committee in September. Among the points made in the report was that '*application of the declared principles of economic management* in the specific system introduced in 1968 *was severely limited by circumstances* . . . Consistent and full implementation of the principles of the party resolution on economic management has still not taken place to this day.'

The closing chapter, entitled 'Conclusions' and containing the position taken on continued development of the reform, is worth quoting:

> *The main task at present is fuller application of the original concept for the management system* . . . Efforts should primarily be concentrated on resolving the issues which have already come to fruition and been sufficiently clarified . . . concerning the preparation of measures . . . in line with the scope available. The operation should be arranged so that the modifications can be introduced comprehensively in 1975.[11]

So the development of a price system that better reflected value relations and international market influences, the preparation of an institutional reform of company organization that would improve the conditions for market competition, the strategy for making the currency convertible and the creation of the conditions and institutions for a freer flow of capital and labour between companies were all placed on the agenda between 1968 and 1970. The examinations undertaken in 1971–2 provided the groundwork for a political decision to take the reform further. To have done so would have removed many of the compromises and breaks built into the 1968 system and brought substantial, if gradual, further progress towards a consistent and homogeneous reformed economic system that took the political and social conditions into account.

Something different happened instead. In the early 1970s the plans and preparations were first brought to a halt and then dropped altogether.

20 The reform comes to a halt and reversal

Despite the economic achievements and the preparations for further reforming measures in the first years after the new economic reform system was introduced, it was not long before signs of uncertainty and recoil could be recognized. Tensions built up, criticisms of the reform were expressed and debates broke out. To some extent this reaction was already apparent at the turn of the 1960s and 70s when the original scheme for profit-sharing was dropped (with its strong financial incentives for managers), and the government introduced measures to oblige companies to supply certain goods and curb the free movement of labour again. When the fourth Five-Year Plan was being prepared an 'allocation' problem arose, since it was proposed that development of raw-material production should be encouraged by central intervention.

The supporters of reform were somewhat defensive in responding to criticism of the 'petty bourgeois attitudes', income differentials and unjustified earnings engendered by the reform. Largely rhetorical attacks were made. 'Great attention must be devoted to revealing the new or strengthening negative phenomena in society . . . and stepping up the battle . . . to curb them', it was pointed out in the report of September 1972 to the Political Committee which has already been quoted.[1] This was intended to further the reform and it was clearly for this very reason that it sought to take the wind out of the sails of those who were coming out against it on the grounds that 'negative phenomena' were becoming stronger. But the process of reform had already faltered in the early seventies, halted and soon went in to reverse. Even though it had only been implemented in part, the reform was comprehensive enough to set some new and difficult tasks and to overturn some habits, including some ingrained doctrines. There were plenty of misunderstandings as well, reinforced by pioneering inexperience and mistakes which were not corrected in good time. Most of all, the functioning of the new mechanism, in a number of areas and at a number of levels, conflicted sharply with the vested interests of certain groups. It was these threatened interests that lay, to no inconsiderable extent, behind the tensions and the criticism. Rewards for better and more valuable performance through income differentials were diametrically opposed to the interests of those unwilling or unable to do any better than average or less; what suited them was a levelling of incomes. This situation provided support for these groups in positions of power who monopolized influence, prerogatives and extremely useful connections. They felt that their existence was jeopardized by the emphasis on knowledge and expertise and by the breaking up of the highly centralized system.

It suited untalented people in the different levels of party, state and managerial apparatus not to have to take decisions on their own or responsibility for what they did. So they tended to obstruct the work of 'fanatics' who set their sights high and took risks, and sought to conserve the existing institutions and power structure which gave them security and ensured them 'connections'. The emphasis on expertise, qualifications and professionalism alarmed these tens of thousands of people who dominated the rank and file of the economic and political apparatus, since their connections, and their reputation for being politically and ideologically trustworthy, were all they had to recommend them.

Clearly, some quite extensive interests were placed in jeopardy by the reform. It was a further weakness that the persistence of the political and ideological views deriving from the Stalinist concept of socialism, and the fact that it was impossible to criticize them – in the conservative Brezhnevian period – proved that there was a conflict between the Hungarian practice and the 'socialist principles'. All this produced attacks. Perhaps it would be more precise to say that the situation provided an opportunity for rallying under the banner of 'the working man's interest' and the 'defence of socialism'. The social tensions that certainly existed could be exploited to provide a kind of mass support for a political offensive against the reform position. Some groups espied a resurgence of capitalism in the economic reform, and spoke of a denial, or at least a serious weakening, of the planned economy. When it came to incomes policy, they criticized what they saw as a neglect of the workers' interests. They fulminated against 'the private entrepreneurial paradise' and spread concern about the 'growing insolence' of the cooperative farms, which they said were undermining state industry by their own industrial activity. The growth of income differentials could be blamed and labelled as a threat to 'socialist principles'. They had no desire to embrace 'economism', the profit principle. Instead their spokesmen cried out for reinforcement of 'socialist ownership', an egalitarian, 'socialist' incomes policy and a collectivist, 'socialist' way of life.

The situation was complex and confusing in many ways. For instance, the reform had given priority to better public supplies and the elimination of shortage, and so it sought to give more scope to small-scale industry, or a combination of large and small, until such time as a developed state industry and service network, along with large-scale cooperative farming, should become capable of and interested in producing the range of products and services required. To this end, the reform wanted to reintroduce market competition for customers, and so began diversifying the corporate structure to produce far smaller (and more flexible) companies and a better mix of large- and small-scale production capacity. Naturally, this would mainly benefit the consumers, and thus the workers who accounted for the majority of the population. It was certainly in the 'workers' interests', for instance, to eliminate the recurrent shortages of meat and other foodstuffs and to remedy the lack of repair and other services. Objectively speaking, it did good, not harm, to the workers' interests to encourage the cooperative farms or small-scale private business.

It should be added that politicians were obliged to try to put this connection across even while the reform was being prepared back in the mid-1960s. The party leaders had persevered with the task of convincing the party membership and the workers that to give recognition to agriculture and farmers and assert their interests was ultimately a pro-worker policy as well. In early 1966, when the prices for farm produce were being raised, Lajos Fehér had argued against those who 'object to "support on this scale"' for the peasantry. 'Many also add', he said, 'that "it is essentially the workers who are paying for the rise in the peasantry's living standards". From time to time, a kind of anti-peasant sentiment arises in the towns. This sentiment is now getting stronger.'[2]

Three days earlier János Kádár had stressed in his New Year statement:

> Superficial assertions that we are solving our problems at the expense of the town are very subjective and contain emotional elements. Remarks have also been made to the effect that the peasants are speculating, not working . . . Our party membership has to understand above all . . . that these measures are parts of a considered

> concept which serves the interests of the working class, the working people, in line with our policy so far.[3]

Not only personal credibility but the facts – the rapid end to the meat shortage, the big improvement in supplies – were convincing in the short term. But a few years later, as wider income differentials appeared, the 'anti-peasant sentiment' increased again. There can be no doubt that peasants' earnings were growing faster than workers', even though the latter were growing faster than ever before. Nor can there be any doubt that some people seized the new opportunities to exploit shortage. Tremendous profits, for instance, were made out of a housing boom that coincided with a serious shortage of construction capacity in the state sector. Since the general rise in living standards meant there was money available, clever entrepreneurs could amass a small fortune in two or three years. Taxation or other measures that might have restrained the heightening conflicts and social tensions from which political capital was made were not taken. A degree of mass backing was won by the growing number of demands that 'order should be restored'. Interests or doctrinaire pedantry motivated such views that the economy should be subordinated to incomes policy, the peasantry prevented from growing richer from their household farms than the workers were from honest toil, the private businessmen from earning vast sums, and the intelligentsia and managerial strata from making extra money, either officially or 'on the side'. This, it was said, was to be done in a way that still encouraged initiative, risk-taking and diligence, while ensuring there were no corrupt practices. In the event, no such rational compromise could be found.

In the autumn of 1972 the leading critics of the reform and advocates of cutting back its 'excesses' took the battle into the political leadership itself. No doubt scholars in later periods will have a chance to study how this happened by exploring the archives,[4] but we already know that when János Kádár became sixty in the spring of that year he offered his resignation as first secretary to the Central Committee, which turned it down and asked him to stay.[5] None the less, certain conservative political forces were at work, and the most obvious ideological tools for them in their quest for power were championship of 'the working man's interest' and the 'values of socialism', for which genuine mass support could be procured.

The attack was aimed first of all at the reversal of the line of reform of the HSWP, hallmarked by the names of Rezső Nyers and Lajos Fehér. If the popular personality of János Kádár who had brought about an oeuvre of historical importance in fifteen years could not be discredited, the fire had to be concentrated on the main representatives of reform of Kádár's policy, and the first secretary had to be 'liberated' from the leading personalities of the party's reform wing. (It is part of the logic of the one-party-system that within it – unless a dictatorship of the Stalin type exists – several trends may coexist, or, as Gramsci put it, if there is one party, there may be two parties within it.) The unchanged political structures made it easy for these forces to organize themselves. And their successes broke up the internal 'coalition' of the party and weakened the centre on the platform of reform.

It is, of course, true that many things got mixed up: it was not simply the 'good' and the 'bad', the 'reformers' and 'anti-reformers' who clashed. Obviously, not everybody knew which side he took or even perceived that different sides existed. It should be obvious that those taking different sides equally made mistakes. But this must not obliterate the impact of and responsibility for actions. True, it was a mistake to believe that far-reaching compromises could be made in order to defend the reform, or that the impact of the oil price explosion could be halted at the western frontier of the country. But these mistakes cannot excuse the 'mistakes' of the devastating attacks on the household-plot farms, the enterprising spirit of cooperatives and the acknowledgement of expertise. The mistakes made in the course of different actions, of different direction, cannot be brought to a common denominator. In spite of all that, there were genuine front lines. Certainly, for the attack against the reform international support was also forthcoming: after 1968 the Hungarian reform had become an isolated process that provoked mistrust and even drew open or concealed criticism from a number of other socialist countries in the columns of *Kommunist*, *Neues Deutschland* or *Rudé Právo*.

However, Prime Minister Jenő Fock spoke openly on the subject at a national propaganda conference in 1971, mentioning reservations expressed by other socialist countries about Hungary's abolition of compulsory plan indicators, its incorporation of some elements of the market and the limitations it had placed on state intervention, which they saw as potential threats to socialism. In September 1972 a resolution appraising the reform passed by the Political Committee stated: 'During the exchange of information (with other socialist countries) . . . concern is also apparent from time to time. This is chiefly in connection with whether . . . the planned nature of the economic processes and the central hold over them, and the development of socialist international economic cooperation, can be sufficiently ensured.'[6]

In December 1973 an article referring to these 'friendly concerns' appeared in the *Népszabadság*:

> Though to a decreasing extent, we have encountered among our friends in recent years some concern alongside the confidence in our system of economic management. How can there be a planned economy if there is no compulsory plan for companies? How can the role of the state be asserted if over half the investments are in the companies' hands? These and similar questions are put not infrequently, particularly in debates among economists.[7]

It is difficult to judge (and today the facts are still not yet disclosed) what mass of ice can be found below the tip of the iceberg, also seen by the public in the form of direct and indirect criticism and even strong pressure.

Let me refer, from among the many, to just one article in *Pravda* (August 31, 1972). Under the title 'Delights and Difficulties of the Hungarian Search for Ways' it projected, in an unparalleled manner, the stand taken by the Central Committee of the HSWP three months later. The newspaper quoted a few sentences from the article by Rezső Nyers on the successes of the reform and then asked the question: 'Why, then, are still worries?' (It mentions among these the flow of experts from the state industry into cooperatives, wage differentiation, the unjustified private incomes, but also the petty bourgeoisie.) 'The next plenary session of the CC of HSWP will soon convene' – the article continued – 'and preparatory work is directed at a thorough analysis of the economic reform . . . Such measures are being elaborated which will increase the role of central planning and state control.' This unusual 'forecast', clearly relying on Budapest sources, obviously strengthened the internal opposition to reform, caused uncertainty among those belonging to the centre and in the majority, considerably weakened the positions of reform and supported the conservative wing on the November plenary session.

Though it may well be that mistakes and even intentional exaggerations were made in assessing the dangers, the external impact still cannot be exaggerated. Violation of the norms of relations among countries perceptibly indicated precisely in 1968, the year when the Hungarian reform was introduced, that 'friendly warnings' must be taken seriously. I may also add that in the post-1968 medium of international 'cooling down' both systems of alliance made efforts to close ranks.

The direct or indirect criticisms that surfaced in various forms in the early 1970s (and may be assumed to be only the tip of the iceberg) certainly put the leaders of the Hungarian party on the defensive. Politicians were obliged to declare constantly that they were not aiming at substantial changes and that the reform had not resulted in an economic model that diverged from those of the other socialist countries. The existence of a 'Hungarian model' was denied.

In October 1972 the central daily of the party found it necessary to underline in a leading article:

> *One of the newest methods employed by anti-communists* . . . is coming to the fore these days: propagation [of the idea that there are] *various 'models' of socialism* . . .
>
> The purpose of this is . . . to arouse nationalism, to exhort to national isolation, and to undermine the confidence among the countries building a new society. In accordance with this double purpose the 'models' too can be divided into two groups. To one belong the so-called species of socialism to which . . . such epithets as 'democratic' and 'with a human face' are attached, while in the other are ranged the 'national types', for instance 'Russian' or 'Hungarian' socialism . . .
>
> *The models of 'national' socialisms are an attempt to set national characteristics up against the general laws of socialist construction* . . . With the aid of the 'models' they 'lend credence' and encouragement to national separatism and belittle the international significance of the Soviet experiences in building socialism. *The purpose of the theory that there are various national models of socialism is to incite nationalism and anti-Soviet feelings.*
>
> Bourgeois propagandists are also proclaiming the existence of some kind of 'Hungarian model', counterposing it against the construction work in the other socialist countries . . . In this respect our position is unequivocal: we reject the unfounded notions developed about the so-called 'Hungarian model'.[8]

Supported and provided with a point of reference by the conservative trends in the other socialist countries and their suspicion towards the Hungarian reform, its critics at home achieved an official and public breakthrough in November 1972, with a resolution adopted by the Central Committee. Although the resolution described 'the system of economic management introduced on January 1, 1968' as 'a serviceable and effective means of furthering socialist planned economic activity and the purposes of socialist construction', it emphasized that the implementation of the earlier decisions had not been entirely satisfactory; 'indeed, in certain respects the implementation is not taking place in the direction and way desired'.[9]

Two-and-a-half years later, Central Committee Secretary Árpád Pullai referred to that meeting in his address to the Eleventh Congress of the Hungarian Socialist Workers' Party, which did not, he said, 'hesitate to examine the rectitude of some of its earlier decisions'. It had 'the strength and courage to carry through some corrections' in accordance with the interests of society and 'our principles'. 'It amended the line, where it was not satisfactory.'[10]

The argument was expressed most openly by Zoltán Komócsin, the party Central Committee secretary responsible for foreign affairs, in the spring of 1974, when he wrote the following in an article in the *Népszabadság*, revealingly entitled 'With Policy Unchanged':

> Countless Central Committee statements and also the resolution of the Tenth [party] Congress stated that the system of economic management applied in this country since 1968 was sound . . . But we cannot think dogmatically and *we cannot adhere rigidly to every word uttered . . . What was good yesterday, can become outworn by today, and changes must be made to it* . . . Nor can the justified delight and pride felt over the successes accomplished prevent us from learning – if we can, as much as possible – *from the tried methods of the other socialist countries* . . . It is well known that the system of economic management in the fraternal [socialist] countries of Europe . . . differs from ours in no few respects.

Although it had been laid down that the principles of the economic management system must be 'kept pure', Komócsin argued, re-examination of the reform had underlined the conclusion that 'we are advancing unswervingly along the path we have begun, constantly adjusting and developing [our] practice to the changing requirements of life'.[11]

Two intentions were clearly mingled in the debates and actions in the autumn of 1972 and the years that followed: of taking corrective measures *on behalf of* the reform to try to resolve the tensions that arose, and of abolishing and reversing the main advances that the reform had made. But major groupings inside the political leadership favoured a 'struggle on two fronts', emphasizing the dangers from both extremes. In January 1973 the editor of the *Társadalmi Szemle*, the party's main periodical, denied 'rumours' concerning the decision of the Central Committee that there had been any clash 'between views touching on essentials, let alone representative of distinct political platforms. Before the Central Committee session – and sporadically even now after the resolution – there were those who spoke as if advocates of two fundamental conceptions, groups representing radically different objectives from each other, were "colliding" . . . [and] referred to a clash, a battle between "reformers" and "dogmatists".'[12]

Whatever the case, those opposed to the reform were obliged to compromise. János Kádár, several times and in public, stated quite firmly: 'Our economic policy, our agricultural policy and our cultural policy are unchanged; we are maintaining our well-tried system of economic management.'[13]

So the November resolution of the Central Committee was something of a disappointment to certain opponents of the reform. At the beginning of December 1972 the *Társadalmi Szemle* put some questions to four leading party officials on 'the reception given to the highly significant declaration of the Central Committee's position'. One of the interview subjects was Pál Romány, first secretary of the Bács-Kiskun County party committee, who said:

> There are some who were expecting a 'restoration of order' of some kind . . . [and] hoped it would be confirmed that the error was only 'at the top' and . . . that the economic mechanism or perhaps the education policy were wrong . . . Such expectations were not fulfilled . . . Those constantly and exclusively urging forcefulness, those voicing pseudo-radical opinions, craved that our party might retract.[14]

The first secretary of the party committee in Budapest's Thirteenth District saw things similarly: 'There were those who expected the session to verify their opinion that the system of economic management had failed and our policy had been erroneous.'[15]

The journal returned to these questions later, stressing in an editorial: 'So, the "left-wing" seekers after self-justification are making the wrong calculations . . . Our party has blocked for good and all the road back towards sectarian, dogmatic policy and methods.'[16]

Although the attempt to question the fundamental institutions of the 1968 reform – the abolition of the command economy, the market orientation of companies and the use of economic regulators as the basic means of state control and influence over the economy – was a failure, highly important decisions of principle on recentralization and a conscious turning back were made in the guise of corrections to the reform. One of the major policy changes was to propose that the economic authorities 'should examine in particular and follow attentively the activity of the forty to fifty largest state companies which account for a significant proportion of the country's industrial production, and where necessary take special measures to ensure them the conditions required for proper working'.[17]

Indeed in 1973 the government did order direct, central supervision of the fifty largest industrial companies (representing 60 per cent of industrial fixed assets, half of production, over 60 per cent of exports, and employment for 700,000 people). Formally, the largely indirect, market-related system of managing the economy remained in force, but major elements of a command economy began to creep back informally into the mechanism. This shows up clearly in some statements made by the secretary of the Budapest party committee in the *Népszabadság* in December:

> For us the political purpose of the [Central Committee] resolution is the prime factor. And this is nothing other than a consistent application of our workers' policy . . .
>
> An opportunity has opened up for the organizations of economic management to receive direct, authentic information on the activity, economic position and production, investment and business policy of these [fifty] companies. In possession of this they are able to monitor more effectively whether the activity and motivating interests of the most important large industrial companies comply with the interests of the national economy, the objectives of the national economic plan and the requirements of our party's economic policy. Moreover, they are now able to provide assistance in good time in coping with unexpected problems encountered by these companies . . .
>
> The sectoral ministers are mainly responsible . . . for implementing the decision. They . . . report on the companies' activities . . . to the Council of Ministers.
>
> I should like to mention as an example that the investment concepts of these companies for the years 1976–80 will also be discussed separately by the supervisory bodies concerned early next year.[18]

The Central Committee had also called on the government to draw up 'an amendment to the economic regulators that provide for the planned development of the national economy'.[19]

The preparations for modifying the regulators began immediately and from January 1976 onwards new measures actually came into force. While making some genuine corrections and repairs to the mechanism, they also embraced a recentralization process. There was a 5 per cent rise in the proportion of corporate net income that was centrally appropriated. Ottó Gadó explained in a book published at this time: 'A degree of centralization of decisions and financing can be expected during the period of the [1976–80] plan. The large, so-called development-credit investments previously planned and financed as company investments have now come under the central, state sphere of decisions.' Moreover, the 'informal' central interventions became institutionalized, since it was stated, as a reinforcement of the role of the supervisory organizations, that 'the ministries will give an opinion and consult on the major company investment decisions'. These ministerial 'planning panels' were among the quasi-institutional methods of direct intervention. Indirectly, the leeway available to companies was reduced by cutting import subsidies and increasing payroll taxes, causing company profits to fall by 30 to 50 per cent. Lip-service was still paid to efforts to combat 'egalitarianism', but the new regulations placed strict limits on the incentive benefits companies could pay their employees: these (including profit shares) were not to exceed 20 per cent of the wage bill in the preceding year. At the same time, the tax on company profit-sharing funds was set at 800 per cent in the uppermost bracket, so that 'formation of a profit-sharing fund in excess of forty days' wages [per employee] would lead to the total elimination of investment opportunities'. The new tax system radically levelled off the rates of profit-sharing, so that the actual differences from company to company could vary only between 15–18 and 36–42 days' wages. At the same time, a new linear tax on increases in the average wage a company was paying imposed a rate of 600 per cent if the average wage rise was over 6 per cent. 'This system also . . . "levels off" and reduces dispersal', Gadó said, summing up his presentation of the new system of regulators, and conceding that 'this makes the distortion of wage relations inevitable . . . [and] admittedly limits incentive to some extent.' Since many of the achievements of the reform were blunted or set aside, it became possible to say plainly again that 'ministers may avail themselves of their rights of command defined legislatively in relation to state companies in cases where specific objectives of the national economic plan cannot be adequately applied through the system of regulators and to do so is justified from the point of view of asserting the national economic interest'.[20]

So the corrections gave plenty of scope for direct state intervention and curtailment of company autonomy. In the autumn of 1975 Árpád Pullai had also emphasized strongly the importance of party control:

> There have emerged . . . views and positions that may not in so many words have cast doubt on the leading role of the party, but if they were applied that role would be relegated. For instance, some were of the opinion at the time the economic reform was introduced that the regulators would, so to speak, direct the economy automatically in the direction of socialism. As a result of the mistaken views and certain erroneous measures, the leading role of the party in several areas of economic life, in factories, companies and cooperatives, became temporarily uncertain. We too committed the mistake at the

> time the reform of economic management was introduced of saying more about what party organizations should *not* interfere in and less about what they should do.[21]

Passions were aroused on the issue. As a newspaper report on a party meeting in Budapest's Thirteenth District (Angyalföld) in February 1975 commented:

> It is hard to convey the atmosphere and mood at the . . . meeting in words. What was at issue was made plain mainly by the secretaries of the party committees at Angyalföld's two largest, so-called priority companies: *the Hungarian Shipyard and Crane Factory and Láng Engineering Works.* Both criticized sharply in their contributions the practice of certain state bodies, which is to base the management of the socialist economy unilaterally on the automatic workings of various regulators and to consider the direct methods of management to be outmoded in the intensive stage of economic development. This practice has given rise in the last few years to several economic decisions in the reaching of which the political consequences of them have patently not been taken into account. In this way the collective [i.e. workforces] of large companies of first-rank importance to the national economy have been placed in an extremely difficult position.

The speakers at the meeting harked back to the revolutionary slogans of the workers and described the two factories as bastions of the revolutionary working class. It was in the most conservative terms of defending vested interests that they voiced their objections to the efforts at changing the structure of production. In the decisions, which they saw as bringing their companies on 'hard times' and threatening their livelihoods, they discerned a conspiracy against the workers. 'We can thank the November 1972 resolution of the party's Central Committee for the fact that this did not succeed.'[22]

But defence of the great state-owned 'bastions of the working class' did not feature among the arguments for intervention merely at local party or union level. As secretary Béla Biszku told the Eleventh Congress of the party in April 1975: 'Development of the large state factories is not simply an economic issue, it is an important constituent of our party policy . . . Thereby we are also doing good service in strengthening the class basis of the society building socialism.'[23]

That same summer a newspaper article on how party control over large factories was going reported a favourable change since the previous year: 'Some company managers thought then it would be enough for the party organization to agitate on behalf of the objectives put forward and the accomplishment of them, and the rest, so to speak, was the management's affair . . . The party secretary could easily be rebuked for "unauthorized interference" . . . These days it is a rare occurrence for some manager or other to cast doubt on the right of the party organization.'[24] In the same month the *Társadalmi Szemle* published Károly Földes's view:

> We should be discrediting the very notion of indirect regulation if we took a correct idea to extremes and sought to use it to solve everything. Planned economic management . . . also involves direct means of attaining the set objectives. Direct control of some of the processes actually taking place is applied on the basis of the national economic plan, through indicators prescribing the fulfilment of certain production programmes via state investment projects, by the expression of 'expectations' and the setting of quotas, and in other forms.[25]

One could hardly have declared more openly in favour of restoring the command economy than Central Committee secretary Árpád Pullai did in a speech to Parliament in December 1972:

> We shall continue to ensure corporate autonomy. However, every company, even the biggest, has a part in our economic processes. They are autonomous, but not independent of what goes on in the country's economy from time to time. The ministries concerned should not leave these companies to their own tasks and problems to the extent they have done in recent years. *Every large company has a responsibility for its economic performance. But every ministry likewise has a responsibility for the work and development of the production units that belong under it.*
>
> Planning involves every competent body and person in coming forward and acting with expertise and decisiveness whenever a divergence from the valid plan arises, whether in the case of a ministry, a company or a plant. If operational willingness to act and step forward serves the purposes of the plan it is not artificial 'outside' interference . . . but a part and a tool of normal activity.[26]

As an almost symbolic step to strengthen central control, the government in 1973 set up the State Planning Committee, supposedly to reinforce the significance and effectiveness of planning.[27] Equally symbolic was the raising of the National Planning Office's status and the promotion of its president to the rank of Deputy Prime Minister. At the same time, a Department of Industry, Agriculture and Transport was set up within the apparatus of the party Central Committee, alongside the existing Department of Economic Policy, as an expression of the aim of tightening the party's direct hold on what was going on in the economy. The November 1972 session of the Central Committee also saw a justification for making certain changes in price policy. Though the reform principles were still emphasized, it was stated that 'the stability of prices must be maximally ensured . . . Price monitoring . . . must be broadened and toughened. The obligation to report price changes must be extended . . . The proportion of set prices in the construction industry must increase from the present 60 per cent to 90 per cent.'[28] The result, when coupled with the greater fluctuations of world-market prices after late 1973, was the collapse of the 1968 price system. As Finance Minister Lajos Faluvégi wrote in the late summer of 1973, 'the flexibility of producer prices has diminished markedly . . . Once more, profit does not express realistically a company's actual efficiency, since the prices and costs are not real either. The support element in prices is large . . . The sums spent on support account for almost 30 per cent of budgetary expenditure; over half of the aggregate company profits derive from support.'[29]

Much of the brunt of the criticism of the reform was borne by peasant wealth and a perceived brazen assertion of 'agricultural cooperative group interest' at the expense of 'the overall interest of society'. The cause of the workers was proclaimed as calls for limiting income from household farming and farms' industrial sideline activity came to the fore. In general terms of ideological intent, the purpose was to eradicate the characteristically Hungarian cooperative model that had arisen out of the reform process and re-establish the classic *kolkhoz* type of Soviet model. As in industry, state intervention was to intensify, and accordingly, local councils received greater powers to intervene directly in the affairs of the ostensibly autonomous, self-managing cooperative farms. In June 1976 the central party authorities declared concerning the previous few years that 'the need to assert the will of the state more powerfully has given councils far more tasks in the direction of production which have not been laid down in legal regulations (assistance in executing priority agricultural programmes – for cattle, sugar beet, vegetables – and specialization and mergers).'[30]

It is particularly worth noting in this resolution the reference to a return to informal, non-institutional intervention by the central authorities, to an informal recentralization that was all too easy to accomplish under the socio-political structure of that time. Particular pressure to do this was applied by the campaigns to weed out profiteering and abuses.

None the less, it must be stressed once again that there were a great many justifications to be found for such a policy: the appeal of opportunities that seemed suddenly to arise was coupled with an uncertainty about how long the chances for entrepreneurship would last. So safe, long-term business policy was pushed out by speculation.

Not least, the very complexity and restrictiveness of the legal regulations put almost every kind of economic activity on the brink of violating the law. The purification campaign that developed uncovered a great many *real* abuses, but the way matters were handled, made public, manipulated and clothed with ideological and political implications along with the practical signs that the reform mechanism needed correcting, created a climate of opinion favouring a return to the Soviet model. In February 1973 the party daily paper *Népszabadság* began a series of articles entitled 'Investigation into Price Matters', in which the reporters sniffed out unjustified price rises. In connection with one case, the reporter asked the party secretary at the cooperative farm which had increased the price of a plastic shopping bag whether it had really been justifiable to do so, or to do so to such a degree. The secretary, whose full name was given, replied that 'he was primarily concerned with the problems of the cooperative. In other words, the group interests', the reporter added.[31] In another article a few weeks earlier – 'Illegal Profit ; Lawful Downfall' – the reporter had presented the case of an ostensibly official private venture with a new fodder concentrate, Univerz 1, which was a conspicuous case of price hiking.[32]

The papers were inundated with similar stories, and a year later were able to report proudly that the number of detected crimes against public property had dropped from 34,000 in 1972 to 29,000 in 1973.[33] A good example was a case reported in December 1973 of a private driving school. In the autumn of 1972 there had been an article reporting that the public sector was unable to meet the demand for driving lessons as the number of private cars rose sharply: people were queuing up at the driving schools. The only solution, it was concluded then, was to set up some private ones. 'Well, since then the private schools have burgeoned. But in the meantime they have earned none too good a reputation: the notice *"Closed on Account of Fraud" has been symbolically pinned on the door of two Budapest schools, and the "official liquidation" of a third has begun.'* (All three charged more than the official rate for tuition and fiddled their books, the extra fee usually being collected directly by the instructor with no receipt given, the paper said.) The report went on to say that those who had already read accounts of such crimes, heard something about the fledgling private driving-school business or perhaps even had some personal experience of it, might easily feel the Ministry of Transport had *'released a dangerous genie from the bottle* when it provided a legal opportunity for private driving schools to be set up in 1971'.[34] Of course it was added that there was no need to eliminate the form, only to tighten up supervision and stamp out abuses, but the press campaign contributed to creating a climate of public uncertainty, even though it treated the specific instances quite correctly. This was particularly true in the case of the cooperative and state farms, where cases of 'irregularities' were publicized frequently. Indeed, preparation of lawsuits was begun against the managing directors and chairmen of state and cooperative farms for alleged abuses. So the press campaign did more than uncover abuses, it helped to elicit measures against private enterprise and engender intense hostility to an autonomous and flexible business spirit as such.

It need not be emphasized that the individual articles may have been correct and objective in themselves; they could speak about real abuses, since there were plenty. But the press campaign – in which every newspaper participated – wanted to prove, tendentiously, that the small ventures, the complementary workshops of cooperatives and household-plot farming were hotbeds of abuses. At the same time, the indignation of the press almost completely bypassed the abuses of power, committed regularly, the abuses of position and the profiteering. And, as fully as it scourged the 'excesses' of the reform, equally it failed to mention the uncompleted state of the reform and the conflicts deriving from it.

The weapons for restriction were actually provided by legal regulation, price policy, taxation and similar instruments, of which the state amply availed itself in 1974–5. The restrictions and the public unease arising out of the campaign precipitated a sudden halt in the rise of production on household farms. In 1967 household farms had sold 220,000 pigs; in 1974 the figure was 2.4 million. In other words, the number of pigs on household farms had multiplied by more than ten after the reform. But in the summer of 1975 the *Népszabadság* published surprising news:

> [The figures] do not, however, mean that all is well in household farming. There are cooperative chairmen who say the household farms lure the members away from the collective task, and so these chairmen *do not sufficiently encourage* household production . . .
>
> The problems that can arise . . . are shown precisely by the change that happened last year in pig-breeding. For last year there came an end to a fine, steady, upward trend in household farming, best exemplified by the fact that in the second half of 1974 the stock of sows on household and auxiliary farms fell from 417,000 to about 290,000 head.
>
> The basic reasons are known. A part was played, for instance, by a

> relatively high fodder price, disruptions in supplies of feed, a fall in the price of piglets and young fatstock . . . A number of rumours spread, and the combined effect was to dampen the ardour to produce.[35]

From the newspaper article it becomes clear that the stock of sows on household farms in 1974 had *fallen by no less than a quarter*. Nor is the hesitant explanation very convincing. Far more is revealed by another report in the same paper a few weeks later ('Is the Past Returning?'):

> The subject that has been stirring up controversy for some time in the village . . . is progressive taxation. Let us look at this, too.
>
> *Zoltán Szél and family* have created a fine little world for themselves. A mechanized home, mechanized farming . . . a horse, two cows, a moped, a Polski [car]. Behind the fine things lie a decade of drudgery. Zoltán Szél's double life: both as a haulier and a farmer; his wife ploughed until midnight and he after midnight . . . but it means suffering and torture even when a person's gripped not by the throat but by the chest or the head by something.
>
> 'Like this special tax now. I'm not going to work just to pay most of it back in taxes', he says with quiet determination. A few days earlier his wife had left her downy bed to spend three nights sleeping in the sty: and the sow did not crush one skull among her twelve piglets! Last year they raised that number of pigs and two calves; now they are giving it up. (Could similar decisions have played a part in the fact that the number of sows dropped by 30 per cent in the Szeged district last year?)
>
> In Zákányszék there were thirteen payers of the special tax in 1973. Last year it was found that on fifty-one farms the annual net income of 50,000 forints had been overstepped. What an upheaval! . . .
>
> It's a hard story, Could the world be such that the past might simply be brought back by any kind of measure? But people say this is like the *kulak* list used to be: 1. It is just as before except that the limit is not 25 *hold* [about 14 ha] but 50,000 forints . . .
>
> So Zoltán Szél is stepping out of the ranks of the special taxpayers . . . He will not work fourteen hours a day any more, he will have more time for the choir, the theatre and other things. From the cultural side that is certainly a good thing. From the supply side, I doubt it.[36]

In fact the tone taken by the press changed a great deal in the summer of 1975, due to the reaction of the pig breeders and the prospect of a sudden shortage of meat. From our point of view the facts recorded are the important thing.

The ideological basis for the measures against household farming and the auxiliary activities of the cooperative farms was the belief that the socialist production relations had to be reinforced and reappearances of capitalist behaviour had to be nipped in the bud. One of the great advocates of this was Béla Biszku, who ranked second in the party hierarchy. He devoted a lecture to it at the national agitation and propaganda meeting in Balatonaliga in September 1975. His point of departure was the public nature of *state ownership* and its declaration as '*the more advanced form of socialist ownership*': 'State ownership is ownership by the general public because it is not ownership by one group, one stratum or one social class but ownership by a whole people . . . It serves the interests of the whole society because the fruits of it are enjoyed not by one group or stratum but by the whole society.' So it '*can be regarded as a higher degree of socialization*'.[37] It is worth noting that even at this starting-point for the presentation of his ideas Biszku was already at variance with the conclusion of the introductory historical survey to his lecture. As he rightly declared at the beginning, the achievements of Hungarian farming were inseparable from the clarification after 1956 of 'the most important issues of principle and theory concerning cooperative ownership'. He quite rightly pointed out: 'We must cleanse our theories of the distortions which mainly accumulated in the early 1950s. One such distortion was to consider cooperative ownership . . . as an inferior form of socialist ownership', a false tenet that was then 'taken to extremes in practice'.[38]

Biszku seems to have forgotten about this almost as soon as he said it, because he went on to take up a position practically indistinguishable from this very distortion. Paying little regard to reality, he argued against those who spoke of the 'advantages of cooperative ownership over state ownership' and of its greater mobility and flexibility of functioning. 'Certain economists', he complained, '. . . tried to prove that cooperative ownership was the more effective, saying that better economic use was made of the means and labour there than in state plants . . . From this apparent "superiority" they . . . drew the conclusion that cooperative ownership is "more democratic" and "more social" than state ownership.' As a counter-argument Biszku was content to say: 'We are concerned not with a form of ownership, but with the real or imaginary advantages of a form of economic activity', that 'precisely owing to the group ownership character of cooperative ownership [the inputs] are exploited less for the benefit of the whole society . . . than for that of the group.'[39] Turning to the future path of development of the cooperatives, he saw it to lie in an 'intensification of the socialization of labour', the leading of them towards 'steady higher forms', and a 'strengthening of the socialist traits in the cooperatives'.

What Biszku actually meant in practice emerges in the subsequent theoretical expatiation: '*We cannot regard the household farm as a socialist farm.*' He took issue with those whose conclusion from the fact 'that the household farms of cooperative members in this country are becoming tied more and more closely to the collective farms' was that 'these are "social smallholdings". This is nonsense. Household farms are not public property . . . the income is the members', not the cooperative community's.' Although Biszku emphasized that support should continue to be given to household farming, his point of departure – ownership relations – and his designation of stronger socialist traits in the cooperatives as the central task made his ultimate political goals quite plain.

The other major issue concerning 'the strengthening of the socialist traits' was restriction of industrial side activities pursued by cooperative farms. 'By the early 1970s this activity . . . began to produce numerous negative tendencies as well', according to Biszku, including 'a negative process from the point of view of ownership relations. In the cooperatives where such side activity assumed significant proportions, substantial surplus income was received.' Biszku spoke at length about fourteen cooperative farms in the Budapest area whose situation had been analysed by the Political Committee. In them, only 20 per cent of income was originating from agricultural activity, and although their various industrial activities

> met important demand from the national economy and in part from the general public, *they in fact diverted several thousand former workers in large companies from the Budapest factories* . . . The auxiliary plants . . . were able to offer substantially higher personal incomes than those of the workers in large companies. These incomes, which . . . are based on the cooperatives' business profits, cannot be regarded as socialist distribution according to work [performed] . . . The regulations and regulators must be adjusted, so that phenomena such as this should be forced back instead of spreading further.

As ideological aspects came to the fore, the ground was laid for a policy of practical restrictions. As a result of the measures following the autumn 1972 resolutions, it was possible for the party to state in the spring of 1973, with a degree of satisfaction, that 'the auxiliary industrial and commercial activity of the cooperative farms is moving in the direction indicated by [them] . . . and the unfavourable accompaniments have been confined'.[40]

The *Népszabadság* devoted another leading article to the need to curtail the cooperatives' side activities in the summer of 1973. A number of activities out of line with the statutes of cooperatives were discovered, it said, when the county people's control committees were looking into them:

> The machinery maintenance associations [run jointly by a group of farms] have begun to look out for other business partners so as to make full use of their capacity. These days they are undertaking a wider and wider range of industrial, personal and commercial services that *not infrequently conflict with the purposes laid down in their founding charter*.
>
> A similar situation is beginning to emerge in the construction associations. Often these no longer serve their original purpose . . . of meeting the building institutions and private individuals . . . It is in the public interest that the specialized agencies exercising administrative control over these associations should everywhere require them to *operate in conformity with the regulations* and not allow any departure from this anywhere.[41]

Ultimately, the limits, restrictions and closer supervision introduced to curb the 'excesses' were aimed at reinforcing the 'socialist traits' of the cooperative farms. Biszku had a kind of institutional convergence in mind, which would 'bring state and cooperative ownership closer together and subsequently develop a homogeneous communist public ownership out of the merger of the two'. But he made plain which form the converging was to take: it was to be 'not a mutual convergence but a development of cooperative ownership towards a higher level of socialization'. He mentioned the agrarian industrial association formed in the Soviet Union: 'Under *sovkhoz* supervision, the *kolkhozes* . . . have formed associations on a larger scale.' He plainly stated that 'the establishment of up-to-date, homogeneous, large-unit farms' was the direction for the 'further development' of the cooperatives. Based on this principle, he considered it necessary to merge the cooperative farms and form units as large as possible.[42]

These principles were accepted by most of the party's leaders, and the eleventh Congress of the Hungarian Socialist Workers' Party in the spring of 1975 stated in a resolution: 'We should continue our agricultural policy, further strengthen the socialist character of the production cooperatives in agriculture . . . [and] continue the rational amalgamation of the agricultural cooperatives.'[43]

Another important ideological weapon, alongside the emphasis on stronger central planning and a 'higher level' of socialist ownership relations, was the call to reinforce and restore the 'system of socialist distribution', which included the objective of raising the incomes of the workers to a greater extent while imposing stronger controls and restrictions on the incomes of the peasantry and the intelligentsia. Particular targets were 'undeserved incomes [and] opportunities seized for profiteering and hoarding', as well as a 'just, general and equitable distribution of the tax burden'. The trade unions put great emphasis on the representation of workers' interests. This activity of theirs extended to both the 'defence of big companies' and the raising of the wage level. This programme, too, won the support of most party leaders.

The November 1972 resolution had already proposed steps to check the income differences which had widened since the reform:

> Of the main classes and strata of the employed, it is in general the workers and in particular the workers in the large-scale industrial companies whose incomes have risen to a relatively lesser extent . . . From March 1, 1973, the wages of workers and foremen in state industry must be raised by an average of 8 per cent . . . through a central wage measure.
>
> To achieve a more equitable distribution of the tax burden, we must . . . examine as the next step the possibilities of devising and introducing a suitable comprehensive taxation system to cover income not deriving from work (inheritance, gifts, etc.) and also chattels and real estate.[44]

Inheritance and gift taxes were indeed increased substantially in 1973, and the property tax on second homes with more than two rooms was raised by 50 per cent. On family houses worth more than 800,000 forints and holiday homes worth more than half a million forints, the existing property tax was joined by a tax on the value of the house. A stiff graduated tax was imposed on sales of real estate. The taxes on secondary earnings and on certain property like private cars were increased as well.

Béla Biszku reiterated the objectives in April 1975:

> Incomes must be so regulated that they do not build up to an unjustified size . . . The sources [of income] that fuel these non-socialist tendencies must be restricted and then blocked. Concurrently with this, the social recognition accorded to work must be raised . . . We must devote ourselves more seriously to restricting the possibilities of earning easy money. We cannot turn a blind eye to the fact that . . a not inconsiderable proportion of young people . . . prefer careers that offer quick and easy affluence to the creative joy of work . . . The non-socialist features in society's thinking have become stronger.[45]

Back in January 1973, the party's periodical, the *Társadalmi Szemle*, had already seen a need for a debate in the spirit of the 'two-front' efforts, lest all the negative phenomena in society be laid at the door of reform: 'Many take the view that self-centredness, the materialistic spirit, did not exist before or influenced a far smaller sphere.' Two years later the editor-in-chief was using a similar argument:

> Why don't we abolish the group interests? I was asked in one place, and in another: 'Why did the group interests have to be brought in?' . . . We did not invent the group interests, we did not introduce them, and they are not merely . . . the concomitant of company independence either . . . We . . . are not fighting against [particular] occupations and sectors but against profiteering and hoarding, and large incomes not procured by work or disproportionate to the social usefulness of the work involved.[46]

But in the mean time Biszku had shifted his emphasis, writing in the spring of 1974: 'One must mention first and foremost as a deciding, characteristic feature that the policy of the party is a *worker policy*.' On that basis he regarded it as justified to restrict peasant and private-sector income when it derived, for instance in the case of the industrial side activities of the cooperative farms, from 'the exploitation of the market growth to an undesirable extent'. The same went for the private sector, which was 'still capable today of satisfying certain social needs more flexibly than large-scale industry and state and cooperative trading. So a proportion of those working in the private sector earn more than the value of their actual work. We shall also limit unjustifiably high incomes by administrative means.'[47]

Here and in the foregoing I have frequently quoted some characteristic personalities in the party leadership who played undeniable leading roles in the turn presented. Of course, this does not at all mean that the doctrinaire views quoted – the policy not dispensing with elements of truth, yet serving the conservative restriction of reform – was represented by them alone. Several other members of the political leadership might be quoted since the centre of the party leadership who had earlier taken the side of reform accepted these views – even if with obvious reservations and abiding by the basic reform achievements. This is also reflected by the resolutions of the Political Committee, the Central Committee and the congress, and this was echoed by the press, too.

In the mean time advocacy of worker policy had inspired a resolution from the Political Committee on the party's social composition and cadre policy. This pointed out that the problems which sometimes 'emerged during the implementation of the party's policy . . . obstruct the approach of the manual workers closer to the party . . . The demand for higher standards of professional expertise and management is accompanied in some places by an ascription of greater importance than appropriate to the intelligentsia and those in various leading positions belonging to the party.'[48] A veritable crusade was launched to promote workers quickly to managerial and professional posts, by side-stepping the established institutional paths for this, for instance through the education system. In 1973 the measures which had abolished a decade earlier the discrimination against youth who did not have a worker or peasant background with the idea of promoting social unity were partially reversed again. The university entrance system was revised to give preference to the children of manual workers. After a one-year preparatory course, some 200 to 300 young workers a year were admitted to universities without secondary school-leaving certificates.[49] In March 1974 the Central Committee stated: 'The party regards it as a political issue of principle for the children of manual workers and peasants to be given special support in education and further education.'[50]

Various management training courses were organized centrally. The Fejér County party committee's courses were 'primarily to ensure the training of a new generation of cadres'. In March 1974 the Central Council of Hungarian Trade Unions ran five-month residential training courses for worker cadres. The Communist Youth League ran similar courses, beginning in 1976. The Central Committee Secretariat, examining the matter on February 2, 1976, 'came to the conclusion that the majority of initiatives allow the number of manual workers who become managers to increase in a relatively short space of time'.[51]

The expertise and professional knowledge which had so often been stressed and valued more highly after the reform now came under suspicion. In the wake of those earlier managers who had been largely unprepared for their tasks and appointed primarily on a political basis came a new wave of political appointees. In a comment on the government resolution concerning the political extension training of managers, the *Népszabadság* noted: 'According to the resolution, the proportion of teaching time devoted to political studies must be significantly increased . . . *One of the commonest mistakes is to place qualifications and professional talent in first place* and give assessment of political preparedness and suitability a second or third place in the selection of managers.'[52] These were plain words, and the typical process of local 'overfulfilment' duly ensued, with large numbers of manual workers, especially those on company party committees, being appointed to leading managerial positions. Even the party's central daily had to object in the summer of 1975. An article entitled 'Without Haste' began thus:

> One of the district party committees in the capital examined how the new manual workers on party committees are helping in the factories. It turned out that over the past few months several dozen of these committee members had been appointed to managerial positions; indeed there were factories where almost all of them had been promoted . . . The large number of workers promoted with such haste lend credence to the assumption that many had received the honour unexpectedly, and above all unprepared . . .[53]

The reform process was seen as causing the spread of bourgeois attitudes and habits. To combat this and promote a 'genuine worker policy', the party daily published in its 'Forum' column in the spring of 1973 a discussion of the relationship between the proletariat and the intelligentsia. The author of the article, putting things 'as we workers see them', pointed to 'tension between the intelligentsia and other working strata. And this . . . could slowly degenerate into a serious conflict . . . As the workers see it . . . *our intelligentsia is overvalued both financially and morally*. At the same time, workers are held in a very great deal less esteem by society.' If the intelligentsia thought the wages for hard manual work were excessively high, they should go and work there themselves. ('And they talk of those who have done so already, but "quickly escaped back".') Doctors were upbraided for despising their patients and acting quite differently in their private surgeries. He went on to note that the form of address '*úr*' (sir) was being 'smuggled back'. (It had been replaced by expressions like comrade, colleague and other, partly newly created terms in the early 1950s.) The aim of this, the writer said, was to 'distinguish', and 'these gentlemen [*urak*] begin to feel themselves to be gentlemen in the old sense'.[54] One contributor to the discussion took the argument further: 'It follows from the nature of socialism that the leading class, in other words the proletariat, must be provided for . . . We have not devoted adequate attention to this precept in the last few years . . . That is how so many clear grievances, which the manual worker has suffered at the hands of the intelligentsia, still surface even today.'[55]

The emphasis placed in various forms and by various means on 'worker policy' also gave rise to direct administrative measures of ideological struggle. The objectives announced in November 1972 were taken as a starting-point for propaganda warfare against 'burgeoning bourgeois-cum-petty bourgeois' views 'alien to socialism'. The cultural policy group at the party Central Committee came out against 'the anti-Marxist views of certain social scientists',[56] and a purge in the field of sociology followed soon after.

In March 1975 the Eleventh Congress of the Hungarian Socialist Workers' Party summed up the main ambitions behind the political line that was emerging: 'Our state is the main instrument for socialist construction . . . The role of our socialist state in the development of the national economy is increasing . . . Because of the growing requirements, central control must be made more effective.' Elsewhere it was declared that 'the public interest is decisive [and] group and individual interests must ultimately be subordinated to it. We must take action against an interpretation of individual or group interest that is detrimental to the community and the country.' The congress 'concludes that the assertion of socialist planning must be considered the fundamental task in the development of the national economy'. One can also pick out from the key phrases and statements in the resolution that the Eleventh Congress stated the need 'to prevent disproportions that give rise to social tensions. In doing this great scope must be provided for central wage measures.' This was to be underpinned by ideological work: 'Our socialist perspectives must be outlined more clearly, the superiority of the socialist way of life over the capitalist one must be demonstrated', wherefore a struggle was to be waged against 'various bourgeois and petty bourgeois views and attitudes which retard development'.[57]

A massive campaign was launched against 'wanton consumption', and wide-ranging debates broke out on the need to 'devise a socialist model of consumption and way of life'. An excellent account of these debates appeared in the summer of 1975 in the *Társadalmi Szemle*. Remnants of the earlier, 'ascetic' outlooks that emphasized 'limits on consumption . . . devoted work and willingness to make sacrifice . . . survive', according to the journal, and are often seen as 'socialist principles': 'Over the last ten years, when supply levels and [personal] consumption have significantly increased, uncertainty about consumption . . . has constantly appeared' in the form of 'protests in the name of socialist values against the so-called bourgeois and petty bourgeois tendencies manifest in consumption.' It noted that 'the appearance and spread of certain new needs is presented as imitation of the capitalist model of consumption', producing a demand 'that we should devise a socialist model of consumption. There are those who believe this to be among the most important tasks.' The writer notes a 'presupposition that the elaboration of the "consumption model" is a task for theory; theory is capable of resolving such a task by relying on the values of socialism (equality, collectivism, etc.) which have emerged historically.' If such a model or system of values is lacking or is not transmitted to the masses through ideological and cultural impact or education, the result will be, as living standards rise, that only 'the material needs will increase, [only] the possessive mentality tied to material goods grow stronger . . . the so-called consumerist outlook and behaviour gain ground . . . in which lie the root of several negative phenomena of which much is said nowadays and which are often described as a "petty bourgeois" tendency.'[58]

For months and years the newspapers and periodicals had been inundated with contributions chastising petty bourgeois, materialistic behaviour. In December 1972 one could read:

> There is no doubt that the reform of economic management has opened new paths to opportunities for personal prosperity. In general they are of a kind that have offered an occasion in keeping with the greater interests of society and the goals of socialism. But complex and indirect influences have also opened up paths by which materialism and petty bourgeois selfishness have begun to enter our society in greater strength.[59]

A few days later the secretary of the Békés County party committee mentioned in an interview the case of a profiteering cooperative director who had now received his deserts: 'But we must also draw farther-reaching conclusions from the case. This is how I put the question: Does the chance of money, of a bigger income, always tend in the direction of socialism?'[60]

In October 1973 the author of an article exposing the case of a corrupt business manager asked how someone could have been led into dishonesty having 'survived difficult, critical situations hundreds and hundreds of times without having his political conviction or loyalty to the party shaken for one moment?'. The reason, we are told, was simply

> the acquisitive urge which has the effect at a certain point of a drug: it not only intoxicates you, it actually lures you away from yourself. Could someone in their right mind sacrifice his past, his whole career in life, his decency and his honour for a few fashionable rags or even a fairy castle of a private home?
>
> No, this is a sickness. It is like an insidious fever that slowly, almost imperceptibly gains power over the body and ruthlessly devours the very last remnants of stamina.[61]

In the summer of 1973 'petty bourgeois' behaviour was the subject of a long debate in the *Népszabadság*. Contributors resorted to scientific arguments, philosophical or historical explanations and personal examples to back up their views. A letter from a worker at one of the Ocsárd cooperative farm's timber yards was published on July 25:

> There have been lively debates where I work as well about petty bourgeois behaviour. Some call it a right-wing outlook, while others say 'leftism' conceals a petty bourgeois outlook too. They also say the petty bourgeois elements are middle-of-the-roaders . . .
>
> I think we shall be closer to understanding it if *we contrast with the fundamental traits of the petty bourgeois those of the class-conscious workers in large-scale industry* . . . Briefly . . . the basic characteristics of the petty bourgeois are: *vacillation*: he always inclines towards the class in the more powerful position; *indolence*: in everyday life he always prefers the easiest possible ways; *distrust*: since his personal aspirations are directed at exploiting others, he assumes this of others as well; *selfishness*: his mental ideal is the capitalist bourgeois, and so he is selfish and inclined to hoard; *inwardness*: he is disinclined to do a collective task from which he gains no direct advantage; *imitation*: he imitates the old ruling classes.[62]

Not only petty bourgeois behaviour but petty bourgeois ideology came under fire. Géza Ripp gave a rather broad interpretation of this: '*Petty bourgeois ideology . . . is as manifest in the theoretical justification of the petty bourgeois attitude as in seemingly extremely radical criticism of it.*'[63]

In an editorial summary of this debate that sought to preserve a balance, there was a mention of the 'challenge of the living standard' which arose out of the conflict between material increase and a human awareness that lagged behind it: 'Thanks to socialism, we have essentially, if not wholly, extricated ourselves from poverty. Now we must learn (or rather everybody must be taught) to live in a new way, a socialist way!'[64] Once again the debates were centring on how to educate people to make healthy use of possessions, to follow a structure of consumption characteristic of socialism and to live their lives after a socialist pattern.

During the same campaign came a powerful offensive against the promotion of 'group interest' over the interests of the national economy. László Szabó wrote that in some cases even local party organizations were failing to take action against unjustified price increases by companies, even though 'it is absolutely impermissible to allow oneself to be under the thumb of the supporters of local, group interests at the expense of broader, social interests'.[65]

The weapons of persuasion, education, discipline and threats were used to convince company and cooperative executives to work for the perceived common good instead of their company's. An editorial in the *Népszabadság* argued:

> This must be emphasized very strongly in the present situation, because there are managers at various levels who cannot or will not understand: they make the group interest absolute and prefer it over the overall interests of society, and in practice this often means they violate the laws and twist the regulations. *Their own* company, *their own* sector, *their own* field or organization is their 'god'; they 'rope in' their influence, authority, connections and everything to assert the interests of the sphere under their control; some so abuse their power as even to interfere in the work of other organizations, not even shrinking from corruption and fraud, etc.[66]

Three weeks later the paper wrote:

> We are talking of those who refer to their honest intentions and selflessness when it emerges that their measures and manoeuvres violate the principles and rules of our socialist economy . . . They insist that no unlawful advantage remained in their hands, they were motivated solely by a wish to serve the interests of the group they belong to more effectively.

The paper's solution was to put forward a hierarchy of values:

> It is a fact that a variety of interests exist and exert a mutual influence in our society. The individual interest of a single person, the group or local interest of a state company, institution or cooperative and the overall interest of the people that embraces them and points far beyond them can all provide a momentum, but clearly not to the same degree. All these indisputably conflict with each other from time to time and from case to case: they seek a standing, a supremacy at the expense of the other interests. In this situation the only way out is consistently to give the green light to the interest of society.[67]

Of course the tensions and conflicts were approached in many different ways, and the discussion did not remain at the level of surface symptoms, evil human characteristics or chastisement of natural interests. It is worth quoting at greater length a 1974 article in the *Társadalmi Szemle*, the party's theoretical journal. Author Lenke Bizám observed the general line in the campaign against the petty bourgeois mentality of attacking the acquisitive instinct: 'a curious voraciousness, a constant yearning for money, an insatiable appetite for durable and less durable consumer goods, that conspicuous trait of seeing value only in what is tangibly and directly one's own. The same can be recognized in tastes as well . . . The petty bourgeois have mere entertainment requirements instead of cultural ones.'[68]

But the author does not content herself with so superficial a critique, since her argument is that 'here we encounter the manifestations' of the petty bourgeois attitude 'to a far greater extent than the proportion of petty private property-owners would warrant'. People then resorted to original sin, bad human characteristics or 'imported' influences from the West as an explanation, which the author said was 'not only inadequate but wholly erroneous'. Instead of taking consumer or moral behaviour as her point of departure, she started out primarily from the behaviour of producers, deducing that in spite of the prevalence of collective ownership, broad strata in society were actually 'undertaking petty private ventures at "public" expense'. 'Out of the collective proprietor grows the small proprietor, as soon as . . . he comes to regard the machine, the tool, the desk . . . the area required for his work as an instrument for asserting his direct private interest and is able to use them accordingly', she wrote.

> He is the one whose direct, private interest shorts the great circuits in the social transmission of the socialist organization of production . . . In effect he moonlights instead of performing the production task he has undertaken in the socialist division of labour . . . When tools and labour are not being utilized he attends to . . . the chance of using them privately . . .

The author reached the following conclusion, therefore:

> The truly dangerous form of petty bourgeois attitude indigenous to this country is nothing other, in fact, than the way a small proprietor relates to socialist public property, something capable of influencing the reality of the building of socialism . . . to such an extent that socialist distribution, in its economic foundation, is asserted only deficiently and inadequately . . . The key word in overcoming the petty bourgeois mentality is not the deprival or limitation of goods but real respect for goods and common-ownership expansion of them.[69]

Alongside the concept of 'common ownership' arose an attempt to devise collective forms of employing leisure time. The secretary of the party committee in the city of Pécs told an interviewer:

> We have asked ourselves whether one can expect the individual who receives more free time from our state to use it in accordance with the aims of our society, in other words spend this time sensibly and usefully in a cultivated way . . . More and more people spend it tilling their plots and gardens . . . Work in the open air is both relaxing and

> very healthy . . . Still, one cannot deny that gardening isolates one from the community.

The solution: follow the pattern of the 'garden cooperative' set up at Komló where the families are working allotments still owned by the state and not fenced off from one another. 'This is now communal life', as is a do-it-yourself workshop set up by the Power Station Company, which 'means an opportunity opens up for communal life even in spare time'.[70]

A wave of rhetoric broke over the most diverse areas of social and political life. The spread of it was certainly helped along by a grain of truth in the criticism. Having become accustomed over decades to egalitarianism, the masses reacted sensitively to the growth of income differentials and social differences, particularly if big money could be earned without actually working, through palpable wheeler-dealering. Those who wanted the 'distortions of the reform' rectified were voicing a real resentment in society. Still more popular, of course, was to take practical measures: wage increases for manual workers, greater social respect, help with housing, promotions to managerial posts, etc. All these things clearly helped to forge a political alliance around these aspirations, all the more because those who supported the criticisms and initiatives were obviously, in many cases, less against the economic reform as such than in favour of curing certain undesirable side-effects of it which had so far been ignored.

However, there were quite a few who argued against a policy centred on income distribution, against a doctrinaire approach to ownership relations and against a focus on 'petty bourgeois attitudes'. They sought to defend the reform and what it had achieved. This group and their arguments will not be discussed at this point but in relation to the following years, when they were instrumental in bringing about a revival of reform.

For the fact remains that from the autumn of 1972 onwards the conservative views and groups which had been relegated into the background in the wake of reform surfaced again, and – independent of the fact that many of them were led by their concern for socialism, by the wish to eliminate repulsive social injustices and 'deformities' – brought the reform process to a halt. The 'second stage' of the reform which had been planned and prepared for introduction in the 1970s was removed from the agenda. In other words, the brakes which had been temporarily built into the reform in 1968, as guarantees of a smooth and gradual transition, were not removed after all. So the consciously created ambivalence of the reform system solidified and what had been believed to be transitory by those initiating the reform now became rigid and strengthened the contradictions; this automatically reinforced the trends towards recentralization. In the absence of a consistently normative system of regulation, the exception-riddled regulations in force so to speak reproduced the command system in other ways. What is more, the modifications to the regulators, the strengthening of direct intervention, particularly in the case of the fifty largest industrial companies, the centralization of more of the company profits and the effort to make the cooperative farms more like the traditional Soviet *kolkhoz* crippled a reform system which had already been seriously weakened by compromise.

A final contribution was made by changes in the top political leadership in 1974–5. Prominent exponents of reform – Rezső Nyers, the Central Committee secretary responsible for economic affairs, Deputy Premier Lajos Fehér, architect of the special cooperative model, Prime Minister Jenő Fock, members of the Political Committee, and Deputy Premier Mátyás Timár – were removed from their posts. György Lázár was elected Prime Minister, Károly Németh secretary of the Central Committee – responsible for economic affairs – and Ferenc Havasi was appointed Deputy Prime Minister.

Thus, between 1972 and 1975, based on the determinant role of external factors, the strong political attack of the leading group – motivated by strivings for domestic power – gave the initial push for reversal towards the Stalinist economic model. Conditions for the latter did exist, of course, in consequence of the inconsistent and interrupted reform. As stated by László Antal, the unchanged political structures secured that 'the interests attached to the reproduction of the system can assert themselves and organize themselves'.[71]

'The Hungarian reform begun in 1968 was slowed down in the early seventies' – writes László Szamuely – 'because in the power structure left unchanged – in addition to the maintenance of the earlier economic development and strategy and insistence on the petrified ideological dogmas – it could not get any further than bringing about a centralized indirect system of control and management.'[72] Accordingly, the internal causes for the reversal should be sought in what 'the reform has not done and did not intend to do'. The unchanged system of economic and political institutions and the similarly unchanged official ideology created a sort of social and political schizophrenia when the reform started. This secured the internal mechanisms for the braking of the reform, and that the transitory reform system should become 'a rigid self-sustaining system'.

21 The oil crisis and its consequences

From the turn of 1973–4 onwards the situation was exacerbated by the shocks to the world economy. The oil crisis in the autumn of 1973 had raised oil prices fivefold in a very short time. This triggered price increases in raw materials and a relative decline in the price level of industrial finished products embodying a medium level of technological input. For the Hungarian economy, very sensitive to foreign trade and dependent on foreign energy and raw materials, the consequence was serious inflationary pressures. The impact of this lasting structural crisis in the world economy was particularly hard on backward countries and those at an intermediate stage of development which had been following a strategy of import-substituting industrialization and concentrating their effort on quantitative growth, so that for lack of motivation to compete on the world market their industries had neglected the technical standards, quality and competitiveness of their products.

Moreover, a general reaction to the alarming price increases was to revive protectionism, which again hit the middle-technology products hardest. For Hungary, the combined effect in the first six years after the oil price explosion was an average increase of some 70 per cent in the prices of imports, while the prices of exports rose by only 30 to 40 per cent.

The balance of trade and the balance of payments, which had been righted in the previous years, sank into deficit. The trade gap was widened by an initial deterioration in the terms of trade of 20 per cent, which subsequently surpassed 30 per cent. To plug the gap, Hungary borrowed abroad a total of about $8,000 million during those years.

The situation was exacerbated by a lack of understanding (caused by false ideology) of what was going on in the world economy. Initially, it was thought (as the first statement by the government stressed) that the crisis disrupting the capitalist world economy would leave

Hungary and other socialist countries unaffected – that it could be halted at the frontier. Quite a long time passed before it was realized that the factors behind the crisis were not temporary or rooted in political sanctions against oil-producing Arab countries, but a structural change that would be determinant in the world economy for a long time.

Initially those in charge of the Hungarian economy did not react at all. They kept on with the same policy of maintaining a rapid growth rate of about 6 per cent. Real wages continued to rise when there were no domestic resources to back this, and no 10 or 12 per cent growth rate in foreign trade to match the 6 per cent increment of the GNP. Even at the end of 1976 it was decided to sustain the growth rate and fulfil the original targets of the 1976–80 five-year plan. As the terms of trade deteriorated the growth of the deficit speeded up. In 1978 foreign debts grew twice as fast as they had in the previous year.

To halt the trend, restore equilibrium and adjust to the new world-market requirements required a far more radical and urgent response. Under such circumstances state intervention, *initially*, was an inevitable reflex reaction. Faced with this emergency, quite a number of free-market countries also used powerful state intervention to avert the impact. There was a demand for central measures and centralized solutions. Reform and a market orientation, it was argued, had been all very well in the mid-1960s, but concealed dangers in the new world-market situation that justified a reversal of them. Some argued that Hungary should isolate itself by cutting off links with the world market as far as possible, since their influence was damaging.

It was not only these subjective, conservative reactions but the objective trauma in the world economy itself that undermined the process of reform. The need to ease the inflationary pressure of the world market and the effort to cut off its influence torpedoed the 1968 price reform. The rises in world-market prices were cushioned by extremely high subsidies built into prices at home, which became unfitted again to reflect real value relations. The oil and raw materials bought at higher and higher prices on the world market were sold to domestic companies again for far less.

By the mid-1970s the Hungarian economic reform was in a parlous condition.

Nevertheless, it should be remembered that the basic institutions of the reform – the absence of compulsory plan indicators and the institutionalized market orientation of companies – managed to survive, and that, very soon, was to prove of historical significance.

The experiences of the half-decade after the oil crisis had made it perfectly plain that the existing policy would lead to insolvency. The Hungarian economy had no choice but to adjust to the world market and restructure its exports and production as a whole. An export orientation and competitiveness on the world market had become decisively important. Restoring the balance of payments required a greater market orientation and market sensitivity of companies. But all this was closely bound up with the price system and the economic mechanism, the factors through which market influences ought to be perceived and a flexible reaction to them ought to be ensured. This recognition became clearer and clearer as the government realized at last the real character of the world economic crisis, including the fact that it was no temporary affair affecting only capitalist countries. They were forced to recognize there was no stopping the crisis at the Hungarian border; it was a lengthy structural crisis which challenged every country to respond. Whether a particular country caught up, held its ground or – if the response was partially or totally unsuccessful – fell back depended on their response. The institutional continuity which had been salvaged from the reform mechanism was shortly to prove a good base from which to take up the reform again. Despite the temporary victory of the reform's opponents, the political and personnel conditions for this change were provided by the leading group in the party and government, whose determining influence was János Kádár. This group proved sufficiently powerful to remove the most prominent anti-reformers, among them Béla Biszku and Árpád Pullai. Several others revised their opinions and turned back to moderate reform. The change was made manifest in the jettisoning of the policy which had gained the upper hand in the mid-1970s. Rallying behind the need for changes and further reform were economists and economic staff at various levels, along with broad sections of the intelligentsia. Finally, a further turn of events took place between the autumn of 1977 and 1979, although it was far from free of ambiguities like direct intervention, new company mergers and efforts to give central government preference to particular spheres.

Part III

The third phase of the reform process, from 1979 onwards

22 Changing political conditions

The protracted crisis in the world economy had a determining effect on the position of the Hungarian economy. By the end of the 1970s the failure to adjust was causing serious turmoil. Not only could the deterioration in the terms of trade, the accumulating foreign trade deficit and the rise in foreign debt not be stopped, they seemed to be speeding up. It became obvious that primitive state intervention to 'restore order', measures to equalize incomes and doctrinaire concepts of ownership were no way to handle the economic difficulties and in fact contributed to them considerably. For instance, the income curbs introduced under the 'worker policy' had dramatically reduced the incentive to keep livestock in household plots. When the significant, moreover retroactive increase in the tax on keeping pigs was introduced, a large part of the pig stock was slaughtered almost overnight, including some of the breeding sows. In fact the national pig stock fell in 1976 by some 20 per cent. From the facts it was clear there was no way back to autarky and isolation from the world market.

The economic deterioration was general in the socialist countries, which confirmed the verdict that this was no merely capitalist crisis, but a world economic turmoil, a technical 'change of regime' to which every country with a modern economy, irrespective of its social conditions, was obliged to adjust. By the early 1980s there were grave economic disruptions in Poland accompanied by an unprecedented political crisis leading to the introduction of a military government. Disruption of supplies to the public caused the introduction of rationing not only in Poland, but in Romania and Yugoslavia. All three countries soon became insolvent and had to renegotiate and reschedule their debts.

The perils of economic and political crisis coincided with a period of strong international polarization and threats of conflict. The process of détente was interrupted and Soviet–US relations reached a low point after the 1979 intervention in Afghanistan. The heightening of confrontation and the new stage in the arms race made it particularly difficult to tackle and solve economic problems.

Around the turn of the 1970s and 1980s new criticisms were made in a number of socialist countries about the system of running the economy, and proposals for experiments with reform were put forward both by economists and from within the apparatus of government. Suddenly the Hungarian reform, which had aroused doubts and even criticisms before, began to be valued more highly abroad as well, as something that might serve as a model and for experiments with reform. In November 1977 Professor D. V. Valovoy, a deputy editor-in-chief of *Pravda*, published a three-part article entitled 'The Path to Perfection of the Economic Mechanism'. At the meeting of the CPSU Central Committee in November 1978,[1] Leonid Brezhnev stated that 'the improvement of planning should be accompanied by measures aimed at perfecting the entire economic mechanism'.[2] At Moscow State University, the Department of Industrial Management staged an all-union conference in November 1978 on 'the comprehensive perfection of direction, planning, financing and economic incentive' in industry. On the other hand, those opposed to comprehensive reform made a decisive stand at the conference. Among them were T. S. Khachaturov, editor-in-chief of *Voprosi Ekonomiki*, and V. M. Ivanchenko, a leading staff member at the State Planning Commission who 'came out against reform efforts aimed at weakening central planning or seeking to divorce financial incentives from the plan'. But A. G. Aganbegyan, director of the Economic Institute of the Soviet Academy of Sciences in Novosibirsk, disputed with these views and went so far as to call for a new kind of relationship between the plan and the economic instruments. He referred to Hungary as a demonstration of how reform offered a chance to mobilize great resources. The price system occupied an important place in his line of argument, and he urged that the example of socialist countries where domestic prices were linked with export prices through the exchange rates should be followed. He emphasized the positive Hungarian results with a profit incentive in combating a shortage economy. Under the specific Soviet conditions, he advocated gradualism, stressing that 'obligatory plan indicators cannot be entirely abolished'. Hungarian economists reporting on the conference concluded that if a decision to reform were taken, the ensuing measures 'would probably not extend to an increase in the role of value categories and profitability, or to the activation . . . of market links', but they added that 'quite lively interest has recently been shown . . . by some Soviet economists . . . in Hungary's economic reform'.[3]

At the Twenty-sixth Congress of the CPSU the effectiveness of Hungarian agriculture and the importance of studying its mechanism were mentioned in the main report, and similar interest was shown in the Hungarian price system. Poland's new political leaders also announced their interest in the Hungàrian economic reform and their aim of implementing a similar reform after consolidation.

During the same years a study was made in post-Mao China of various socialist experiences, including the Hungarian one. A major step towards comprehensive reform of the Chinese system was the 1979 'village reform'. Many lessons of the Hungarian agricultural mechanism were studied when it was being devised.

23 Returning to reform

The turn towards reform had been aided particularly by the changes of personnel and policy in the Soviet Union in the mid-1980s. The concept emerged after the election of Yuri Andropov as general secretary of the party, and led to a declaration of the need for 'radical reform' at the Twenty-seventh Congress after Mikhail Gorbachev took over, and then to transformations of historical purport, to the comprehensive reform programme adopted at the National Party Conference in summer 1988. Though the process was far from unequivocal or free from compromise, economic reform was soon in the air again in a number of socialist countries. It is as yet impossible to write the history of this most recent process just evolving in our days. In what follows I can merely attempt to outline the Hungarian debates about reform and the reform processes in the eighties.

There is a parallel with these events abroad in the fact that the conservatives, who had gained ground between 1972 and 1975, began slowly to retreat in Hungary after 1977–8. Rezső Nyers had been replaced as party Central Committee secretary responsible for economic affairs in 1974 by Károly Németh, who discussed the main issues on the workings of the economy with a small economic advisory committee. There the opinions steadily came to favour a return to the reform.[1] Also placed on the agenda were the tasks of adjusting to the new world economic environment and the response which inescapably had to be made. In 1976 the party's Political Committee set up a number of working committees,[2] whose report was discussed in October 1977 by the Central Committee, which adopted a resolution: 'Guidelines for Our Long-Term External Economic Policy and the Development of the Product Structure'.[3] This new strategy still relied on central decisions and directives, so that it cannot yet be regarded as a return to the reform as such, although a few years later it was to become an element in that return.

So it is worth summing up the ideas this important document contained. After an introduction relating the stages of post-war economic development, stressing that manpower reserves were now exhausted and the external economic conditions had radically changed, came a formulation of the new principle for economic policy. Here the leitmotif was the central place to be taken by foreign trade. 'The export capacity of industry and agriculture is not in proportion to the opportunities and requirements', it said. The impetus for development must come 'from a change in the structure of production in accordance with domestic conditions and international requirements and satisfying the demands of the foreign market'. For 'more active participation in the international division of labour' was an 'indispensable precondition' for the development of the Hungarian economy, and the opportunities for it could only be exploited through 'a marked expansion of exports'. Consequently, 'external economic criteria become decisive to the framing of a growing number of development objectives' whose attainment 'demand a selective policy . . . [whereby] we develop intensively the sectors of great weight in our exports and substantially raise the ratio of highly processed products'.

The document stated that 'profitable production and development of the production structure will be accompanied by a growth in the imports of products which cannot or can only uneconomically be manufactured domestically', which ties in very closely with cutbacks in the 'unjustifiably broad product structure' brought into being by decades of industrialization based on import substitution and with 'the reduction or elimination of certain production sectors, crops and groups of products existing today'.

Like many Latin American and Asian countries in the post-war period, Hungary and the socialist countries had adopted an industrial strategy of import substitution. The upheavals on the world market in the 1970s led to a recognition that import substitution had to give way to an export orientation. The idea, of course, had been around for some time, because the processes at work in the economy had shown in the mid-1960s the importance of achieving intensive growth and the sensitivity of the Hungarian economy to its foreign economic relations. The technical and structural changes in the world economy combined with the disequilibrium that appeared to reinforce this recognition.

But to place exports at the centre of development strategy had clear implications for the whole system of economic operation and management. The resolution states:

> Changing the structure of production and increasing the interest in the foreign economy requires greater initiative . . . All this can only be achieved through more purposeful incentives and company and individual income differentials. It is particularly important to develop the price and support system in a direction that contributes more to resolving our structural tasks . . .
>
> We must build foreign economic relations better into the system of regulators, while reinforcing the price and financial system . . . and [providing] incentives that support our foreign economic objectives. An important principle in developing our price system is to bring producer-price relations . . . closer to price relations prevalent on the world market.
>
> The impact of the lasting price changes on the world market . . . should be perceived more fully by domestic producers and consumers . . . and changes in producer prices must be applied more consistently in consumer prices and price relations . . . There must be a reduction in the broad sphere of financial discrimination, which still imposes strong limits, results to a large extent in a levelling down, fails to recognize exceptional achievement and impedes the attainment of greater results.

At the same time the resolution expressed a need to expand the 'normative constituents of the financial system'. The logical consequence of an export orientation for economic management is also stated:

> We must strengthen the ability of the institutions of the management system to recognize changes in internal and external conditions more quickly at every level and to respond to these more flexibly . . . The regulatory system must provide companies with a way of making . . . all the moves required for more flexible foreign-market activity and the emergence of a spirit of enterprise with requisite speed.

These principles were to be applied, according to the final sentence of the resolution, under the Sixth Five-Year Plan, i.e. from 1981 onwards.

Yet the party leaders, looking back on the resolution in the spring of 1984, were quite right in saying that although it had 'outlined the major tasks and the system for implementing them . . . it was not effective enough. On the one hand it tried to achieve market successes by central designation, and on the other . . . tried to improve the structure of production . . . in a direct way.'[4] The Central Committee resolution of October 1977 was self-contradictory, and it remained ineffective. A decade later it had still not been put into practice.

None the less, the time had come for a return to reform. The damage done by the economic policy of the mid-1970s had rendered it inevitable and the need for it patently obvious. At the end of 1977 the economic weekly *Figyelő* (Observer) published an interview with

Deputy Premier Ferenc Havasi to mark the tenth anniversary of the reform. Instead of repeating the oft-made statements about 'distortions' in implementing the reform, Havasi concentrated on the excessive degree of compromise it contained and the inconsistent way it had been applied:

> Partly for reasons beyond our control and partly through our own weakness and inexperience, *we were not consistent enough* in implementing the reform, or in other cases we aimed at an excessive degree of safety and caution over hypothetical dangers from which we sought to protect society. An example was the system of monitoring average wages, which we used, among other reasons, to prevent an excessive growth of purchasing power, to ensure a balance between the money in circulation and the goods on the market . . . [and] impede what it was then assumed would be a large-scale fall in employment. In the mean time it emerged that the last of these dangers had never really existed . . . As far as inconsistency is concerned, we gave excessive protection – through various subsidies and supports – to uneconomic or insufficiently profitable production, and *thereby limited in advance the attainment of one of the reform's fundamental objectives, an improvement in economic efficiency.*
>
> When the economic reform was introduced we did not, unfortunately, take sufficient account of the subjective and attitude factors. We did not calculate correctly the time it would take to bring about the required change in outlook.[5]

A few years later, as Central Committee secretary responsible for economic affairs, Havasi also referred diplomatically to the 'uncertainty in the political sphere' in 1972–4 as well, in an article in the *Népszabadság*:

> In that climate of opinion it was understandably hard enough to seek, and still more to apply, the more radical solutions that would suit our system of managing the economy. The quest for a way out was marked . . . by efforts in which the solution was seen in the revival of methods and concepts employed earlier . . . Intensive development of the economy can only be attained by improving the economy's ability to adjust and by increasing its foreign economic activity. The indispensable requirement for this is to develop continuously the system of economic management and every major element of it.[6]

The whole tone of the party's principal daily changed in the late 1970s. The very criticisms of 'distortions', 'mistaken implementation' and 'petty bourgeois attitudes' made earlier and the conservative practice that arose from them now came in for criticism. In October 1978 István Földes wrote that 'instead of gradually removing the brakes of a "temporary nature" built into the reform on its introduction and giving scope for income differentials that would reflect differences in performance, we assisted the companies that found it hard to prosper under the new circumstances'.[7] In the spring of 1981 came an even clearer denunciation of the former anti-reform policy:

> Our reformed system of management has since shown itself to be a useful means of resolving the tasks of intensive development under our conditions. *And even if attempts have been made to restrict the extent of its influence and distort its fundamental principles, life has shown it is not the incorporation into it of further brakes or the smuggling back of the old subjective methods of deciding and judging that lead to success, but the contrary, the gradual elimination of the initially inescapable constraints, the reduction of specific exemptions and subsidies and the broad application of normative prescriptions* . . . It has emerged . . . that assistance to which no economic conditions are in practice attached and which contradict the fundamental principles of the reform can lead only to the conservation of the old production structures and delay the vitally necessary structural change.[8]

The vice-president of the National Planning Office made particularly strong criticisms of the regulatory system in force in the late 1970s, as one of covert direct regulation:

> Experience shows a regulatory system cannot work effectively if it contains too many specific elements, in other words if it regulates in practice at company level. The remnants of *the direct system of management* are easy to discern. *In fact it is hardly here nor there whether we give production indicators to individual companies or intervene in their financial relations directly*. These methods and the effect of them hardly differ from the *plan bargaining* criticized so frequently, and all the harmful consequences of it. The system of regulators must therefore function in a *normative* way.[9]

The trend towards reform that regained supremacy at the turn of the 1970s and 1980s had already led at the end of 1978 to some important new decisions. At the Central Committee meeting in December 1978, when the routine report on the fulfilment of the plan for 1978 and the budgetary guidelines for the 1979 plan were being discussed, some major decisions of principle were reached. It was stressed that the standard of economic activity and the structure of production 'have not adjusted sufficiently to the changed and more demanding requirements', that 'the economic regulators have not helped sufficiently either . . . to accomplish the several tasks of outstanding importance in 1978'. So the Central Committee declared that 'our practice in economic policy and economic management is slow to adjust to the requirements of a changing situation'. Centring on the objective of righting the economic balance, the meeting called for a major reshaping of the management mechanism and the system of regulators.[10]

The statements and newspaper articles quoted so far make it clear that criticism of the setback to reform and the demand for further progress intensified greatly in the early 1980s. Heated debates broke out again. Arguments were put not only for a return to the policy of 1968 but for a new development of that policy. In the summer of 1981 Miklós Pulai of the State Planning Committee declared in the *Figyelö*:

> In the view of the State Planning Committee we must devise proposals aimed at a comprehensive and coordinated change in the system of economic management . . . The fundamental issue . . . remains to define the sphere of application of goods – money relations that accords with the level of the economic development, and on that basis the direction and relations for determining state and company decision-making.
>
> Substantial though the changes commenced may be, they represent only the first step in the process. The experiences gained with the operation of the economy justify further development of the institutional system of economic management and the system of company structures.
>
> The comprehensive development of economic management makes it necessary to investigate what further development of the system of structural institutions will increase the effectiveness of that management . . . While altering the structural-cum-institutional system we must ensure the organizational frames for the emergence of enterprise [and] make the economy more open to an abundance of organizational forms.[11]

There was scarcely any disagreement in the early 1980s that substantial further reform was needed. Béla Csikós-Nagy, president of the Materials and Prices Office, wrote in the same paper: 'It is abundantly clear from the debates so far that it is not a matter of how to apply the principles expressed in the economic reform of 1968 but of how to develop its concept further.'[12]

24 A new chapter in the debates on reform: the reform decisions of 1984 and 1987

However, strongly divergent views arose about the direction and extent of further reform. As one contributor, László Antal, put it in the *Figyelő*: 'One can also size up the present situation by saying that alterations in course are always cumbersome; the new regulators still need refining . . . There is much truth in this: by improving certain elements of direction and taking measures aimed at particular areas, one can achieve temporary successes, and these are important too.' But the author goes on to quarrel with this argument, saying that even the 1968 concept had to be surpassed.

> The present economic mechanism *has not proved sufficiently suited to creating the operating conditions for the market* within the frames of a planned economy: to assuring effective utilization of *individual abilities and talents*, such as a spirit of enterprise, an ability to innovate, inventiveness and a proprietorial motivation; to ensuring in the *harmonization of interests* that the role of control by society is strongly asserted.
>
> Resolution of these tasks could liberate new and lasting growth forces. The model I am thinking of accords with the basic principles of the 1968 reform, but learning precisely from the experiences of the past twelve years its aim is not simply to realize them consistently but to move significantly beyond them on a number of points.

As the principal element in substantive further development, Antal lists the following measures of reform:

> In the company (and cooperative) sphere it is necessary *to eliminate direct dependence* on the directing organizations . . .
>
> I also consider . . . *the regulating role of the market* to be important *in a far broader sphere*, not merely in the distribution of products but in the allocation of capital, the regulation of wages . . .
>
> *In the state function of economic management* the spheres ensuring the general framework for economic activity (normative regulation) and intervention in market relations *become separated* . . .

> The key point in the development of the economic mechanism is *the transformation of the company management system* . . .
>
> People in top positions have an interest in ensuring longer-term income. Their appointments are only for a fixed term. So managerial incentive includes – no longer as an abstract possibility – the risk of failure as well . . .
>
> Another possible 'company' form is the cooperative. In this form the functions of ownership are practised by the whole workforce, or more precisely by the body (for example, a council) that is elected directly by it . . .
>
> The elected body possesses the right of decision or at least the right of veto on major company issues. It appoints the manager, it endorses the company plan and the structure of company organization, it controls the management of the company's finances . . .
>
> The third type is the entrepreneur (or entrepreneurial group) that *rents* social property . . . The potential entrepreneurs obtain the leading position by open tender, in the form of bidding, and units capable of autonomous goods production can also be run in this form.

The proposal extended to a transformation of the price system, the total elimination of subsidies and the introduction of graduated income tax.

> An important feature of my proposal is that *the company sphere is an ensemble of heterogeneous organizational forms capable of growing into each other and competing with each other*. This breaks up the unilateral, vertical dependence. The operation of the economy would essentially be governed by substantially more forces (planning centre, fiscal policy, entrepreneurial interests, trade unions, market) in a relation of partnership to each other.[1]

As Antal's article demonstrates, a debate had begun on the need for 'reform of the reform'. In a quite unusual way it was a popular economic weekly, the *Heti Világgazdaság* (Weekly World Economy), that began to run in October 1982 a debate on the subject that lasted for over seven months. 'Is the slowing down of the development of the Hungarian economy sufficient reason for renouncing a further development of the economic mechanism?' the paper asked as it launched the discussion. 'Can we be content with treating the symptoms? Shall we not lose further valuable years by referring to the dire situation of the world economy, the untimeliness of the reform of the reform?'[2]

In his introductory article in the same number, Márton Tardos, an economist, stressed emphatically the need for a swift and substantial wave of further reform. The lead in this would be played by autonomy for companies, their removal from the hierarchy of public administration, reinforcement of the role of the market and market prices, transformation of the banking system, establishment of a plurality of domestic and foreign trading channels, and reshaping of income regulation.[3]

A number of those who took part in the debate, including Tardos and later Antal, wanted a transitional period, a 'period of consolidation' lasting for a few years. 'Above all, a short-term programme is necessary', Antal wrote, 'one suited to the partial . . . dynamization of the economy, for the relief of those pursuing economic activity from the increasingly minute and rigid restrictions. This we could call the programme for activating the economy.'[4]

Before the debate in the paper had ended, a working group of professionals had published its position in the *Társadalmi Szemle*, the party's theoretical journal. This was entitled 'Further Development of our Economic Mechanism in the Service of Socialist Construction'.[5] Again in the *Társadalmi Szemle*, Tamás Bauer criticized the moderate concept of further reform that the article proposed. He stressed particularly that the central momentum for boosting the reform was 'the severance of companies, as business ventures, from the umbilical cord of hierarchical relations attaching them to the administration of the state'. But Bauer also regarded it as essential to create a democratic and institutionalized mechanism for coordinating the interests of the various strata in society, and to undertake an ideological clarification, so that the approach of the kind 'the excesses of the reform must not weaken the socialist nature of our society' should be unable to imperil the reform's progress.[6]

In these debates it was clearly stated that economic reform should be accompanied by social and political reforms. In the autumn of 1981 Rezső Nyers delivered a lecture on the interaction between the economy and politics. He underlined the need to 'think out and rethink many, many tasks', and 'the line of action of *the whole society*', since 'the economic sphere in itself would be unable to accomplish the success one can only create – I could also say "sweat out" – by the total effort of society'.[7]

One revealing moment in the debate came in the January 1984 issue of the economics journal *Közgazdasági Szemle*, when András Hegedüs launched a frontal assault on the top management of the large state companies: 'One of the most serious chronic diseases in our economy', he declared, 'is that it is in almost unchanging immobility . . . there lie large companies one might call corporate empires, whose managers still dream over and dandle their mighty plans.' According to

Hegedüs, the majority of the managers of large companies were opposed to the reform and resisted real changes. 'It does not follow from all of this that a radical reform must necessarily be anti-large company, but it does follow that the reform cannot sidestep the problem of the large companies.'[8]

It would go beyond the scope of this book to present in full the heated debates that raged between 1982 and 1984, or review all the more moderate proposals for developing the reform that were set up against the 'reform of the reform' in its various forms, either for principled or tactical reasons.[9] Let us be content instead with looking at the most authoritative position of all, taken up in the spring of 1983. It was put forward in an extensive and extensively covered statement by János Kádár, first secretary of the party:

> We have heard opinions expressed that we should now reform the reform as well. Nothing could be further from our thoughts: we shall apply a socialist system of management which has been proven in practice. Our task in this respect is to follow the experiences with attention and if the institutions and methods need adjusting and developing as well we shall do so. But we will not replace this system of management by anything radically different.[10]

The standpoint unambiguously formulated by the first secretary of the party clearly expressed the line of reform policy in the eighties: although the government returned to the road of 1968, it wanted to proceed along it only extremely cautiously, ponderingly. Accordingly, the system of reform – burdened with compromises – was to be further developed only by partial and gradual corrections.

The arguments in the early 1980s ranged very widely between developing a radically new economic model and rejection of one different in substance from those in the other socialist countries. In early 1982, while at one extreme the 'Liska debate' (which we shall come to in a moment) was taking place within Budapest's Karl Marx University of Economic Sciences, the *Népszabadság* carried an interview with the rector of the party's Political Academy. Asked whether there was a 'Hungarian model' of any kind, his answer was this:

> I think I have to reply with a firm *no* to this question so often expressed or left unexpressed. In my view, what is termed the 'Hungarian model' is merely *the adaptation to Hungarian conditions* of the general laws of Marxism–Leninism and socialist construction and of the experiences – I stress this – of other socialist countries . . .
>
> Articles and studies published in the West about the'Hungarian model' attempt above all to 'prove' that Hungary is different from the other socialist countries. They claim that what is being done in the

> economy here differs widely from the practice in the other socialist countries [and] stands opposed to the 'classical' theory and earlier concept of socialism . . . *So there is no 'Hungarian model', although there is a Hungarian praxis,* which entails adapting the various recognitions to the specific Hungarian conditions.[11]

As in the seventies, policy-makers again thought it was important to deny the existence of a Hungarian model. Obviously, this line of policy also squeezed the continuation of reform between narrow limits and downgraded it into patchwork. In this partly considerations of foreign policy, partly tactical reasons played a role.

At the same time, in contrast to this standpoint, Tibor Liska came up with an economic approach which was something quite different from the road of reform followed up to that time, indeed a radical departure from it. In fact it was less a radicalization of the reform than an entirely new model of 'entrepreneurial socialism'.

To Liska socialism was in fact a higher grade of commodity production than capitalism was: 'It creates, by eliminating the bonds of private property and liberating labour on a basis of public ownership, a far broader opportunity for democratic and free enterprise' than capitalism.[12]

So Liska's purpose was not merely to modify certain aspects of the previous mechanism or to make it consistent with itself but to change the entire economic system: only under socialism was it truly possible, without any restraint, to create free competition. For this to build up and operate it would be necessary for all the means of production to be taken into totally social ownership – in other words, not into those of the state or any bureaucratic stratum acting in its name, so as to ensure that no one should gain any prior rights over them. On this basis it was precisely and exclusively under socialism that an opportunity could open up for an unlimited expression of the spirit of enterprise and competition, since real social ownership would allow everyone to measure and utilize their abilities in various enterprises. Moreover, the country had to enter the mainstream of the international division of labour and prices had to follow the laws of supply and demand through the creation of real money and a real market. It would be vitally important to guarantee the freedom of competition, for which the main instrument would be democracy, and also for 'the sole criterion of achievement in competition to be the performance rendered to society'.

Liska firmly distinguished his concept of socialist enterprise from small private business. For 'although flexible small businesses in principle come into being as a civil right, they additionally require capital in most cases, which is not a desert accompanying that civil right'.[13] Under the Liska system ownership may appear as a strong economic, incentive-giving motif, but it cannot become a monopoly.

This entirely new concept of social ownership, and within it what he called *'personal social property'*, would be a social unit of property which, primarily in the form of means of production (machinery, trucks, etc.), could be taken into a personal enterprise by anybody at all. Companies potentially available as personal enterprises would possess a *minimum nominal capital value*. This value (the bid price) would be determined on the first transfer of the company to a personal enterprise (by auction), in such a way as to reflect the 'likely profit of the specific company unit, presupposing there has been painstaking economic activity'.

What Liska termed the *plan-market value* was to be set by the prevailing market situation. Liska considered it important to point out: 'It is always the possessor whose realistically guaranteed plan concept bids the highest plan-market property value who is entitled to conduct autonomous economic activity with public property and to the personal and social appropriation of surplus achievements.'

Liska described as *'moral capital'* the nominal capital value with which the entrepreneur would seek to increase the price of public property by bidding higher. ('Moral capital is a sum total per entrepreneur of the increments to the property undertaken through valid bidding.')

The *plan-market of entrepreneurs* would be a value market in which 'competition decides whose is the right and obligation to conduct autonomous private economic activity with public property'. The opportunity for subsequent 'higher bidding', 'self-bidding' and 'reverse-bidding' would ensure the automatic selection of entrepreneurs, so that ownership could not be monopolized.[14] Through these auctions the management of a company or the operation of a machine tool could alike be won on the basis of competitive bidding, while anyone could take this away from the previous 'tenant' at any time by 'bidding higher'.

The financial resources and guarantees of the entrepreneur would partly be his own *'human property'*, consisting of his *'social inheritance'* (i.e. a part of collective wealth) from the moment of his birth, and partly of his *'moral capital'*, which accumulates in the course of his work. Under Liska's system everything, including medical and educational services, can be bought by people according to their needs, at the market price. By contrast, the entrepreneur would possess as a potential starting capital for the ventures his own 'social inheritance', i.e. his share of the totality of the country's existing means of production and infrastructure. Or as Liska put it: 'The financial return from the personal inheritance capital, which constantly grows, is the germ in the present of a communism conducting an advanced money economy, except that it is still largely wrapped up in the form of benefits in kind and "cheap" benefits.' At the same time, this would also mean that every member of society, as part of this 'social inheritance', would possess, as a 'civil right', a minimum wage irrespective of his work.

How would the state profit from all of this? Among other things through economic growth, improving performance and greater competitiveness on the world market. Incidentally, the 'annual sum of interest' which the 'tenant' of social property would have to pay into the bank 'would far exceed that of today's taxes'.[15]

The handling of social property could be entrusted to a system of banks that functioned on an enterprise basis. They would in fact be fulfilling the functions of a revenue office, a public notary, a savings bank and a keeper of current accounts.

The state, on the other hand, would wholly withdraw from the economy, and to use Liska's term merely fulfil 'the function of a referee', i.e. ensure that the regulations were kept without playing the least part in the game itself.

Although Liska was thinking in terms of a closed system, he did not regard 'enterprise socialism' as something complete and immutable. He considered experiments and verification in practice as indispensable to its development, and in 1982 he conducted an experiment on the Felszabadulás (Liberation) cooperative farm in Szentes precisely for this purpose, the chairman of the cooperative having agreed.

At the first public tender in October 1981 some ten units of production (a chicken hatchery covered with PVC film, a truck with a trailer, a tractor and so on) were leased out as enterprises. As a gauge of efficiency, the cost, book, sale and planned-market values of the assets offered were considered in setting the reserve price, and each tender was won by the entrepreneur who made the highest bid. The surplus value he was to produce raised his 'moral capital'. (This sum was deposited in a closed account.)

In the Szentes model, the cooperative's headquarters acted as a bank for the entrepreneurs, keeping the current accounts of the enterprises. The money set aside for maintaining or replacing the assets which composed each enterprise was known as the asset-depreciation fund.

The adjustment of each entrepreneur to market changes could be regulated by his making another bid himself or by someone else making a bid. The fund for development was the entrepreneur's credit limit. He was responsible both for the assets he took over and for the financial obligations incurred by the venture. Should he be unable to pay and exhaust his credit, insolvency proceedings would be taken against the venture.

Under Liska's scheme the entire system of production and services was to function as communal property leased out to individual entrepreneurs in this way.

During a series of debates held in 1982 Liska's intellectual contribution to reform and extremely useful specific ideas were acknowledged, but economists committed to reform almost unanimously rejected entrepreneurial socialism as a consistent system.[16] The arguments for doing so were of many different kinds. One was that the actual power of disposal over the fixed assets could not be decided purely by the *promise* of the entrepreneur represented by his bid. The uncertainty factor was too great. For instance, an entrepreneur had no way of knowing that somebody would not *bid higher* (promise more) the very next day. The scheme reckoned initially with separate, competing entrepreneurs, but 'association, the forming of coalitions and cartels, is inevitable'.[17] In other words, 'Will the enterprises not lead to the formation of large-scale business monopolies?'[18] It was emphasized that most of the elements recommended were acceptable in one sector of the economy or another, but the consistent enterprise system proposed was a Utopia. 'The enterprise model can take root in areas where the conditions are favourable for it, but if it is expanded into a general, comprehensive principle, it will immediately collide with the unaccounted-for facts of reality, of which Tibor Liska takes no note at all in his abstract concept for creating the system.'[19] It was said to be unrealistic of Liska, for instance, to assume a complete 'withdrawal' by the state and elimination of central intervention. Others emphasized how Utopian it was to suppose that 'everything in the economy can be organised and operated as an enterprise' (including single machine tools or trucks); 'within this it is particularly unrealistic to conceive of society solely as a mass of bidding and competing individuals.'[20] As one contributor asked: 'What will become of those who do not want to undertake an enterprise? . . . If not everybody wants to, society will contain both entrepreneurial and non-entrepreneurial members. Surely the latter, the plain employees, will end up in an unjustifiably disadvantageous position compared with the entrepreneurs?'[21]

So this market model with extreme free competition and an absence of state intervention, under which consistently communal property, ranging from a big factory to a single lathe and from a truck to the school, would be managed in the form of individual enterprises based on consistently competitive tenders, was rejected by the vast majority of Hungarian economists. However, several parts of the system were accepted, and even applied in practice.

Ultimately the extensive debates and the often radical differences of view all contributed in their own way to the emergence of a system of ideas for the third stage in the reform process. But from what has been said so far it is clear that nothing more emerged between 1978 and 1987 than new ideas for reform. In terms of policy and action one is more justified in speaking of the emergence of a further period of gradual correction in the process of reform which had lasted for several decades. This is a better interpretation of a number of measures intended to restore the 1968 reform system and adjust it in a number of fields. On the level of political decision-making, the party Central Committee's resolution on reform in April 1984 appeared to be central to a new turn in the reform process.[22] After two years of preparatory work this comprehensive concept, devised with the help of expert committees,[23] and embodied in a resolution in the spring of 1984 had as its central purpose the real emergence of more efficient economic activity from the grave problems of the Hungarian economy, as opposed to the restrictions which had been applied in the preceding years (and still are):

> The fundamental requirement for catching up with those in the international forefront in future is to achieve the main objectives of our economic policy by increasing efficiency and not by reducing domestic spending. This requires further development of the system of economic management. Measures must be taken to mobilize collectives and individuals and so release energies for improving economic efficiency.

For this reason structural modernization continued to feature as a task in developing the system of managing the economy: 'Company dimensions should be adjusted to the requirements of economic operation and production', it said. And elsewhere: 'One must work towards the emergence of a banking system in which the functions of a bank of issue, of state financing and of commercial banking are separated.' Meanwhile 'the division of labour is needed between the organizations of state and the management of companies in the exercise of the right to dispose over state property and the right to act as an employer'. A complete overhaul of the system of company management was called for in order to increase corporate independence. It was decided there should be two new management forms for state companies, essentially in order to diminish the direct influence of the ministry and increase the autonomous function of the company staff by setting up company councils and introducing the election (instead of the appointment) of top management. This was expected to produce an attitude of proprietorship among those working for the company: 'In the long run this could also give employees an interest not only in profit and personal earnings but in the growth of the company's assets and the shape of the factories' future.' It was underlined that 'the proprietorial sense and behaviour of the employees can be reinforced in this way'.[24]

The resolution called for further development of the price system, greater assertion of socially justified costs, efforts to eliminate state subsidies in the longer term and the introduction of a far more flexible system of regulating incomes. More efficient companies were to receive a bigger incentive to maximize profits: 'The economic entities should receive a greater share of the greater performance than they do today so that their profit incentive increases.' The intention was the same with income regulation. As the resolution put it, 'We must change to methods aligned to company performance and ensuring more flexible management by companies of wages and labour. Extra performance should be accompanied by proportionally higher personal earnings.' Guidelines were also given for transforming the personal tax system by introducing a comprehensive, progressive system of personal income tax. At the same time, stronger company autonomy was intended to be linked with a freer flow of manpower, capital and means of production, aimed at 'a regrouping . . . among the economic organizations'.[25]

At this point one should add that the proportion of the proposals in the 1984 resolution actually realized in the following few years was to prove insufficient to produce a real turning-point in the reform. This period of corrective measures, like the one after 1956–7, turned out to be ambiguous and self-contradictory, one in which there was substitution for and evasion of the requisite comprehensive stage in the reform but also one of theoretical and practical preparation for it. Throughout the middle and into the second half of the decade the direly needed comprehensive and radical measures were missing. Although experts and even certain government circles urged that the elaboration of price, wage and currency reforms, and of a new comprehensive reform, should be started, in the end the government did not undertake it. The procrastination clearly demonstrated that the economic and structural transformation made urgent by the pressures from the world economy and the adjustment required by the technological revolution could not be carried out without a market and financial mechanism, and a price and wage system to match. In other words, the imbalance of the Hungarian economy could not be restored in the long term by restrictions and brakes.

Around the turn of 1986–7 a group of economists and sociologists, the collective of the Financial Research Institute (Pénzügykutató Intézet), worked out a study entitled 'Change and Reform', in which they expounded a programme that linked the rational tasks of short-term stabilization with the long-term evolution of the reform as well as with political reform and the bringing about of the necessary social openness.[26]

The document – at first considered to be contrary to government intentions and more or less even 'oppositionist' – was discussed by the Economic Panel operating beside the Central Committee of the HSWP which supported it in every major question.[27] In the wake of these new recognitions a new platform entitled 'A Programme for Economic and Social Development' was adopted by the party Central Committee in July 1987.[28] The resolution obtained emphasis by the changes simultaneously made in the central economic management: the prime minister and the secretary of the Central Committee responsible for economic affairs were relieved of their office and Károly Grósz and Miklós Németh were elected to replace them.

The introduction to this resolution, whose title reflects the comprehensiveness of its purpose, stated this clearly:

> We have been late in adjusting to the changed situation. Economic management as a whole has failed to encourage and compel sufficiently transfer to the intensive stage [and] a transformation of the production structure. [So] the confused system of subsidies and taxes [levies], which disguise efficiency, needs to be changed . . . Loss-making activity cannot in the longer term be financed at the expense of the efficient companies.

So the Central Committee came out in favour of 'a broad development of the process of economic reform' after a fairly short period of two to three years' stabilization. Under the longer-term programme, 'commodity and money relations, supply and demand, credit, prices, exchange rates, profitability and profit must play an active part in the economy'. That meant that companies 'must turn into organizations of economic activity possessing genuine independence and directly interested in the expansion of income and wealth [property]'.

Point II (4) of the resolution stated that 'a price system and price mechanism expressing international competitiveness must be established'. It also said a 'wage reform' was necessary and that 'wage relations that express the social usefulness of work should be created in the longer term'. Point II (7) concerned the 'purposeful development of socialist market relations', and Point II (9) the need for 'a diverse combination of forms of ownership'. Point II (8) stated unequivocally that 'auxiliary and side activities on farms, and also private activity, constitute an integral part of the socialist economy'.

At the same time, this Central Committee resolution stressed the correlation between the economic sphere and the socio-political conditions: 'To realize our social and economic programme it is imperative to develop socialist democracy and modernize the way the system of political institutions operates.'

So the decisions on economic strategy and economic reform taken in 1977, 1984 and 1987, along with debates on the reform that took place in the 1980s, had, finally, led first to professional and then to party and governmental recognition that further comprehensive reform was required.

For the most part implicitly, the debates and resolutions had focused and reached conclusions primarily on the question of whether the indirect system of central planning that was to replace planning based on commands should be one of partial, gradual further corrections or an entirely new, comprehensive reform. If the latter could institutionalize a *regulated market economy*, a substantial advance would be made. In this case company regulation that reproduced elements of the command economy and was riddled with special cases would give way to consistently normative state regulation of the market. Furthermore, this would be accompanied by the safeguards for the functioning of automatic processes and by the environment of socio-political institutions that an economy of this type would require. So it would also entail a substantial development of the political system and a profound democratization of the old, largely 'command' forms. This would indeed amount to a new stage of the Hungarian reform. All of this requires that the reform process should expand to cover the legal and institutional spheres of politics, the self-restraint and pluralization of power.

In the eighties the government's platform had been, while acknowledging to various degrees the need to continue developing the reform, essentially to confine itself to correcting the reform system. The July 1987 resolution, on the other hand, inherently contained the framework for a programme of substantive advance towards a comprehensive reform.

A genuine breakthrough in this direction has occurred only in the national party conference of the HSWP held in May 1988. It represented a powerful critique of earlier policy, and a demand for abandoning the economic and political system obtained particular emphasis from the radical personal changes in the party leadership, from the significant reshuffling of the old guard of the preceding period. With the implementation of this resolution at the end of the 1980s and the beginning of the 1990s, a new chapter in the history of the Hungarian reform process could open. Obviously it depends on the outcome of further debates, political struggle and international influences whether this chapter will amount to a real turning-point in the long process of Hungarian reform. In this case the measures to reconstruct and correct the reform in the decade between 1977 and 1987 could come to be seen as preparations for that turning-point, and it is in this light that we can survey the main processes at work during this corrective phase.

25 The price reform of 1979–1980

Meanwhile the detailed elaboration of the 1977 outline proposals for developing the whole economic system, primarily the price system, had been continuing in the working committees set up in 1976. The result in April 1978 was a resolution that criticized the price policy followed since 1973. Although it noted, and marked down as an achievement, that 'the state was able to curb the cumulative influence of the high world-market prices by central means', the resolution had harsh words for the 'complicated system of state supports and deductions' and the unrealistic general level of consumer prices it had produced: 'Producer and consumer prices do not reflect real costs, which hinders clarity of vision, effective economic activity, transformation of the production structure . . . ' The resolution confirmed the Central Committee's view that 'it is necessary to perfect our pricing system in accordance with the economic policy objectives'.[1] This revision was all the more necessary because the price reform originally envisaged as gradual and covering a longer period had suffered a setback in the latter part of the 1970s. As Béla Csikós-Nagy remarked about those years in 1980, 'The pricing policy concept of the Fourth Five-Year Plan, embracing the period between 1971 and 1975, and the first phase in the switch to value-related prices was contained in the first concept for the Fifth Five-Year Plan, which had, however . . . to be removed from the agenda.'[2]

The guidelines for the new price reform were finally settled in 1979, and summed up by the president of the Prices Office as the formation of an integral link between domestic and world-market (foreign trade) prices; restoration of the two-tier pricing system (abolition of the contribution on assets tied up, reduction of the wage contribution incorporated into prices and reduction of the profit tax rate); and finally, the ensuring of flexibility in the price system so that changing foreign trade prices and the domestic market's estimation of value could be asserted.[3]

It amounted to no less than the restoration of the price system introduced in 1968, and the development of it planned earlier but never implemented, since the 1968 system had practically collapsed in the 1970s. The new price reform was instituted in two stages, in July 1979 and January 1980. It covered both producer and consumer prices.

In the case of producer prices it went further than the 1968 price reform, which had sought to reflect domestic production costs and genuine value relations, since it aimed for the first time at a linkage with prices and price movements on the world market. A system known as *international competitive prices* was established in the producer-price sphere. However, this still did not amount to the assertion of a world-market price mechanism.

The linkage was rather a complex one, since efforts were made to prevent companies from shifting export losses on to a domestic market in which they held a monopoly. The domestic prices for energy and raw materials were set on the basis of world-market import prices, not Comecon ones. That raised the price of energy by 56 per cent (and of heating oil by 75 per cent) between 1979 and 1980. Chemical base materials became 30 per cent more expensive, metallurgical products 15 per cent, leather and hides 90 per cent and building materials and timber 20 per cent dearer.

Overall, the prices of raw materials and basic semi-finished products rose by 57 per cent. As a study presenting the new system pointed out,

> A relative increase in the price of materials has been a mark of our pricing system since 1975. Since 1973–4, the price level for materials has risen by 110 per cent by comparison with the prices of finished products, and almost half of this increase took place on January 1, 1980. So the 1980 change in price ratios is greater than any carried out under a previous major adjustment of prices.[4]

However, the price of adjustment was not a one-off affair that would allow the gulf between domestic and world-market prices to open again, because the changes in the domestic prices of materials were linked to the longer-lasting movements of world-market prices. The domestic prices of raw materials and basic semi-finished products were allowed to change freely in line with convertible-currency import prices and exchange rates, but the price of energy was set centrally, and adjustments to world-market prices made periodically. The result was to make energy and raw materials rather expensive resources for companies; by comparison with the combined cost of equipment and wages, the ratio of material costs rose by 22 per cent. So unlike the previous principle of relating prices to production costs, the new system compelled companies to economize on energy and materials.

The system of competitive prices worked differently in the case of manufactures: companies whose non-rouble exports accounted for at least 5 per cent of their sales were allowed to calculate their domestic prices according to the rate of profit attained on their hard-currency exports,[5] i.e. they could not raise their domestic prices at a higher rate than their export prices rose, and they were obliged to reduce their domestic prices when their export prices fell. The prices set in this way and linked through export prices to price movements on the world market covered 75–80 per cent of engineering products, 50 per cent of chemical products, 15–20 per cent of food products and some two-thirds of all manufactures.

As a result of the new measures, not least the reduction in the profit and other taxes on producers, the prices of manufactures fell (particularly those of engineering and textile products). This linkage of domestic prices with export prices was an attempt to expose companies' domestic marketing to the bracing wind of world-market competition, but like all regulations, it immediately created opportunities for evasion of it. In many cases where export prices were unfavourable, companies preferred not to export at all, so as not to have to reduce their domestic prices. So the competitive price system became an express disincentive to exporting, at a time when exporting was vitally important to the economy.

The international competitive price system was in any case introduced only in the so-called competitive sphere – industries which accounted for some 35 per cent of national income. There was no intention at all of allowing international prices to affect such sectors as construction, haulage or the services generally. Any such linkage was considered equally impossible in agriculture and most of the food industry (where international prices were largely manipulated and compensated for by substantial domestic price support). So the prices of food products and the principal services remained largely unchanged, with 70 to 80 per cent of such goods and services being sold at an officially set price. However, it was stated that from time to time these prices would also be regulated centrally with an eye to adjusting them flexibly to market conditions.

The price reform increased the buying prices for agriculture by an average of more than 10 per cent, and the producer price level for foodstuffs by 11 per cent (at a time when state subsidies were also cut by some 70 per cent). Adapting to the cost relations, the price level of transport and services to the population rose by 10 to 20 per cent, bringing a reduction in state subsidies along with it.

The two-stage consumer price reform (introduced in the summer of 1979 and in January 1980) was an attempt to bring prices nearer to values. During the 1970s the subsidies built into the pricing system and the efforts to curtail international inflationary influences had brought about an unprecedented situation: by 1978 the overall consumer price level was 4 per cent lower than the producer price level. (This defence against inflation was aimed against the symptoms rather than the causes, and ultimately compounded rather than remedied the difficulties.) Major price increases, the partial elimination or reduction of subsidies and the extensive introduction of uniform rates of turnover tax brought the overall level of consumer prices 3 per cent above that of producer prices, so producing to a meagre extent the usual two-tier character of a pricing system. (Food consumer prices were 14 per cent below producer prices, as compared with 18 per cent in the first half of 1979. On the other hand, the consumer prices of clothing and other consumer articles rose respectively to 5 to 9 per cent and 4 to 12 per cent higher than producer prices. Meanwhile the state subsidies on fuels, electricity, gas and communal services were increased, so that in the case of fuels, for instance, consumers were paying 67 per cent less than producer prices, instead of 42 per cent less.)

The outcome was only partial progress towards consumer prices proportionate to value. However, one indication of the loosening in the price system is that 50 per cent of retail turnover in 1980 was in goods whose prices were not controlled, compared with 37 per cent in 1979.

To coincide with the price reform, a uniform exchange rate for the forint was introduced. The exchange rate had assumed importance from the point of view of price formation, because the international competitive prices were converted on the basis of import and export prices. At the same time, the exchange rate was important as a brake on inflationary influences. Moreover, if Hungary was to join the International Monetary Fund, which it planned to do, it was a condition of joining that it establish a uniform exchange rate in place of the widely different commercial and tourist rate (the former was double the latter even in 1968).

In fact the uniform exchange rate came after a long process of change. Before the 1968 reform the exchange rate system had become irrevocably confused because of price levelling and price skimming that affected almost every product. There were significant simplifications in 1968, when a three-tier rate of exchange was introduced: a formal rate based on a parity with gold (which had no practical significance), a tourist rate (30 forints to the US dollar) and a commercial rate (60 forints).

Further progress came in the early 1980s. According to the president of the National Bank,

> The price reform . . . of 1979–80, under which we established a closer link between domestic producer prices and world-market prices, created from the angle of the price the conditions for bringing in a uniform exchange rate . . . To dampen the unfavourable impact of capitalist inflation, which had speeded up in the years after the oil-price shock, we revalued the forint several times; from 1979 onwards we also began to bring the commercial and non-commercial exchange rates closer together. In this way it became possible after eliminating a difference of a mere 8 per cent to establish on October 1 [1981] a *uniform* exchange rate of 35 forints to the dollar for both the commercial and non-commercial spheres.
>
> Basically, the uniform exchange rate now introduced has been set at the old commercial exchange rate.[6]

The uniform rate was achieved after a period of almost half a century, since the 1930s, when a variety of concurrent rates had been used. The process was connected with preparations for what was called the external convertibility of the forint, envisaged as part of the reform. 'We make no secret of the fact', Ferenc Havasi said in the press a few weeks later, 'that we are taking steps, dependent on external and internal conditions, towards making the forint convertible.'[7] In the event the move did not materialize, however.

Other regulators connected with the price system were also adjusted, in some cases in a contradictory way. One of the measures taken to reduce the budget deficit was to regulate company income – profits tax rose to 45 per cent and the local development contribution to 10 per cent. Other taxes were raised as well. But central regulation of investment was limited to a narrower sphere of 'major central investments', largely confined to the infrastructure, raw material production and energy. Another form of state intervention in investment, covering funds for schemes in specific areas targeted for development by the government, was reduced. These measures shifted the emphasis on to self-financing by companies, and primarily on to credit, particularly development credits extended on a competitive basis.[8]

Of the various ways used to control wages, the new system of regulators gave greater importance to regulation of the wage bill. This had been introduced partially and experimentally in 1972, and by the end of the decade applied to 70 to 75 per cent of industry and to the sphere of profit-oriented companies. Although four forms of wage control remained in force, regulation of the wage bill became the predominant one, with an important change: it was no longer the average wage per employee that was controlled (causing companies to pad out their labour force with superfluous low-paid workers) but the actual size of the total wage bill. Under the new scheme, every percentage point of growth in performance gave an automatic entitlement to increase the wage bill by 0.3 per cent. But if the wage bill was increased by more than this, penal rates of graduated payroll tax were levied. Average wages could be increased by up to 9 per cent a year without attracting extra company taxation. This limit was raised to 12 per cent in 1982. The tax on increases in excess of this ranged from 150 to 800 per cent.

In theory regulation of the wage bill gave companies more leeway, but it had some unfavourable features. For one thing it perpetuated the habit of thinking in terms of a base-figure. The level of the wage bill depended not only on the growth of productivity but on the base – the wage bill in the preceding year. In effect, efficient companies were at a disadvantage compared with inefficient ones. Both were still paying similar wage rates, but the latter had a better chance of raising their productivity. However, other intricate mechanisms operated at the same time, since the temporary fall in profit levels inevitably suffered by companies undergoing structural modernization meant a low rate of wage increases, acting as a counter-incentive to companies to invest. To counteract this, central intervention was used: preferential wage treatment was given in cases where the government thought it justified by granting exemptions from the norms of wage control. That meant the supervisory authorities were interfering again on a case-by-case basis.[9]

Experiments with further ways of developing the wage control system began almost immediately after the change in the regulations and continued through the early 1980s. In January 1983 twenty-nine companies employing 100,000 people were included in two new, more flexible schemes for regulating wages. This experiment was expanded to cover fifty-four companies and 225,000 employees in 1984, while a further seventy-two companies with 350,000 employees joined yet another experimental regime.[10]

Although the 1980 changes in the regulations had their positive features, their effect was less to develop the system of managing the economy than to act as a vehicle for central financial restrictions and redistribution. Two economists who examined the matter arrived, quite rightly, at the conclusion that the 1980 changes 'amounted to intervention in the system on a large scale'. There were radical consequences for the amounts companies had to pay into the budget and the amounts companies received from the budget in subsidies. 'In other words, the redistribution continues to be aimed . . . steadily at withdrawing higher incomes that appear in industry.'[11]

Havasi, as Central Committee secretary responsible for economic matters, spoke of 'rapidly deteriorating external conditions' that meant 'we had to use the kind of compulsory measures which from the companies' point of view, to put it mildly, were against the rules of the game'.[12]

26 Partial reform of the system of institutions

The change in the price system made in 1979–80 demonstrated very well that a new phase in the process of reform had begun after the setbacks and reversals of the 1970s. The plan was now to implement directly the further measures of reform (the 'second stage') which had been prepared and placed on the agenda in 1968–70.

Another aspect that came to the fore again was one of the major compromises made in the 1968 reform: the retention of the existing system of economic institutions. As we have seen earlier, those directing the process of reform had pencilled in a change in the system of institutions (the abolition of the large monopoly companies and transformation of the banking system) for the end of the 1960s. It is worth recalling that some elements of institutional reform had even featured in the reform proposals of 1957, for instance the establishment of a unified, trans-sectoral ministry of industry.

A decisive reversal of the process of centralization came in the early 1980s. (Although the development of an overly centralized industrial structure, as mentioned already, took place mainly in the early 1960s, company amalgamations had resumed after 1972. Industrial companies employing over a thousand people had accounted for 15 per cent of the industrial workforce in 1960, over 35 per cent in 1970, and scarcely less than 45 per cent by 1979!) The dismantling of the large monopoly industrial and service-industry companies that started in the early 1980s was one step towards more favourable conditions for market competition. In Havasi's words at the time, 'The modernization of the system of organization and company management is in progress. This task is based on a recognition that there is space in our industrial structure both for larger-sized economic entities with a compound structure and for small and medium-sized companies.'[1]

In 1980 there were altogether 546 state industrial companies under ministerial supervision, but of these twelve were by Hungarian

Table 1

Year	State industrial companies No.	1980=100
1975	779	111
1980	699	100
1982	726	104
1984	891	127
1985	956	137

Source: Statisztikai Évkönyv 1985 (Budapest, 1986), p. 89.

standards vast 'trusts' (groups) that controlled 40 per cent of the fixed industrial assets between them.[2] The process of breaking up these horizontal monopolies controlling whole sectors of industry began. The brewery trust was broken up into four companies, and the individual breweries regained some of the independence they had originally had as separate concerns. In the spring of 1983 came the government's decision to dismember the Csepel Works, a giant engineering group. Similar measures had soon created 137 new companies out of trusts and large monopoly organizations. But the process did not stop there. The figures show that after continuing to fall even in the late 1970s, the number of state industrial companies grew sharply (see table 1).

The decentralization in the service sector was even more marked. The monopoly national companies for servicing cars and domestic appliances were each broken up into several hundred units, some of which were merged with units owned by town or district councils. The Engineering Industry Electrical Maintenance Company (Gelka) operated nationally, and in 1982 ran 320 service depots for domestic appliances. In January 1983 the county Gelka service depots were changed into small council-owned companies and the smaller depots were leased out. A newspaper report in the spring of that year declared, 'The centrally decided "atomization", in other words the organization of the Gelka network . . . into units of a rational size, has taken place.'[3]

So the number of small and medium-sized firms grew appreciably but the decentralization process did not stop at restructuring the state-owned sector. At least as significant was an even faster growth in the number of industrial cooperatives, which had been falling between 1975 and 1980 (see table 2).

Table 2

	Industrial cooperatives	
Year	No.	1980=100
1975	793	120
1980	661	100
1982	715	108
1984	811	123
1985	935	141

Source: Statisztikai Évkönyv 1985 (Budapest, 1986), p. 89.

After a period in which the side industrial and servicing activities of the cooperative farms had been hounded and squeezed, the new wave of reform reversed the position again at the end of the 1970s. The *Népszabadság* described the situation thus in the autumn of 1979:

> The assessment of supplementary activities has not always been uniform in this country. From time to time the debate has flared up and arguments and counter-arguments have clashed over whether it is worthwhile [or] permissible for cooperative and state farms to develop supplementary activities . . . It is of great importance to us that it has been clarified: supplementary activity is not a distortion of agriculture but an honest and useful endeavour.

The paper quotes at length from a report by the chairman of the Sárfehér cooperative farm in Izsák, József Szemők:

> The Izsák farm deals with a great deal besides its main activity. An annual 1,355,000 shoe uppers a year are made on the cooperative for the Duna, Alföld and Szombathely footwear factories, whereby it is able to provide employment for 400, mainly women. Its activities extend to construction and haulage; it has its own shops in Izsák and Budapest; it sells its own wines in eight wine bars in Budapest; it has its own brewery and spirit-bottling plant.

The newspaper goes on to say there is another side to what farms are involved in on the side:

> The other significant sphere of supplementary activity is light industry, engineering, plastics and other industrial activity. A sizeable proportion of large-scale farms, almost 80 per cent of them, undertake activity of this kind. In cooperation with industrial fac-

> tories, they manufacture a variety of components, part-assemblies, finished products and rubber articles in large quantities or to special order. They have established production relations with major industrial companies like Ikarus [bus company], United Incandescent Lamps and the Bakony Works [engineering, car parts] of Veszprém, and deliver to them the components they require in their production.[4]

Following the Central Committee resolution of March 1978, there was a new expansion of these side activities. 'According to estimates', the economic weekly *Figyelő* reported, '*the number of workers in auxiliary plants rose by ten thousand in 1979 and the first two months of 1980.* Behind 40 per cent of this growth in the number employed lies new supplementary activity, and behind 60 per cent the expansion of existing auxiliary plants.'[5]

By the summer of 1983 a quite different situation had arisen: 'What has this activity so necessary in prohibitory and freer times alike developed into in recent years? According to the latest figures, it accounts for 34 per cent of the value of cooperative farms' production, the ratio being about 40 per cent in the case of state farms.'[6] The benefits of providing work for local people, of the profit generated by greater processing of produce and of extra production and services for the good of the country became everyday topics in the press. So the industrial sidelines of the cooperative farms gained a new momentum as well, increasing, in fact, by 70 per cent between 1980 and 1985.[7]

A big contribution to the expansion of the cooperatives was made by the 1982 amendment of the act on cooperatives, which swept away a number of restrictions. It allowed them to pursue any kind of economic activity not expressly prohibited by law or ministerial order, or expressly reserved for the state sector.

So the small and medium-sized plants in the cooperative sector became an increasingly important complement to state-owned industry, once the doctrinaire prejudices about ownership relations prevalent in the mid-1970s had been swept away. (This reappraisal and the spurt of growth in small-scale and private activity will be discussed later on, to provide a fuller picture of how the structure of the Hungarian economy was changed, substantially decentralized and indeed pluralized in the early 1980s.)

In general, the 1980s witnessed a return to the reform of 1968 and a continuing development of it. But the environment ran counter to this, with more direct state intervention and restrictive policies aimed at restoring the balance of the economy. This shows up clearly in the process of institutional restructuring, where years went by before a decentralized, competitive structure could be established, an institutional system tailored to the requirements of a command-oriented planning system could be transformed, and the reorganization of the banking system mooted back in 1968 could actually take place. Only in 1986 was the insurance monopoly broken up, and despite a Central Committee resolution in 1984, it was not until January 1987 that the changes in the banking system got under way. The latter brought an end to the monopoly of the National Bank over credit and to the overly centralized banking system characteristic of command based planning, by establishing a *two-tier* system of banking better matched to the autonomy of state companies and better able to ensure the flow and redistribution of capital among freer companies that was demanded by the new economic policy concept. The National Bank reverted to its original functions as a central bank and a bank of issue with responsibility for monetary policy, international credits transactions and control of the domestic money market. The extending of credit to companies and the overall banking tasks connected with the management of company finances passed into the hands of new commercial banks established expressly for this purpose and operating under a competitive, profit-based system. Companies are now able to turn to any of the five commercial banks, and to have business relations with several of them at once. However, the links of the commercial banks with the international money market are still severely restricted under the reformed banking system.

The institutional restructuring in industry, the services and banking was related closely to a central principle of the 1968 reform: fuller assertion of company independence. For this reason, the institutional reform was not confined to decentralizing the corporate, institutional structure.

During these years further steps were taken to establish a more flexible system of institutions. The right of companies to conduct foreign trade, for instance, was gradually extended. As early as August 1978 a leading article in the *Népszabadság* could report:

> Whereas the tasks in relation to the exports and imports required by the economy were handled exclusively by a few '-impex' companies, the number of specialized state and cooperative foreign trade companies is steadily rising today. Quite a few partnerships have formed in the past few years, and to encourage effective marketing, *numerous companies have been allocated occasional rights to independent trade activity.*
>
> Another great incentive to organizational development has been given by the resolution of the party Central Committee last October . . . As regards foreign trade in the engineering industry, for

> instance, 38 per cent of its exports and 27 per cent of its imports are no longer handled by the specialized [foreign trade] companies.[8]

By 1984 over 200 companies had the right to trade abroad on their own account. However, the organization of foreign trading which had been established in the period of the command economy was adjusted to the new operating system rather than abolished root and branch.

Other restrictions on companies were also relaxed to give them more institutional freedom of movement. In 1981 they obtained the right to pursue economically useful activities not defined as their sphere in their charters. In other words, what were known as the company profile limitations, under which the sphere of production was laid down centrally, were abolished. In the same year, companies were granted the right to establish subsidiaries whose activities could be freely determined by the companies. To encourage 'more effective use or augmentation' of fixed assets and working capital, a decree in 1982 allowed bonds to be issued.[9]

In the spring of 1983, the *Népszabadság* reported:

> Although the decree is still very recent, one already hears of several kinds of initiative. The associations of cooperative farms and their joint companies and new small organizations have been remarkably quick to recognize the opportunities inherent in applying for bonds, but one or two well-known large industrial companies are also experimenting with this method. The gas bonds of the National Oil and Petroleum Trust and the issue to finance the brick industry's concrete tile development are foremost.
>
> Communal bonds provide an opportunity to make economic use of personal savings for a common purpose. Here it should be noted that the method has already been tested experimentally in ten communities since the autumn of 1981. During the experiment, the communal bonds were issued by the National Savings Bank in order to finance out of the proceeds some development projects designed to improve the living standards and social welfare provision of the local population in the communities concerned. They planned to issue bonds to a value of some 63 million forints in denominations of one thousand and five thousand forints. So far communal bonds to a value of some 35 million forints have been subscribed to, and the proceeds used, among other things, for improving the sewage system, for road construction, for the building of kindergartens, for medical surgeries, for day-care centres for the elderly, and in one place, for an indoor swimming pool.[10]

In the autumn of 1981 the economic weekly *Figyelő* had published as an 'article for discussion' a piece by Sándor Kopátsy entitled 'The Role of Joint-Stock Companies', in which he recommended the socialist joint-stock company as a major institution for bringing about an effective flow of capital within the economy.[11]

Institutional reinforcement of corporate independence was also furthered by changes in the institutions of supervision and direction. In this way a proposal made by an expert committee set up back in December 1956 to abolish the strongly centralized system of sectoral industrial ministries was realized at last. These ministries, which controlled industry at company level, were to be combined into a single Ministry for Industry which was to act as an industrial policy-making and supervisory body. However, when the idea of institutional reform was rejected, the conditions for accomplishing this failed to come out in 1957. With the abolition of the system of compulsory plan indicators under the 1968 reform, a demand naturally arose for the abolition of ministerial paternalism and direct control. Again nothing happened, because of the compromises reached at that stage and the obstacles to further progress in the 1970s, which have already been discussed. Only in 1980 did the government abolish the branch ministries, under Decree No. 19/1980, published on December 6, which established a single Ministry for Industry in their place. As from January 1, 1981, the Ministry of Metallurgy and the Engineering Industry, the Ministry for Light Industry and the Ministry for Heavy Industry were closed.[12] The central institutions for controlling industry by directive had been abolished.

However, this measure of institutional reform was by no means a consistent one, since the managers of the formally independent state companies were still appointed and dismissed at the behest of the minister; in other words, company managers were directly dependent on the ministry and accountable to it, not to their company workforce. This element in the reform process is in itself a fascinating case-study, since at the time the Hungarian economic reform was mooted in 1956–7 company workers' councils were a fact of life under specific historical conditions, and at that time even the government had wanted to incorporate them into the new system of economic management. Then the political and power struggles and the consolidation of the new government in the spring of 1957 had led to the winding up of the workers' councils. The company councils formed to replace them never actually functioned in practice. By the end of the 1950s the institution of self-management had become tainted by the label of 'revisionism' and so ideologically and politically taboo. However, the self-contradictory process of reform did not exclude self-management in the single sector of the agricultural cooperatives after agriculture was collectivized in the early 1960s, and particularly after the 1965 decision to go ahead with the reform. Self-management on the farms contributed substantially to the development of a proprietorial incentive and awareness, and so to creating a vested interest in long-term development. But all this was still lacking in the state sector. As with other elements of the reform process, the pioneering experiences and achievements of reform in agriculture led to conclusions being drawn about the functioning of other sectors of the economy. This aspect was openly expressed by Ferenc Havasi in his speech proposing the Central Committee's reform resolution of April 1984:

> Will company autonomy, its extent, and the ensuring on our part of extensive rights to companies of disposal over property not lead to a weakening of the central state intention, to an undesirable strengthening of group interest? In answering this question it is worth referring to the experiences of the Hungarian cooperative movement . . . Today we already know how this greater independence furthered the emergence of responsible entrepreneurial behaviour in economic activity . . . It was in this sector that a few commendable methods of economic activity emerged and became general practice . . . These, now that the system of management is being further developed, we want to utilize in a broader sphere.[13]

So the transformation of the system of managing state companies returned to the agenda and was accomplished in the course of 1985–6.

For the measure – an amendment of the Company Act of 1977 – that provided for elements of self-management only appeared in October 1984. In the case of some three-quarters of the companies, the regulation left it to company councils set up at this time, and in the case of small companies with up to 200 employees to the general meeting of company workers, to appoint and dismiss company managers, which had previously been a minister's prerogative. Moreover, it was decreed that in companies which did not remain under direct state supervision (mainly those involved in the defence industry or with a public service or communal profile) 'the general management of the company' was to be carried out by the company council or general assembly of workers. In such cases, according to Article 15 of the amended act, 'the decision concerning the election and dismissal of the manager rests with this body'.[14]

The post of company manager was placed on a competitive basis. With a term of office of five years, company managers were made accountable to the company itself instead of to the minister. Here one cannot of course say that the system of self-management as such has been applied, since with the exception of agriculture it is valid only for the smallest companies. But elements of self-management were built into the structure of the overwhelming majority of state companies, since both the workforce and the management were represented on the company council. (It is worth noting at this point that company councils were originally envisaged as possessing a corporate character: a third of the members would have been delegated by the workers' representatives, a third by the manager and a third by the central authorities of the state. Eventually the idea of the central authorities being represented was thrown out: 'We cannot restrict the company independence that we wish to extend by sending . . . outside experts into the companies . . . We can adequately ensure the central intention is asserted . . . by the instruments of regulation as well', it was stressed by Central Committee Secretary Ferenc Havasi.)[15]

27 Internal contradictions and delays in the process of reform

From the late 1970s onwards it became quite clear that Hungary was returning to its earlier course of economic reform. More was involved than a rehabilitation and reinstatement of the 1968 reform. In the case of the price system and of the system of economic institutions, there was a discernible continuation and further development of the earlier phase, which had been heavily laden with compromise.

Yet this third phase of reform – hallmarked by the decisions of principle taken between the October 1977 outline of a strategy for foreign economic and structural transformation and the Central Committee's radicalizing resolutions of April 1984 and July 1987 and by the practical measures to apply them which remained partial even in the mid-1980s – cannot be considered an unequivocal continuation. For one thing, the measures to continue and develop the reform, all of which were aimed ultimately at strengthening commodity and money relations and market conditions and influences by increasing company independence and the competitive environment, were accompanied and weakened by government activity that worked in the opposite direction. For another there were long delays in pursuing and carrying out the reform objectives once they had been identified.

Both these assertions require further explanation. As for the self-contradictions, the picture was perfectly clear. The disruption by recession and domestic upheavals of a growth trend which had lasted a quarter of a century, coupled with the lessons of the anti-reform trend in the mid-1970s, made it quite clear the reform had to be continued, but the government was propelled, by its short-term restrictive measures to restore the balance of the economy, into a course whose every detail worked against the recognized reforming objectives. The main purpose of the 1979–80 price reform was to expose companies to more market, indeed world-market influences. The government that applied the reform thwarted it by using the prevailing functional mechanism and system of regulators to divert some 90 per cent of the extra profits earned by highly profitable companies through direct intervention, whilst keeping inefficient companies afloat with regular subsidies from the budget. In 1986 and in the first six months of 1987 alone, the government spent 50,000 million forints on financing loss-making companies – a sum almost equal to the budget deficit in the same period. The policy of improving the balance of the economy led, particularly during the grave liquidity crisis of 1982–3, to the use of an almost unprecedented degree of direct control which extended to the minutest of details, right down to specific, compulsory export assignments at company level, to similar prescriptions covering income, to centrally determined diversion of funds, to import and investment curbs, and from time to time to almost solo centralization by a single 'crisis manager'. Clearly this was, to some extent, inevitable, and even effective in keeping the country solvent and ensuring its economic survival. But in the face of all expectations, this kind of restrictive, direct control turned out not to be the temporary, emergency measure intended. It persisted throughout the first half of the 1980s, and it remains true even as this book is written that it has become, over the last eight years, the fundamental obstacle to the genuine emergence of the reform process.

The other factor – the procrastination in pursuing the reform objectives once they had been identified – arose out of the overall political conditions in the first half of the 1980s, and gave rise to strong criticism of the economic administration. There was often a gulf between the steps needed and the steps taken. Often measures with social repercussions that would have run counter to a quarter of a century's social policy in areas like living standards and employment were required to avert the consequences of the economic disruption. Instead the inertia of traditional political reflexes persisted.

So some heated debates on reform were triggered off during this ten-year period. Some contributors traced the problems and difficulties to the tampering with the traditional model for a socialist economy: there was too much talk of markets, an excessively liberal economic policy and an inadequate use of central planning and regulation, they said. Others criticized the inadequacy of the reform and an economic management system which in spite of the regulators bore a remarkable resemblance to the one under the command economy of yore. They declared that further reform was required, and recommended a 'reform of the reform', a free-market system purged of state interference, the introduction of 'entrepreneurial' socialism'.

The debates were a natural consequence of the complexity of the situation, of the slowness in adjusting to the new conditions and the conflicting steps taken, and of a general desire to have a set course that could be firmly implemented. At the same time, various forms of discontent were expressed over the ambiguity of the reform process in the first half of the 1980s. Despite all the genuine progress, one cannot speak of any substantial new development of the Hungarian economic model, even in the 1979–87 period. In fact, the beneficial effects of eliminating some of the 1968 compromises were largely cancelled out by the brakes imposed.

The linkage of central planning with market elements and the operation of a regulated market contained the inherent danger of incongruent economic activity based on plan-based directives and operated through special regulators. In the event this occurred more intensely than ever in several important areas. 'Special regulation', a leading official at the Planning Office pointed out, 'is usually a specific form of the system of planning directives.'[1]

Having said all that, one must add that the period was marked by an unprecedented development of small-scale private business, which gained a new role as an integral and institutional incorporation of the second economy into the functioning of the economy as a whole. This was among the salient developments of the reform process, and perhaps the only one that can be regarded as a major breakthrough.

28 A new role for small business

From the beginnings of the Hungarian economic reform it can be observed that every wave of reform was accompanied by a reappraisal of the role of the private sector involving a more liberal attitude or even an encouragement of it. This found expression not only in the expansion of private, small-scale industry and retail trading but in the emergence of new forms for it that in some cases paved the way to some kind of private activity within the framework of common ownership. In 1957 there was the leasing out of state-owned shops, for instance, and in the 1960s the special role assigned to household farming.

After 1979, small private business in general, and an extensive combining of public ownership with private activity in particular, acquired a significant role. This was due not least to the favourable experiences during the previous waves of reform, particularly with the special symbiosis established between cooperative and household farming. Once again, a reappraisal of the significance of household farming to the cooperatives, with the revision and rejection of the doctrinaire restrictions placed on it in the mid-1970s, blazed the trail for the private sector.

For the 'theoretical' exclusion of household farming from socialist cooperative ownership, as described above, had caused a dramatic fall in production and the mass slaughter of livestock. The 13 per cent drop in the number of small farms between 1972 and 1978, in the wake of the various restrictive measures, was a warning and an omen. This response by the peasantry was the reason why household farming was the area in which the speediest turn against the anti-reform campaign of the mid-1970s took place. By the beginning of 1977, the central party daily was signalling this:

> In the second half of last year the government . . . examined the position in several branches of agriculture. The areas of farming put

on the agenda were those in which . . . the desire to produce had waned . . . [and] a fallback was noticeable . . . Cases in point were the production of vegetables, the planting of orchards and vineyards, the production of pigmeat and the breeding of cattle.

After listing the measures and price increases introduced, the *Népszabadság*, without putting forward a formal argument, came out against the preference given to incomes policy two or three years earlier and restated the priority for production characteristic of the reform: 'As regards the tax policy affecting household farms and the practice to be followed with it, the following principle applies: *The prime thing is not the tax revenue, but the production. What we expect of small-scale production is not more tax, but more produce and products.*'[1]

In the autumn of that year, the *Népszabadság* published a theoretical article under the characteristic title 'Further Development of Socialist Property Relations' (in other words conforming to the rhetoric of two years earlier). This declared household farming to be indispensable at the prevailing level of development, and reversed the argument of the preceding years:

> It is in society's interest to develop, not to repress, the household farms. With the strengthening of the cooperatives, substantial changes can also be seen in the nature of the household farms. Relying on the cooperatives (and on the state companies) and in integral connection with them, they play a more intensive, production-complementing part, whereby they also contribute to the growth of the commodity stocks, [and do so] moreover in accordance with the material interest of the country, the cooperative and the individual. Not only does this make the household farms more intensive, it presumably prolongs the period of their existence substantially.[2]

So the 'further development of socialist property relations' was no longer associated with an approach by the cooperatives to state ownership, or with any declaration that household farming was unsocialist by nature. In fact it called for a link between collective and household farming of a lasting kind.

Thereafter the press was full of contributions indicating the change of line: Household farming 'is *the most sensitive area of agricultural production* . . . It adapts extremely quickly to factors influencing production, not only to favourable phenomena but to uncertain ones . . .' Should it not see its way financially with a certain product 'it will not experiment with it the following year . . . And this is the better case. There is worse trouble if it ceases production altogether.' After the deterioration of production security and the will to produce in the preceding years, there was an emphatic return to the reasoning of the late 1960s: 'We all have an interest . . . in creating the right conditions for *strengthening the security of production and will to produce in this area as well.*'[3]

The example of the Haladás (Progress) cooperative in Forráskut was given of how a cooperative 'undertook the organization of production for the small units'. In this case the backing of a 'strong, evenly developing collective farm allows more attention to be paid to small-scale production as well'.[4]

The party Central Committee took up a new position in its resolution of March 1978: the cooperative and state farms were to assist household farmers and establish close ties with them. The concept of the symbiosis between collective and household farming was clearly expressed, or rather reaffirmed:

> The greatest change has been brought about by the spread of a variant of household and small-scale production which is better than traditional household farming in many respects, and this is *small-scale production linking with the large farm* . . . For a sizeable proportion of the large farms these days employ methods and procedures for organizing small-scale production and marketing, whereby only individual parts or elements of production are taken over by the household or auxiliary farms. These large farms provide the services required to develop this production on a long-term basis, providing the household farms with good quality seed, seedlings and breeding materials, looking after the plant protection and organizing veterinary services, and purchasing and sales of goods produced on the small-scale farms.[5]

In the summer of 1980 a head of division at the Central Statistical Office announced triumphantly:

> A special pattern of Hungarian household farm has emerged, in which, characteristically, the collective and the household farm form an integral cooperating entity . . . *Some 2,300 million hours* a year are spent [working] on the household and small farms, more than on all the large, mechanized socialist farms put together . . . The household, auxiliary and other small farms [smallholders] account for *one-third* (and in some years a still greater proportion) of total agricultural production . . . In recent years the value of all the agricultural produce turned out by small producers *exceeded 60,000 million forints,* which is roughly equivalent to [the value of] the Hungarian economy's agricultural and food exports.[6]

The experience built up in agriculture and the renewed combination of collective and private activity that was emerging began to exert a stronger influence than agriculture had ever done over other sectors of the economy, as the third wave of reform arrived.

Of course there was a link in the 1980s between the encouragement of small-scale private activity – the legalization of the 'second economy' in the 1980s – and the deteriorating economic balance, the sharp fall in the growth rate and the plunge in the rate of investment. It became necessary to open and expand opportunities to earn extra income in order to forestall or at least alleviate a fall in living standards. It was equally important that services to the population could be improved in this way without any state investment. Since the investment rate had fallen from 25 to 10 per cent of national income, it would not have been possible to develop this backward service sector in any other way. Finally, the private sector was where the extra labour input required by the economy and for family finances could best be encouraged. So a paradoxical situation emerged: in a deteriorating economic situation the working week was cut back (first to a 44-hour five-day week and then to a 40-hour week) in order to improve living conditions, yet in the same years there was a marked increase in the input of labour into the economy, due to the extensive development of second jobs and other side activities.

So small-scale private activity assumed a role of a different quality, becoming an important new feature of the Hungarian economic system. In February 1980 the HSWP Political Committee adopted a major resolution 'On the Role and Opportunities for Development of the Secondary Economy', and this immediately became the starting-point for practical processes of change.

The proposal on which the resolution was based drew attention to the fact that some 16 to 18 per cent of the total time spent in society on work was accounted for by the secondary economy. This was equivalent to a quarter of the total time worked in the state and cooperative sectors. Taking part in this were some 3.5 million active earners and some million to a million-and-a-half people not in regular employment, in other words about half the country's population.

The Political Committee had this to say about a sector whose existence until recently has been ignored, or even banned and persecuted in many fields: 'By and large useful activity is being pursued within the second economy: it relieves shortages [and] it is a major supplementary source for our development. A proportion of the real demand and needs are being met, alongside the socialist sector, by the secondary economy.'

The train of thought in this realistic resolution was as follows:

> The secondary economy must be placed in the service of social progress in a more organized way . . . [It] must be integrated more closely into the socialist sector so that social organization should prevail in this area as well . . . This can produce a greater diversity in the form and size of companies, a spread of small and medium-sized plants (cooperatives, forms of casual association, business partnerships, etc.), and a simplification of the conditions under which small and medium-sized plants may function . . . Hungarian agriculture can serve as a pattern for suitable forms of the division of labour, having established a specific form of integration between the socialist large farm and the secondary economy. The principles applied there can also be asserted more generally, principally in the realm of the construction industry, commerce and the services.
>
> In spheres of activity where integration with the socialist sector is not economically expedient, the matching of supply with demand and the elimination of monopoly situations must be regularized by issuing more operating permits and through economic competition . . . Economic, legal and ideological barriers to the development of organizational ability that is not centrally initiated must be steadily eliminated. For this purpose, socialist organizational forms may be combined with individual initiative and with the shouldering of risk by the general public using their own savings . . . Recognition must be accorded to high incomes acquired by work and in proportion with it – including income from the secondary economy . . . The earning and accumulation of income which can be accorded social recognition should be regulated through taxation in such a way that the scale of deduction from income does not obstruct the efforts to engage in [economic] activity.

The resolution also stated clearly that the structural changes which were inevitable in the socialist (i.e. state and cooperative) sector would involve a restructuring which would release labour. Some of this labour could find new job opportunities in the second economy, it said.

The Political Committee made an effort to define clearly the boundaries and limits to the development of this sector. A consistent attitude should be taken in assessing the social utility of activity in the second economy, but it had to be pointed out that political recognition implied not 'an expansion of private activity to the detriment of the socialist sector, but a more effective linking of it into the overall economic system, the sphere of authority of the planned economy'. The Political Committee made it clear that 'the legal and organizational settlement of the links between the socialist sector and the second economy' must be coupled with 'firm action, using both socio-economic and legal means, against all damaging phenomena discernible in the activity of the secondary economy that undermine the credibility of our achievements to date, are alien to the socialist order of society, do harm to social ownership and so give rise to a bad socio-political climate of opinion and impede our subsequent development'.[7]

It is worth noting that a position on amending the labour legislation in a way that conformed with the line put forward in the Political Committee resolution had been devised a few months earlier, in September 1979. In the resolution itself it was stated that this

> should contribute to effective utilization of working hours and reveal supplementary employment opportunities . . . To this end it must become possible for regular, voluntarily undertaken work outside normal working hours to emerge at the original [place of] employment either connected with the [normal] sphere of work or even in the form of other activity unrelated to it. We must allow, wherever the nature of the work allows it and [the work] cannot be undertaken within working hours, preparatory and completing tasks connected with the sphere of work to be undertaken outside working hours for payment . . . Within justifiable limits certain restrictions on the employment of manual workers outside their main jobs must be eased.[8]

With this the government had in fact put into practice the lessons to be drawn from sociological findings. One of the foremost scholars in the field argued as follows:

> The heightening of the contradictions also results from the second economy's in many respects unclarified situation and varying official estimation and treatment. As a result the sector, still to this day, functions largely on the margin between legality and illegality . . . From the research findings one can draw the most important conclusion, which can be regarded as the guideline for practical action. The economic policy of the 1980s in general, and labour policy in particular, must ascribe greater importance and assign a more important role than it has to production and service activity outside the socialist economic organizations, particularly if economic growth in the socialist sector and the inevitable slowing of the rate of improvement in living standards are taken into consideration as well. If one accepts this, the right starting-point seems to be the conjecture that if one creates *legal* functional frameworks and forms more suitable and more diverse than the present ones, and to assure the sector more balanced treatment, this will improve the performance of the second economy and at the same time alleviate the current conflicts arising out of its existence.[9]

The legalization of the 'second economy' that was actually implemented had an effect on very broad areas of the economy. As a result of all this (and in this respect in a way similar to what had happened during the previous waves of reform) the growth of small, private industry and retailing was triggered off by a range of preferences and incentives. There had been slightly fewer than 36,000 self-employed artisans in 1975. By 1985 there were over 43,000. Counting those they employed, the figure rose from 83,000 to 96,000.

The growth in the private retail trade was bigger still. There had been just over 9,000 self-employed shopkeepers and 900 operators of private catering places in 1975, but in 1985 there were around 20,000 and over 5,000 respectively. The number of the two combined, therefore, shot from 10,000 to over 25,000.[10]

As a growth in the number of private craftsmen, shopkeepers and caterers and their employees of almost 40 per cent goes to show, the expansion of the private sector was sufficient to affect its importance significantly, even though its weight in the economy as a whole remained small. Between 1980 and 1985, the private sector's share of national income almost doubled from 3.5 per cent to 6.3 per cent, which can still be regarded as low in comparison with a number of other socialist countries and with earlier periods in Hungary. (In 1960, the year in which the collectivization of agriculture was completed, the private sector had accounted for 9 per cent of Hungary's national income.)[11]

Nor was this expansion of the private sector the most noteworthy feature of the reform process in the 1980s. Far more important, as the Political Committee resolution quoted earlier emphasized, was the establishment of specific and novel combinations between private activity and the various forms of public ownership. It was through these, for instance, that the experiences in agriculture were drawn upon in the service industries to produce a system whereby small state-owned shops and catering places could be operated on contract or leased by private families. In 1981 only a little over 400 state shops were operated on a lease, but by 1985 the number was almost 4,500. In catering, the number of leased units rose from a little over 1,500 to over 7,000 in the same period. Taking the two together the increase was from just over 2,000 to almost 12,000. The leases had to be bid for, but under the system loss-making units started to yield a trading profit and the standard of service improved.

To run a shop on contract one had to have been employed by the 'landlord' company. Both the contracts and the leaseholds were for a maximum of five years, after which the right to keep the contract or lease for another five years had to be won through another public tender. The bidding took place in the presence of a notary public, and the unit went to the person prepared to pay the highest fee out of the takings. Very often it was previous unit managers with a good local knowledge who applied. One sign of the interest is that there were more than fifty bidders for ten units offered by the South Buda Catering Company, and bidding often pushed the price 20 or 30 per cent above the reserve. 'One hopes that this is the birth of a socialist form of enterprise whose experiences can be utilized in other sectors of the economy as well', one newspaper report said, 'above all in the sphere of [maintenance] *services*, and which is likely to increase the income of the economy by several thousand million forints in the coming years.'[12]

Having run at a loss before, the catering units concerned were soon making substantial profits for the state now that they were free of any cumbersome apparatus and able to operate in a flexible way. For instance, the 10 per cent of restaurants run under a lease or contract accounted for 18 per cent of the sales turnover in the first six months of 1982, and their combined operating profits of 500 million forints were equal to those of the other 90 per cent still run directly by the catering companies.[13]

In certain respects one can consider as a kind of combination of the public and private sectors the rapidly emerging system that released the legal and other constraints on repair and service work done after hours by those in full employment. Typical part-time activities were television and radio repairs, plumbing, manual work on building sites or the use of private cars as taxis, and they and many others greatly contributed to the services available to the general public. The licensing of private taxis was a typical case: in Budapest, for example, a stroke of the official pen succeeded in more than doubling the number of taxis during the early 1980s, without the state investing a penny. Indeed there was a considerable gain for the state in terms of tax revenue.

A curious, experimental combination of public and private activity emerged in large state-owned factories, where 'intra-company economic working partnerships' (in other publications the terms 'economic workteams' or 'economic working communities' are also used) were set up. In 1980 this form of enterprise had not even existed. In November 1981, after central approval, the management at Csepel Auto issued a circular to its workforce asking them to 'make proposals about the type of small enterprises, within the large company, they consider justified and feasible'. As the *Népszabadság* reported, 'The proposals were not long in arriving. As a start, the workers of the large company recommended setting up *eight small cooperatives and 33 economic partnerships.'* An engineering partnership to prepare newly purchased machine tools for making power-assisted steering units was formed, and put in fifty extra hours of work a month. The single-purpose machine constructors set up two partnerships.[14] In summer 1982 there were press reports that fifty-six partnerships had been formed among employees at the Duna Steelworks, with 'startling' results:

> Productivity in the small enterprises averaged one-and-a-half times the level and in some cases is three times the level of productivity in normal working hours. Among the reasons are some quite tangible ones. After all, the first partnerships were set up by the best and more enterprising workers. They were very choosy about who they allowed into the team. Another indisputable fact is that . . . extraordinary care is taken everywhere to ensure the partnership does not have to stop work for lack of materials, machinery or tools . . . A great impetus is provided by higher earnings as well . . . Potter about the job from six in the morning till two in the afternoon, really put on the pressure from two till six, and have the same person in the same factory earn three times as much: it's a typical case of schizophrenia . . . But what has actually happened is one of the things the new measures had sought to achieve: to provide the opportunity to pay proportionately for a higher performance.[15]

By the following spring, 1,500 people at the Duna Steelworks were working in 125 economic partnerships within the company. But great concern was already expressed by the trade union secretaries at each plant:

> The small enterprises at the works are spreading a materialistic attitude, and robbing the family, private life, study of the arts, voluntary work and political activity of time; they are weakening the trade union movement and the cohesive force of work competitions, helping some to achieve undeservedly high incomes, endangering the balance between goods supply and purchasing power, upsetting the system in the factories, weakening the work ethic, and ultimately attacking our socialist values.

Others put it like this:

> The trouble is that there is a great deal of confusion in people's minds. Many feel that work done in official working hours is socialist, and what is done in a small enterprise is *not* socialist. Yet the workers are producing with the same means of production that are in socialist

> ownership, for the benefit of the socialist plant. The difference is merely that the small enterprise is at least twice as productive and pays them better. Could that be why it is not socialist?[16]

Pressing for a greater compulsion to perform, the state secretary for industry pointed out that the directly motivated performance within the intra-company partnerships after working hours, using precisely the same equipment, was not infrequently 25 to 40 per cent higher than it was in regular working time.[17]

The tensions produced by the new institution within companies and society as a whole became a subject of daily discussion all over the country. Why are there not adequate incentives to perform better in regular working hours? A contributor to the weekly economic paper *Figyelő* put the view of many: 'I *consider it unfavourable*, or at least *question* whether it is tolerable in the long term for a quasi-dual level of performance and payment to emerge within one and the same organization.' The intra-company partnerships (workteams) became at once controversial and indispensable. They raised the companies' capacity and provided the needful conditions for supplementary activities. But as the journalist just remarked with justification, they were 'almost an indictment of company labour management' that 'illuminates the limitations and performance-restricting influence of wage and income regulation'.[18] The experiences at the Duna Steelworks and the fact that 60 per cent of the partnerships were engaged in maintenance, revealed that their establishment had primarily 'been intended to evade the obstacles posed by the present regulation of wages', as the same writer pointed out in an earlier article.[19]

One cannot yet say how viable the experiment has been or what benefits, direct and indirect, it brings, but one can say the partnerships struck root very rapidly. After the measures were taken at the end of 1981, there were 1,634 of them in 1982 involving scarcely more than 18,000 workers and engineers. By 1985 there were well over 13,000 partnerships (workteams) inside companies involving around 168,000 people. They have been carrying out work for their companies which in some cases is a substitute for cooperation with other companies, even foreign ones, and in a number of major factories and sectors they have made a substantial contribution in important areas of production. This they have been doing after hours and at weekends, in some 3 per cent of the hours worked in industry, under contracts with companies whose machinery and facilities they use.

Mention must finally be made of the extra-company 'economic working partnerships' and the not dissimilar 'small cooperatives' and 'civil-law companies' founded privately in both the production and service sectors. Again, there had been no such institution in 1980, but in the autumn of 1981 the *Népszabadság* was reporting on keen interest:

> Although the starting pistol for the new [forms of] small enterprise will only go off at the beginning of next year, the recent publication of the legal regulations has already led to preparatory, organizing work in a number of areas . . . *Vilmos Mithaleczky*, now retired, was previously a commercial consultant with the National Petroleum and Gas Industry Trust.
>
> 'I and thirty associates of mine who are full of ideas want to establish a small cooperative to organize other small enterprises. We have started out from the existence in the country of vast potential whose tapping would also be in the national economic interest, but up to now, for a variety of reasons, the people who will actually do it have not met. We are digging up obvious ideas of this kind, and then we shall bring the business partners together . . .'
>
> The 'Soft-Coop' small cooperative, on the other hand, was actually formed in mid-September, with *László Pintér*, a distinguished figure in Hungarian computer technology, as its chairman.
>
> 'We design basic and applied software, in other words we prepare computer programmes to orders from home and abroad. We undertake all the orders great and small which have not been "worth the while" up to now of the big computer organizing institutes . . . An indication of the demand is the fact that we already have contracts worth 1.4 million forints. For the time being there are twenty-six of us, in most cases not beginners but experienced, middle-aged professional computer systems engineers and designers.'[20]

At the beginning of 1983, a year after the frames had been provided, there were 11,000 new small organizations, more than half of them being in commerce and catering.[21] As opposed to 800 in 1982, there were almost 3,000 private industrial partnerships by 1985, and the number of people they employed rose from slightly less than 4,000 to 16,000.

If one also counts in the traditional combination of collective and household farming, dating back to the 1960s, which had stood the test of time and begun to flourish in the late 1970s, there was a very extensive development of auxiliary private activity in production and the services, in most cases amounting to a private–public symbiosis rather than a straight private sector. Whereas the private sector proper accounts for only 6 per cent of national income, it is estimated that the contribution of auxiliary private activity is several times that proportion.

As early as the spring of 1980, István Földes was assembling some startling figures in a summary of the various calculations and estimates of the role of this auxiliary private activity:

> If one takes as a basis the full range of activities classified under the secondary economy, i.e. from second jobs to household and auxiliary farms and moonlighting . . . and if one also includes in this category small-scale industry and retailing, the estimates are that some 75 per cent of active earners (3.5 million people) and one-and-a-half million of those not in full employment, in other words at least half the population of the country, take part in the secondary economy in some form. That also means that about 70 to 75 per cent of families receive secondary-economy income. According to the various calculations and estimates, 10 per cent of those in managerial positions, 20 to 25 per cent of the intelligentsia, one-third of other white-collar workers, 60 to 70 per cent of non-agricultural manual workers, 80 to 90 per cent of agricultural workers and 40 per cent of the non-employed do regular extra work, i.e. earn additional income within the secondary economy. But in the case of some 70 per cent of the families involved this only brings the family income up to around the average level, and only a few tens of thousands of families earn very high incomes under our conditions.
>
> The household and auxiliary farms, with wide-ranging assistance from large socialist farms and the state, account for a third of gross *agricultural* production. Within the framework of this economy *35,000–45,000 family houses,* or 40 to 45 per cent of all new dwellings, are built per year. The secondary economy meets approximately three-quarters of the needs in the *service* sector, while *private* accommodation provides nearly half of all commercial accommodation . . . We must rid ourselves of the misconception, reflected in Hungarian conditions, that socialist production is synonymous with large-scale production.[22]

Taking private small-scale industry, intra-company partnerships (workteams) and other forms of private activity into account, the private sphere also plays a part in industrial production.

Based upon all this, one can say that by the mid-1980s small-scale private activity had become an extremely important contributor to national income, accounting for about a third of it.

These facts demonstrate in themselves that an essential change, a hidden pluralization, has started in the ownership structure of the Hungarian economy, even though the supplementary private activities have primarily developed in forms that are combined into collective, public ownership. By correcting the 'over-nationalizations' carried out in the late forties and early fifties, this could lead from the previously monolithic theory and practice of ownership relations to the emergence of a new, mixed structure of ownership (property) relations.

The above listed dominating forms of private activities, while bringing about changes amounting to a model and starting substantial transformation processes, undeniably carried the signs of strong compromise as well. The government did not want to face the ownership relations and property structure developed in consequence of the 'over-nationalizations' – with the demand for theoretical and political clarification and rethinking – and thus the various complementary private activities could be mainly realized in the second economy. The latter, however, not only offered a ground for but also set narrower-than-justified limits to private activities.

A thorough analysis of these processes suggests that the institutional framework of private activities should be substantially expanded.

29 From reform towards a change of system

The relatively long history of the Hungarian economic reforms came to an historical turning-point in 1987–9. The overly gradual, cautious, stop–go process of reform had been unable to produce a system flexible enough to react to challenge of the world economy. The economic crisis which developed in the 1970s and 1980s halted the impressive rate of economic growth and led by the 1980s to a typical 'stagflation' accompanied by a halt and then a decline in the previously continuous increase in the real incomes of the population. Steadily increasing budget, foreign trade and balance of payments deficits reflected a lack of equilibrium in the economy, and the foreign debts which accumulated in an almost intolerable repayment burden. Yet all these problems remained unanswered: instead of painful modernization and adjustment of the Hungarian economy there was continuous erosion and an increasing relative lag behind the West.

Hungary's economic failure in the 1970s and 1980s discredited the reformed system too. It proved that the philosophy of combining the concepts of a planned and a market economy and simulating a market by using what were referred to as regulators was unable to match the requirements of the last third of the twentieth century, even though it created a better and relatively more flexible model for a socialist economy. The need for a much more radical reform became clear. Needless to say, the dismantling of obsolete ideological barriers and the correction of the Utopian misunderstandings had implications far beyond the economic arena. To the reforming wing of the ruling party the importance of ensuring the political requisites for change became plain. The supporters of reform had learned from their own historical experience that the monolithic ownership and economic system could not be destroyed, and a real market and real incentives introduced, while the monolithic political framework of the 'party state' remained in place.

The first phase in the Hungarian process of reform, which could be no more than a set of corrective measures to 'improve' the command economy or make it more efficient, led to recognition of the need for essential reform of the economy. So in the middle to late 1960s the reform process passed from its introductory, 'corrective' stage to a second stage of real reform; whereas corrections had not conflicted with the existing, orthodox ideology of 'socialism', that ideology was attacked and revealed as obsolete by essential economic reform. The incompatibility of the two became more and more evident, but it was the reforms that were trimmed to fit the mould of Soviet-type socialism.

By 1987 the imperative, unpostponable and undeniable need to 'reform the reform' with a comprehensive strategy that coupled political reform with economic had visibly undermined the rigid structures and eroded the official ideology.

The old leadership was swept away in a peaceful revolution. There was a revolt against half-measures by the party intelligentsia and some of the leading members of the party apparatus. The green light for a more radical transformation had been given by the opening up in the Soviet Union under Gorbachev. That new situation of *perestroika*, *glasnost* and warmer international relations strengthened the forces for reform in the HSWP. It not only weakened the position of the party's conservative rank and file, but swept away the biggest external barrier to radical reform. The path was clear. The party conference of May 1988 announced a turn towards a mixed ownership structure (i.e. strong privatization of the economy), a market economy shorn of the adjective 'socialist' which had hitherto signified strong curbs on the market, and above all a programme that combined economic with political reform. The declared aims of political pluralism and constitutionalism of the system (*Rechtsstaatlichkeit*) came to the fore. Within a year they had led to the acceptance of a multi-party system of parliamentary democracy. Once the opposition parties had emerged and reached outline agreement with the ruling party, the road was open for free, representative elections, without restrictions on nominations or other traditional means of control. At the time of writing, general elections early in 1990 will close the chapter of Hungarian history in which the monolithic Soviet type of political system held sway and represent an attempt to establish democracy. Meanwhile private ownership almost without restrictions, guarantees for foreign investment (even 100 per cent foreign ownership), a beginning of privatization of some state-owned firms and the chance for members of cooperative farms to decide whether to continue collectively or on private farm basis, look highly likely to lead to a mixed economy. A programme of transition to a market economy was devised by an expert committee appointed by the government in the summer of 1988, and published a year later. The task, historically, is unparalleled. The world knows how to run a market economy, but never before has one been 'introduced' in a matter of a few years. The steps towards liberalization of imports and wages, deliberate 'deregulation' and an end to corporate subsidies have begun to be taken.

However, the traps and dangers are quite daunting. Disregarding the possibility of a restoration of 'traditional' socialism by conservative forces inside or outside the country, even the path of peaceful transition is extremely difficult and untrodden, especially in a period of economic crisis, rising inflation and falling living standards. Adjustment to the world economy, reorientation of foreign trade away from the non-market Comecon system to the competitive world market, and preparations for making the Hungarian currency convertible must go hand in hand with economic stabilization and restoration of budget, foreign trade and balance of payments equilibrium. Combined with all these tasks is the immense undertaking of political transformation.

Meanwhile the developments in Hungary are generating conflicts with some neighbouring socialist countries. Hungary's alliance system forms part of the post-war arrangements fixed by the great powers. Although economic ties within a Comecon framework are diminishing, they are still quite important. All in all, Hungary is strongly dependent on its socialist neighbours, where there are a great many uncertainties. The old unity has ceased to exist.

Hungary's foreign policy is becoming increasingly independent and mindful of national interests. Another blow to orthodox ideology has been struck by a thorough re-evaluation of the past, notably the dramatic events of 1956 and the role of Imre Nagy. This led to a polarization of opinion in the Hungarian Socialist Workers' Party and ultimately its change towards a West European socialist type party. The reburial of Imre Nagy and his comrades and the death in the same summer of 1989 of János Kádár, the country's paramount leader for a third of a century, brought an era of Hungarian history to a close, symbolically and actually. What has begun and continues is nothing other than a comprehensive transformation, a fundamental change in the concept of socialism and in the political, economic and social system of the country.

This framework of events is opening up a new road and stage of reform. The new system will certainly not be a traditional capitalism and decidedly not a semi-reformed taditional socialism. The marks of the economic system will be mixed ownership, a market economy and strong social guarantees. However, this road will be strongly influenced also by external factors and by domestic political struggles.

The history and lessons of the economic reforms remain a living factor in the future course of events in Hungary, and no doubts in the efforts and trends towards reform in other socialist countries.

Notes

Introduction

1 György Ránki, *Magyarország gazdasága az első 3 éves terv időszakában /1947–1949/* (Hungary's Economy in the Period of the First Three-year Plan) (Budapest, 1963), pp. 110–11.
2 *Statisztikai Évkönyv* (Statistical Yearbook) *1949–1955* (Budapest, 1957), pp. 128–9 and 252.
3 The new system of material management was established between 1949 and 1951 on the basis of Resolution No. NT. 371/1949 and then Decree No. 103/1950.IV.6.MT, and Enabling Resolution No. 384/1950.NT.
4 Cf. Béla Csikós-Nagy, 'Az ipari termelői árak ujjárendezése' (The Restructuring of Industrial Producer Prices), *Közgazdasági Szemle* (Economic Review, hereafter *KSz*), No. 8–9, 1957, pp. 818–19.
5 On the system of bonuses see Lacfalvi-Wagner, 'A prémiumok alakulása és a premizálás hatása az iparban' (The Changes in Bonuses and the Impact of the Bonus System on Industry), *Statisztikai Szemle* (Statistical Review, hereafter *SSz*), July 1955.
6 Based on a personal communication by Ernő Gerő.
7 *Adatok és adalékok a népgazdaság fejlődésének tanulmányozásához. 1949–1955* (Data and Contributions to the Study of the Development of the National Economy), KSH (Central Statistical Office) (Budapest, 1957), p. 12.
8 *P. I. Archivuma* (Archives of the Institute of Party History, hereafter *PIA*), 2/9-230.2156, 'Példák iparunkban uralkodó jellegzetes tünetekre' (Examples of the Typical Symptoms Prevailing in Our Industry), September 14, 1951, Memo of the Hungarian Working People's Party's Department of Public Finances.
9 Miklos Somogyi, 'Az ipar feleslegesen gyártott és elfekvő késztermékéről' (On Industry's Superfluously Manufactured and Frozen Stocks of Finished Products), *SSz*, May 1955, p. 414.
10 Cf. Antal Radó, 'A hazai szénbányászat közgazdasági sajátosságai és mai helyzete' (The Economic Features and Current Position of Domestic Coalmining), *KSz*, No. 1, 1957, pp. 19–22.
11 *PIA*, 2/9-145.00454, Report of the Council of the Ministry for Heavy Industry, May 20, 1950.
12 *PIA*, 2/9-230, Report by Ernő Gerő to the June 4, 1951 Meeting of the National Economic Council on the Foreign trade position.

13 Sándor and Wágner, 'A szocialista bérezés elveinek érvényesülése az iparban' (The Application of the Socialist Wage Principles in Industry), *SSz*, September 1954, pp. 674–5.
14 Ibid., p. 545.
15 *PIA*, 2/9-274.2699, Minutes of the November 1, 1951 Meeting of the Council of the National Planning Office.
16 Julia Zala, 'Statisztika és bürokrácia a pártkongresszus megvilágitásában' (Statistics and Bureaucracy in the Light of the Party Congress), *SSz*, June–July 1954, p. 449.
17 *PIA*, 2/9-281.2740, August 17, 1951 memo of the party Department of Public Finances.
18 Sándor and Wágner, 'The Application of Socialist Wage Principles', p. 668.
19 Cf. János Kornai, *Overcentralization in Economic Administration* (Oxford, 1959).
20 Relying on the tenets of the Polish economists Kalecki and Brus, the Czechoslovak Josef Goldmann proved this tenet by analysing data from Czechoslovakia, Hungary, Poland and the GDR. He published his conclusions in two articles entitled 'The Periodical Fluctuations in the Pace of Growth in the Economies of Certain Socialist Countries' and 'The Pace of Growth and the Model of Economic Management of Certain Socialist Countries', published in Nos. 9 and 11, 1964 of *Planovane Hospodarstvi* (Economic Planning). For the debate that the articles aroused, see *KSz*, No. 9, 1965.
21 The production of national income, calculating at constant prices, rose from 27,700 million forints in 1949 to 59,000 million in 1953. It is not now possible to give exact figures for the items mentioned here. The growth in stocks and the trend in the number of uncompleted investment projects are recorded statistically in the balance sheet for the economy under current assets. On the other hand, current assets rose between 1949 and 1953 from 3,100 million to 6,900 million forints, although it must be noted that it had peaked at 9,100 million in 1951 and reached a trough of 4,100 million in 1952. Separate statistics on uncompleted investment projects make these figures seem impossibly small, since this item alone soared from 2,300 million to 10,900 million forints between 1950 and 1953. However, these figures are stated at current rather than constant prices. Although it is highly probable that these figures are inaccurate, their significance is unquestionable.
22 Based on a personal communication by György Aczél.

1 The first moves to correct the economic mechanism

1 June 28, 1953. *Propagandista* (Propaganda), No. 4, 1986, pp. 144 and 156.
2 On this subject, see Iván Petö and Sándor Szakács, *A hazai gazdaság négy évtizedének története 1945–1985* (History of Four Decades of the Hungarian Economy 1945–1985), Vol. I (Budapest, 1985), pp. 321–39, which provides a brief summary of the 'rationalization' aimed at correcting the functioning of the economy.

2 The critique of the command economy: towards a new concept of the economic system

1 Tibor Liska and Antal Máriás, 'A gazdaságosság és a nemzetközi munkamegosztás' (Economic Viability and the International Division of Labour), *KSz*, No. 10, 1954, pp. 75ff.

2 Kálmán Szabó and Sándor Kopátsy, 'A mezőgazdasági árak képzésének néhány kérdése' (A Few Issues in the Setting of Agricultural Prices), *KSz*, No. 11, 1954, pp. 144–5.

3 László Stenczinger, 'Vita a háztáji gazdaság kérdéséröl (A MTA Agrártudományok Osztályának ülése)' (Debate on the Issue of the Household Farm – Session of the Hungarian Academy of Sciences' Department of Agricultural Sciences), *KSz*, No. 12, 1954, pp. 338–41.

4 Sándor Balázsy, 'Javitsuk meg szervezési módszereinket' (Let Us Improve our Methods of Organization), *Többtermelés* (Surplus Production), November 1954, pp. 2–12.

5 György Péter, 'A gazdaságosság jelentőségéről és szerepéről a népgazdaság tervszerü irányitásában' (On the Significance and Role of Profitability in the Planned Management of the National Economy), *KSz*, No. 3, 1954.

6 Ibid., pp. 301–22.

7 János Kornai, *Overcentralization*, pp. 3–4. Page references in notes 7–11 relate to the Hungarian original.

8 Ibid., pp. 185 and 25.

9 Ibid., pp. 56, 36 and 169.

10 Ibid., pp. 44, 202 and 171.

11 Ibid., p. 174.

12 János Kornai, *Növekedés, hiány és hatékonyság* (Growth, Shortage and Efficiency) (Budapest, 1982), pp. 35 and 59–60.

13 Tamás Nagy, 'Előszó' (Foreword), in György Péter, *A gazdaságosság és jövedelmezőség jelentősége a tervgazdálkodásban* (The Significance of Economic Efficiency and Profitability in the Planned Economy) (Budapest, 1956), pp. 13–30.

14 Péter Erdős, 'A népgazdaság központi irányitása és a gazdasági mechanizmusok' (The Central Management of the Economy and the Economic Mechanisms), *Szabad Nép* (Free People), September 14, 1956.

15 János Kornai's article in *Szabad Nép*, October 14, 1956.

16 László Szamuely, 'The First Wave of the Mechanism Debate in Hungary, 1957', *Acta Oeconomica*, Vol. 29, No. 1–2, 1982, pp. 1–23.

17 'Feladataink a Központi Vezetőség márciusi határozatának megvalósitásában' (Our Tasks in the Realization of the Central Leadership's March Resolution), *KSz*, No. 3–4, 1955, pp. 262–5.

18 József Nyilas, 'A szocialista iparositás időszerű elvi kérdései' (The Topical Issues of Principle Concerning Socialist Industrialization), *KSz*, No. 3–4, 1955, pp. 292ff.

3 The turn: reform goals of the government and the practice of correction

1 *A Magyar Szocialista Munkáspárt határozatai és dokumentumai 1956–1962* (The Resolutions and Documents of the Hungarian Socialist Workers' Party, hereafter *Resolutions 1956–62*) (Budapest, 1964), pp. 13, 14, 22 and 23.

2 István Friss, 'Gazdaságpolitikai problémáink és az 1957. évi terv' (Our Economic Policy Problems and the 1957 Plan), *KSz*, No. 7, 1957, p. 704.

3 István Friss, 'Az MSZMP VII. kongresszusa és a közgazdaságtudomány feladatai' (The Seventh Congress of the HSWP and the Tasks of Economic Science), *KSz*, No. 5, 1960, pp. 527–8.

4 *A Magyar Szocialista Munkáspárt Országos Értekezletének jegyzőkönyve, 1957. junius 27–29* (Minutes of the National Conference of the Hungarian Socialist Workers' Party, June 27–29, 1957, hereafter *HSWP Conference 1957*) (Budapest, 1957), p. 148. The italics are mine.

5 *PIA*, 288.f.23/1957, Minutes of the Meeting of the Economic Committee (Gazdasági Bizottság) on December 10, 1957.

6 István Varga, a professor at the Karl Marx University of Economic Sciences in Budapest, had been the director of the Economic Research Institute before 1945 and a state secretary (deputy minister) under Ferenc Nagy, the Minister of Reconstruction in the coalition government. He also served as an economic adviser to the Smallholders' Party, although he was not a member of it, and subsequently presided over the Materials and Prices Board until its abolition in the late 1940s.

7 According to proposals made by István Friss on December 12 and 15, 1956, the broader Economic (Gazdasági) Committee would first 'work out a more concise programme to serve as the guideline' before the Economics (Közgazdasági) and other expert committees set about 'devising the more detailed programme . . . The experts should preferably include several people outside the party, and members of the older generation who gained a good professional reputation before the liberation.' Finally, Friss said the proposals of the expert committees should be coordinated by the government's Economic Committee itself, which would work out 'the whole draft programme'. *PIA*, 288.f.23/1957. Proposals for the 'Working Out of the Government's Programme' (December 15, 1956) and the 'Committee to be Established for Working Out the Government's Economic Programme' (December 12, 1956).

8 Ibid., Current Issues in the Organization and Management of the National Economy, Ministry of Finance, December 5, 1956. The italics are mine.

9 János Bokor, Ottó Gadó, Pál Kürthy, Tamás Meitner, Mrs Sándor Sárosi and Jenő Wilcsek, *Javaslat az ipar gazdasági irányitásának uj rendszerére* (A Proposal for a New System of Economic Management for Industry), *KSz*, No. 4, 1987, pp. 371–92.

4 Economic reform and the workers' councils

1 *PIA*, 288.f.23/1957.

2 Sándor Balázsy, 'Üzemi munkástanács, vállalati önállóság, iparvezetés'

(The Factory Workers' Council, Company Autonomy, Industrial Management), *KSz*, No. 11–12, 1956, p. 1297.

3 Decree No. 25/1956 of the Presidential Council of the People's Republic, *Magyar Közlöny* (Hungarian Gazette, hereafter *MK*), November 24, 1956.

4 'Ujévi gondok – ujévi remények' (New Year Cares – New Year Hopes), *Népszabadság* (People's Freedom), January 1, 1957.

5 Zoltán Gombás, 'A népgazdaság igazgatásának alapja a munkásönigazgatás' (The Foundation of Direction of the National Economy is Worker Self-Management), *Népszabadság*, December 25, 1956.

6 Konrád Baller, 'A felelősség és a hatalom kérdései az igazgató és a munkástanács kapcsolatában' (Questions of Responsibility and Authority in the Relationship of the Manager and the Workers' Council). *Népszabadság*, January 10, 1957.

7 László Pesti, 'Munkástanács és vállalati tervezés' (The Workers' Council and Company Planning), *Népszabadság*, January 16, 1957.

8 Tivadar Láng, 'Vizsgáljuk felül a technikai felkészültséget és a gyártási profilt' (Let Us Reappraise Technical Preparedness and the Production Profile), *Népszabadság*, February 15, 1957.

9 'Két malomkő között?' (Between Two Millstones?), *Népszabadság*, February 6, 1957.

10 'Ülést tartott a munkás-önkormányzatot előkészitő bizottság' (The Preparatory Committee for Worker Self-Management Holds a Meeting), *Népszabadság*, February 1, 1957.

11 Kádár's presentation of the Central Committee report on the political situation and the tasks facing the party, *HSWP Conference 1957*, p. 57.

12 *PIA*, 288.f.23/1957, Address by Jenő Fock: 'A népgazdaság helyzete és az 1957. évi terv fő feladatai' (The Situation of the National Economy and the Main Tasks of the 1957 Plan), containing the report of the Provisional Executive Committee to the HSWP Central Committee's meeting on May 17. The position taken in the spring by the party leadership was the same as the statement made in January. 'We must strive', Kádár had told a meeting of activists in Csepel on January 27, 'to transform the [workers'] councils correctly, so that they serve the interests of workers' power everywhere . . . The workers' councils can do truly useful and effective work so long as . . . the party of the working class leads them. This, however, cannot be achieved by command. What is needed is for the party membership to work devotedly for the accomplishment of this objective.' János Kádár, *Szilárd népi hatalom: független Magyarország* (Stable People's Power: Independent Hungary) (Budapest, 1962), p. 24.

13 Contribution by János Kukucska, *HSWP Conference 1957*, p. 130.

14 Contribution by József Révai, ibid., p. 153.

15 Address by János Kádár, ibid., pp. 57–8.

16 *PIA*, 298.f.23/1957, The Party's Economic Policy, HSWP Department of Public Finances, May 27, 1957.

17 Bokor et al., 'Proposal for a New System', p. 375.

18 *PIA*, 288.f.23/1957, Second Proposal of the Economics Committee for the

Economic Programme of the Revolutionary Worker-Peasant Government, May 29, 1957.

19 The workers' councils were in any case soon eliminated as an institution. In November 1957, Decree No. 63/1957 of the Presidential Council annulled Decree No. 25/1956, in other words abolished them (*MK*, November 17, 1957). On the same day resolution No. 1086/1957.XI.17 of the Presidium of the National Federation of Free Hungarian Trade Unions, on factory councils, was issued, saying in Point I(1) that the new institution was to replace the workers' councils. It declared that 'the further development of factory democracy . . . is the honourable duty . . . of the trade unions, which possess a wealth of experience'. The factory councils were set up under union control 'for the purpose of involving factory workers more intensively in the economic management of companies and the social control of production'.

5 The principle of the substantial reform

1 *Népszabadság*, January 5, 1957.
2 *Népszabadság*, January 12, 1957.
3 *Népszabadság*, February 7, 1957.
4 *Népszabadság*, February 17, 1957.
5 *PIA*, 288.f.23/1957, Central Council of Hungarian Trade Unions Economic Bulletin, Preliminary Bulletin on the Economic Situation in January, February 11, 1957.
6 Ibid., The Summary Proposal of the Economic Committee for the Government's Economic Programme, June 1, 1957.
7 Ibid., Proposal for the Formation of the Economic Structure and Mechanism, March 2, 1957. Its authors were István Antos and István Varga.
8 In other words, the extension of company autonomy 'cannot in any area involve a relinquishment or loosening of central control. For instance in the case of investments, companies will be able to make proposals but . . . the setting of investment tasks will be fully centralized. Unless this were so it would be impossible to ensure that the economy developed in the right direction.'
9 If the supply of goods were adequate, 'the prices of articles available in abundance could be decontrolled . . . However, it must be emphasized that even in the most distant future this can only occur in the case of articles of lesser importance in the supply to the general public.' The prices of materials, industrial articles and the main services 'must always be set (maximum-minimum)'.
10 *PIA*, 288.f.23/1957.

6 A counterproposal for partial corrective measures

1 István Friss, 'Our Economic Policy Problems', p. 704.
2 *PIA*, 288.f.23/1957, The Party's Economic Policy, May 24, 1957, HSWP Department of Public Finances.

3 Ibid., May 27, 1957.
4 Ibid., Some Current Issues in the Management and Economic Activity of Industrial Companies, July 8, 1957, presented by István Friss.
5 Ibid., Report of June 18, 1957.
6 Ibid., Report of June 15, 1957.
7 Ibid., Some Current Issues.
8 Ibid.
9 Up until October 1956, two-thirds of the workers were on piece-work, whereas from November onwards hourly wages set on the basis of earnings in the third quarter of that year became almost general. But companies soon began experimenting with a number of other schemes such as individual, performance-linked hourly wages, bonuses linked with particular tasks, piece-work again and plain hourly wages. The previous, almost totally centralized distribution of bonuses was abolished in favour of schemes financed out of set company bonus funds, part of which could be freely disposed of by the management, and the rest of which could be distributed once the company had met a set of ministerial stipulations.
10 The proposal did not consider that the similarly new system of profit-sharing could be appraised because 'the increase in the autonomy of companies is taking place under a producer price system which wrongly reflects costs, and this practice leads to a great many contradictions and damaging consequences. The investigation has therefore confirmed the need to set producer prices in order.'

7 Immediate corrections to the operation of the economy

1 *PIA*, 288.f.23/1957, Proposal to the Economic Committee on the Establishment of a Prices Board, December 14, 1956.
2 Ibid., Proposal of the President of the National Prices Board to the Economic Committee, January 31, 1957.
3 Resolution No. 1029/1957 of the Hungarian Revolutionary Worker-Peasant Government, *MK*, March 10, 1957.
4 *PIA*, 288.f.23/1958, Proposal to the Hungarian Revolutionary Worker-Peasant Government, May 2, 1958, from the Minister for Food.
5 Ibid., July 22, 1957.
6 Ibid., Proposal to the Economic Committee, March 26, 1957. The italics are mine.
7 *PIA*, 288.f.23/1959, Changes in Economic Management Activity since 1957, Primarily with Respect to Industry, Appendix No. 1, National Planning Office, April 17, 1959.
8 The remark was made during János Kornai's defence of his dissertation for the degree of Candidate of the Academy of Sciences in September 1956. See *KSz*, No. 11–12, 1956, pp. 1490–2.
9 *PIA*, 288.f.23/1957, Proposal to the Economic Committee, Modification of the System of Price Equalizing in Foreign Trade, January 25, 1957, written by István Antos and Jenő Incze. Price equalization 'has emerged in

accordance with our export policy of focusing exclusively on volume'. It provided an automatic offset for the difference between the low export price level of goods and the domestic price level of them. (In 1955–6 some 10,000 million forints was spent from the budget on this.) It was therefore essential, they argued, to align the pricing system and the foreign exchange rates with realistic value relations.

10 The official exchange rate was 11.75 forints to the US dollar. The surcharge proposed would offset the difference between this official rate and the 'shadow' rate of 30 forints. It was proposed that automatic offsets should be replaced by fixed price-offset rates, so that companies would only be able to offset their sales losses abroad to a degree fixed in advance according to types of goods and on an empirical basis, rather than being able to pass on any trading loss they might incur.

11 Ibid., December 14, 1956, Proposal by the National Planning Office, presented by Árpád Kiss.

12 *Népszabadság*, January 5, 1957.

13 *MK*, January 26, 1957, Resolution No. 1014/1957/I.26 of the Hungarian Revolutionary Worker-Peasant Government on the Development of Private Small Industry.

14 *MK*, February 24, 1957, Resolution No. 1023/1957/II.24 of the Hungarian Revolutionary Worker-Peasant Government.

15 *PIA*, 288.f.23/1957, the February 1, 1957 Resolution of the Economic Committee and Minister János Tausz's Proposal of January 18, 1957.

16 *MK*, February 10, 1957, Resolution No. 1022/1957 of the Hungarian Revolutionary Worker-Peasant Government.

17 Róbert Hoch, 'A magánszektor szerepe a kereskedelemben' (The Role of the Private Sector in Trade), *KSz*, No. 3, 1957, p. 271.

18 *MK*, April 21, 1957, Decree with the Force of Law No. 28/1957 of the Presidential Council of the Hungarian People's Republic.

19 *PIA*, 288.f.23/1958, The Regulation of the Sale of Smaller Housing Property in State Ownership, December 1, 1958.

8 Intervention against the comprehensive reform plans as 'economic revisionism'

1 Bokor et al., 'Proposal for a New System', pp. 371–92.

2 The chance and necessity of planning, as one of the basic traits of the socialism of the future, had been derived by Marx and Engels from the analysis of the capitalism of their time. The rapid socialization of production which commenced with the emergence of large-scale mechanized industry made the social regulation of production indispensable. Following the proletarian revolution, Engels stressed, once the means of production were freed of their capital character, 'social production according to a previously set plan becomes possible'. 'A szocializmus fejlődése az utópiától a tudományig' (The Development of Socialism from Utopia to Science), in *Marx-Engels Válogatott Müvek* (Selected Works of Marx and Engels), Vol. II (Budapest, 1949), p. 150. The specific form of the planned

economy remained, of course, undefined for a long time, and a number of variants appeared in the practical economic-policy activity pursued by Lenin after the October Revolution. (Five-year plans were drawn up for certain specific tasks like the restoration of transport, but long-term goals were expressed to the greatest extent in the long-term electrification programme.)

From the turn of the 1920s and 1930s the characteristic method of planning and management through five-year plans emerged, and was closely bound up with the forced pace of industrialization which was placed on the agenda at this time, with the tasks of a war economy set by the external threat, and with the purpose of speedily making up a development lag of a century, which was vital for defence. In an article entitled 'The Tasks of the Economic Leaders', written in February 1931, Stalin formulated the correlations with particular clarity: 'In ten years at the most, we must cover the distance by which we have lagged behind the leading countries of capitalism . . . It is time we put a stop to the exploded idea of non-intervention in production. It is time . . . we adopted a position suited to the present time: that *intervention is necessary everywhere.*' *Sztálin Müvei* (The Works of Stalin), Vol. XIII (Budapest, 1950), p. 44. It was in this specific situation and with this specific purpose that a system of planning and management which rejected 'plan proposals' and 'plan forecasts' in favour of commands came into being. During the three decades that followed, this system ossified into what was claimed to be the sole possible model for a socialist economy.

3 *PIA*, 288.f.11/85, Ideological Struggle against Revisionist Economic Views, May 24, 1957, a draft of a study by Andor Berei.

4 Ibid.

5 'Vita a gazdasági irányitás tökéletesitéséről az Országos Tervhivatal közgazdász körében' (Debate on the Perfecting of Economic Management among the Economists at the National Planning Office), *KSz*, No. 5, 1957, pp. 568–77.

Albert Katócs said that since the aim was to create a new industrial structure, and this could only be accomplished in a planned way, 'the elimination of planning's attribute of having specific addressees would not be a viable course'. István Bartos and Tamás Morva argued that 'only quantitative changes are needed in the development of the economic mechanism', and methods of incentive based on utilization of the law of value could only play an auxiliary role. Reiterating the same position, Pál Füsti drew the conclusion that 'our task is now to rectify the mistakes and not to remove the foundations of the planned economy'. Among other remarks, József Soós asked, 'How can we ensure through the mechanism the goods supply to match the purchasing power we have planned when the companies are essentially planning to do what is more profitable to them?'

6 *Gazdasági Figyelő* (Economic Observer, hereafter *GF*), March 28, 1957.

7 *GF*, April 5, 1957.

8 *GF*, May 2, 1957.

9 Ilona Bieber, József Fábián and Emil Gulyás, 'Megjegyzések a Közgazdasági Szemle 1956. 11–12. számának vezércikkéhez' (Remarks on the Leading Article in the 11–12/1956 Number of the *Közgazdasági Szemle*), *KSz*, No. 4, 1957, p. 396.

10 György Varga, 'Gazdasági mechanizmus "vagy" gazdaságpolitika?' (Economic Mechanism 'or' Economic Policy?), *KSz*, No. 7, 1957, p. 767. Described as a debate contribution.

11 *Társadalmi Szemle* (Social Review, hereafter *TSz*), No. 6, 1957, pp. 51–4 and 57.

12 István Friss, 'A technikai haladás társadalmi-gazdasági következményei' (The Social and Economic Consequences of Technical Progress), *KSz*, No. 11–12, 1956, pp. 1350 and 1353.

13 István Varga, 'Az "egyesek" és a "kettesek"' ('Some' and 'Others'), *GF*, June 6, 1957.

14 László Háy, 'Vagy alusznak, vagy nem hallják . . .' (Either They Are Sleeping or They Cannot Hear . . .), *GF*, June 6, 1957. Replying to István Varga.

15 Tamás Bácskai, 'Az értéktörvény jobb felhasználása még nem revizionizmus' (Better Utilization of the Law of Value Is Still Not Revisionism), *Népszabadság*, August 14, 1957.

16 *Népszabadság*, September 8, 1957.

17 *Népszabadság*, October 2, 1957.

18 Edit Varga, 'A tervezés módszereinek megjavitása' (Improvement of the Methods of Planning), *KSz*, No. 7, 1958, pp. 696, 697 and 700.

19 István Szurdi, 'Néhány észrevétel a közgazdasági szakértőbizottság elgondolásaihoz, javaslataihoz' (A Few Observations on the Ideas and Proposals of the Economic Experts' Committee), *KSz*, No. 7, 1958, p. 694.

20 Of the three authors just quoted, Friss and Szurdi were Central Committee department heads, while Varga was a deputy department head there. Looking back on this period almost two decades later, Friss pointed out: 'Following the inauguration of the economic reform of 1968 there were some who thought how good it would have been to introduce it back in 1957, but then "the advocates of the new mechanism were silenced". The facts . . . show that this assertion is, to say the least, a considerable exaggeration. In actual fact *in 1957 no professional regarded the introduction of the reform as possible*. Those who insisted on change were, it is true, accused of revisionism by certain argumentative opponents, but neither the party nor the government stigmatized or condemned them.' The official positions put forward above conflict with Friss's statement and recollection, in István Friss (ed.), *Gazdaságpolitikai tanulságok. Gazdaságpolitikánk tapasztalatai és tanulságai /1957–1960/* (Economic Policy Lessons. The Experiences and Lessons of Our Economic Policy, 1957–1960) (Budapest, 1976), p. 332.

I would like to stress in this connection that it was almost exclusively the research team headed by Friss that investigated the economic policy experiments of the period comprehensively and in depth, and their findings were published in the anthology of studies just cited. The authors of the studies in the book – Miklós Hegedüs, Mrs Miklós Ungvárszki, Aranka Rédei and Judit Barta, Zsuzsa Esze, János Gyenis and István Friss himself – broke new ground and studied primary sources and documents as well. I agree with them on many of the details in their assertions and on several issues contained in their line of thought. But on numerous points I see and evaluate the processes differently. This is due on the one hand to the fact that in my work I have processed far more source material, and on the other to the fact that I did not break off my investigation at the year 1960, so that I could see the whole decade as an entity. Finally, instead of taking individual, separate themes, I aimed at a homogeneous treatment of the issues investigated. However, I prefer not to make this work of mine more cumbersome by detailing its points of agreement and disagreement with the works of others and its additions to them.

21 It is indicative of how swift the consolidation process was that Friss, who was still reporting on January 10, 1957 that there was 'no production of any significance at the plants under the ministries of Metallurgy and Engineering', that 'the brick industry is not receiving coal at the moment', and that 'clinker and lime-burning are at a standstill at every cement factory . . . In the glass industry seven factories are at a standstill', could assert in February that 'the country's economic situation promises to be more favourable in 1957 than would have been judged possible either in mid-December or even in the middle of January.' *PIA*, 288.f.23/1957, The National Economic Plan for 1957, February 5, 1957.

22 *Népszabadság*, April 14, 1957.

23 Resolution No. 1046/1957/IV.28 of the Hungarian Revolutionary Worker-Peasant Government on Coal Mining, *MK*, April 28, 1957. In the wake of the consolidation of production, the institution of government commissioners for coal, introduced in December 1956 and controlled by Lajos Fehér and Károly Papp, was abolished with effect from May 1, 1957.

24 *PIA*, 288.f.23/1957, The Main Features of the Country's Economic Situation, June 15, 1957.

25 Ibid., Report on the Economic Situation in January, February 19, 1957, presented by István Friss.

26 In his reply to the contributions at the party conference, János Kádár stated: 'When Comrade Révai stepped up to the rostrum, he held the flag of the party – figuratively speaking – in his hand . . . Later, however, he waved the broken flag of the fallen leadership in the hall . . . By repeating these slanders he unwittingly voiced the slogans of the fallen leadership . . . Comrade Bakó puts things very well in my opinion, when she said that the December resolution must not be trifled with. According to some, this resolution was not entirely good, that of February was better, the subsequent one better still . . . Comrade Révai criticized the December resolution . . . Even if there are faults in the December resolution, in its main points the Central Committee's evaluation has proved correct, and today

nobody can work usefully for the party who does not fully identify himself with the essentials of this resolution.' *HSWP Conference 1957*, pp. 215 and 220.

In a sharp debate with Révai, György Aczél put his position like this: 'Today there are already many who kept a low profile in November and December and now stridently criticize comrades who stood by the party precisely in that most difficult period, but who did not see clearly on certain issues, or formulated their message in an erroneous way. At that time we were working under difficult circumstances . . . Comrade Révai also said that "circumstances exempt no one". I do not think that our party's leadership needed excuses in any way . . . Comrade Révai is not right theoretically . . . We are Marxists who . . . believe that "any phenomena can become meaningless if we investigate them removed from their context, separate from it".' Ibid., p. 172.

27 Ferenc Münnich, 'Az MSZMP tapasztalatai a revizionizmus elleni harcban' (The Experiences of the HSWP in the Struggle against Revisionism), *TSz*, No. 11, 1958, pp. 28, 29 and 31.

28 *Resolutions 1956–62*, p. 75.

29 István Friss, 'Népgazdaságunk vezetésének néhány gyakorlati és elméleti kérdéséről' (On a Number of Practical and Theoretical Issues in the Direction of our National Economy), *Népszabadság*, October 2, 1957. The italics are mine.

30 *PIA*, 288.f.23/1958, Report on the Work of the Economic (Gazdasági) Committee in 1957 (draft), compiled by the committee's Secretariat, February 4, 1958. The italics are mine.

31 Ibid., Observations on the Proposals of the Economics (Közgazdasági) Committee. The italics are mine.

32 *PIA*, 288.f.23/1959, Changes in Economic Management Activity since 1957, Primarily with Respect to Industry, National Planning Office, April 17, 1959.

33 Ibid.

34 'Thus the ministries determine in accordance with the professional conditions, within their own sphere of authority, the kind of obligatory plan indicators to be approved for companies. Some ministries avail themselves of this right to a greater extent, others to a lesser. At present the Ministry for Light Industry is working with the fewest indicators. In light industry four fundamental indicator systems are being prescribed, namely (1) sale of goods . . . (2) material supply for priority materials, (3) the average wage, and (4) investment and renovation funds.' István Antos, 'Gazdaságpolitika és gazdaságirányitás az ellenforradalom után' (Economic Policy and Economic Management since the Counter-Revolution), *TSz*, No. 10, 1959, p. 12.

35 *PIA*, 288.f.23/1959, The National Planning Office's Report of April 17, 1959. The place of plan stipulations for products 'was taken over by a specification agreement between industry and trade . . . by commodity exhibitions staged by each industry directorate, and delivery contracts concluded on the basis of these'.

36 Whereas a national material balance was drawn up for 1,271 products in 1954 and for 567 even in 1956, from 1957 on material balances were done for some 290 products 'excluding priority foodstuffs and consumer articles included in economic activity'.

37 Certain ministries, for instance those of Metallurgy and Engineering, had the plans drafted by the companies, whilst other ministries planned collectively, utilizing company proposals.

38 The company received a share of the price equalization made more favourable by the price-equalizing rates, which differed according to groups of commodities. But as the Planning Office pointed out, the linkage between production companies and foreign trade was not consistent, since 'at these companies, too, there is to date a separate system of material incentives for industrial activity and another for foreign trade activity'.

39 Admittedly the companies could receive a modest share of up to 10 per cent of the surplus profit obtained, from which they could set up a development fund. Moreover, companies' independent opportunities were increased by the fact that certain investment activity of a non-construction nature could also be charged to the renovation funds.

9 Minor corrections to the mechanism between 1958 and 1964

1 Béla Csikós-Nagy, 'The Restructuring of Industrial Producer Prices', p. 819.

2 Róbert Hoch and Aranka Rédei, 'A fogyasztói árképzés fő elvei' (The Main Principles of Setting Consumer Prices), *KSz*, No. 1, 1957, p. 4.

3 Edit Jávorka, 'Az ipari árrendszer egyes kérdései' (Certain Aspects of the Industrial Price System), *KSz*, No. 2, 1957, p. 123. 'In this case', the author adds, 'the producing company has a stake in manufacturing as many easily saleable items as possible.'

4 The price propositions of the Polish Economic Councils were put forward by W. Brus, and shared by M. Kalecki, Z. Augustovski and others. For a summary of the various types of producer-price system that surfaced in the international and Hungarian price debate, see Imre Vincze, 'A jelenlegi termelői árrendezés alapelvei' (The Principles of the Present Setting of Producer Prices), *KSz*, No. 9, 1958, pp. 993–1007.

5 *PIA*, 288.f.23/1957, Committee of National Economy, July 1, 1957 Resolution of the State Economic Committee on the General Reorganization of Industrial Producer Prices in 1958.

6 Cf. Imre Vincze, 'Az uj termelői árak és az értékben kifejezett népgazdasági mutatók' (The New Producer Prices and the Economic Indicators Expressed in Value), *KSz*, No. 7, 1959.

7 *PIA*, 288.f.11/481, Bulletin for the Political Committee on the Experiences to Date in the Setting of Product Prices, May 14, 1959, written by István Friss.

8 *PIA*, 288.f.23/1959, The Proposal of the National Price Office to the Economic Committee: The Economic Assessment of the Setting of Producer Prices, December 1, 1959, written by Béla Csikós-Nagy.

10 Organizational corrections – the transformation of company structures

1 Sándor Balázsy and György Varga, 'A szocialista iparirányitás szervezeti kérdéseiről' (Some of the Organizational Issues in the Socialist Management of Industry), *KSz*, No. 8–9, 1959, p. 847.
2 'Vita a gazdaságirányitás tökéletesitéséről az Országos Tervhivatal tervgazdász körében' (Debate on the Perfecting of Economic Management among the Economic Planners at the National Planning Office), March 19, 1957, *KSz*, No. 5, 1957, p. 577.
3 Bokor et al., 'Proposal for a New System'.
4 Tibor Botka, 'Iparági irányitás vállalati formában (A Magyar Selyemipari Vállalat tapasztalatai)' (Industrial Sector Management in Company Form. The Experiences of the Hungarian Silk Industry Company), *KSz*, No. 1, 1960, p. 93.
5 *PIA*, 288.f.23/1958, Proposal to the Economic Committee, The Founding of a National Brewery Company, October 18, 1958.
6 *PIA*, 288.f.23/1959.
7 'Közgazdaságtudományi előadások a Magyar Tudományos Akadémia 1960. évi nagygyülésén' (Lectures in Economics at the 1960 General Assembly of the Hungarian Academy of Sciences), *KSz*, No. 6, 1960, p. 751. Contribution by Jenő Fock, HSWP Central Committee Secretary and Political Committee member, to the lecture by István Friss.
8 Ibid., pp. 752 and 754.
9 András Hegedüs, 'A tervgazdaság konkrét rendszeréről' (On the Specific System of the Planned Economy), *KSz*, No. 12, 1960, pp. 1429, 1430 and 1438.
10 Tibor Liska, 'Kritika és koncepció' (Criticism and Conception), *KSz*, No. 9, 1963, pp. 1058 and 1068.
11 Béla Csikós-Nagy, 'Kritikai megjegyzések a világpiaci árbázisu árrendszerhez' (Critical Remarks on the Price System Based on World Market Prices) and Tamás Nagy, 'Egy kritikáról és koncepcióról' (On a Criticism and a Conception), *KSz*, No. 9, 1963.
12 Ibid., p. 1078.
13 *PIA*, 288.f.11/1019, Memorandum of the September 5, 1962 Meeting of the Economic Committee, September 8, 1962.
14 Ibid.
15 *PIA*, 288.f.23/1963, Proposal for the Economic Committee, The Reorganization of the KGM Car and Tractor Industry Directorate into a Trust, September 1963; 288.f.23/1962, Proposal for Economic Committee, Establishment of the Diósgyőr Engineering Works, October 17, 1962; 288.f.11/1290, Information Report for the Political Committee on the Execution of the Central Committee's Resolution of February 2, 1962, May 5, 1964; 288.f.23/1963; 288.f.11/1901, Report on the State of Implementation of the Resolution on the Further Development of Economic Management, February 21, 1963.
16 István Szurdi, 'Az ipari vállalatok összevonásáról' (On the Merger of Industrial Companies), *TSz*, No. 3, 1963, p. 11.

17 *PIA*, 288.f.11/1290, Information Report for the Political Committee, May 5, 1964.

11 The new model for agricultural cooperatives

1 Ernő Csizmadia, 'Átmeneti formák és megoldások mezőgazdaságunk szocialista nagyüzemi rendszerének épitésében' (Transitional Forms and Solutions in the Building of the Large-Scale Socialist Farm System in Hungarian Agriculture), *KSz*, No. 11, 1960, p. 1275.

2 Imre Szabó, 'Hogyan fokozhatjuk a szövetkezeti tagok szorgalmát?' (How Can We Increase the Diligence of the Cooperative Members?), *Népszabadság*, February 9, 1960.

3 Lajos Major, 'Családokra osztották a kapások területét, és prémiumot adnak a paksi járás tsz-ei' (The Root-Crop Area Has Been Divided Up among Families and the Cooperatives of the Paks District Will Pay Bonuses), *Népszabadság*, May 11, 1960.

4 Lajos Major, 'A közös állattenyésztés kialakitásának problémái. Látogatás Kapospula tsz-községben' (The Problems of Establishing Collective Stockbreeding. A Visit to Kapospula Cooperative Village), *Népszabadság*, April 10, 1959.

5 Lajos Fehér, 'A termelőszővetkezetek megszilárditásának feladatai' (The Tasks in Consolidation of the Cooperatives), *TSz*, No. 6, 1960, p. 8.

6 *PIA*, 288.f.11/1959, Information Report for the Political Committee on the State of the Cooperative Movement, June 26, 1959.

7 Lajos Fehér, 'The Tasks in Consolidation', p. 10.

8 Ernő Csizmadia, 'Transitional Forms and Solutions', p. 1286.

9 Lajos Fehér, 'The Tasks in Consolidation', p. 12. The italics are mine.

10 *PIA*, 288.f.23/1959, National Planning Office Proposal to the Political Committee on the Main Problems Connected with the Second Five-Year Plan, August 26, 1961, written by Árpád Kiss.

11 Ferenc Szabó, 'A háztáji gazdaságok helyzete és megitélése' (The Situation and Standing of Household Farms), *TSz*, No. 1, 1964, p. 31.

12 Károly Németh, 'Mezőgazdaságunk fejlesztésének feladatai' (The Tasks in Developing Hungarian Agriculture), *TSz*, No. 4, 1964, pp. 126–7.

13 Cf. Mária Sárosi, 'Az állami gépállomások politikai és gazdasági szerepe a mezőgazdaság szocialista átalakitásában' (The Political and Economic Role of the State Machine Stations in the Socialist Transformation of Agriculture), doctoral diss. (Karl Marx University of Economic Sciences, Budapest, 1981), pp. 226–7. I have also drawn on this study in the pages that follow.

14 *MK*, March 2, 1957.

15 *PIA*, 288.f.23/1957, Resolution adopted at the February 28, 1957 Meeting of the Economic Committee on the Regulation of the Functioning of the Machine Stations.

16 Imre Dimény, *Mezőgazdaságunk traktorszükségletét meghatározó tényezők* (Factors Determining the Tractor Needs of Hungarian Agriculture) (Budapest, 1961), p. 14.

17 *Népszabadság*, April 9, 1957.
18 *Népszabadság*, April 11, 1957.
19 *Népszabadság*, April 13, 1957.
20 *Népszabadság*, April 17, 1957.
21 *PIA*, 288.f.23/1957, Jenő Fock's Address at the HSWP Central Committee Session of May 17, 1957.
22 *Resolutions 1956–62*, pp. 107–8.
23 The resolution pointed out that 'it must still be possible for cooperatives which are functioning efficiently . . . where the conditions of large-scale machine utilization exist . . . and which fulfil their obligations to be able to buy universal tractors and working machinery from their own resources'. *PIA*, 288.f.20/1957, Resolution of the Political Committee on the Political, Economic and Organizational Consolidation of the Cooperatives, August 13, 1957.
24 *Resolutions 1956–62*, pp. 390 and 487.
25 *PIA*, 288.f.20/104, Report for the Political Committee on the Experiences with the Implementation of the PC Resolution on the Sale of the Machines of the Individual Machine Stations, and a Proposal on the Actions to be Taken, March 8, 1962.
26 *A Magyar Szocialista Munkáspárt határozatai és dokumentumai 1963–1966* (The Resolutions and Documents of the Hungarian Socialist Workers' Party 1963–1966, hereafter *Resolutions 1963–6*), p. 65.
27 Cf. Ferenc Erdei, 'A termelőszövetkezeti munkadijazás és jövedelemelosztás kérdéséhez' (On the Issue of Remuneration for Work and Income Distribution in Agricultural Cooperatives), *KSz*, No. 8–9, 1957.
28 *PIA*, 288.f.20/9, Resolution of the Political Committee on the Political, Economic and Organizational Consolidation of the Agricultural Cooperatives, August 13, 1957.
29 Sándor K. Nagy, 'Az elosztási formák fejlesztése termelőszövetkezeteinkben' (The Development of the Forms of Distribution in Our Agricultural Cooperatives), *TSz*, No. 2, 1961, p. 74.
30 Antal Márczis, 'Hasznositsák szövetkezeteink az első félév tapasztalatait' (Let Our Cooperatives Make Use of the First Six Months' Experiences), *Népszabadság*, August 2, 1960.
31 'Hogyan fokozhatjuk a szövetkezeti tagok anyagi érdekeltségét?' (How Can We Increase the Material Incentive of Cooperative Members?), Discussion, *Népszabadság*, February 15, 1960.
32 Ibid. The change of attitude was not unrelated to the replacement of the previous minister of agriculture, a traditionalist, by Pál Losonczi, the chairman of the Barcs cooperative.
33 'Eszmecsere' (Exchange of Views), *TSz*, No. 3, 1961, pp. 64 and 68.
34 Sándor K. Nagy, 'The Development in the Forms of Distribution', p. 75.
35 Imre Dimény, 'A magyar mezőgazdaság fejlődésének néhány kérdése' (Some Questions in the Development of Hungarian Agriculture), *TSz*, No. 11, 1963, p. 16.
36 *Resolutions 1956–62*, p. 108.

38 *PIA*, 288.f.15/1965, Report to the Public Finances Committee on the State of the Agricultural Cooperatives on the Basis of the Final Figures for 1965, April 2, 1965, written by Imre Dimény.
39 *PIA*, 288.f.20/1965, The Political Committee Resolution of July 6, 1965 on the Further Development of the Agricultural Price, Tax and Financial System.
40 *PIA*, 288.f.11/1967, Report for the Political Committee on the Settlement of the Credits of the Agricultural Cooperatives, May 15, 1967.
41 Ibid.

12 First criticisms of the ineffectiveness of the corrective policy

1 *PIA*, 288.f.11/1290, Information Report for the Political Committee, May 5, 1964.
2 *PIA*, 288.f.11/1451, Briefing on Some Experiences with the Implementation of the February 9, 1962 Central Committee Resolution on the Further Development of Economic Management, December 18, 1964. The italics are mine.
3 There was an obligation to pay the charge attaching to 85 per cent of the fixed assets in industry. The intention was also to give companies a direct motivation to invest effectively, since it would only be worth a company's while to invest if the return would more than cover the charge. In the event, with the system of planning and economic management basically unchanged and producer prices set officially, the introduction of the charge had no effect in persuading companies to husband their assets or be selective about their investments, since net income depended, after all, on the producer-price system, which bore no correlation to the efficiency with which fixed assets were being used. Thus the charge eventually became a price-setting factor.
4 *PIA*, 288.f.23/1960, Report for the Economic Committee, January 29, 1960, presented by Árpád Kiss.
5 *PIA*, 288.f.11/1548, Assessment of Our Economic Development, April 29, 1965.

13 Disequilibrium, tensions and shortcomings in the workings of the economy

1 Of the more recent Hungarian studies of these issues, let me recommend Tamás Bauer, *Tervgazdaság, beruházás, ciklusok* (Planned Economy, Investment, Cycles) (Budapest, 1981), and János Kornai, *Economics of Shortage* (Amsterdam/New York/Oxford, 1980).
2 *PIA*, 288.f.15/1962, Report on the Experiences with the Fulfilment of the 1962 National Economic Plan, April 2, 1963.
3 *PIA*, 288.f.11/1962, Briefing for the Political Committee on the Country's International Financial Situation, Work So Far on Drafting Next Year's

National Economic Plan, and Certain Issues Concerning the Development of the Standard of Living, 1962.

4 Ibid., Proposal Discussed and Endorsed at the Political Committee's Meeting on April 13, 1965 on the Position with the Drafting of the Third Five-Year Plan and the Further Tasks Ahead.

5 Ibid., Briefing for the Political Committee on the Experiences with the Fulfilment of the 1964 Plan, March 5, 1965. (In the first half of 1963 a price gain of 102 million forints in convertible currency and 79 million forints in rouble-based currency, in other words a total of 181 million forints of foreign exchange was recorded. Ibid., Report on the Main Experiences with the Fulfilment of the First Six Months of the 1962 National Economic Plan, August 16, 1963.)

6 Tibor Kiss, 'A szocialista nemzetközi munkamegosztás továbbfejlődése' (Further Development of the Socialist International Division of Labour), *Népszabadság*, July 31, 1957.

7 *PIA*, 288.f.23/1958. The italics are mine.

8 *PIA*, 288.f.15/1964, National Planning Office Guidelines for the Drafting of the Third Five-Year Plan, May 12, 1964, compiled by Miklós Ajtai.

9 Ibid., Main Issues of Our Industrial Development, May 11, 1965, compiled by Péter Vályi.

10 Ibid., National Planning Office Proposal on the Third Five-Year Plan of the Hungarian People's Republic, April 1966.

11 Ibid., National Planning Office Proposal on the Draft Third Five-Year Plan, February 28, 1966.

12 József Bognár, 'Külkereskedelmünk problémái' (The Problems of Our Foreign Trade), *KSz*, No. 8–9, 1957, pp. 850–1.

13 *PIA*, 288.f.15/1963, Memorandum on the Meeting on November 4, 1963 of the Public Finances Committee of the HSWP Central Committee.

14 *PIA*, 288.f.20/1964, The Political Committee's January 21, 1964 Resolution on the Utilization of Long-Term Capitalist Credits for Investment Purposes.

15 Ibid., The Political Committee's September 20, 1960 Resolution Concerning the Tensions Discernible in the National Economy.

16 Ibid., The Political Committee's November 29, 1960 Resolution on the Economic Organizing Activity of the Regional Party Committees.

17 *Népszabadság*, December 25, 1959.

18 *PIA*, 288.f.20/1963, The Central Committee's December 5, 1963 Resolution on the National Economic Plan for 1964.

19 *PIA*, 288.f.15/1965, March 17, 1965.

20 *PIA*, 288.f.23/1958, Examples Taken from the Material Gathered in the Investigation of State-Owned Trading, May 1958.

21 Ibid., Proposal to the Economic Committee by the Central People's Control Commission.

22 *PIA*, 288.f.20/1957, Report on the Economic Situation.

23 *PIA*, 288.f.23/1960, National Planning Office Proposal to the Committee on the Economy, January 4, 1960.

24 *PIA*, 288.f.23/1958, Briefing for the Economic Committee. Situation Report on the Trend in Industrial Stocks, July 8, 1958.
25 *PIA*, 288.f.11/1961, Information Report on the Development of the Economic Situation in May 1961, June 17, 1961.
26 Ibid., Briefing on the Development of the National Economic Situation in January 1962, February 20, 1962.
27 *PIA*, 288.f.15/1965, Assessment of our Economic Development and the Experiences in Applying our Economic Policy, March 17, 1965.
28 *PIA*, 288.f.23/1958, July 8, 1958.
29 Ibid., Proposal for Settling Certain Issues of Technical Development, November 11, 1958.
30 'Fontos döntés a müszaki fejlesztés segitésére' (Major Decision to Assist Technical Development), *Népszabadság*, September 27, 1957.
31 *PIA*, 288.f.23/1957, Some Problems in the Planning and Financing of Company Renovations, November 29, 1957.
32 *PIA*, 288.f.23/1960, Proposal for the Economic Committee, January 4, 1960.
33 'A technika százada és a magyar ipar' (The Century of Technology and Hungarian Industry), *Népszabadság*, August 7, 1957.
34 *PIA*, 288.f.11/1961, Briefing for the Political Committee on the Trend in the Economic Situation in April 1961, May 18, 1961.
35 Ibid., Information Report to the Political Committee on the Development of the National Economy in the First Three Quarters of 1962, October 23, 1962.
36 Ibid., Briefing for the Political Committee on the First Quarter Development of the National Economy, May 7, 1964.
37 Ibid., Report of December 18, 1964 on the Implementation of the Central Committee Resolution of February 9, 1962.
38 Lajos Rév, 'A külkereskedelem feladatai a második ötéves tervben' (The Tasks in Foreign Trade under the Second Five-Year Plan), *TSz*, No. 4, 1962, p. 59.
39 *PIA*, 288.f.23/1966/60, On the Controversial Issues Concerning the Reform of the Economic Mechanism and on the Situation with the Drafting of the Reform, Lecture by Rezső Nyers at the HSWP Central Committee's Political Academy, December 12, 1966, shorthand record.

14 Plans and preparation for reform in other socialist countries

1 Liberman, [Y. Liberman], 'Terv, nyereség, prémium' (Plan, Profit, Bonuses), *TSz*, No. 12, 1964, pp. 107–8.
2 G. Popov, 'Szovjet közgazdászok az uj gazdasági reformról a Szovjetunióban' (Soviet Economists on the New Economic Reform in the Soviet Union), *KSz*, No. 1, 1967, pp. 128–32.
3 'Közeledik-e egymáshoz a Kelet és Nyugat gazdasági rendszere?' (Are the Economic Systems of the East and West Coming Closer to Each Other?), *KSz*, No. 6, 1966, pp. 763–4. Interview with Professor Ota Šik taken from the March 1966 issue of *Wirtschaftsdienst*.
4 Cf. *Voprosi Ekonomiki* (Economic Problems), No. 2, 1966.

5 Cf. *Economist*, August 19, 1967. The paper also said that if the Czechoslovak and Hungarian reforms materialized, the world would witness for the first time the operation of the kind of 'market socialism' outlined by Oskar Lange in the 1930s.
6 'A gazdaságirányitási rendszer átalakitásáról' (On the Transformation of the Economic System), *Népszabadság*, April 25, 1965.
7 János Kádár, 'Felszólalás a Központi Bizottság november 24-i ülésén' (Contribution at the November 24 Session of the Central Committee), *TSz*, No. 12, 1967, p. 27.

15 The political background to the reform

1 Cf. editorial in *Pravda*, October 21, 1961.
2 Cf. Ferenc Münnich, 'Az MSZMP tapasztalatai a revizionizmus elleni harcban' (The Experiences of the HSWP in the Struggle against Revisionism), *TSz*, No. 11, 1957, pp. 28, 29 and 31.
3 Cf. *Resolutions 1956–62*.
4 Ibid., Resolution of the August 14–16, 1962 Session of the HSWP Central Committee.
5 Cf. *A Magyar Szocialista Munkáspárt határozatai és dokumentumai 1963–1966* (The Resolutions and Documents of the Hungarian Socialist Workers' Party, 1963–1966, hereafter *Resolution 1963–6*) (Budapest, 1968).

16 The reform decision

1 Rezső Nyers, 'Az ötéves terv derekán' (Halfway Through the Five-Year Plan), *TSz*, No. 2, 1964, p. 19.
2 Károly Földes, 'A marxista közgazdaságtudomány fejlesztéséért' (For the Development of Marxist Economics), *TSz*, No. 2, 1964, p. 77.
3 *PIA*, 288.f.15/1964, Memorandum on the June 22, 1964 Meeting of the Public Finances Committee of the HSWP Central Committee.
4 Ibid., Memorandum of the January 10, 1966 Meeting of the Public Finances Committee of the HSWP Central Committee.
5 Personal communication by Rezső Nyers.
6 *PIA*, 288.f.15/1964, Proposal to the Public Finances Department of the HSWP Central Committee on the Direction and Programme of Work Concerning the Further Development of Economic Management, July 15, 1964.
7 Ibid., Memorandum on the July 21, 1964 Session of the Public Finances Department of the HSWP Central Committee.
8 István Friss, 'Laws and Control of Socialist Economy', in *Economic Laws, Policy, Planning* (Budapest, 1971), pp. 41–55.
9 *Resolutions 1963–6*, p. 107.
10 *PIA*, 288.f.23/1966/40, Briefing for the Working Groups Set Up for the Reexamination and Modernization of the Economic System, January 7, 1965.

11 *PIA*, 288.f.29/1966/41, Memorandum on the January 7, 1965 Meeting of the Committee.
12 *PIA*, 288.f.23/1966/40.
13 Ibid.
14 *PIA*, 288.f.23/1966/42, Memorandum for the HSWP Central Committee's Committee for Preparing the Economic Mechanism; Debate over the Second Variant of the Initial Concept, June 9, 1965.
15 Ibid., Memorandum on the May 28, 1965 Meeting of the HSWP Central Committee's Committee for Preparing the Economic Mechanism, June 9, 1965.
16 *PIA*, 288.f.23/1966/40.
17 *PIA*, 288.f.24/1967/64, The Main Legal Issues in the Reform of the Economic Mechanism, July 14, 1967.
18 *Resolutions 1963–6*, pp. 234–9ff.
19 Ibid., p. 240.
20 Ibid., pp. 451–2.
21 Ibid., pp. 306–7. The italics are mine.

17 Debates on the reform and compromises before its introduction

1 *PIA*, 288.f.15/49, National Planning Office Report for the Public Finances Committee of the HSWP Central Committee, The Development of the Living Standard of the Population under the Twenty-Year Plan, 1961.
2 István Huszár, 'A második ötéves terv irányelveiről' (On the Guidelines for the Second Five-Year Plan), *TSz*, No. 2, 1960, p. 10.
3 Mihály Váci, 'Se az atombomba, se az isten!' (Neither the Atom Bomb, Nor God!), *Uj Irás* (New Writing), No. 9, 1961, pp. 579–80.
4 János Földeák, 'Hüség a néphez és a marxizmus-leninizmushoz!' (Loyalty to the People and to Marxism-Leninism!), ibid., No. 1, 1962, p. 51.
5 Endre Gerelyes, 'Huszonegy karóra' (Twenty-One Wrist Watches), ibid., No. 11, 1961, p. 840.
6 Imre Takács, 'Egyéniség és társadalom' (Personality and Society), ibid., No. 1, 1962, p. 160; Pál Salamon, 'Mivel él az ember?' (What Does Man Live On?), ibid., No. 12, 1961, p. 936.
7 Péter Veres, 'Néhány szó a kollektiv gondolkozásról' (A Few Words on Collective Thinking), *Népszabadság*, October 15, 1967.
8 Péter Veres, 'A hajszoltságról' (On the Hectic Pace of Life), in *A gondviselő társadalom* (The Caring Society) (Budapest, 1979).
9 Ibid., 'A "guvernamentális" gondolkodásról' (On Governmentalist Thinking), pp. 138–9.
10 Ibid., p. 145.
11 Mihály Várkonyi, 'Szine és visszája' (Inside and Outside), *Népszabadság*, October 9, 1965.
12 Mihály Várkonyi, 'Magunk becsülete' (Our Own Honour), *Népszabadság*, October 29, 1965.
13 Jenő Faragó, 'Közösségben a közösségért' (In the Community, for the Community), *Népszabadság*, September 15, 1966.

14 László Rózsa, 'Összetőrt kőtáblák felett?' (Over Broken Tablets of Stone?), *Népszabadság*, December 17, 1967.
15 *Élet és Irodalom* (Life and Literature), November 25, 1967.
16 Ibid., December 2, 1967.
17 László Rózsa, 'In the Community, for the Community'.
18 Miklós Szatmári, 'A reform propagandájának helyzete és feladatai' (The Position and Tasks of Propaganda for the Reform), *TSz*, No. 10, 1967, p. 99.
19 *PIA*, 288.f.24/1967/60, Memorandum on the Experiences at the Political Academy of the Propaganda on the Economic Mechanism between September 1966 and October 1967, October 10, 1967.
20 *PIA*, 288.f.23/1966/63, Report on the Experiences Concerning the Debate on the Central Committee Document Entitled 'The Initial Guidelines on the Reform of the System of Economic Management', Political Committee Briefing, April 22, 1966.
21 *PIA*, 288.f.24/1967/58, Report on the Preparations in the District's Production Plants for the Introduction of the Reform of the System of Economic Management, Nineteenth District Committee of the HSWP, April 15, 1967.
22 *PIA*, 288.f.24/1967/57, The Economic Supervision Activity of Party Organizations in Foreign Trade Companies within the Frames of the New Mechanism, May 4, 1967.
23 Károly Németh, 'A reform előkészitésének tapasztalatairól' (On the Experience in Preparing the Reform), *TSz*, No. 10, 1967, p. 8.
24 Gábor Somoskői, 'Hozzászólás "Az uj gazdasági mechanizmus várható társadalmi és politikai kihatásai" cimű cikkhez' (Comment on the Article Entitled 'The Likely Social and Political Impact of the New Economic Mechanism'), *TSz*, No. 7, 1968, p. 52.
25 József Bálint, 'Pártszervezeteink a gazdasági reform bevezetéséért' (Our Party Organizations on Behalf of the Introduction of the Economic Reform), *TSz*, No. 8–9, 1967, p. 11.
26 József Sólyom, 'Mi lesz a sorsuk?' (What Will Be Their Fate?), *Népszabadság*, October 3, 1967.
27 János Dojcsák, 'Vita az üzemi pártmunkáról' (Debate on Party Work in the Factories), *Népszabadság*, May 21, 1967.
28 Ferenc Frank, 'Vezető szerep és meggyőzés' (Leading Role and Persuasion), *Népszabadság*, October 8, 1966.
29 István Földes, 'A tennikészek, az aggódok és a csodavárók' (The Willing, the Anxious and the Awaiters of Miracles), *Népszabadság*, December 25, 1966.
30 Rezső Nyers, 'Az uj gazdasági mechanizmus várható társadalmi és politikai kihatásai' (The Likely Social and Political Effects of the New Economic Mechanism), *TSz*, No. 3, 1968, pp. 20–1.
31 *Resolutions 1963–6*, p. 133.
32 *PIA*, 288.f.41/1966/59, Minutes of the June 1, 1966 Meeting of the Agitation and Propaganda Committee of the HSWP Central Committee, Proposal on the Tasks in the Reform of the Economic Mechanism and the Propaganda for the Third Five-Year Plan, May 26, 1966.

33 *PIA*, 288.f.11/1966/63, Briefing on the Preparatory Work for the Reform of the Economic Mechanism among the Party Membership, November 10, 1966.

34 *PIA*, 288.f.11/2654, On the Experiences in the Study of the Topic Entitled The Role of Party Organizations in Economic Work, June 7, 1969.

35 *PIA*, 288.f.24/1967/70, Memorandum on the 1967 Agitation and Propaganda on the Reform of the Economic Mechanism, Secretariat of the Central Council of Hungarian Trade Unions, October 10, 1967.

36 *Resolutions 1963–6*, p. 134.

37 Éva Terényi, 'Eszméinknek megfelelően' (In Accordance with Our Ideas), *Népszabadság*, December 16, 1967.

38 Béla Csikós-Nagy, 'A gazdaságirányitási reform küszöbén' (On the Threshold of the Economic Management Reform), *KSz*, No. 12, 1967, p. 1398.

39 Rezső Nyers, 'Beszámoló a Központi Bizottság november 23-i ülésén' (Report at the November 23 Meeting of the Central Committee), *TSz*, No. 12, 1967, pp. 9–10.

40 János Kádár, 'Felszólalás a központi Bizottság november 24-i ülésén' (Speech at the November 24 Meeting of the Central Committee), *TSz*, No. 12, December 1967, pp. 22–3. The italics are mine.

41 Béla Csikós-Nagy, 'On the Threshold of the Reform', p. 1398.

42 Rezső Nyers, 'Gazdaságpolitikánk néhány kérdése' (Some Issues in Our Economic Policy), A Report at the June 23 Meeting of the Central Committee, *TSz*, No. 7, 1967, p. 66.

43 Béla Csikós-Nagy, 'On the Threshold of the Reform', p. 1399.

44 Ibid., pp. 1400–1.

45 *PIA*, 288.f.23/1966/41, Memorandum on the November 26, 1964 Meeting of the Committee.

46 *PIA*, 288.f.20/464, Political Committee Resolution on Some Organizational Measures Concerning the Economic Mechanism Reform, November 16, 1966.

47 *PIA*, 288.f.23/1966/55, Examination of the Position on the Subject of Involving Employees in the Management System, compiled by the Working Group of the HSWP Central Committee's Committee for Preparing the Economic Mechanism, April 1965.

48 Ibid., Proposal for the HSWP Central Committee's Committee for Preparing the Economic Mechanism, January 10, 1966, Scheme for Making the Involvement of the Workers in the Management System More Effective.

49 *PIA*, 288.f.23/1966/61, Briefing on a Comprehensive Reappraisal of Our Economic Management System and the Preparation for the Reform, November 17, 1966.

50 László Rózsa, 'A reform gondolata – gondolkodásunk reformja' (The Idea of Reform – A Reform of Our Thinking), *Népszabadság*, March 27, 1966.

18 The main features of the new reform system

1 *PIA*, 288.f.23/1966/61.
2 *PIA*, 288.f.24/1967/4, Economic Policy Guidelines in the Period of the Introduction of the New Mechanism, Rezső Nyers, May 31, 1967.
3 *PIA*, 288.f.23/1966/63, Report on the Position of the Preparatory Work for the Reform of the Economic Mechanism, November 15, 1966, for the Political Committee.
4 Ákos Balassa, 'Uj módszerek a népgazdasági tervezésben' (New Methods in National Economic Planning), *KSz*, No. 3, 1968, p. 289.
5 Jenő Wilcsek, 'A tervszerü iparfejlesztés szabályozói a gazdaságirányitás uj rendszerében' (The Regulators of Planned Industrial Development under the New System of Economic Management), *KSz*, No. 2, 1968, p. 131.
6 Márton Tardos, 'Az uj gazdasági mechanizmus szabályozó rendszerének modellje' (The Model of the Regulating System for the New Economic Mechanism), *KSz*, No. 10, 1968, p. 1188.
7 Ottó Gadó, 'Az 1968. évi népgazdasági terv és a gazdasági szabályozók' (The 1968 National Economic Plan and the Economic Regulators), *KSz*, No. 10, 1967, p. 1151.
8 Béla Csikós-Nagy, 'Az uj magyar árréndszer' (The New Hungarian Price System), *KSz*, No. 3, 1968, p. 284. The remainder of this account of the new price system relies on this study.
9 *PIA*, 288.f.24/1968/2, Memorandum on the Economic Management Reform, Central Statistical Office.
10 Béla Csikós-Nagy, 'The New Hungarian Price System', p. 277.
11 Ibid., p. 278.
12 *PIA*, 288.f.24/1967/61, Proposal to the HSWP Central Committee's Economic Policy Committee, Subject: Guidelines and Preparation Schedule for the 1968 Reform of Consumer Prices, February 13, 1967.
13 Ibid., Proposal to the HSWP Political Committee on the 1968 Reform of Consumer Prices, October 1967.
14 Ibid., Proposal to the HSWP Central Committee's Economic Policy Committee, September 22, 1967.
15 Béla Csikós-Nagy, 'The New Hungarian Price System', p. 269.
16 Within industry, using the same basis of comparison, the figure for heavy industry and engineering products rose from 60 to 110 per cent, for light industrial products from 120 to 155, for foodstuffs from 70 to 94 and for the construction industry from 70 to 106 per cent.
17 Béla Csikós-Nagy, 'The New Hungarian Price System', p. 268.
18 *PIA*, 288.f.24/1969/59, Memorandum on the Further Development of the Distribution System for Cash Share-Outs, June 2, 1969; Certain Issues Concerning the Division of the Profit-Share Fund, May 14, 1969.
19 Gábor Havas, 'A beruházási hatáskör és források megoszlása' (The Sphere of Investment Authority and the Distribution of Resources), *KSz*, No. 9, 1968, p. 1063.
20 *PIA*, 288.f.24/1967/62, The Likely Effects and Problems of the Investment

Reform, Magyar Beruházási Bank (Hungarian Investment Bank), October 18, 1967.

21 *PIA*, 288.f.23/1966/60, On the Controversial Issues Concerning the Reform of the Economic Mechanism and on the Situation with the Drafting of the Reform, Lecture by Rezső Nyers at the HSWP Central Committee's Political Academy, December 12, 1966, shorthand record.

22 'Kezükben a szövetkezetek jövője. A ceglédi járás tapasztalataiból' (The Cooperatives' Future in Their Hands. From the Experiences of the Cegléd District), *Népszabadság*, February 9, 1966. The italics are mine.

23 Cf. *Resolutions 1963–6*.

24 Benedek Tóth, 'Miért helyes bővíteni a termelőszövetkezetek gazdasági tevékenységét?' (Why Is It Correct to Expand the Economic Activity of the Agricultural Cooperatives?), *Népszabadság*, May 12, 1966.

25 Lajos Baranyi, 'Bátran élnek lehetőségeikkel. Jövedelmező melléküzemágak a nagykovácsi termelőszövetkezetben' (They Seize Their Opportunities. Profitable Auxiliary Activities at the Nagykovácsi Cooperative Farm), *Népszabadság*, January 27, 1966.

26 'A mezőgazdaság fejlesztésének fő irányai' (The Main Lines of Agricultural Development), Lecture by Lajos Fehér at the HSWP Political Academy, *Népszabadság*, April 8, 1966.

27 Lajos Major, 'A háztáji gazdaságok jelentősége Somogy megyében' (The Significance of Household Farms in Somogy County), *Népszabadság*, January 25, 1966.

28 'A termelőszövetkezeti törvény' (The Act on Production Cooperatives), *Népszabadság*, October 6, 1967. The Act set the size of household farms at the equivalent of 2,856–5,712 sq.m per cooperative member, even when there were several members in one family. 'The number of livestock which can be kept on a household farm will be laid down in a separate order. The principle is that one cow, one or two young cattle, one or two sows with their litters, three or four fattened pigs a year, five sheep or goats and an unlimited number of small livestock should be allowed on a household farm.'

29 *PIA*, 288.f.24/1967/58, Proposal for the Conference of Deputy Ministers, Subject: The Position and Role of Private Retail Trading under the New System of Economic Management, August 2, 1967.

30 In many trading companies larger units used a 'tight' accounting system and smaller ones a 'free till' system, meaning that the takings were not checked and the manager could be held responsible for matching the cash takings with the stock as determined at periodic stocktakings, rather than for the takings on a day-to-day basis. At the time of the reform new systems were proposed for these smaller units. Over 79 per cent of the retail units and almost 69 per cent of the catering units used the 'free till' system. These units accounted for 38 per cent of retail and 40 per cent of catering turnover.

31 *PIA*, 288.f.24/1968/10, Proposal to the HSWP Central Committee's Economic Policy Committee, November 11, 1968, compiled by István Szurdi.

32 *PIA*, 288.f.15/137, Memorandum on the December 13, 1967 Meeting of the Economic Committee.

33 Ibid., Proposal to the Economic Committee on the Economic Policy Guidelines for Regulating Private Small-Scale Industry and Private Retail Trading. The italics are mine.

34 Cf. Antal Stark, *Tervezés és valóság* (Planning and Reality) (Budapest, 1973).

35 László Csapó, 'Central Planning in a Guided Market Model', *Acta Oeconomica*, Vol. 1, No. 3–4, 1966, pp. 237–53.

19 The plan and preparations for continuing the reform after 1968

1 *PIA*, 288.f.15/150, September 30, 1968.

2 *PIA*, 288.f.24/1968/2, November 14, 1968.

3 *PIA*, 288.f.15/163, Proposal to the HSWP Central Committee's Economic Policy Committee on the Long-Term Issues of Pricing Policy, National Materials and Prices Office, May 17, 1969; also the Economic Policy Committee's resolution.

4 *PIA*, 288.f.15/164, June 28, 1969.

5 *PIA*, 288.f.15/193, Report to the HSWP Central Committee's Economic Policy Committee on the Implementation of the 1969 EPC Resolution on the Further Development of the Large-Company organization, December 14, 1970.

6 'Taking the practical requirements into consideration, a monopoly type of organization seems justified for certain public services (e.g. Hungarian State Railways, the Post Office), in cases where optimum size of unit (international competitiveness) requires it, and where domestic and international load distribution require direct operative measures (e.g. the electricity generating industry, aluminium smelting, the meat industry). 'The monopoly situation should not be maintained for consumer articles and services of a non-communal character, in which the monopoly situation is detrimental to provision to the general public and to prices.'

7 *PIA*, 288.f.24/1970/3, Proposal for the HSWP Central Committee's Economic Policy Committee on the Further Development of Large-Company Organization.

8 In metallurgy a proposal was made to reorganize the Alloy Factory and the Smelting Company, and in the engineering industry the Tool and Machine Part Factories Company, the United Electrical Machinery Factory Company and the Electrical Equipment and Appliance Works; in light industry, it was proposed that there should be a reappraisal of the organization of the Cotton Printing Industry, Leather Industry, Paper Industry and Fine Cloth Companies.

9 *PIA*, 288.f.24/1970/1, Briefing on the Planned Regulation of the Flow of Social Capital, HSWP Central Committee Economic Policy Department, October 26, 1970.

10 *PIA*, 288.f.24/1970/34, Proposal for the Deputy Ministers' Conference, Subject: Further Development of Wage and Income Relations, November 27, 1970, Ministry of Labour.

11 *Az ötödik ötéves terv gazdaságirányitási feladatainak elemzése. Az uj irñyitási*

rendszer eddigi tapasztalatai (Analysis of the Economic Policy Tasks Under the Fifth Five-Year Plan. The Experiences So Far with the New System of Management, hereafter *Analysis 1973*), published by the HSWP Central Committee's Economic Policy Department (Budapest, 1973), pp. 12 and 43. The italics are mine.

20 The reform comes to a halt and reversal

1 Ibid., p. 41.

2 'Fehér Lajos beszéde a várossá alakult Gödöllő ünnepi tanácsülésén' (Lajos Fehér's Speech at the Festive Council Meeting in Gödöllő, Incorporated as a Town), *Népszabadság*, January 4, 1966.

3 'Kádár János nyilatkozata nemzetközi kérdésekről, kül- és belpolitikánkról, népgazdaságunk helyzetéről és az idei feladatokról' (János Kádár's Statement on International Issues, Our Domestic and Foreign Policy, the State of Our National Economy and the Tasks This Year), *Népszabadság*, January 1, 1966.

4 As I write, the material in the Party Archives up to the end of 1970 is open to researchers, but not the material for the rest of the 1970s.

5 This fact was recalled by Kádár himself at a celebration to mark his seventieth birthday in May 1972, in reply to a toast.

6 *Analysis 1973*, p. 36.

7 István Földes, 'Fogadatlan prókátorok' (Meddlers), *Népszabadság*, December 24, 1973.

8 Tamás Pálos, 'A negyedik dimenzió' (The Fourth Dimension), *Népszabadság*, October 15, 1972.

9 *A Magyar Szocialista Munkáspárt határozatai és dokumentumai 1971–1975* (Resolutions and Documents of the Hungarian Socialist Workers' Party 1971–1975, hereafter *Resolutions 1971–5* (Budapest, 1978), p. 377.

10 Árpád Pullai, 'A párt vezető szerepe, a pártélet kérdései' (The Party's Leading Role, the Issues of Party Activity), *TSz*, No. 4, 1975, pp. 106–7.

11 Zoltán Komócsin, 'Változatlan politikával' (With Policy Unchanged), *Népszabadság*, March 23, 1974. The italics are mine.

12 Valéria Benke, 'Egységes értelmezés, kommunista kiállás, közös cselekvés' (United Interpretation, Communist Stand, Collective Action), *TSz*, No. 1, 1973, p. 5.

13 *TSz*, No. 5, 1974, p. 7.

14 'Pártmunkások nyilatkozatai a Központi Bizottság novemberi határozatáról' (Statements by Party Activists on the Central Committee's November Resolution), *TSz*, No. 1, 1973, p. 46.

15 Ibid., p. 50.

16 'Kongresszusra készülődve' (Preparing for the Congress), *TSz*, No. 5, 1974, pp. 7–8. This editorial followed a strict 'struggle-on-two-fronts' line, referring in the very same sentence to the simultaneous rebuttal of 'all revisionist attempts'.

17 Ibid., p. 376.

18 'Üzemek a politika mérlegén. Beszélgetés Nagy Richárddal, az MSzMP

Budapesti Bizottságának titkárával' (Factories in the Political Balance. A Discussion with Richárd Nagy, Secretary of the HSWP's Budapest Committee), *Népszabadság*, December 16, 1973.

19 *Resolutions 1971–5*, p. 377.

20 Ottó Gadó, *Közgazdasági szabályozó rendszerünk 1976-ban* (Our Economic Regulatory System in 1976) (Budapest, 1976, pp. 157, 40, 51 and 158. Also in English: *The Economic Mechanism in Hungary – How It Works in 1976* (Leyden/Budapest, 1976).

21 Árpád Pullai, 'A pártélet, a pártmunka időszerü kérdései. Előadás az országos agitációs és propagandaértekezleten' (Topical Issues in Party Activity and Party Work. Lecture at the National Agitation and Propaganda Conference), *TSz*, No. 11, 1975, pp. 43–4.

22 Éva Terényi, 'Angyalföld neve kötelez. Jegyzetek a XIII. kerületi pártértekezletről' (The Name of Angyalföld Imposes an Obligation. Notes on the Thirteenth District Party Conference), *Népszabadság*, February 18, 1975.

23 Béla Biszku, 'A munkásosztály vezető szerepe, a szövetségi politika és a szocialista demokrácia' (The Leading Role of the Working Class, the Policy of Alliances and Socialist Democracy), *TSz*, No. 4, 1975, p. 64.

24 Éva Terényi, 'Segiteni a végrehajtást. A nagyüzemi pártellenőrzés tapasztalatairól' (Helping with Implementation. On the Experiences of Party Control in Large Factories), *Népszabadság*, July 2, 1975.

25 Károly Földes, 'Tervgazdaságunk szabályozási elvei, a szövetségi politika és a szocialista demokrácia' (The Regulatory Principles of Our Planned Economy, the Policy of Alliances and Socialist Democracy), *TSz*, 1975, pp. 31–2.

26 'Az 1973. évi költségvetésről tárgyal az országgyülés. Pullai Árpád: "A helyes döntések megvannak, most a tetteken a sor"' (Parliament Discusses the Budget for 1973. Árpád Pullai: 'We Have the Right Decisions, Now Is the Time for Deeds'), *Népszabadság*, December 13, 1972.

27 *Törvények és Rendeletek Hivatalos Gyüjteménye* (Official Repository of Acts and Regulations), 1973, p. 425: Resolution No. 1023/1973.VI.30 of the Council of Ministers (government).

28 *Resolutions 1971–5*, p. 379.

29 Lajos Faluvégi, 'Development of the Financial Regulators and the New Hungarian Five-Year Plan', *Acta Oeconomica*, Vol. 16, No. 1, 1976, pp. 19–34.

30 *A Magyar Szocialista Munkáspárt határozatai és dokumentumai 1975–1980* (Resolutions and Documents of the Hungarian Socialist Workers' Party 1975–1980, hereafter *Resolutions 1975–80*) (Budapest, 1983), p. 233. The italics are mine.

31 László Szabó, 'Oknyomozás árügyekben' (Investigation into Price Matters), *Népszabadság*, February 18, 1973.

32 *Népszabadság*, January 7, 1973.

33 László Szabó, 'A köztulajdon védelme' (Protection of Public Property), *Népszabadság*, April 21, 1974.

34 László Medveczky, 'Szellem a palackból: Mi van és mi lesz a "gebines" autósiskolákkal?' (Genie from the Bottle: What Is Happening and What Is to Happen to the Private Driving Schools?), *Népszabadság*, December 30, 1973.
35 Ferenc Cserkuti, 'A közös és a háztáji' (Collective and Household Plot), *Népszabadság*, June 4, 1975.
36 Árpád Pünkösti, 'Mienk a dió? Visszatér a Mult?' (Is the Walnut Ours? Is the Past Returning?), *Népszabadság*, July 13, 1975.
37 Béla Biszku, 'A XI. kongresszus a társadalmi viszonyok fejlesztéséről' (The Eleventh Congress on the Development of Social Conditions), *TSz*, No. 11, 1975, p. 11. The italics are mine.
38 Ibid., p. 10.
39 Ibid., pp. 12–13.
40 *Resolutions 1971–5*, p. 486.
41 József Sólyom, 'Az alapszabály szerint' (According to the Rule Book), *Népszabadság*, August 8, 1973.
42 Béla Biszku, 'The Eleventh Congress', pp. 14–15.
43 *Resolutions 1971–5*, pp. 917, 918 and 926.
44 Ibid., pp. 381–5.
45 Béla Biszku, 'A munkásosztály vezető szerepe, a szocialista demokrácia' (The Leading Role of the Working Class, Socialist Democracy), *TSz*, No. 4, 1975, p. 68.
46 Valéria Benke, 'Egységes értelmezés, kommunista kiállás, közös cselekvés' (United Interpretation, Communist Stand, Collective Action), *TSz*, January 1973, pp. 12–13; idem, 'Szocialista eszmeiség, müvelődés, közösségi erkölcs' (Socialist Idealism, Cultivation, Collective Morality), *TSz*, No. 4, 1975, pp. 82–3.
47 Béla Biszku, 'Pártunk politikájának időszerü kérdéseiről' (On the Topical Issues in Our Party's Policy), *TSz*, No. 3, 1974, pp. 3, 6 and 7.
48 Resolution of the HSWP Central Committee's Political Committee on the Growth of Party Membership and the Changes in Its Social Composition, November 21, 1972, in *Resolutions 1971–5*, pp. 394 and 401ff.
49 Government Resolution No. 2026/1973/VIII.8/Mt.h on higher education for youth with skilled worker qualifications, in *Határozatok Tára. Gyüjtemény* (Repository of Resolutions. Collection), pp. 358–9.
50 *Resolutions 1971–5*, p. 657.
51 Ibid., pp. 908–9. However, to curb the plainly excessive zeal being shown, the Central Committee secretary added: 'In the longer run . . . it will continue to be more expedient to use the institutional forms of school-system adult education. The aim of the various initiatives is merely to complement state and party education and not to substitute for them. The attention of the Central Council of Hungarian Trade Unions and the Communist Youth League has also been drawn to this.'
52 Éva Terényi, 'Egyenrangu követelmények. Kormányhatározat a vezetők politikai továbbképséséről' (Requirements Equal in Rank. Government Resolution on the Political Extension Training of Leaders), *Népszabadság*, January 8, 1975. The italics are mine.

53 Ferenc Komornik, 'Kapkodás nélkül' (Without Haste), *Népszabadság*, August 15, 1975.
54 Béla Nagy, 'Munkásság és értelmiség' (Working Class and Intelligentsia), *TSz*, No. 4, 1973, pp. 58–64. The italics are mine.
55 Lajos Baráth, 'Beidegződés vagy urhatnámság' (Habit or Snobbery), *TSz*, No. 4, 1973, p. 66.
56 *Resolutions 1971–5*, pp. 456ff.
57 Ibid., pp. 920, 921, 927, 930 and 933.
58 Imre Szabó, 'Szükségletek és érdekek a szocializmusban' (Needs and Interests Under Socialism), *TSz*, No. 6, 1975, pp. 36, 42 and 43.
59 László Rózsa, 'A pártban és a párton kivül' (Inside and Outside the Party), *Népszabadság*, December 17, 1972.
60 Jenő Faragó, 'Szigoru mércével. Beszélgetés dr. Szabó Sándorral, az MSZMP Békés megyei Bizottságának titkárával' (By a Rigorous Yardstick. A Talk with Dr Sándor Szabó, Secretary of the HSWP's Békés County Committee), *Népszabadság*, December 29, 1972.
61 József Sólyom, 'A szerzés ördöge' (Demon of Acquisition), *Népszabadság*, October 18, 1973.
62 'Vita a kispolgáriságról. Három vélemény' (A Debate on Petty Bourgeois Attitudes. Three Views), *Népszabadság*, July 25, 1973.
63 'Vita a kispolgáriságról' (Debate on Petty Bourgeois Attitudes): Géza Ripp, 'A kispolgári ideológia szélsőségei' (Extremist Examples of Petty Bourgeois Ideology), *Népszabadság*, July 5, 1973.
64 'A szerkesztőség összefoglalója' (Editorial Summary), *Népszabadság*, September 23, 1973.
65 László Szabó, 'Politika és végrehajtás' (Policy and Implementation), *Népszabadság*, November 24, 1972.
66 'Teljes szélességben' (Full Breadth), *Népszabadság*, December 2, 1973.
67 'Érdek de kié?' (Interest, But Whose?), *Népszabadság*, December 24, 1973.
68 Lenke Bizám, 'Mitől kispolgár?' (Whence Petty Bourgeois?), *TSz*, No. 7, 1974, p. 44.
69 Ibid., pp. 45–8.
70 'Interju Szentiványi Józseffel' (Interview with József Szentiványi), *TSz*, No. 1, 1973, pp. 60–1.
71 László Antal, 'Hogy többé ne ismétlődhessen meg' (It Must Not Happen Again), *Valóság* (Reality), No. 5, 1988.
72 László Szamuely, 'Szándékok és korlátok' (Intentions and Constraints), *Valóság*, No. 5, 1988.

22 Changing political conditions

1 *Pravda*, November 10, 11 and 12, 1977. In the December 4, 1977 edition of *Népszabadság*, there was a full-page article on the Soviet debate over reform, entitled 'What Do Incentives Encourage? On the Further Development of the Soviet Economic Mechanism'.
2 *Pravda*, November 28, 1978.

3 Tamás Bauer and Károly Attila Soós, 'Szovjet közgazdászok vitái a gazdaságirányitás szükséges átalakitásáról' (The Debates of Soviet Economists on the Necessary Transformation of Economic Management), *KSz*, No. 6, 1979, pp. 728–31.

23 Returning to reform

1 As a member of this body, I can state this from personal experience.
2 Béla Csikós-Nagy, 'Az árpolitika szerepe gazdaságpolitikai céljaink végrehajtásában' (The Role of Pricing Policy in the Implementation of Our Economic Policy Objectives), *KSz*, No. 7–8, 1980, p. 932.
3 *Resolutions 1975–80*, pp. 561–91.
4 Ferenc Havasi, 'A gazdaságirányitási rendszer továbbfejlesztése. Előadói beszéd a Központi Bizottság 1984. április 17-i ülésén' (Further Development of the System of Economic Management. Address delivered at the April 17, 1984 Meeting of the Central Committee), *TSz*, No. 5, 1984, p. 17.
5 'Tiz esztendő. Interju Havasi Ferenccel' (Ten Years. Interview with Ferenc Havasi), *Figyelő* (Observer), December 28, 1977.
6 Ferenc Havasi, 'Gazdaságunk az uj növekedési pályán' (Our Economy on the New Growth Path), *Népszabadság*, May 15, 1982.
7 István Földes, 'Merjünk differenciálni' (Let Us Dare to Differentiate), *Népszabadság*, October 29, 1978.
8 István Földes, 'Politika és gazdaság' (Politics and the Economy), *Népszabadság*, May 1, 1981. The italics are mine.
9 Dr László Horváth, 'A szabályozórendszer fejlesztése' (The Development of the System of Regulators), *Figyelő*, April 4, 1979.
10 Communiqué on the Meeting of the HSWP Central Committee, December 6, 1978, in *Resolutions 1975–80*, pp. 906–12.
11 Miklós Pulai, 'A gazdaságirányitás fejlesztése' (The Development of Economic Management), *Figyelő*, June 17, 1981.
12 'A gazdaságirányitás továbbfejlesztése' (The Further Development of Economic Management), *Figyelő*, February 16, 1984.

24 A new chapter in the debates on reform: the reform decisions of 1984 and 1987

1 László Antal, 'Okulva a tapasztalatokból. Gondolatok a gazdasági mechanizmus továbbfejlesztéséhez' (Learning from Experience. Ideas for the Further Development of the Economic Mechanism), *Figyelő*, April 14, 1982.
2 *Heti Világgazdaság* (Weekly World Economy), October 2, 1982.
3 Ibid., Márton Tardos, 'Mit tegyünk eredményeink védelmében?' (What Shall We Do to Defend Our Achievements?).
4 László Antal, 'El kell mozdulni a holtpontról' (We Must Break Out of the Impasse), *Heti Világgazdaság*, October 15, 1982.

5 *TSz*, No. 11, 1983.
6 Tamás Bauer, 'Eszrevételek a 'Gazdaságirányitási rendszerünk továbbfejlesztése a szocialista építés szolgálatában' cimü tanulmányhoz' (Observations on the Study Entitled 'The Further Development of Our Economic Management System in the Service of Socialist Construction'), *TSz*, No. 4, 1984.
7 Rezső Nyers, 'Gazdaság és politika kölcsönhatása' (The Interaction of the Economy and Politics), *Népszabadság*, October 6, 1981.
8 András Hegedüs, 'A nagyvállalatok és a szocializmus' (The Large Companies and Socialism), *KSz*, No. 1, 1984, pp. 63 and 68.
9 Worth noting are two pieces of writing in the *Heti Világgazdaság*, December 11, 1983: the article closing the reform debate – János Hoós, 'Ne feledkezzünk meg a gazdaságpolitikáról!' (Don't Let's Forget about the Economic Policy) – and the editorial position – 'Vitazáró helyett' (Instead of a Debate Closure).
10 'Folytatjuk a bizalomra épülő nyilt, tisztességes politikánkat' (We Are Continuing Our Open, Honest Policy Built Upon Trust), *Népszabadság*, April 30, 1983. Statement on radio and television by János Kádár.
11 Dénes Kovács, 'Az ideológiai harc és a gazdaság' (The Ideological Struggle and the Economy), *Népszabadság*, January 19, 1982. Discussion with József Szabó, rector of the HSWP Central Committee's Political Academy.
12 See the book containing the Liska debate: *Koncepció és kritika* (Concept and Critics) (Budapest, 1984), pp. 31–2.
13 Ibid., pp. 40 and 46.
14 Ibid., pp. 51, 57, 117–18 and 141.
15 Ibid., p. 70.
16 Ibid. See particularly the criticisms of János Kornai, Iván T. Berend and Márton Tardos.
17 Ibid., p. 317.
18 Ibid., p. 437.
19 Ibid., p. 340.
20 Ibid., p. 355.
21 Ibid., p. 365.
22 'Az MSZMP Központi Bizottságának 1984. április 17-i állásfoglalása a gazdaságirányitási rendszer továbbfejlesztének feladatairól' (The April 17, 1984 Position of the HSWP Central Committee on the Tasks in the Further Development of the System of Economic Management, hereafter 'CC Position 1984'), *TSz*, No. 5, 1984, pp. 3–14.
23 The process is described by a well-informed participant in Tamás Sárközy, *Egy gazdasági szervezeti reform sodrában* (In the Midst of an Economic Organizational Reform) (Budapest, 1986).
24 Ferenc Havasi, 'A gazdasági irányitási rendszer továbbfeijlesztése' (Further Development of the System of Economic Management), *TSz*, No. 5, 1974, p. 23.
25 Cf. 'CC Position 1984'.
26 László Antal, Lajos Bokros, István Csillag, László Lengyel and György

Matolcsy, 'Change and Reform', *Acta Oeconomica*, Vol. 38, No. 3–4, 1987, pp. 186–213.

27 Stand taken by the Economic Panel of the Central Committee, Hungarian Socialist Workers' Party, *Acta Oeconomica*, Vol. 38, No. 3–4, 1987, pp. 263–372.

28 Cf. 'Az MSZMP KB 1987. julius 2-i állásfoglalása' (The HSWP Central Committee's Statement of Position of July 2, 1987), *Népszabadság*, July 14, 1987.

25 The price reform of 1979–1980

1 'Az MSZMP KB határozata a XI. Kongresszus óta végzett munkáról és a párt feladatairól, 1978. április 19–20' (Resolution of the HSWP Central Committee on the Work Done since the Eleventh Congress and on the Party's Tasks, April 19–20, 1978), *Resolutions 1975–80*, p. 768.

2 Béla Csikós-Nagy, 'Az árpolitika szerepe' (The Role of Pricing Policy), *KSz*, No. 7–8, 1980, p. 833.

3 Ibid., p. 832.

4 László Rácz, 'Az uj árrendszer' (The New Pricing System), *KSz*, No. 2, 1980, p. 133. I also rely on this study in the rest of this presentation of the price reform.

5 Thus the price of a product sold at home was calculated from a profit margin based on the production cost of the foreign exchange earned from exporting it.

6 Mátyás Timár, 'A forint egységes árfolyama' (The Uniform Forint Exchange Rate), *Népszabadság*, October 2, 1981.

7 'Interju Havasi Ferenccel' (Interview with Ferenc Havasi), *Figyelő*, November 25, 1981.

8 László Horváth, 'Az 1980-as gazdasági szabályozók' (The 1980 Economic Regulators), *KSz*, No. 1, 1980, pp. 8–9.

9 Cf. János Lökkös, 'A keresetszabályozás néhány problémája és a továbbfejlesztés lehetőségei' (Some Problems of Income Regulation and the Possibilities for Further Development), *KSz*, No. 2, 1978; Béla Balassa, 'Az uj gazdasági mechanizmus reformja Magyarországon' (The Reform of the New Economic Mechanism in Hungary), *KSz*, No. 9, 1987, p. 837.

10 Ferenc Havasi, 'A gazdaságirányitás továbbfejlesztése' (The Further Development of Economic Management), *TSz*, No. 5, 1984, p. 25.

11 Ágnes Matis and József Temesi, 'Szabályozóváltozások és vállalati reakciók' (Changes in Regulators and Company Reactions), *KSz*, No. 6, 1983, pp. 689 and 691.

12 Ferenc Havasi, 'The Further Development of Economic Management', p. 17.

26 Partial reform of the system of institutions

1 Ferenc Havasi, 'Gazdaságunk az uj növekedési pályán. Előadás a XXI. közgazdász-vándorgyülésen. 1982. május 10.' (Our Economy on a New

Course of Growth. Lecture to the Twenty-first Itinerant Conference of Economists, May 10, 1982), *KSz*, No. 7, 1982.

2 György Varga, 'Vállalati méretstruktura a magyar iparban' (Company-Size Structure in Hungarian Industry), *Gazdaság* (Economy), No. 1, 1979, p. 28.

3 István Sáfrán, 'Volt egyszer egy országos vállalat' (Once There Was a National Company), *Népszabadság*, March 16, 1983.

4 Ferenc Cserkuti, 'Hasznos az üzemeknek és a népgazdaságnak. Mezőgazdasági nagyüzemek vezetői a kiegészitő tevékenységekről' (Useful to the Farms and the National Economy. Managers on the Supplementary Activities of the Large-Scale Agricultural Units), *Népszabadság*, November 29, 1979.

5 Dr Mária Frey, 'Mellékes a melléküzem?' (Are Side Activities a Side Issue?), *Figyelő*, January 14, 1981.

6 Benedek Tóth, 'Mindenkinek előnyös' (To Everyone's Advantage), *Népszabadság*, July 5, 1983. Part of a series of articles on supplementary activities by farms.

7 Yearbook 1985, p. 149.

8 József K. Nyirő, 'Vállalati külkereskedelem' (Company Foreign Trading), *Népszabadság*, August 31, 1978.

9 Legal Decree No. 28/1982 on Bonds, *Törvények és rendeletek hivatalos gyüjteménye. 1982. I.k.* (Official Repository of Acts and Regulations, 1982, Vol. I) (Budapest, 1983), p. 246.

10 Katalin Bossányi, 'Az eszközáramlás uj lehetőségei' (New Opportunities for Asset Flows), *Népszabadság*, March 30, 1983.

11 *Figyelő*, November 4, 1981.

12 *Törvények és rendeletek hivatalos gyüjteménye. 1980* (Official Repository of Acts and Regulations, 1980) (Budapest, 1981), p. 214.

13 Ferenc Havasi, 'A gazdaságirányitás továbbfejlesztése' (The Further Development of Economic Management), *TSz*, No. 5, 1984, p. 21.

14 Legal Decree No. 22/1984 on the Amendment of Act No. VI/1977 on State Companies, *Törvények és rendeletek hivatalos gyüjteménye 1984* (Official Repository of Acts and Decrees, 1984) (Budapest, 1985), p. 120.

15 Ferenc Havasi, 'Further Development', p. 23.

27 Internal contradictions and delays in the process of reform

1 László Horváth, 'Az 1980-as gazdasági szabályozók' (The Economic Regulators for 1980), *KSz*, No. 1, 1980, p. 3.

28 A new role for small business

1 István Almási, 'Kedvezőbb feltételek között' (Under More Favourable Circumstances), *Népszabadság*, February 3, 1977.

2 Aladár Sipos, 'A szocialista tulajdonviszonyok továbbfejlesztése' (Further Development of Socialist Property Relations), *Népszabadság*, October 4, 1977.

3 Ferenc Cserkuti, 'Az érzékeny háztáji' (The Sensitivity of Household Farming), *Népszabadság*, December 29, 1979.
4 Tibor Sándor, 'A nagyüzem és a kistermelők együttmüködése' (The Cooperation between the Large Farm and the Small Producers), *Népszabadság*, July 19, 1978.
5 Ferenc Cserkuti, 'A közös és a háztáji' (Collective and Household), *Népszabadság*, June 22, 1979.
6 Béla Fazekas, 'A mezőgazdasági kistermelés uj vonásai' (New Features of Small-Scale Agricultural Production), *Népszabadság*, August 6, 1980.
7 *Resolutions 1975–80*, pp. 1113–16.
8 Political Committee Resolution on Amendment of Labour Law Regulation, September 18, 1979, *Resolutions 1975–80*, p. 1069.
9 István R. Gábor, 'Második gazdaság. Szabályozásra várva' (The Second Economy: Awaiting Regulation), *Figyelő*, November 12, 1980.
10 *Yearbook 1985*, pp. 89 and 208.
11 Ibid., p. 24.
12 Tamás Schagrin, 'Vállalkozás a kereskedelemben' (Entrepreneurship in Trade), *Figyelő*, March 4, 1981.
13 Ernő Merner, 'Jó üzlet a szerződéses üzemeltetés' (Contract Operation Is Good Business), *Figyelő*, September 23, 1982.
14 Katalin Bossányi, 'Kisvállalkozások a Csepel Autógyárban' (Small-Scale Business at the Csepel Auto Factory), *Népszabadság*, March 12, 1982.
15 László Karczagi, 'Tudathasadás kettőtől hatig' (Schizophrenia from Two to Six), *Népszabadság*, July 7, 1982.
16 László Karczagi, 'Aggályok és vállalkozások' (Anxieties and Ventures), *Népszabadság*, May 6, 1983.
17 Ádám Juhász, 'Teljesitménykényszert' (Performance Imperative), *Népszabadság*, March 5, 1983.
18 György Varga, 'Termelő munkaközösségek a Dunai Vasmüben' (Production Partnership [Workteams] at the Duna Steelworks), *Figyelő*, March 10, 1982.
19 György Varga, 'A vállalkozás előiskolája' (The Preparatory School of Business), *Figyelő*, December 9, 1982.
20 Katalin Bossányi, 'Három kicsi elindul. Nem könnyü kisvállalkozást alapitani' (Three Little Ones Start Out. Not Easy to Establish a Small Business), *Népszabadság*, October 14, 1981.
21 Katalin Bossányi, 'Kerekasztal a kisvállalkozások első évéről' (Round-Table Discussion on the First Year of the Small Businesses), *Népszabadság*, February 12, 1983.
22 István Földes, 'Másodlagos' (Secondary), *Népszabadság*, May 1, 1980.

Index of subjects

Index of names

Soviet and East European Studies

54 DAVID GRANICK
Job rights in the Soviet Union: their consequences

53 ANITA PRAZMOWSKA
Britain, Poland and the Eastern Front, 1939

52 ELLEN JONES AND FRED GRUPP
Modernization, value change and fertility in the Soviet Union

51 CATHERINE ANDREYEV
Vlasov and the Russian liberation movement
Soviet reality and émigré theories

50 STEPHEN WHITE
The origins of détente
The Genoa Conference and Soviet-Western relations 1921–1922

49 JAMES MCADAMS
East Germany and détente
Building authority after the Wall

48 S. G. WHEATCROFT AND R. W. DAVIES (EDS.)
Materials for a balance of the Soviet national economy 1928–1930

47 SYLVANA MALLE
The economic organization of war communism, 1918–1921

46 DAVID S. MASON
Public opinion and political change in Poland, 1980–1982

45 MARK HARRISON
Soviet planning in peace and war 1938–1945

44 NIGEL SWAIN
Collective farms which work?

43 J. ARCH GETTY
Origins of the great purges
The Soviet Communist Party reconsidered, 1933–1938

42 TADEUSZ SWIETOCHOWSKI
Russian Azerbaijan 1905–1920
The shaping of national identity in a muslim community

41 RAY TARAS
Ideology in a socialist state
Poland 1956–1983

40 SAUL ESTRIN
Self-management: economic theory and Yugoslav practice

39 S. A. SMITH
Red Petrograd
Revolution in the factories 1917–1918

38 DAVID A. DYKER
The process of investment in the Soviet Union

36 JEAN WOODALL
The socialist corporation and technocratic power
The Polish United Workers Party, industrial organisation and workforce control 1958–1980

35 WILLIAM J. CONYNGHAM
The modernization of Soviet industrial management

34 ANGELA STENT
From embargo to Ostpolitik
The political economy of West German–Soviet relations 1955–1980

32 BLAIR A. RUBLE
Soviet trade unions
Their development in the 1970s

31 R. F. LESLIE (ED.)
The history of Poland since 1863

30 JOZEF M. VAN BRABANT
Socialist economic integration
Aspects of contemporary economic problems in Eastern Europe

28 STELLA ALEXANDER
Church and state in Yugoslavia since 1945

27 SHEILA FITZPATRICK
Education and social mobility in the Soviet Union 1921–1934

23 PAUL VYSNÝ
Neo-Slavism and the Czechs 1898–1914

22 JAMES RIORDAN
Sport in Soviet society
Development of sport and physical education in Russia and the USSR

14 RUDOLF BIĆANIĆ
Economic policy in socialist Yugoslavia

The following series titles are now out of print:

1 ANDREA BOLTHO
Foreign trade criteria in socialist economies

2 SHEILA FITZPATRICK
The commissariat of enlightenment
Soviet organization of education and the arts under Lunacharsky, October 1917–1921

3 DONALD J. MALE
Russian peasant organisation before collectivisation
A study of commune and gathering 1925–1930

4 P. WILES (ED.)
The prediction of communist economic performance

5 VLADIMIR V. KUSIN
The intellectual origins of the Prague Spring
The development of reformist ideas in Czechoslovakia 1956–1967

6 GALIA GOLAN
The Czechoslovak reform movement

7 NAUN JASNY
Soviet economists of the twenties
Names to be remembered

8 ASHA L. DATAR
India's economic relations with the USSR and Eastern Europe, 1953–1969

9 T. M. PODOLSKI
Socialist banking and monetary control
The experience of Poland

10 SHMUEL GALAI
The liberation movement in Russia 1900–1905

11 GALIA GOLAN
Reform rule in Czechoslovakia
The Dubcek era 1968–1969

12 GEOFFREY A. HOSKING
The Russian constitutional experiment
Government and Duma 1907–1914

13 RICHARD B. DAY
Leon Trotsky and the politics of economic isolation

15 JAN M. CIECHANOWSKI
The Warsaw rising of 1944

16 EDWARD A. HEWITT
Foreign trade prices in the Council for Mutual Economic Assistance

17 ALICE TEICHOVA
An economic background to Munich
International business and Czechoslovakia 1918–1938

18 DANIEL F. CALHOUN
The united front: the TUC and the Russians 1923–1928

19 GALIA GOLAN
Yom Kippur and after
The Soviet Union and the Middle East crisis

20 MAUREEN PERRIE
The agrarian policy of the Russian Socialist-Revolutionary Party
From its origins through the revolution of 1905–1907

21 GABRIEL GORODETSKY
The precarious truce: Anglo-Soviet relations 1924–1927

24 GREGORY WALKER
Soviet book publishing policy

25 FELICITY ANN O'DELL
Socialisation through children's literature
The Soviet example

26 T. H. RIGBY
Lenin's government: Sovnarkom 1917–1922

29 MARTIN CAVE
Computers and economic planning
The Soviet experience

33 MARTIN MYANT
Socialism and democracy in Czechoslovakia 1944–1948

37 ISRAEL GETZLER
Kronstadt 1917–1921
The fate of a Soviet democracy

For EU product safety concerns, contact us at Calle de José Abascal, 56–1°, 28003 Madrid, Spain or eugpsr@cambridge.org.

www.ingramcontent.com/pod-product-compliance
Lightning Source LLC
LaVergne TN
LVHW090306210926
848480LV00001B/156